W9-AEF-001

Other Books by Burke Davis

Biography:

THEY CALLED HIM STONEWALL

GRAY FOX: R. E. LEE & THE CIVIL WAR

JEB STUART, THE LAST CAVALIER

MARINE! THE LIFE OF LT. GEN. LEWIS B. (CHESTY) PULLER, U.S.M.C. (RET.)

History:

TO APPOMATTOX

OUR INCREDIBLE CIVIL WAR

THE COWPENS-GUILFORD COURTHOUSE CAMPAIGN

Novels:

THE SUMMER LAND

WHISPER MY NAME

THE RAGGED ONES

YORKTOWN

The BILLY MITCHELL AFFAIR

The BILLY MITCHELL AFFAIR

by Burke Davis

RANDOM HOUSE *New York*

First Printing

 Published in New York by Random House, Inc., and simultaneously in Toronto, Canada, by Random House of Canada Limited.

Library of Congress Catalog Card Number: 66–21474

Manufactured in the United States of America by Kingsport Press, Inc., Kingsport, Tennessee

to BRODIE S. GRIFFITH

and EDWIN PARSONS YOUNG, JR.

Contents

The BILLY MITCHELL AFFAIR

1

With the Air of a Conqueror

The Cunard liner *Aquitania* rolled westward in the last days of February 1919, carrying American troops home from war. She had left Liverpool when the Armistice was a hundred days old and now ran to New York at 22 knots, in a lane that had so recently been a hunting ground for German submarines. Her voyage resounded with bugle calls. Every morning for two hours an officer marched the 900-foot decks to inspect the ship, with fanfares echoing before him. The flourishes began on the upper decks, to the dismay of passengers in first class, and descended until the bugles pealed faintly from the hold, where troops were quartered.

Percy Hammond, a Chicago *Tribune* correspondent returning from the Versailles Conference, took note of this officer: "Young, handsome, and with the air of a conqueror, he personified war in much of its pristine grandeur. He was better dressed than Pershing—a plumed fellow with the aura of banner, spear and shield. He flecked his boots with his handkerchief and committed many martial gestures annoying to his cargo of confirmed civilians.

"Every morning he and his little retinue gladly inspected the vessel, preceded along the decks and corridors by outriders and a bugle corps. No one ever had a better time being a general."

When the handsome officer was passing, Hammond and his friends smiled at his "ingenious splendors," but were impressed by the order and discipline on the ship, and by enjoyment of the troops in his "ornamental visits"; the soldiers seemed to "grow militant again under the influence of his princely glances." Hammond never forgot this striking soldier.

The officer was Brigadier General William Mitchell of the Air Service, U.S. Army. He was then little known outside the American military services and the Allied air forces in Western Europe, but on shipboard he attracted more attention than the distinguished passengers—J. Pierpont Morgan and his family; the suite of Lord Reading, the new British ambassador to Washington; a party of British publishers; Commodore C. E. O. Charlton of the Royal Air Force mission; or Miss Gertrude Pershing, sister and official hostess of the widowed commander of the American Expeditionary Force.

The passengers had seen no American officers turned out as Mitchell was; he might have been British, uniformed on Savile Row. He wore, instead of the bobtailed American tunic, a handsome blouse with a long flared skirt and patch pockets; his breeches were British pinks and the cordovan boots gleamed like dark mirrors. He was recognizably American only from his clear, high-pitched Midwestern accent.

He was a few days past his thirty-ninth birthday, spare and athletic, weighing about one hundred and fifty pounds, five feet nine and one-half inches tall. His movements were graceful and his posture notable among the younger officers aboard. There was quick humor on his dimpled boyish face, whose mouth was clasped by deep lines. His eyes were intensely brown, his chin was cleft, his nose long and sharp, and his ears grew almost flat against his skull. There was about him, even in repose, an air of vital animal energy, and an infectious enthusiasm in his speech.

He had spent twenty-one years in the Army and come through three wars—and seen fourteen major engagements in France—but he wore only a pair of Air Service silver wings on his chest. He had been the first American officer under fire, the first to fly over enemy lines, and he was one of the most decorated men in the A.E.F. He was the first American to be given a Croix de Guerre, and Marshal Pétain had awarded him the Legion of Honor. At St. Mihiel he had commanded almost 1500 Allied planes. He had taken the Prince of Wales for a flight, and had recently been given an audience by George V.

One man aboard who watched Mitchell with open admiration was the skipper, Sir Edward Charles, the line's senior captain. Charles had begun the voyage with a case of nerves, remembering his last run across the Atlantic when Canadian troops overran their officers and raided the upper decks for steamer chairs, dirtied his ship and left her a shambles. He had expected worse from the American Negroes he now carried; these men had been loaded at Brest, where they had been mutinous. On the last day of the war, thrown against German lines by inept officers, the green troops of the 92nd Division had broken, and had since been treated harshly. Captain Charles had felt relief the moment he saw Mitchell pace down the division's lines at Brest, followed by smiles of recognition from young Negro officers. The troops had abruptly come to soldierly attention.

Mitchell had assured the captain: "They will not only cause no trouble. They'll do better than any other troops you ever saw." They had policed the ship daily, submitted to Mitchell's inspections, and the only sounds of their presence came up from their quarters—mass singing and the wail of jazz bands.

Mitchell had organized a small staff on shipboard as if he were still at war; his chief of staff, who had served him in France, was Colonel Thomas Milling, a sandy-haired flier from Louisiana. On the daily inspections, which began with a dozen officers, the staff dwindled away, one by one, until, in the hold, there were only Mitchell, Milling and the Negro buglers.

At other times, civilians passing one of the salons saw Mitchell in another role, more like a Chautauqua lecturer than a homecoming soldier. He seemed to have a message for the American people, and was practicing it with the fervor of an evangelist. He held small audiences of officers before photographs of planes, diagrams of air battles, charts, graphs, tables of organization for air forces, and Royal Air Force posters. His manner revealed none of the relief that everyone else felt at the end of the war. He never mentioned the peace plans that President Wilson was then putting to paper—he was talking only of more war.

The next war, he said, would come in the air. Planes would strike at cities and factories and not simply at armies—if the war had lasted a few months longer he would have shown them. The air was now the first line of defense, and without air power to shield them, armies and navies would be helpless. He must go home and wake up his countrymen.

Mitchell lingered over a battle map of the engagement at St. Mihiel, explaining with swift gestures: "I sent five hundred planes across like this, and as soon as they were over, five hundred more from this side, like a boxer, hitting right and left. We cut them off in the rear, deep along this line, and bombed their airdromes and roads and rail yards. We drove them out of the air . . . Think of the next war, when we can hit with two or three thousand planes at once. It will be decisive."

His speech was colored with phrases in the American vernacular: "The General Staff knows as much about the air as a hog does about skating . . . A standing army that's stood too long . . . The war's over. The generals in Washington got out of their swivel chairs and went over to watch and they're going back to sit down again. They've learned nothing and forgotten nothing."

Germany had thrown in the sponge too soon, he said, before she was truly defeated. He wondered how long it would be before American troops must return to Europe.

One of his listeners was a Navy man, Jerome C. Hunsaker of Boston, a plane designer now on his way home with the Naval Armistice Commission. Officially, Hunsaker had observed the disarming of German ships and planes at Kiel, Wilhelmshafen and Hamburg; unofficially, he had worked for naval intelligence, inspecting details of German armament before they disappeared from view.

Hunsaker saw Mitchell with the eyes of a naval partisan, and one with long experience in aviation. Hunsaker had designed the NC flying boats which would make the first flight of the Atlantic before the year was out, and was to become the designer of the Navy dirigible *Shenandoah*. Six years earlier he had inaugurated the first American course in aerodynamics, at Massachusetts Institute of Technology. Hunsaker saw Mitchell's effectiveness in the salon of the liner and felt that he would be a dangerous adversary: "Mitchell was intelligent, persuasive and good-tempered, even when his assertions were objected to. He liked to try out some of these papers on me and the other passengers. He would give close attention to objections and criticisms."

Hunsaker was the first Navy man to report Mitchell as an enemy: ". . . a very attractive fellow . . . a politician in uniform. We, who were somewhat prejudiced, thought the cause was Billy Mitchell himself, and not air power." Other passengers had no such reservations, and among them gossip about Mitchell's career in France had a heroic quality, as if he were a legendary new kind of American military hero.

Passengers got their first glimpse of the American shore through wisps of fog, for the *Aquitania* was caught in a vast gray bank and lay for hours off Sandy Hook, waiting. When it began to clear, the ship went gingerly ahead at 6 knots, past still-wailing horns of other ships, until the towers of the city loomed up the river. No passenger looked more eagerly ahead than Mitchell.

Self-assurance had marked every move of his life, and now, at the end of a unique and spectacular career in the skies of France, his confidence was unbounded. He had kept few of his secret hopes to himself; by now many passengers saw at least the outlines of his dream—an American air force of such power that it would one day dominate the world.

On that same morning Woodrow Wilson was in the midst of his battle for the League of Nations; returning from France, the President and Mrs. Wilson had landed a week earlier, with his Assistant Secretary of the Navy, Franklin D. Roosevelt, to the greeting of cheering crowds. Only later, in the summer to come, when he had to face hostile senators, would the mood change.

Wilson had little time. Within another week he would return to Paris to pursue his plans for peace. In the end he would try to by-pass the stubborn men of the Senate and take the issue to the American people, who were determined to end war. Mitchell, who would one day take the same course in his own crusade, saw his country's future in a very different light. A few days before he left London he had heard world government proposed for the first time, and rejected it. He had made careful notes for his journal of this occasion, when he was the guest of Sir Hugh Trenchard, chief of the Royal Air Force:

"General Trenchard gave an interesting dinner for me in the House of Commons at which leaders of various factions were present and I was very much surprised at Lord Robert Cecil's ideas on internationalism. I could not get at exactly what they were but he seemed to want to have everybody merged into one general organization. Whether this should be for the purpose of having England run the world I could not find out. Lord Londonderry, the treasurer of the air force, I liked very much. He belongs to the Castlereagh family and it was his great-uncle who had been the British envoy to Europe during Napoleonic times, and it was he that sat with Metternich in Vienna when the first league of nations was devised after the fall of Napoleon. I doubt if any league of nations works any better now than it did then."

As the *Aquitania* came within sight of her dock, Mitchell thought of peace in terms of planes. He was returning to become Chief of Military Aeronautics, as Pershing had promised; he meant to make the arm more powerful than the Army and Navy combined. As if to reassure him, a flight of planes from Mitchel Field, on Long Island, circled over the ship to welcome him home. He waved to them, joined by happy but puzzled passengers.

While the planes still wheeled overhead, the *Aquitania* blundered into a collision. She swerved to avoid a freighter in the channel, and as she did so, bore down on the *Lord Dufferin,* a sugar cargo ship, cutting her in two like a "knife cutting cheese," it seemed to Mitchell. Bags of sugar toppled into the water; a crewman, caught by a running rope, was flung into the harbor and drowned. The *Dufferin* went down within twenty minutes, before the liner had crept to her berth.

Mitchell's young sister Harriet met him; she had climbed up an elevator shaft to get a better look, and her clothing was smeared with grease. She watched him come down the gangplank, with Lewis Brereton, Tom Milling, Bill Sherman, Harold Hartney and Alan Winslow around him. Mitchell took her back aboard, despite her smudges, to meet Captain Charles.

There was little in the way of an official welcome. The Mayor's Welcome Committee, the Women Police Reserves and the Police Band were on a nearby pier to meet an incoming engineer regiment; the city was already weary with the incessant arrivals and parades of troops. The *Aquitania* docked at Thirteenth Street without ceremony.

A *New York Times* reporter came, but he was drawn only by J. P. Morgan, who reported that his trip had been mostly for pleasure. When he was asked about foreign trade in the postwar world, Morgan fixed the reporter with the glance of a jolly brigand and advised caution: "We'd better see, first, if they have the money to pay for the orders." The writer thought that Mr. Morgan had put on weight.

Otherwise the *Times* found little of interest aboard. It mentioned the British diplomatic mission but said nothing of Commodore Charlton, who was the first attaché of the Royal Air Force in America. The reporter found Gertrude Pershing and the British publishers, and wrote a few lines in praise of the Negro troops, gleaned from officers. The reporter seemed not to have heard of General Mitchell, who was identified as "Brigadier General James Mitchell, who has been in command of American air forces in France."

Newspapers ashore offered a few signs of the national mood: President Wilson said he might retire from politics in 1921. Henry Cabot Lodge attacked the League of Nations. Charles Frohman, the theatrical genius who was lost on the *Lusitania,* had left an estate of $451. The Navy was testing the NC-1 flying boat for a transatlantic crossing. An air exposition was drawing crowds to Madison Square Garden and to the 69th Regiment Armory, where Douglas Campbell, the first American to have shot down a German plane, was the chief attraction.

Men from the exposition seized Mitchell at dockside, and that night, as a surprise addition, he spoke to a crowd in the Garden, a throng drawn by radio-controlled planes circling the building during the day. Mitchell was escorted by the staff of Hazelhurst Flying Field to a platform erected over a huge new bomber built by the Glenn L. Martin Company, just too late for use in Europe.

Mitchell spoke of American aviation during the war, "drawing much applause when he asserted that at that moment the American air forces had gained the ascendency in tactical operations over all their allies." Americans, he said, were superior in aerial gunnery, photography, signaling, patrolling, artillery-spotting and almost all else. He drew cheers when he said American pilots brought down Germans in a proportion of four and a half to one over those of ours forced down by the enemy.

He left a good deal unsaid, and evidently thought that this was not the moment to complain that not a single American combat plane had gone into action, except for about 250 observation planes. Mitchell still thought of the Air Service, which had grown so miraculously in the brief months of the war—almost 2800 pilots, 20,000 officers and 150,000 men. He could not have foreseen that the nation, as if embarrassed to find itself in arms after victory, would disband its Army of 2,000,000 almost overnight, and that the Air Service would dwindle to 1300 officers and 11,000 men by the end of the year.

He spoke from a setting decorated with symbols of the dawning air age, against a backdrop on which was painted a landing field and a sky dotted with aircraft. Before him the crowd was almost lost among airplanes—the Martin and Handley Page bombers dwarfed other exhibits, but there was also an inflated kite balloon, a Spad, a Breguet, a Caproni bomber, an SE-5 pursuit and an American-made De Havilland.

When it was over, Mitchell hurriedly left for Washington, caught by a vision that was to dominate his life and become a cause that would haunt his country long afterward.

2

I Am Naturally a Sort of Soldier

Mitchell came from a clan of strong-willed and unpredictable Scotsmen. His grandfather, Alexander Mitchell, "the Rothschild of Milwaukee," had left a bank clerk's post in Aberdeenshire in 1839, and at twenty-one arrived in the Wisconsin village of fifteen hundred to seek his fortune.

Alexander nurtured a tiny insurance firm into a bank and survived the savage raids of Chicago competitors and the panics of 1857 and 1873. At the time of the Civil War he was president of the world's largest rail system, the 5000-mile Chicago, St. Paul & Milwaukee. In an era of wild economic gyrations he made "Mitchell money" a symbol of sound currency in the Midwest, and his bank grew into the modern Marine National Exchange Bank. Alexander served two terms in Congress, then declined further public office, even that of governor.

When the Wisconsin legislature fixed railroad rates he thought too low, Mitchell blandly notified the governor, in the best Robber Baron tradition, that the old rates would remain in effect until the courts had settled the case. Mitchell won. The progressive senator "Fighting Bob" La Follette said of this: "A more brazen defiance of the law could scarcely be conceived." A Milwaukee historian remembered Alexander as "a stoutish man with a broad round face, a double chin fringed with a gray beard that extended in a semicircle from ear to ear. He walked slowly, his hands behind his back . . . something proud and defiant in his manner . . . he did not look as happy as I believed a millionaire should look."

His wife was drawn to the American past. She was one of three founders of the women's group which saved Mount Vernon as a national shrine and was active in affairs of the Society of Mayflower Descendants and the Colonial Dames.

Their son, John Lendrum Mitchell, was educated in Geneva, Dresden and Munich, spent much of his youth traveling and spoke five languages. He went to the Civil War in a Wisconsin volunteer regiment, became chief of ordnance on the staff of a general, but was discharged from the Army because of an eye ailment and went into the family business. He was not an empire builder; his interests were philanthropy, politics, literature and the arts, and experimental farming. His manor house on a country estate, Meadowmere, was a Milwaukee showplace housing art works and fine furnishings from many countries.

The contrasts between father and son became part of Wisconsin folklore. A citizens' committee seeking funds for a local hospital once called on Alexander, and when he pledged only $1000 the indignant spokesman said: "Why, Mr. Mitchell, we expected so much more of you. Your son has pledged us five thousand dollars."

"Ah," the old man said. "I hadn't the good fortune to have a wealthy father."

When his first marriage ended in divorce, John Mitchell married Harriet Danforth Becker of New York. Their first child arrived while they were in Nice, on the French Riviera, on December 29, 1879, in an apartment on Place Grimaldi. They named him William Mitchell.* He was the first of ten children, only three of whom were boys.

The baby was three years old before the Mitchells returned to Milwaukee; he spoke French as naturally as English, and with the other children, who came rapidly, he was trained in German, Spanish and Italian. Back at Meadowmere, where John Mitchell experimented with agriculture, his children were raised with pedigreed dogs, saddle and harness horses and prize farm stock.

Mary Alexander, a Scotch governess, was put in charge of Willie, as the future airman was called by his family, and spent "the most hectic years" of her life trying to control him. He was small, wiry and utterly fearless. When he was forbidden to climb

* Though he was often identified as William Lendrum Mitchell, he bore no middle name.

on the greenhouse he made it a daily practice to scale it, by some miracle never falling or breaking a pane of glass. He was not a joy to Mary: "He absolutely never stopped."

He was given an air rifle at the age of five, and a few weeks later, when he came down with scarlet fever, shot at targets on the walls in his room; the house had to be redecorated after his recovery. Willie was never afterward without guns. He camped and hunted in the Wisconsin woods, often alone, and shot and stuffed two hundred native birds, with the aid of a Milwaukee taxidermist, Carl Akeley, who was to become a well-known naturalist. A neighbor, Eleanor Mercein Kelly, a future novelist, remembered life at Meadowmere as an idyll, with ponies to ride, cows to milk, a private race track and "a private lake quite large enough to play corsair upon."

Willie's course was set by his mother. Eleanor Kelly saw her as "a woman of such force and dignity that she rarely needed to suppress her young—a glance or a quiet word and they suppressed themselves automatically." She also held Willie to his duty. Once when he was quite small he came home dirty and discouraged after an effort to ride a pony, and complained: "Mummy, I can't handle that nasty beast."

"Then you go on riding it until you can."

The failure was temporary. Before he was fourteen Willie was playing polo, and long before he reached manhood he had many broken bones and dislocated joints.

When he first went to school, speaking his native French, boys laughed at him and called him "Froggie," so that he did not utter another word in the language for years afterward. He was not quite ten when he went off to an Episcopal prep school, Racine College. His school letters to "Mummy" revealed him as one of the least inhibited of spellers, but his grades showed a 9.2 average in spelling, a standing of second in his class, and, on one occasion, "perfect" in conduct. He begged for books on electricity and physical experiments, and for a magnet. His reports were not always models. He was charged with "talking before grace in the dining room, boisterous conduct at the table and disorder in the dormitory."

His father was elected to Congress in 1891, and became a Democratic National Committeeman. In the crash of 1893, when many banks were closed, among them "The Mitchell Bank," John saw to it that depositors recovered their money, though it cost him all of his ready assets, about $1,350,000, and the family fortune was affected to such an extent—at least temporarily—that the breeding of horses at Meadowmere was no longer a hobby but a serious business.

John Mitchell entered the Senate in the year of the crash and pioneered in social legislation, "wildly visionary" schemes such as the eight-hour working day and the income tax; despite his background in banking, he supported the monetary program of William Jennings Bryan, advocating unlimited coinage of silver.

Willie begged to be freed from Racine, and was brought to Washington's Columbian School, to prepare for its college division, the forerunner of George Washington University. The Mitchells lived for ten years in a large house on Capitol Hill, in the block now occupied by the Old Senate Office Building.

Mary Alexander had new problems as governess here; when she tried to enforce the maternal edict that Willie attend dancing school, he hid his slippers—but she sent him anyway. In defiance, the boy carried frogs to school and dropped them into the pockets of friends. "Very rarely, when he had been a good boy," he was allowed at the dinner table with important guests, and always found a way to intrude into the conversation.

There was an air of freedom in the household which encouraged the young Mitchells to grow up in their own way. Some dignitary who once invited himself home with the senator aroused Mrs. Mitchell's indignation, and when her housekeeper nervously suggested that other eminent guests must be summoned in honor of the interloper, Mrs. Mitchell agreed. "We'll make an occasion of it. All the children shall come to the table, even the baby." The guest was treated to performances by each of the children speaking "their quaint little Mitchell minds" or rendering their specialties, recitations, songs and dances. Mary Alexander strummed the finale on a zither. The dignitary never forgot the Mitchells.

Willie felt a growing sense of American history in the new home. He developed a proprietary interest in Capitol Hill, so long his playground, and he often went to Mount Vernon with his grandmother. His sister Ruth, who was very close to him, remembered that Willie was so moved when he spoke the words "America" or "the United States" that his voice changed, became hesitant, with "a shy . . . painful warmth." She thought that his foreign birthplace had made him more "passionately" American. The talk at home was of America's past, of great historic moments, or of the days of Grandfather Mitchell, or sometimes of America's present, as in the Congress, where their father played a leading role. Ruth wrote: "All this enterprise, integrity, and enthusiasm was . . . the very air we breathed. America, its inspiring past and glowing future, became the very warp and woof of Bill's own mind."

There was also talk about war. Mitchell's father was of two minds about the subject; he fought jingoism and imperialism in the Senate and struggled for peace—and yet, as a Civil War veteran, he was fascinated by old battles, and so often entertained comrades of the Grand Army of the Republic that Willie began to feel that he had himself been a participant.

During his tenure in the Senate, John sometimes took the family to Europe, and to the disgust of his daughters, carried the stair-step children to the "most unlikely un-get-at-able places . . . dreary, once-gory old battlefields." The girls were bored and sullen, but Willie's small, pointed face was alight.

One memorable day he took the children on a wearying train ride, thence into the country a few miles from Caen, on the Normandy coast, to a remote village called Dives, smelling of fish and kelp. He spoke in emotional tones, pointing across the bay to the Channel. This, he said, was the spot from which William the Conqueror had sailed for England. Only Willie seemed to share with him the echoes of 1066, the clank of swords against shields and the grating of longboats. "The very last time that England was conquered," John said. "The very last time that an armed enemy ever set foot on English soil." A few miles to the south were beaches which would, long afterward, bear names neither Norman nor English—Omaha Beach, Utah Beach.

On another day they were dragged off to Waterloo, down "that damned sunken road," as Ruth recalled it. The children had gorged themselves on bananas that hot day and came to grief on the battlefield, all except Willie. Ruth had the idea that Willie could see the old battles going on as if they were unfolding before his eyes. He was a reluctant scholar, but seemed to forget nothing he read of his own accord. He knew the *Travels of Marco Polo* practically by heart.

As the war with Spain approached, John Mitchell became one of the most outspoken pacifists in the Senate. He resisted American involvement in 1898, but after the episode of the battleship *Maine* in Havana harbor he saw that resistance to the war tide was useless and wrote to a constituent: "There are some things worse than war." Even after war had been declared, and his son had joined the campaign that would abruptly extend American influence as far as the coast of Asia, Senator Mitchell continued to chide the Senate for the hypocrisy of American policy in Cuba, Puerto Rico, Hawaii and the Philippines: "Europe already questions our sincerity in the declaration touching Cuba . . . The seizure of Hawaii would remove any doubt as to our all-around land-grabbing intentions . . . Since the advent of the white man every leaf in the history of Hawaii is either red with blood or black with intrigue and jobbery."

He was scornful of the slogans of the war hawks: "Manifest Destiny" and "Mastery of the Pacific." Mitchell drew laughter with his quip: "There is no demand for more troops in the United States proper, as distinguished from the United States improper." One of his challenges before the Senate, on the eve of the Spanish-American War, was a memorable call to the conscience of his country: "No soldier should be mustered in for the purpose of shooting our ideas of liberty and justice into an alien people."

One of the most enthusiastic young soldiers at that work was Willie, who was eighteen when war was declared, in his junior year at college. He had been in the Senate gallery when the noisy session ended with passage of the declaration. Determined to see action at the first opportunity, Willie ran home, and by the time his father arrived with several friends, he had packed his clothes. Before a crowd that included "Fighting Joe" Wheeler, the old Confederate cavalry general, Willie announced that he was off to Wisconsin to join a regiment.

"You're not going to let this little boy go to war, John," Wheeler said, "especially as he's your oldest child?"

"He's eighteen," Senator Mitchell said, "and sound physically and mentally. I'd rather have them under twenty than over forty, if I were running a war."

Willie left that night for Milwaukee and was soon off to Florida with his regiment, a departure witnessed by a friend of the family who reported: "I soon recognized him by a certain swing to his walk and the extreme badness of his hat—the very worst hat I ever saw. He gave a shy little jerk of his hand in response to our frantic handkerchief wavings . . . We just . . . laughed and joked and pretended it was all a picnic . . . And so we left him—gay and debonair—a typical soldier boy off to the wars."

William Mitchell began his career of twenty-eight years in the U.S. Army by becoming a second lieutenant within a week, the youngest officer in service. He waited in Florida for a chance to get to Cuba, even after the fighting was over, resisting his father's advice to resign and come home. He was made first lieutenant. He often wrote home about camp life, praising his men, but was already critical of the command system: "I really do believe that if we had been up against a first-rate power, they would have whaled the mischief right out of us."

When he finally got to Cuba, he won his first commendation for a report on a foray into the interior. "It is a very creditable report," his superior wrote, "and indicates that this officer, despite his youth, is a man of ability, energy and intelligence. I have seen few reports giving so much information in clear-cut form on a technical subject of such range."

He became bored by inactivity, and wrote home about the Army: "I would not make it my life's work," but suddenly, when he learned of the campaign in the Philippines against the rebel chief, Emilio Aguinaldo, he besieged Washington with requests for a transfer. He also wrote to his father: "Here I have been since the war without any foreign service to speak of and have not been in any engagements as yet. How would you have felt in the Civil War if you had been out of the way somewhere?" He was soon on his way to the Pacific. His father's influence largely shaped his early military career.

As he passed through the United States, still short of his twentieth birthday, his father thought the Army had made a man of him "physically and mentally," and John Mitchell wrote proudly to his wife: "He stands straight and talks straight, and, I may say, entertainingly. The impression he has made here on everybody is very favorable."

Young Mitchell stopped for a few days in Milwaukee, where he was treated as a war hero; he saw many old friends at parties, among them Douglas MacArthur, who was soon to leave for West Point as a cadet, and whose father, General Arthur MacArthur, commanded a division in the Philippines. An older woman wrote Billy's mother after this visit: "How handsome and fascinating all the girls found him . . . He seems the perfect type of the ideal American soldier."

At the turn of the century Mitchell spent seven months in the Philippines, in the hectic campaign to subdue the guerrilla band of Aguinaldo which was terrorizing the islands. He served under MacArthur, and for several months led an independent column in the jungle. One of his first important military accomplishments was the laying of a telegraph line for seventy-five miles through rough country infested by the enemy. Mitchell fabricated insulators of bamboo and broken bottles, and pushed the line through tenaciously, warning tribesmen along the route that if a break occurred in their territory, he would return to burn and kill. He led fifteen Negro soldiers in a night raid and captured Aguinaldo's adjutant, Captain Mendoza, but the chief himself eluded him. Before it was over, Mitchell's signalmen had broken up several rebel bands and captured more than seventy insurgent flags.

Mitchell caught malaria, and apparently while depressed by the disease, wrote his mother, who was traveling in Germany, that he had again thought of resigning from the Army. He wanted to "have a home, some settled aim, business and association and try to earn one's self-respect and of one's neighbors." Still, he foresaw the promise of action, and told his mother: "There will be a big stir-up somewhere one of these days and not far away, and probably with the country in which you are now, among others."

He spent his six months' leave going home through the Middle East and Europe. He had planned to resign after he got back to Washington, but instead General Adolphus W. Greely, the Signal Corps chief, persuaded him to volunteer for duty in Alaska.

The Army had long tried, and failed, to link the interior with the Alaskan coast by telegraphy, and Mitchell worked all summer scouting the rugged route. For the next two winters, in weather often 70 degrees below zero, in snow forty feet deep, surmounting cruel terrain, difficult labor and savage dog teams, he completed the 1700-mile line. In his last days in Alaska, Mitchell developed a new interest that was to dominate his life. He and a companion spent weeks in a trapper's cabin, snowed-in, studying engineering and aeronautics, poring over the limited information about Otto Lilienthal's gliders and the aeronautical experiments of Professor Samuel P. Langley.

He emerged from his tour in the Far North as a captain, the Army's youngest. He had gained weight and overcome the effects of malaria, but he had a permanently stiff knee from a fall on the ice. In later years he used a cane but never explained why, so his critics thought it an affectation.

Back in the United States, Mitchell found an Army greatly expanded in his absence—100,000 strong—and he saw his future in the service. He wrote to his father: "If I ever get a chance in the field I think that I can do something . . . I am naturally a sort of soldier."

In 1903, fresh from the Alaskan adventure, he married Caroline Stoddard of Rochester, the daughter of family friends. From the start his bride saw that his first love was a remarkable game of war, strongly visual to him—he played it constantly, even on their honeymoon in Mexico. As Caroline reported to her mother-in-law, Mitchell more often looked about the landscape to find good artillery positions than he took notice of his wife.

His father died in 1904, at a time when Mitchell was deeply involved with experiments in military communications. He set up the first field radio stations, at Fort Leavenworth, Kansas, and by means of a kite carrying his wire over 10,000 feet into the air, received a radio message from Puerto Rico, some 1900 miles away. Mitchell experimented with military photography from kites, with rapid development of pictures in the field, and at twenty-five was an instructor at Leavenworth and author of a text on communications. In 1906 he initiated his role as a military prophet with an article in the *Cavalry Journal:* "Conflicts no doubt will be carried on in the future in the air, on the surface of the earth and water, and under the water." It was three years after the first tentative flight by the Wright brothers and two years before their first plane delivery to the Army.

Mitchell may have been on hand when the first plane joined the Army, but he was not on official duty for the occasion, which passed with little attention from the country at large. For the next six years he was in school, on Western outpost duty or in the Pacific. He was stationed in San Francisco after the earthquake, in Cuba during an uprising, became the first Signal Corps officer to attend the Army's School of The Line, and was one of its "Distinguished Graduates." He was thus involved while Lieutenants Frank Lahm and Frederic Humphreys were becoming the first two Army aviators and the third, Benjamin Foulois, was beginning his flight training at College Park, Maryland, in 1909.

In these years his efficiency reports reflected the admiration of his superiors. For example, his commanding officer wrote: "Captain Mitchell is an earnest, zealous, efficient young officer, intensely interested in his professional work . . . an enthusiast in whatever he undertakes. One of the most indefatigable workers I have ever known. Presentable and agreeable personality; courteous and subordinate, cheerful and sanguine . . . will undertake to accomplish anything; ambitious and willing."

By 1909, when he was sent back to the Philippines as signal officer on Luzon, Mitchell was the father of two daughters, Harriet and Elizabeth. He played polo, and was captain of the Army team which defeated the British for the Eastern Cup in Hong Kong. He soon found even more exciting recreation. He volunteered to take a spying trip around the small islands off Luzon, where the Japanese had wireless stations, apparently reporting on American activities in the Philippines. He went by small boat through the island chain to Formosa, photographing almost everything he saw, despite suspicious Japanese guards. He reported to Washington: "I traveled as a naturalist, measuring birds and fish . . . The Japanese were at first very distant . . . but as they are quite lonely, beer and cigarettes, of which I had a goodly store, had an immediate effect." He was permitted to photograph and sketch without question.

This report from the thirty-year-old captain seemed to draw no attention in Washington, but he did not desist. In August 1911 he began another intelligence mission, traveling through Japan, the battlefields in Manchuria and other scenes of the Russo-Japanese war. He made a voluminous report, with photographs from Port Arthur, Dairen, Mukden and the Japanese home islands. He reported on infantry, artillery, medical corps, cavalry, engineers, the telegraph corps—his details including sights on the new Japanese rifles, their rest periods in marching exercises, accuracy of machine-gun fire, and at the end of his report were pasted scores of photographs and samples of field wire in use by Japanese troops.

He went into the same detail for China, and though he saw that the country was poorly organized, he wrote: "Before many years pass they will be able to take care of themselves." The Chinese war lord Chang Tso-lin reviewed 20,000 troops for Mitchell, who was impressed: "If the uncounted millions of Chinese could be organized, equipped and led properly . . . there is nothing they could not accomplish." The friendly war lord, who was bald, asked Mitchell's advice on how to keep flies off his head; Mitchell suggested a tattooed spider web on the yellow skull.

He forecast the military future in this Eastern arena: "That increasing friction between Japan and the United States will take place in the future there can be little doubt, and that this will lead to war sooner or later seems quite certain." * It was thirty years before Pearl Harbor.

He was astounded by the Japanese interest in aviation. In Kyoto he saw schoolboys being taught the principles of flying with the use of five-foot scale models, and in many cities saw great crowds gather to watch model planes in the air.

Soon after he had returned from the Orient, Mitchell found that he had been singled out as one of the most promising officers in the Army. He was chosen for the General Staff, at thirty-two the youngest man ever selected. He reported it first to his mother: "My Dear Mummy . . . I enclose a telegram which came today as a total surprise . . . It is the most sought-after position which a military man can aspire to . . . of course I have always aspired

* The original of this report, in the War College papers at the National Archives, bears a cryptic anonymous penciled notation in the margin opposite this section: "Arse."

to it, but I did not think for a moment I would get it this time . . . You will note that my name appears first on the list . . . It will be the greatest thing in my career so far . . ."

His second thoughts were pragmatic: "All the general officers I have served with are good friends. My trip to Manchuria and incident report had considerable to do with it, I imagine. This combined with the fact that there is not a spot on my record . . . These combined with a knowledge of horses and shooting have done it." He recognized his opportunity: "I may be a general before many years have passed."

Back in Washington, with his family in a large house on Q Street, Mitchell was soon involved in the social whirl he knew was so important to his future. As one of the most skilled riders in the service, he starred in horse shows and hunts, and acquired a stable of hunters. The Mitchells became familiar figures in Washington, New York and Long Island society; he hunted, rode, fished and played tennis with civilian and military friends, always with insistence upon perfection (his tennis was so good that the international star Bill Larned was a regular opponent). He soon discovered that even the generous aid of a wealthy wife could not support this life. He frequently wrote his mother for help (which she gave), accounting in detail for his heavy expenses, even to the high cost of eggs in Washington. His financial problems made him thoughtful: "I am practically committed to the Army as a career and am already probably too old to change, although I do not feel so myself."

In this period the tone of his efficiency reports from superiors began to change. The first reservation was expressed by his commanding officer in the prewar period: "A careful and industrious officer, but I do not consider him especially qualified for laborious and painstaking staff duties."

Mitchell wrote his mother that he was determined to live up to the traditions set by his father and grandfather, which had always been a stimulus to him: "If we cannot do as well or even better, then we are not progressing as we should." He could match them only in an Army career, he thought, and if he were a success, he expected "no limit in the gift" of the American people.

In 1912 the General Staff assigned Mitchell to Intelligence, in charge of military information coming from Europe during the Balkan Wars. Most of the interesting developments crossing his desk involved aviation: Bulgarian fliers had dropped tiny bombs on Adrianople, in Turkey, and escaped with a few bullet holes in their plane. The Greeks had tried to bomb warships in the Dardanelles, the first attempt of its kind.

Most European nations had gone far ahead of the United States in aviation, despite the American inventions of the airplane and machine guns, and the feat of Eugene Ely in landing on a warship, in 1911. The U.S. Army and Navy combined had six planes; the French were said to have 1200. Mitchell's interest was aroused. He visited the Army's new flying school at College Park, Maryland, and began some of the most important friendships of his life, the first with men of the Aviation Section of the Signal Corps.

He had found the right place. Lieutenant Henry H. ("Hap") Arnold, the future general of the U.S. Army Air Forces and air commander of World War II, was now, in the summer of 1912, in the midst of American efforts to fashion the plane into a weapon. Arnold's West Point nickname came from an ineradicable grin which had lately been tested. He had crashed a plane in the sea off Plymouth Beach, and while hanging in the wreckage saw help approaching—two old men in G.A.R. uniforms who rowed stolidly past; they disapproved of airplanes. Arnold became one of the first five officers rated as Military Aviators in the United States. He had just set a new Army altitude record, 4674 feet. His companions Tom Milling and Charles deF. Chandler had recently fired the first machine gun from a plane, and with a civilian inventor, Riley Scott, were now experimenting with dropping bombs. Arnold and Milling had learned to fly with the Wright brothers a year earlier.

Mitchell's fascination for the work of the airmen was obvious from the first moment. Arnold remembered him as "a sharp-faced eager young captain," full of talk of Alaska and the air forces of Japan, and intent on learning: "His questions about the air were intelligent and to the point; in fact, it was he who did most of the talking, asking questions only to get concrete facts."

Mitchell took such an interest in aviation that when a congressional committee looked into European air power the following year, in 1913, he was called as a witness, with Arnold and Ben Foulois. He was three years away from his first plane ride, but did not hesitate to offer his opinions at length.

As to independence for the Aviation Section, Mitchell agreed with Arnold and Foulois and expressed their idea: it should not be divorced from the Signal Corps. It was a statement that would come back to haunt him: "If we are going to try to build up aviation in this country, what's the use of trying to create a separate branch . . . causing all sorts of complications? I believe it would set aviation back to create a separate organization."

Arnold was struck by the thoroughness and brilliance of the testimony as Mitchell drew on history for illustrations of his argument in a lengthy lecture. Congressmen fidgeted as he instructed them about early European campaigns, Bull Run, Gettysburg and the tactics of Admiral Cervera in the Spanish-American War.

But Mitchell had an intuition that the new weapon might one day outgrow his corps: "Instead, as some people think, of the aeroplane being an adjunct of the lines of information, the lines of information may grow to be an adjunct to the aeroplane, and very probably will."

When the hearing was over, the House Military Affairs Committee not only agreed to leave the Signal Corps in charge of aviation; the chairman asked Mitchell to draft the legislation. He was becoming known on Capitol Hill as a military expert. In July 1914, when German columns marched into the Low Countries and across the French border, Mitchell's role became important overnight. He was in charge of the war maps by which congressmen were given their daily briefings, and it was through Mitchell that the legislators got their impressions of the opening phases of the war.

About two months later he wrote to his mother: "People who have not studied the German organization in every line do not appreciate what a wonderful and coordinated empire it is, both for war and in peace. We may run up against it before many years are over, or against an almost equally well organized one, Japan."

During this time a form of rheumatism contracted in Alaska flared up again. Intense pain in the joints kept him in bed, but he spent much of the time writing; he even became a military expert for the Chicago *Tribune* under an assumed name, to avoid a War

Department regulation. He also contributed an article on the war to *World's Work,* anonymously.

Early in 1915, when German success in the field had become ominous, Mitchell had his first brush with Army discipline over the public expression of his opinions. A Washington newspaper unexpectedly devoted headlines to a lecture he had given to a group of engineers:

SAYS FOE CAN TAKE U.S.
ERE ARMY IS RAISED

Capt. Mitchell, U.S. Army General Staff, Gives Startling Military Facts

NOT SURE WE HAVE A NAVY

The story itself revealed that the headlines had stretched the truth. Mitchell had said that since it took the United States three years to field an effective army in the Civil War, it might take as long for this war. As to his comment on the U.S. Navy, a man in his audience had asked: "Have we got a Navy?" and Mitchell replied: "Well, I'm an Army man and supposed to know very little about the Navy, but I hear we have several pretty good ships."

The War Department called Mitchell to account, and he made a stout defense. The newspaper, he said, gave "an entirely erroneous impression." He sent a copy of the speech and his lantern slides. His explanation was accepted, but as a warning he was sent a copy of a stern order by Major General Hugh L. ("Three Fingers") Scott, forbidding any officer to air his opinions publicly.

In July 1915 Mitchell wrote a long critique that was a hint of things to come: "Our Faulty Military Policy." He proposed a reorganization of the War Department, and the creation of a Council of National Defense, over the Army and Navy: "We would then have the whole national defense brains, so to speak, under one roof." He urged compulsory military service as the only feasible system in a democracy. He warned that America's geographical position was no longer a guarantee against attack, especially by submarine and plane. He also said: "The military policy of the United States is and has been to prepare for war *after such war has actually broken out.*" In debate over preparedness as war approached, there were suggestions that the National Guard be given planes, and Mitchell, aware that the Army itself had so few, made a retort that was to echo for years: "To hell with the National Guard!"

Mitchell's superiors noted his growing impatience with staff work, and his efficiency reports of the period pointed this out to the high command. In 1915: "Very capable, alert. I consider him better suited to active service with troops than on General Staff duty. He would be an efficient aide-de-camp to a general in the field." A year later: "Especially fitted for field service . . . resourcefulness and initiative in an emergency."

In late 1915 Mitchell was forced to give in to his rheumatism, which was now diagnosed as inflammatory (perhaps rheumatic fever). His heart was so weak that he was advised to leave the Army for a less active career, and to give up riding and hunting. Instead, he stayed in bed for three months, almost without stirring, and at the beginning of the year was able to go downstairs once daily. His heart had improved, and though "the rheumatism stays a little in my hands and shoulders and does not seem to want to leave," he simply put the illness out of his mind.

By now he was a major, and when his General Staff duty ended he went into the Aviation Section of the Signal Corps under Colonel George O. Squier, an old friend from Fort Leavenworth days. Now, at thirty-six, he began to fly. He took his first lessons as soon as he had thrown off his illness.

The flying school nearest to Washington was at Newport News, Virginia, operated by Glenn Curtiss, and Mitchell went there with Tom Milling, who gave him his first flight. Milling wrote: "He was crazy about it . . . he went over faithfully every weekend and kept up his flying that way."

Mitchell's instructor was Jimmy Johnson, who was immediately impressed by his pupil. "Let's get this straight," Mitchell said. "You forget I'm an Army major, and treat me like anyone else who's here to learn." Mitchell was quick and self-confident, but Johnson hesitated to let him solo, despite Mitchell's insistence. One day Johnson was ill and Mitchell was turned over to a new teacher, Walter Lees. As Johnson recalled it, "When Mitchell really wanted anything, he could be pretty persuasive," and he "fast-talked Lees into letting him solo." Lees sent Mitchell on two solo flights that day and he did well.

Soon afterward, when he returned for a lesson from Johnson, Mitchell insisted that he be allowed to solo once more, but leveled off too high for his landing on the rough field and flipped the Jenny on its back. Johnson rushed to his pupil as he hung upside down in the small plane: "Are you all right?" Mitchell said only: "What did I do wrong?"

Mitchell later wrote of this crash: "It taught me more than anything that ever happened to me in the air." He flew on weekends for about five months, until mid-January 1917. He had thirty-six flights and fifteen hours of instruction, and was forced to pay most of the $1470 bill himself, since Army regulations forbade the payment of more than $500 in fees to a civilian agency for the benefit of an officer.

Mitchell was sure that the country would go to war against Germany and "decided to seek service in Europe and learn as much as possible"; he badgered his superiors until he was given a place on a five-man party of observers about to go to France. His orders were issued on March 3, 1917; he was to report to the American ambassador in Paris "for the specific purpose of observing the manufacture and development of aircraft," and to report on French methods in combat, training and organization of airmen.*

He sailed on March 17, by way of Miami and Key West, thence to Cuba, where the Spanish minister held a ship for him, the *Alfonso XIII,* bound for Corunna, Spain. He was making his way to France through that spy-infested neutral country when the American entry into the war, on April 6, caught him by surprise. He hurried toward Paris.

* Hap Arnold thought that Mitchell "inadvertently" sped his departure for the war by his criticism of the high command.

3

Good Men . . . Running Around in Circles

Mitchell was depressed by his first glimpse of France at war. The only men to be seen were old, on guard duty in the small towns. The people were depressed and haggard and talked only of the new offensive to be launched in the north, which was to lead to more bloodletting on battered and trench-scarred landscapes. "What a foolish kind of war this seemed," Mitchell wrote, "where an army could not advance twenty or thirty miles for months . . . It seemed to me that the utility of ground armies was rapidly falling to about zero."

In Paris he found Major James Logan and three officers of the U.S. military mission, the only men in the city wearing American uniforms. Logan asked Mitchell to prepare for the coming of U.S. airmen in the months ahead. There was no money, but Mitchell opened an office anyway. French and American officers volunteered for his staff, the American Radiator Company gave him office space, he spent his own money and got contributions from American civilians in Paris. He cabled Washington for $50,000, and there was a long silence. When General Squier finally replied he said it was "not customary" to send so much money to a junior officer. Lieutenant Laurence Miller of Mitchell's staff retorted that "it is not customary to have a world war."

Mitchell bombarded the War Department with suggestions he gleaned from his French friends. The United States should build or buy French planes—Spads, Breguets and Nieuports. These suggestions were also followed by silence, probably because Washington assumed that he had not become an expert on plane performance overnight. But Mitchell was learning quickly. He took lessons from Victor Fumat, a leading instructor of French pursuit pilots, and learned of the superiority of European warplanes firsthand: "I had been able to flounder around with the animated kites that we called airplanes in the United States, but when I laid my hand to the greyhounds of the air they had in Europe, which went twice as fast as ours, it was an entirely different matter." Fumat was the best instructor he had known, and after a month's intensive training under him, Mitchell won the title of Junior Military Aviator, the highest ranking open to him, and second only to the coveted Military Aviator. It was his last instruction.

Like many another incident in Mitchell's career, the new rating came in a rather impromptu fashion. He was in a consuming hurry, and when it appeared that there were no records at hand, headquarters named a two-man board to pass Mitchell (one of them Major M. F. Harmon, who became a World War II air commander). He flew an 80-horsepower Nieuport in simple maneuvers, climbing, gliding, landing within a 100-foot circle, spiraling right and left, and flying figures of eight. He flew a round trip, Paris to Châteauroux, over three hundred miles, in under six hours, using map and compass, and made another, triangular flight from Le Bourget to nearby towns, about 64 miles in fifty minutes, a flight in rough weather, during which Mitchell was forced to dodge clouds and fog.

The board said that Mitchell "handled his machine with ease and very good control . . . is well qualified in every way to be rated as a Junior Military Aviator . . . his technical knowledge and theoretical knowledge and flying ability are well above that of the average applicant."

Mitchell became friendly with many French aviation officials, including Daniel Vincent, the Minister of Aviation, and before he had been in Paris two weeks, was off for the front to inspect French methods. His offensive against Washington was stepped up; he saw everything, photographed everything, and seemed to spare the War Department nothing. He typed so furiously at night in his hotel room that French neighbors thought he was operating some kind of telegraph, and he was forced to demonstrate the machine before the mystery was cleared.

He took part in an infantry attack at the front, was in a dugout during artillery bombardments, and became the first American in uniform under fire, for which he won the first Croix de Guerre given an American. He was fascinated by tanks and crawled over them, noting armor, guns and power, and the affinity of tankers for airmen. He predicted that this was a weapon of the future, and felt the same enthusiasm for other advances he saw in operation for the first time—camouflage, photography, bridge-building and meteorology, all accomplished rapidly and under makeshift conditions at the front, contributing to each operation of the army. He reported on searchlights and anti-aircraft guns, and thought this and other French equipment far superior to that of the U.S. Army.

French officers told him of the need for massed air power, for flights of hundreds to strike the Germans rather than dribbling away strength by assigning small groups to divisions. Commanders emphasized to him that there could be no victory on the ground without victory in the air—a view for which they won no more support in their army than Mitchell later won in his own.

He flew over the lines with a French pilot, an uneventful flight, but one which gave him a view of the ground fighting which no high-ranking American officer of the war would ever have:

"One flight over the lines gave me a much clearer impression of how the armies were laid out than any amount of traveling around on the ground. A very significant thing to me was that we could cross the lines of these contending armies in a few minutes in our airplane, whereas the armies had been locked in the struggle, immovable, powerless to advance, for three years . . . This whole area over which the Germans and French battled was not more than sixty miles across. It was as though they kept knocking their heads against a stone wall, until their brains were dashed out. They got nowhere, as far as ending the war was concerned.

"It looked as though the war would keep up indefinitely until either the airplanes brought an end to the war or the contending nations dropped from sheer exhaustion."

In May, Mitchell became a lieutenant colonel, and began to lead a more active sociopolitical life. He became friendly with two influential Americans, James Gordon Bennett and James Hazen Hyde, who were unofficial ambassadors in Paris, and through them met many French leaders. He later took General James G. Harbord of Pershing's staff to dinner at Hyde's home and the lavish party rather shocked the general. "I was quite overcome," Harbord wrote. He met a French ambassador, the head of an art academy in Rome, an international financier and General Weygand, Chief of Staff to General Foch. Harbord caught the names of only two of the women guests, the Princesses Murat and Lucinge, because of his bad French. Harbord recorded in his diary: "Since last night I realize the meaning of décolleté . . . It was the lowest-necked party I ever attended, I think. The necks were well selected, neither flat nor scrawny." *

Though Washington placed little value on Mitchell's views on aviation (even his friend Hap Arnold thought him prone to exaggeration), the French regarded him as an authority. He once lectured the French Senate committee on aviation, and gave an impressive résumé of military aviation, including the promise of American participation in the war, which was now about to begin. When Henry Franklin-Bouillion, the socialist leader in the Chamber of Deputies, was leaving for America, he sought advice from Mitchell on the outlook of American leaders he must meet. Before Pershing arrived in Paris with his staff, Mitchell was deep in the work of the Inter-Allied Board, which was set up to produce planes for the coming American squadrons. He found himself in frequent arguments with M. Flandin of this board, a relationship which improved when they combined their meetings with luncheons and dinners given by the Marquise de Brantes of the Schneider family, the heiress of an arms-making dynasty who was known as "the Bertha Krupp of France."

One result of such friendships was the Ribot Cable, a message to Washington by Premier Ribot which shocked the War Department with its demands for 20,000 planes and 40,000 mechanics. Mitchell had conceived the plan and persuaded the French to present it—though in Washington only Hap Arnold and a few others recognized his handiwork. The goal was too high for the

* Harbord was later caught in an air raid at Nancy, disdainfully remaining in his hotel room while German bombers were at work, and when one side of the hotel was demolished, Harbord was blown into a bathtub with a window casing about his neck. "If a few more of our General Staff officers could have had this same experience . . . it would have been an excellent thing," Mitchell wrote.

Americans, but it formed the basis of policy, and within a year this stimulus helped to produce an aerial force three times the size of the French.

Just before Pershing's arrival in Paris, Mitchell toured the British sector and met Sir Hugh ("Boom") Trenchard, a former pilot, six feet tall, not yet forty, a brusque, able man who had built the Royal Flying Corps into an arm of 2000 planes. It was Trenchard who gave Mitchell his first lessons in strategic air power; they got on well despite a brief clash of wills at their first meeting. Mitchell arrived unexpectedly, to find Trenchard leaving for an inspection of his squadrons.

"What can I do for you? Have you an appointment?"

"No, General, but I still want to see as much of your organization as you can show me." Mitchell asked to see equipment, stores and the supply system, and to fly with units that were going against the Germans. Trenchard stared at the boyish-looking interloper.

"That's quite a large order. How many weeks have you got to spare?"

"We could take in the equipment and supply today. Tomorrow we could start—"

"One minute, young man. Do you think I've nothing more to do than chaperon you and answer questions?"

Mitchell grinned disarmingly. "I know you've got such an excellent organization that it shouldn't need your leadership for a day or so."

Trenchard's aides expected an explosion, but their chief said only: "Come along, young man. I can see you're the sort who usually gets what he wants in the end." He led Mitchell to his war maps and explained his operations. He traced the evolution of air war against the Germans, from the early days of observation by unarmed planes to the concept of long-range bombing of enemy industrial centers.

Mitchell spent three days at Trenchard's side, absorbing ideas, putting shrewd questions endlessly, learning even more than Trenchard's French admirers had led him to expect. He saw artillery outfits and fighter squadrons, and watched night bombers take off on strikes behind enemy lines. The use of massed bombers convinced him: "This is the proper way to use air power and I am sure the future will see operations conducted in this way by thousands of airplanes."

Mitchell found the British less tradition-bound than the French, more willing to try new weapons, especially tanks. This was a pointed lesson to him: "The great captains are those who thought out new methods and then put them into execution. Anybody can always use the old methods. That is the trouble with old regular army officers; they can never get out of the rut, but always go into a war with the methods of a former war . . . sure to be whipped whenever they come up against an elastic-minded, constructive leader on the other side."

Trenchard followed Mitchell's hectic activities during the next few weeks as the U.S. air arm was organized, and not long afterward said to one of his staff: "Mitchell is a man after my own heart. If only he can break his habit of trying to convert opponents by killing them, he'll go far." *

Mitchell returned to Paris to campaign even more vigorously to persuade Washington to build a great air force. He moved into larger offices, provided by the French, and continued his studies and reports. Among the papers he typed was a personal one, a casual sort of last will and testament: "Please send home what stuff I have . . . especially all pictures and films. Keep what flying clothes and odds and ends anyone wants. Fill out the enclosed check for enough to cover all expenses and set the gang up to a bottle of champagne at the peace."

He met Pershing and his staff when they arrived in Paris on June 13, 1917, "looking a little bewildered" at the almost hysterical welcome given by the French. Mitchell went with the commander on his rounds of visits to French officials; people threw flowers in the party's path as it moved through the city.

Pershing had brought his own aviation officer, Major Townsend F. Dodd, a veteran flier who was Mitchell's junior in rank. Mitchell wrote, somewhat disingenuously: "I'm only over here to fight Germans and I would just as soon be a pilot in one of the

* Like Mitchell, Trenchard was a dogged fighter who put into action the best ideas he gleaned from other men. He was a great leader and organizer, but had none of Mitchell's eloquence. Winston Churchill once said of Trenchard: "He can't write and he can't speak but we can't do without him."

squadrons as anything else," but he was pleased when Pershing recognized his superior rank and installed him as air chief, assigning Dodd to other duty. This was the beginning of a command struggle in American aviation that was to end only after the Armistice.

Less than a month after Pershing's arrival the Secretary of War sent a surprise, an air mission of about a hundred, headed by Major Reynal C. Bolling, which was to study British and French aviation, train about ninety mechanics, and return to America with a proposed organization. The mission, independent of Pershing, worked for about a month, and left Bolling behind. He was an able negotiator, a lawyer for U.S. Steel who had learned to fly, and was invaluable in procuring planes and engines in Europe. He set up the complex system of bases, flying schools and supply centers in the rear for the U.S. air arm which was to come; thus far, there were no American flying units at the front. During the enormous build-up of American forces in France, Bolling's duties kept him near the front, where, in March 1918, he was killed, defending himself with a pistol against a party of Germans.

A result of the Bolling mission was the decision to build one type of plane in the United States—the British two-seater De Havilland light bomber, which Mitchell thought almost worthless. The planes were to be powered by a durable new engine designed for the purpose, known as the Liberty. Mitchell was outraged that his suggestions for use of the fine French pursuit planes had been ignored: "There must have been a lot of inside work somewhere by the English manufacturers to put this thing over on the Americans." He protested that the new engine would not suit the plane, which was far from ideal, even for observation work.

As he wrote to his mother: "I suppose that aviation after my departure from the States was handled worse than anything ever has been."

While these early storms raged within the command, Mitchell had an air force of one plane, a French Nieuport which he used personally. He still lived in Paris, with Major Logan and Major Randolph Churchill, trying to cope with officers of the incoming Army staff: "Few of them had ever been to Europe, and most of them were thinking more about rank for themselves than what to do with the troops . . . they were full of information as to what should and should not be done."

Mitchell's frustrations increased: "We were running into more and more trouble with our own staff over aviation matters. It was such a big subject and ignorance about it was so widespread that each member had to be told, from the bottom up, whenever anything new occurred . . . Incoming papers were passed around from one section to another, just as in Washington, with everyone trying to avoid responsibility."

He thought ground officers were jealous of aviators, because the work was "more spectacular" and brought more rapid advancement and pay. Worse still, he found Pershing slow to act: "General Pershing himself thought aviation was full of dynamite and pussyfooted just when we needed the most action." Mitchell thought the solution was a single American air commander in Europe, "and not have every Tom, Dick and Harry in the United States, who were neither pilots nor had ever seen an armed German, prescribe what should be done against the enemy."

Toms, Dicks and Harrys were en route.

By the time the American command left Paris and moved toward the front, these squabbles had become more intense. The General Staff interfered in air matters, and in its ignorance created problems for Mitchell: "It was terrible to have to fight with an organization of this kind, instead of devoting all our attention to the powerful enemy in our front." He had many talks with Pershing, some of them heated, "with much pounding on the table with fists on both sides of the argument." Pershing once threatened to send Mitchell home if he continued to insist on his reforms.

"If you do, you'll soon come after me," Mitchell said. Pershing only laughed, and as Mitchell recalled it, their talk ended amicably.

In the fall of 1917, in a peacemaking effort, Pershing installed Major General William Kenly as Chief of the Air Service. He was a newly trained pilot who had worked with the Royal Flying Corps, and both Bolling and Mitchell served under him.* However, there

* The involved chain of command of the U.S. air forces in France was made more complex as the war went on; nomenclature became a problem: Pershing

were still clashes, and in November, Benny Foulois, now with a temporary commission of brigadier general, arrived with yet another air mission. The experienced aviator tried for six months to cope with imposing problems of building an air arm, not the least of which was Mitchell.

By now Mitchell lived on the Marne, near Chaumont in a château which was once a hunting lodge of Louis XV's, had acquired a Mercedes racing car, and was beginning to assemble able men about him—men like Lewis Brereton and M. F. Harmon, Clayton Bissell, Harold Hartney, Elmer Haslett, Alan Winslow and Major Thomas Milling. He seemed to attract the most daring spirits, and to find prospective aviators everywhere. One day he had car trouble on a French road, and the Mercedes was quickly repaired by an Army driver who was passing by. When he found that the chauffeur had been a racing driver back home, and wanted to fly, Mitchell helped him into the Air Service. His recruit was Eddie Rickenbacker, soon to become the leading American ace.

In the spring of 1918 Hap Arnold heard in Washington that Mitchell and Foulois had clashed: "Mitchell had created splendid relationships with the French and British . . . and without portfolio had established himself as the leader of the American air force in the war . . . Foulois, with a much more studious, careful, mechanical-minded experience of his own, dating back to the Army's first airplane, still had to make such contacts."

The two adversaries fought it out, and almost at once Foulois asked Pershing to send Mitchell back to America because of his "extremely childish attitude," as "mentally unfitted for further field service, incapable of working in harmony with myself." This outburst was brought on by a confrontation at Toul, when Foulois arrived to take over Mitchell's old post as Chief of Air Service, First

removed aviation in the A.E.F. from Signal Corps control (a year before it was made official in Washington); Kenly's Air Service was not a combat arm then, but one of supply and equipment. Kenly put Mitchell in charge of the Air Service, Zone of Advance. When Foulois arrived he replaced Kenly, who went to Washington—as Director of Military Aeronautics.

In none of these moves was Mitchell considered by Pershing for the post of chief of air operations, but his influence was always felt, and his progress toward a combat command was irresistible.

Army, while Mitchell was to retain command of all active air units at the front. Foulois wrote to Pershing that Mitchell was hostile and insubordinate, and he described the scene: "He informed me that the entire office force, the officers and enlisted men, office furniture, and maps on the wall and even telephones were a part of the 1st Corps Air Service personnel and material and would be removed when he turned over the office."

Foulois made a second visit, with reinforcements, before he got the wall maps and some of the staff—but Mitchell retained his own desk. Foulois complained that Mitchell opposed every policy announced by the General Staff on aviation, that every session with Mitchell ended in a noisy squabble, and that the year of hard service was beginning to tell on Mitchell.

Mitchell scoffed at Foulois and the other newcomers as "a shipload of aviation officers . . . almost none of whom had ever seen an airplane. A more incompetent lot of air warriors had never arrived in the zone of active military operations." As for Foulois: "While Foulois meant well and had had some experience in aviation in the United States, he was not at all conversant with conditions in Europe. As rapidly as possible, the competent men, who had learned their duties in the face of the enemy, were displaced and their positions taken by these carpetbaggers."

Pershing tried to restore order by moving Mitchell up front, under Foulois, who commanded from the rear area. When conflict continued, Pershing took his final step. He called on a West Point classmate, General Mason Patrick, an able but testy engineer, to become Chief of the Air Service. He told the astonished Patrick of his new assignment: "In all of this Army, there is but one thing causing me real anxiety, and that's the Air Service. There are a lot of good men in it, but they're running around in circles. Somebody has got to make them go straight. I want you to do the job."

Patrick found "a chaotic condition of affairs" and soon improved it. The "clash of personalities," as he described it, between Mitchell and Foulois subsided. As soon as Mitchell's gift for tactical command at the front became obvious Foulois, in a manly gesture, wrote to Pershing asking that Mitchell replace him as chief of the First Army Air Service. He praised the "high fighting spirit of morale" in the squadrons and Mitchell's "most efficient service . . . in the organization, battle training, general supervision and guidance of the Air Service units . . . in the Château-Thierry area." *

Mitchell's fliers used French planes, at first worn-out Nieuports in which they suffered heavy casualties in battles with Baron von Richthofen's "Flying Circus." Mitchell appealed to General Foch and was given new Spads as well as British reinforcements, three bomber squadrons and four pursuit. He sent the British to strike enemy ammunition depots behind Château-Thierry and put the enemy on the defensive, forcing him to guard his rear. Twelve British planes were lost, but Mitchell thought he had won an objective: "We had found the Achilles heel of the German position north of the Marne and seized the initiative in the air. What we could have done if we had had 1000 good airplanes instead of a measly 250!"

On July 15, 1918, the last great German attack was launched, across the Marne, and it was Mitchell who discovered the strength and direction of the offensive. He flew along the river through fog and low clouds to the battle area, into which Ludendorff was throwing seventy divisions: "Suddenly as I rounded a turn of the river east of Dormans, I saw a great mass of artillery fire hitting the south bank, and, spanning the river, five bridges filled with German troops marching over." He descended to within 500 feet of these streams of men, without being fired upon, or seeing a German plane. "Looking down on the men, marching so splendidly, I thought to myself, what a shame to spoil such fine infantry."

He flew back and took his information to Malin Craig, chief of staff to General Hunter Liggett, who commanded the First Army. Ground forces were aligned to meet this new threat and Mitchell's squadrons took part in the counterattack which halted the Germans. Major Elmer Haslett, one of Mitchell's most daring pilots, had seen Mitchell skimming along the Marne, and thought this one of the most remarkable flights of the war. He said it was a stroke of luck for the Allied cause that the man who flew over these

* With this gesture, Foulois was content to devote his own talents to supplying Mitchell with men, planes and supplies from the rear. As one aviation historian put it: "Everyone lived happily ever after, except Foulois." The animosity of some A.E.F. officers toward Mitchell dated from this incident in the struggle for command.

Marne bridges was "a rare tactician and strategist" who saw what other officers would not have seen: "He realized the awful truth where the ordinary airman would not have conceived the possibilities . . . when the fliers found out who had made that mysterious flight, our morale was strengthened one hundred per cent."

Mitchell thought his pilots were improving, and he was proud of them despite the losses in the counterattack on the Germans: "Although there were many things left to be desired, I felt that our work at Château-Thierry had been remarkable."

He was now ready for the greatest air battle of his career, in which he tested theories of air power to which he would devote the rest of his life.

The German salient at St. Mihiel thrust deep into Allied lines like a misshapen horseshoe, guarding Metz and the approach to the German Ruhr, a landscape torn by four years of battle. The high command planned to straighten the line in this sector in September 1918 by throwing the Germans back as a prelude to a grand assault on the whole enemy position. Mitchell was ready with a plan to match the occasion; he asked for a force of about 1500 planes, American, British, French and Italian, to drive the Germans from the sky over the salient, seal off the rear, destroy communications, and aid ground troops massing for the attack. Pershing and Foch agreed with him. Mitchell welcomed the new day:

"General Pershing was now in high spirits; we were getting our American army together, and our air people, who for a long time had felt that Pershing did not know, or care to know, very much about aviation, were beginning to change their minds, as he was helping us in every way possible. I guess he couldn't swallow the whole hog to begin with, had to take it easy."

The air units were now well organized, "going like clockwork" under Milling, the best of all possible chiefs of staff, Mitchell thought. While infantry, artillery and other units filled the roads, moving toward the St. Mihiel front, Mitchell scattered his huge air force on fourteen fields, carefully camouflaging his planes and continually moving dummies to deceive the Germans. It was, he said, "the first definite American command organized for grand operations in our history." Of the forty-nine squadrons, twenty-nine were American, and Mitchell found no dissension. He wrote in his journal: "Here we were, a force of four nations, acting together with no discord . . . Such a thing could not have occurred with ground troops."

The British were led by Trenchard—eight squadrons of night bombers. Mitchell wrote his mother about this time: "I am in a new field of activity and command all [Allied] air troops in service in our area. Someday I shall write and tell you about the number of airplanes. Should they fly at once the sky would be black." *

Mitchell began operations in a school building back of the lines. Haslett went there once, to find Mitchell and his staff crawling on the floor around a relief map of the St. Mihiel area: "I was fascinated. It was like toy-soldier stuff, but in deadly earnest." This map had been made in sections by French balloon companies, and once pieced together, revealed every rise and fold, every hill and stream and building or defense position in the salient. Mitchell worked over it for several days: "This, combined with my intimate knowledge of the country . . . by studying it for many years, and now from flying over it with both French and American observers . . . made me feel that I knew this part of the world as well as any man living."

He concealed the concentration of planes from the enemy so that the element of surprise would allow him about two days of unchallenged superiority in the area. His pilots would fly across the salient from each side, bombing the rear in order to halt and disorganize the enemy retreat. He would attack in brigade strength rather than with small flights: "Nothing like this had ever been tried before," he later wrote. "It marked the beginning of great strategical air operations away from the troops."

On September 10 Mitchell flew over the lines and confirmed the suspicion that the Germans knew of the coming attack. He saw columns of the enemy in retreat. By now 400,000 American troops and more than 3000 cannon were in line, accompanied this time

* Tom Milling of Mitchell's staff, in the report on St. Mihiel, said the British were there for "fullest co-operation," but could not be placed under Mitchell's immediate command, since they were directed from London. Mitchell was in effective command, but Trenchard later objected to such claims, saying that he never relinquished control of his squadrons to anyone.

by tanks, some of them under the command of Mitchell's friend George S. Patton, Jr.

When Mitchell went to Pershing's headquarters the night before the attack, he was surprised to hear the Chief Engineer urging postponement: "The rain will slow delivery of ammunition on the railways. It's going to be hard to get up enough water for the troops." The objections were endless, Mitchell thought, "a thousand and one things which could not be done were mentioned." He saw that several of the "old fossils" in the meeting agreed with the engineer and reflected that "you can always trust an engineer officer to go on the defensive whenever it is possible." He was the junior officer present and the last to be asked for his opinion.

"I told them very plainly that I knew the Germans were withdrawing . . . as I had seen them personally . . . furthermore, I said, there wasn't going to be much of a battle at Saint-Mihiel, and our troops might be better off without artillery, as they might shoot a good many of our own men . . . all we had to do was to jump on the Germans, and the quicker we did it, the better."

Pershing ordered the attack on schedule.

The first day, September 12, was gray and rainy, and few of the squadrons got off; there was limited air combat, but Mitchell's planes strafed enemy positions and bombed the rear. Major Carl ("Tooey") Spaatz from Boyertown, Pennsylvania, West Point class of 1914, went up with a fifteen-plane squadron of Spads and got into a dogfight: "The thing really happened so damned fast that the only recollection you have is diving on a plane, or seeing them try to dive on you, and you maneuver to either get away or get on them. I knocked down three Fokkers."

Kenneth Littauer, another of Mitchell's pilots, saw "600 or 700" planes go over in one formation: "I didn't believe my eyes, because we'd never seen such a thing before. I happened to be standing on the air field when this damned thing started to go over. Then it went and it went . . . it was awfully impressive." A few minutes later, when Littauer went up on a mission, he found that Mitchell's big flight had "certainly swept the sky clean of enemy aircraft."

On the second day, when the weather was only slightly better, Mitchell drove his pilots relentlessly, and they flew in conditions many thought impossible. As Milling wrote: "Previous to the St. Mihiel offensive, the American Air Service had seldom departed from the airdrome unless weather conditions were propitious for flying. This precedent was entirely exploded, and the units were ordered to carry out their missions regardless of weather. They made gallant and daring efforts." There were crashes and ruined planes and a few accidental deaths, but the squadrons flew.

The battle had been decided on the first day; all objectives were taken, and within four days the lines had been straightened, the German air force driven from the vicinity, and the final phase of the war was opening. Pershing wrote to Mitchell:

"Please accept my sincere congratulations on the successful and very important part taken by the Air Force under your command in the first offensive of the American Army. The organization and control of the tremendous concentration of air forces . . . is as fine a tribute to you personally as is the courage and nerve shown by your officers a signal proof of the high morale which permeates the service under your command . . . I am proud of you all."

Mitchell wrote his mother proudly, to report that he had commanded the largest air force ever assembled, and added: "I have been recommended to be made a general at once, to be decorated with our Military Cross and the Legion of Honor . . . I enclose letters the like of which are seldom written."

By now, some time after the event, he could write his mother about the death of his younger brother John, who had crashed in a defective plane and was buried in Sevastopol cemetery. Mitchell saw to it that the grave was covered with grass, and put there a wreath of Lorraine thistles: "The grave is near a pretty wood . . . It is the quietest spot around . . . I sometimes fly low over this place to see how it is getting along when I can't get there in other ways."

Without a pause Mitchell prepared for an attack in the Argonne. The French reclaimed their planes but the British remained, and American forces were growing. U.S. squadrons still used French planes, for the only American planes arriving were the De Havillands, of little combat use, Mitchell thought, except in observation. The DH's quickly won a reputation as "flaming coffins"; in the haste to produce standardized models, American manufacturers had not only powered the British design with the new Liberty motor, they had mounted the gas tanks between pilot and observer, and crashes usually resulted in explosions.

Mitchell used his organization plans of St. Mihiel for the new offensive, improving his communications system between airfields and other points by radio, telephone and motorcycle couriers. His tactical problem was new—an attack over parallel battle lines, subject to flanking attacks by the enemy. He massed his planes in the center of the fifty-mile front, which was manned by more than half a million U.S. ground troops.

The Germans were stronger in the air during this engagement, but were kept off the American infantry during most of the advance. Mitchell once spotted a dangerous congestion of truck traffic at a village crossroads, realized that German attack planes would wreak havoc there, and pushed a formation of 320 planes to the area, bombing German troop centers and keeping enemy planes busy. He had Harold Hartney's pursuit squadrons fly just over the heads of U.S. infantry, to shield them from attack.

Reporters who went to his headquarters got exuberant statements from Mitchell, mostly in praise of his fliers. "There is nothing to beat them in the world," he said. On the biggest day of the air battle over the Argonne, sixty enemy planes and twelve balloons were reported shot down, at a loss of about twenty Allied planes. On that day, Mitchell reported, a single wing of his force had flown almost 45,000 miles, fought fifty combats and destroyed nineteen enemy planes without a loss.

Through the long Argonne drive Mitchell's planes hammered the enemy rear, taking heavy toll of airdromes, supply points, bridges and railroads. Though he found this battle "not a particularly interesting one from an air standpoint," it was far more demanding than St. Mihiel and tested the stamina of his organization for the first time. In October, when at the time the still-resisting Germans were beginning to run short of material, Mitchell was promoted to commander of the Air Service, Group of Armies. Milling succeeded him in the First Army.

Mitchell was now one of the most popular men in France. Hap Arnold, who visited him at headquarters during the month of the Armistice, saw that the Army's stories about him were not exaggerated. Billy seemed "on top of the world" as he held court: "Laughing and constantly talking, wearing that blouse with the outside pockets and the famous pink breeches." One airman, Fred Schauss, thought Mitchell looked very much the part of the hero: "He didn't walk like other men, and though he was modest and considerate of everybody, there was pride in every movement. Even if he had only eight or ten feet to walk, he went at it as though he were marching a mile, and was late. He moved at top speed." A stream of fliers, French, British and American, came to see him, and most of the well-known Allied generals too, merely anxious for a look at the renowned aviator.

"The fliers around him would have done anything for him," Arnold said, "and so would the boys out in the squadrons . . . Billy was clearly the Prince of the Air now."

The French government had given him a Renault racer and Mitchell often drove it at 90 miles an hour over French roads, with his chauffeur sitting behind.

By this time his teacher, Trenchard, listened respectfully to Mitchell's ideas, and had recognized him as a master after the Meuse-Argonne offensive: "The most terrific exhibition I have ever seen—you have cleaned out the air."

As Arnold watched Mitchell he realized "how much we needed him back in Washington," where a different kind of war was to be fought; Pershing would move in as Chief of Staff, and Mitchell should join him. Arnold tried to convince Mitchell that he should return home and become the new Air Chief. "Why shouldn't you capitalize on your war record? Can you swing it with Pershing?"

Mitchell laughed and shook his head. His fliers were going to the Rhineland with the army of occupation and he would lead them. "I want to see this thing through."

Arnold gave up ruefully, for he was convinced that there was no one else "who could possibly" take over the job of Air Chief in Washington. Above all others Mitchell had the background, knowledge of operations, prestige and personal courage. Arnold diagnosed the reason for his failure with Mitchell: "He wanted to drive that fastest Mercedes down Unter den Linden."

Only at the very end of the war did Mitchell realize what a strain he had lived under. For six months he had slept no more than three hours a night. Daily reports from his squadrons did not reach him until ten o'clock at night and his orders for the next day went out about two in the morning; by five o'clock he was up to watch the departure of planes before dawn. The internal struggles of command had also taxed him, and he could foresee more of these in the future.

Mitchell visited his squadron commanders on Armistice Day to congratulate them: "This was the first time in the world's history that great bodies of air troops had been brought together and fought as a single organization. We Americans had developed the best system of air fighting that the world had ever seen." (Mitchell attributed some of this to his use of an anonymous officer he kept at headquarters as a guinea pig. He read every order to this man, and "if he could understand them, anybody could. He wasn't particularly bright, but he was one of my most valuable officers for that reason.")

Mitchell was proud of the victory over accomplished German airmen, and told his officers so in exuberant speeches on the day of celebration. "We could look with absolute confidence to the future if our system were maintained," he wrote, "and our men who were trained in actual combat were given charge of the development to make America absolutely safe from hostile invasion." Disappointments were in store for him.

As "everyone was rejoicing" on Armistice night, Mitchell could not bear to miss the riotous scenes in Paris. He gathered some of his French friends and a few officers, and they were off in his largest automobile, along roads choked with traffic, fighting their way to the capital. It was late when they rolled onto the Champs Élysées, where men and women were pulling German cannon along the street, and everyone was dancing, singing, kissing, "the most spectacular outburst of feeling that I have ever seen," Mitchell said. Americans in uniform were hailed as heroes.

Mitchell saw no other cars; only military vehicles were allowed on the streets. A cordon of police barred Mitchell's way until a group of French fliers who had fought at St. Mihiel recognized him: "*Vive notre général américain!*" they shouted. They brushed aside the police, "almost picked up the automobile" and towed it down the boulevards. Men sat on the roof and the hood and clung to the running boards; others joined hands and made rings about them, singing "Madelon" and the "Marseillaise" and gamy air force songs.*

The next day Pershing gave Mitchell orders to head the U.S. air force of the Ruhr occupation, and to take only the oldest units, at full strength. Mitchell drove to Germany in the Mercedes, inspecting bomb damage done by planes along the way, looking over planes the Germans had destroyed on their own airfields, and watched admiringly as German troops crossed the Rhine with banners flying, flowers in the muzzles of their rifles, while bands played "Die Wacht am Rhein."

He made headquarters in a municipal building in Coblenz, overlooking the Rhine, in an office where he found a bust of Julius Caesar, and he became interested in the history of the spot where Caesar had crossed the river: "I spent many hours translating his account of how he placed the bridge and whipped the Germans." Mitchell chose a site near Caesar's ancient crossing for an airdrome, and construction crews began clearing it for runways. His staff worked on operations reports for the war, visited nearby U.S. commands, and accepted several hundred new German planes under the terms of the Armistice.

One day he took the young Prince of Wales for a flight over the valleys of the Rhine and the Moselle, and as they passed the Lorelei rock the Prince yelled: "I think I can see her!"

A few days later Mitchell was called to American headquarters, where he joined several others to receive the Legion of Honor from Marshal Pétain. Afterward he abruptly decided that he wanted to leave Germany. Hap Arnold was still in Paris, and Mitchell called him there: "As soon as you get back to Washington, have orders issued getting me home. I want to get back as fast as possible. Right away. Can you do that?"

Arnold promised to help, but it was probably Mitchell's own influence with Pershing that sent him home—for the following week, on January 14, Pershing advised Washington that when

* Mitchell's associate, Frank Lahm, later a general, recalling this night many years later, thought the Paris scene exaggerated. Lahm and Mitchell dined in Nancy that night, two hundred miles from Paris, and Lahm wondered at Mitchell's ability to negotiate the distance over crowded roads. Colonel C. H. M. Roberts of Mitchell's ordnance, however, though he recalled the roads as jammed, said: "It would have been just like Mitchell to have fought his way through and celebrated in Paris."

Mitchell had been decorated with the Legion of Honor, he had other things in mind for him: "He has applied for authority to return to the U.S. via England to consult with General Trenchard and other officers of the British air service to see what the result of creating a separate branch of aeronautics has been. As it would seem to be in the best interest of the Air Service, Colonel Mitchell * will be given this authority unless contrary instructions are received."

Mitchell was soon off for home with Milling and two old friends, Elmer Haslett and Alan Winslow, who had recently been released from German prisons. They went through Belgium, where they walked the field of Waterloo, and speculated on how a few planes in that battle might have changed history. Mitchell inspected the defensive positions at Louvain, then went to Zeebrugge to see the results of British bombardment of the seaplane base. They were in England by early February.

London seemed outwardly gay but "rather sad and despondent . . . because no one knew what the future held in store." Mitchell was happy to find Trenchard in command of the peacetime Royal Air Force, and was once more impressed by British airmen: "Everywhere the British are, there is system, and this is shown distinctly in their air force. It is the best organized force of its kind in the world . . . If we could have the air organization in the U.S. that the British have we would be so far ahead of the rest of the world that there would be no comparison." He took that impression home with him, determined to convince his superiors and the country at large.

He visited Major Bill Larned, General Biddle, and Fred Guest and David Henderson of the British Air Board, and met Winston Churchill at a dinner party: "Churchill is certainly a go-ahead sort of a person; he may not figure out things in detail, but he looks at the broad aspects of a situation."

His sister Ruth, who was living in London, welcomed him, and when she saw his plain blouse she asked: "Where are all those medals we've been hearing about?" He fished one from a pocket, the Legion of Honor. "Is that all?" With an air of embarrassment he pulled out the others—a Croix de Guerre with Palm; the Italian

* Mitchell's promotion to brigadier general in 1918 was a temporary commission.

Order of Sts. Maurice and Lazarus; the Victory Medal, with clasps for Cambrai, the Somme, Meuse-Argonne, Champagne-Marne; the Distinguished Service Cross and Medal.

He toured British arms factories but took time to see Shakespeare's birthplace at Stratford, and just before sailing for home went to an investiture ceremony at Buckingham Palace, where King George called him aside for a "delightful chat." The Prince of Wales had written his father about his flight with Mitchell, and the King expressed his appreciation. "He also told me that it was his great desire to have the British and American people understand each other so that in future they may be drawn together more and more . . . in case of war." Mitchell proposed more frequent visits between the countries, beginning with a tour of the United States by the Prince of Wales.

Then, after an absence of almost two years, he boarded the *Aquitania* for the voyage home. He returned in a mood as purposeful, as restless and as ardent as that in which he had slipped off to war in advance of his countrymen.

4

It's Mostly the Navy, but It's Old-Fashioned Generals, Too

The Washington to which Mitchell returned was in a giddy mood. There was an exhilarating air of triumph, and of the opening of an era of unbroken peace and prosperity. With the Armistice, there had come a sense of relief that eighteen months of war had, after all, cost the nation so little, and war-built industry promised an unprecedented boom. It was easy for Americans to accept the assurances they heard so often, that the A.E.F. had made the world safe for democracy. Without an enemy in sight, the United States had no need for a war machine, and even in March 1919, when Mitchell reached Washington, the Army was hastily being disbanded, as if it were an obstacle to progress and an embarrassing burden to a magnanimous conqueror.

Mitchell came back to a barely existent Air Service. He had hardly a scrap of paper to document its organization, purpose or extent. Basic manuals must be prepared for every phase of the work. The pell-mell return to peace would soon reduce Air Service officers from 20,000 to about 1300; the planes, most of them De Havillands, were left over from the war, and few new ones could be expected.

Yet Mitchell began as if he had no doubts. The air lessons of the war, he thought, had been overlooked, but he would soon make them clear to the country. He had reason for confidence, under his orders to return and become Director of Military Aeronautics.

Almost before he unpacked his bags he was caught up in the campaign which was to become a seven-year whirlwind. He flew to New York to address the Society of Automotive Engineers and startled them with a wartime secret. If the war had not ended, he would have dropped airborne troops behind the German lines and caught the enemy between two forces. He had been promised a full division, to be carried in 1200 Handley Page bombers, and armed with 24,000 machine guns. He was convinced that it would have demoralized the enemy.

His talk in the hotel ballroom that evening had a dreamlike quality, and the auto engineers, in whose world the Model T Ford was still the wonder of the age, were probably among the first civilians to conclude that Mitchell was unbalanced. One New York newspaper, the *Herald,* gave the speech a brief mention.*

Mitchell returned to an unpleasant surprise in Washington. Although he had orders to report as Director of Military Aeronautics, both title and office had disappeared in a postwar reorganization; the war-born Air Service was moved from France to Washington, and its Chief was not Mitchell, but General Charles Menoher. The new Chief was an infantry hero, commander of the Rainbow Division in France and a celebrated disciplinarian, but he had never flown. It was the first clear sign that the Army had learned none of the air lessons Mitchell was proclaiming, and that it saw the plane as an auxiliary weapon of limited promise.

Mitchell gave no outward sign of chagrin as he began work—he was Menoher's G-3 officer, in charge of training and operations. In the next months Menoher's name was heard less frequently than Mitchell's in Washington. It was the G-3 who became the symbol of the Air Service, which was now a tiny band with only one general (Mitchell was a colonel). Mitchell surrounded himself with a group of veterans who had fought in France, Tom Milling and Chuck Chandler, now colonels, and Lewis Brereton, William Sherman and Harold Hartney, who were lieutenant colonels. Other wartime fliers crowded the office. Tooey Spaatz was one of the few who still had a strong desire to fly (later he took command of the First Pursuit Group in the field).

* Even after World War II, paratroop commanders thought Mitchell's scheme of an air drop in 1918 unrealistic, in view of available equipment. But as Hap Arnold recorded, he tested the idea at Kelly Field soon afterward, dropping 'chutists with machine guns. As Arnold wrote: "After these early experiments, the use of parachute troops languished in this country."

Burdette Wright, an accomplished piano player, was seldom out of Mitchell's sight. The colonel rarely let a day pass without a party of some kind, and Wright was always detailed to find a piano, and play it as long as anyone was about. On each visit to an Air Service post Mitchell asked if a party had been planned, and offered to give one himself if it were not scheduled; the hosts always responded with an impromptu gala.

Reed Chambers, a Kansas farm boy who had shot down seven German planes, came one day to announce his resignation; he was anxious to join Eddie Rickenbacker in auto manufacturing. Mitchell brought him home for dinner and took him down to the cellar, where Chambers detected an improbable odor.

"I'm running a little experiment," Mitchell said. "I thought you'd like to watch. These people passed this Prohibition law while we were fighting for the country. They can't do that to me." And he started a fire beneath a small whiskey still.

Chambers recalled: "Pretty soon this stuff started dripping through and he had a glass and you could get about half a glass. He'd pour out some of this and sniff it and hand me some and we drank this warm white lightning."

In that intimate setting Mitchell persuaded Chambers to re-enlist. "Look here, I got your resignation. You can't do it. Too many old-timers have left and we need you. We've got to keep a cadre of experienced men to get this thing organized. I want you to reconsider. I'll give you command of the First Pursuit Group if you'll stay."

Chambers succumbed. He agreed to command the pursuit at Selfridge Field, Michigan, where Mitchell would send him all the pilots he could find.

Mitchell had been in office only five days when Franklin D. Roosevelt, then Acting Secretary of the Navy, invited him to appear before the Navy General Board, which was considering its future air policy. The session was pleasant enough, but marked the opening of a duel that was to hold the attention of the American people for years.

Mitchell was not backward. He advised the Navy to develop some defense against aircraft. Battleships alone could not defend themselves against planes. The only real defense was other aircraft. Admiral Albert G. Winterhalter, the Navy's spokesman for the board, exchanged views with Mitchell.

"My opinion is that you can make a direct attack on ships from the air in the future," Mitchell said.

"I agree with you there."

"We will get a missile to attack a big ship, whether it takes a ton or two tons," Mitchell said.

"We shall have to tackle both sides of the question," Winterhalter said. "We shall have to find out what your methods of attack are so that we can find means to meet them."

"I think, Admiral, we can try out a good many things around Chesapeake Bay." He suggested that the Air Service and the Navy hold maneuvers, with planes attacking warships.

"There isn't anything . . . to me more important," Winterhalter said.

Mitchell then spoke of coastal defense, insisting that the Air Service, not the Navy, should defend the shores. Winterhalter asked how far out to sea the air cover would reach. "As far out as the Air Service can operate," Mitchell said. "You've got to have a combination of the three . . . The Army, the Navy and the Air Service . . . If we look forward, there will be a Ministry of Defense, combining Army, Navy and Air Force under one direction."

He talked for three hours, and even at the end the naval officers remained friendly. But it was to be his last invitation to come before the Navy General Board; in the future there were few congenial meetings between Mitchell and the Navy's high command. Winterhalter's enthusiastic response to Mitchell's proposal of bombing tests was not to be repeated. The board, as if convinced by Mitchell's testimony, reported that aviation was "an adjunct . . . of such vital importance . . . that no inferiority must be accepted."

Someone in the high command quieted Winterhalter and his companions on the board, for this utterance was the last of its sort. As Mitchell made increasingly stronger claims for the plane, the Navy replied with a more spirited defense of the battleship.

A day or so after this appearance Mitchell began the rounds of travel by air that would carry him more than 200,000 miles in the next four years. At McCook Field in Dayton he flew a new fighter, the Thomas Morse, "faster than any general in any army had ever flown before." Mitchell thought the Morse was the "best all-round fighting single-seater in the world," and ordered it into production.

He flew to Chicago and Milwaukee for public speeches, and with Elmer Haslett to inspect a plane plant on Long Island. Back in Washington, he was soon making a routine of appearing before congressional committees to testify on air power, but found time to re-enter George Washington University and take his retroactive degree, twenty-one years after his studies had been interrupted by the war with Spain. Each day found Mitchell at some new activity—winning ribbons at an Arlington horse show, speaking to a Baltimore Elks Club, flying at Bolling Field, consulting with plane builder Glenn Curtiss and inspecting mail planes.

At the same time he inundated Menoher with his suggestions, many of them looking so far into the future that the Chief was incredulous. Mitchell asked for bombers able to cross the Atlantic and return, as well as dirigibles for "offensive expeditions"; he wanted two Army aircraft carriers with 900-foot decks, with defenses against planes and submarines and capable of "very high speed." Menoher, startled by this invasion of the Navy's field, returned this proposal to Mitchell. There was no end to the others:

He asked for torpedoes and armor-piercing bombs; development of the 37-mm. cannon and a 20-mm. automatic machine gun, both firing thermite projectiles, as well as the ordinary armor-piercing, incendiary and tracer shells.

Many of these were proposed by Mitchell as "emergency measures"; all were ignored at headquarters. Secretary of War Newton Baker and the General Staff thought that the war had deranged Mitchell and that his ideas were beneath serious notice. One day Mitchell asked a staff officer: "What is the Staff doing with my recommendations? I haven't heard about any one of them. I think they're important to the country." The officer laughed. "We're filing 'em," he said. The rumor was that the War Department cellar had a special place for discarded Mitchell proposals, known as The Flying Trash Pile, but the daily bombardment went on, not to cease entirely so long as he remained in uniform:

A force of expert aviation mechanics must be trained, with special pay and status, in order to protect the lives of fliers. Air-raid protection should be given cities, with alarms, food rationing and medical-assistance plans. Air transports must be built to carry ground troops. Combined maneuvers should test coastal defenses against air attack. Commercial aviation should be expanded, to furnish a reserve of pilots in case of war. Chemical Warfare and the Air Service should have a formal exchange of ideas. There must be a pool of amphibious planes for rescue work. Air routes should be set up immediately all across the country, and into South America and Canada. An all-metal bomber must be built; the Pacific Coast must have a defensive shield of air power; special plane-landing equipment, including skis, should be developed.

Few of these ideas were his own—but no one else made an effort to collect them, force them upon the Army's attention or embody them into a concept of the needs of air power. Though Mitchell saw his suggestions ignored, he made no official complaint; he sought other means to implement them.

There were, even now, encouraging signs, and Mitchell's unflagging high spirits were sustained by the success of his tiny band of airmen, especially those at McCook Field. They had developed a variable pitch propeller for greater efficiency in taking off and at high altitudes; a 37-mm. cannon had been fired from a plane. Parachutists were making regular jumps. A DH4B had been used as a dive bomber, plunging down with a 300-pound bomb to strike its target. With the wartime chief of aerial photography, Edward Steichen, he found a young photographer at a Florida base, George Goddard, who had rigged an ingenious camera mount of four tennis balls, to prevent vibration. He installed Goddard in a small laboratory at McCook, where, with the aid of Dr. Kenneth Mees of Eastman Kodak, he pioneered in high-quality photography from planes.

He found a new ally in Major Alexander de Seversky, a Russian emigré who had lost a leg in a bomb explosion during the war, a budding inventor who had been chief of the Russian fighter force in the Baltic region. The two became fast friends. As Seversky recalled it: "We spoke the same airman's language and were eager to compare our experiences." They were soon deep in theories of air war; Mitchell concluded that the Russian would be useful in his plan of campaign.

No sooner had Mitchell begun, however, than the Army put him on notice that it would resist him. Senior officers who had been assigned to study the lessons of the war reported to General Pershing, who was now Chief of Staff, that though aviation was useful for observation, there was no sign that it would become a decisive weapon. As if inspired by the report, Franklin D. Roosevelt published an article which dismissed Mitchell's views as "pernicious."

Mitchell's approach was still restrained, though he saw a fight stretching far ahead of him. He wrote to his mother in the summer of 1919: "If I can get this on a firm basis within the next ten years, I shall consider my work pretty well done to the country."

In the spring, along with a slate of war fliers—Spaatz, Chambers and a few others—he had been given the rating of Military Aviator for his wartime service in France. This designation, originally given to only twenty-four fliers of 1913 vintage, was highly coveted, and the newcomers were resented by old-timers who had won their "wings" in primitive planes. Despite close friendships between the men of the two groups, the wartime Military Aviators were never quite accepted.*

Mitchell was finding the cost of Washington living ruinous, higher than in prewar days, and he still lived beyond his means, entertaining lavishly. He wrote to his mother that he had two alternatives, "to get out of Washington or leave the service and make more money." He could not bring himself to break faith with his supporters, however: "I am practically the only one that can bring about a betterment of our national defense at this time." On several occasions his mother sent him $5000 or $10,000 to help out, and his wife contributed liberally, though she thought Mitchell extravagant. Entertainment, an essential part of his campaign to woo political and military leaders, once pushed his household costs to $30,000 a year.

On July 4 Mitchell saw Hap Arnold for the first time since the war, in El Paso, Texas, where they inspected the work of the Air

* In order of seniority the first twelve Military Aviators were Charles DeF. Chandler, F. P. Lahm, Ben Foulois, P. W. Beck, R. C. Kirtland, H. H. Arnold, Tom Milling, H. Geiger, S. H. McLeary, L. H. Brereton, J. D. Park and L. E. Goodier.

Service border patrol, largely a device to keep the few pilots busy. Flights along the Rio Grande spotted wetbacks crossing illegally from Mexico, and also watched for bandit parties, still active in the wake of Pancho Villa's private war. The Army commander in El Paso was an old horse soldier, Colonel Tommy Tompkins, a legendary trooper who wore ragged side whiskers, a misshapen campaign hat and well-worn spurs. Tompkins admired the air patrol: "Wouldn't it be a great thing if we could fly right over the border down to Villa's home country in Chihuahua and see about that new trouble they say is stirring?"

"Well, come on," Mitchell said. "What're you waiting for?"

The old bandit-chaser was hesitant. "Why, we can't do a thing like that!"

"The hell we can't," Mitchell said. "Come on. Let's get moving. Here's the airplane." Arnold watched them fly away with Tompkins' whiskers whipped by the wind, off on his first and perhaps only flight, in defiance of regulations and international law.

Arnold and Mitchell had long conversations during their Texas meeting. Arnold found him sharper and more alert than ever, but thought him disappointed in Washington life; his office in the capital did not compare with "the gay, triumphant headquarters he had had in France." Arnold also thought he detected in Mitchell "an undercurrent of angry impatience," though it was not yet visible in public. Arnold thought Mitchell overlooked the possibility that most Americans lacked the capacity to grasp his theories of air power. Mitchell also seemed to think that resistance to his ideas was the result of a conspiracy.

"It's mostly the Navy," Mitchell said, "but it's old-fashioned generals, too." Arnold got the impression that Mitchell's ruling passion was to "show them," with spectacular uses of air power, like the border patrol, a cross-country air race, flights to Alaska and around the world. "And above all," Arnold recalled, "to sink those damned battleships!"

Arnold had just returned to his post in San Francisco when Mitchell wrote him: "I am very anxious to push through this flight to Alaska with land planes. Better get oriented along that line . . . This might develop into a round-the-world flight." The result was a flight to Alaska in 1920, led by veteran Captain St. Clair ("Wingbone") Streett, a 9000-mile test without a casualty, flown largely over uncharted lands. Only the unyielding State Department, which feared to arouse Russian suspicions, prevented Mitchell from sending the planes across the Bering Strait.

By midsummer of 1919 the air-power battle was becoming a public issue. Secretary of War Newton Baker, a vigorous reformer from Cleveland, had sent an eight-man commission to study European aviation, led by Assistant Secretary Benedict Crowell. Baker soon had word that the mission was drinking in Mitchell's favorite ideas from men like Sir Hugh Trenchard, and cabled a warning to Crowell that he was to limit himself to fact-finding and submit no conclusions as to air policy. (It was not strange that Baker got this impression; Mitchell had notified air attachés in Europe to befriend and guide this mission.)

The defiant mission returned to Baker with a report urging Mitchell's ideas upon him: ". . . Immediate action is necessary to safeguard the air interest of the United States, to preserve for the government some benefit of the great aviation expenditures made during the period of the war, and to prevent a vitally necessary industry from disappearing."

Crowell said that 90 percent of the aviation industry had disappeared, and the rest was in danger. His commission urged the concentration of all air activity under one government agency, coequal with Army, Navy and Commerce.

Baker was infuriated with Crowell for "flying in the face of my orders" and presenting the case for an air ministry. Behind Baker's reaction was his fear that a strong, independent air arm would lead to indiscriminate bombing of civilians. Only a few days before the Armistice he had sent a stern warning to the Air Service that the United States would not take part in an offensive that "has as its objective promiscuous bombing upon industry, commerce or population, in enemy countries."

It was perhaps for this reason that Mitchell spoke infrequently, and obliquely, of the bombing of civilian centers during 1919. He referred to targets in enemy nations only as "elements which are further back than his troops are."

Baker withheld the Crowell report, refused to endorse it, and did his best to keep it from the public, but there was no secret about the document in military circles. Crowell and Howard Coffin of the mission both saw Admiral Charles Benson, the Chief of Naval Operations, soon after their return, and found him hostile: "You're wasting your time. I cannot conceive of any use that the fleet will ever have for aircraft . . . The Navy doesn't need airplanes. Aviation is just a lot of noise."

Benson was in earnest. On August 1 he issued a confidential order abolishing the Aviation Division of the Navy, scattering its remains throughout other branches. It was a secret even from Assistant Secretary Roosevelt, but some despairing Navy aviator apparently passed a copy to Mitchell, for at his first chance, before the Senate Military Affairs Committee, he spoke up:

"In this country, our Army aviation is shot to pieces and our naval aviation does not exist as an arm, under their new organization. They are even worse off than they were."

This was news to Senator James Wadsworth of New York: "In what respect?"

"In that they have stopped having a separate bureau for aviation and have distributed those duties among six or seven different departments."

Wadsworth was incredulous: "In the Navy Department?"

"Yes, sir."

Franklin Roosevelt came before the committee a few days later, and though he spoke up for aviation in general, challenged Mitchell on several points. Senator Harry New of Indiana asked Roosevelt his views on the role of naval aviation in war; he replied that it was the same as the function of the Navy at large: "Why should it be separated from the Navy?"

"You regard it as an adjunct to the Navy?"

"In the same way that submarines are an adjunct to the Navy. They operate below the surface."

"That is exactly where I think the mistake is made now," New said. "I think submarines are clearly an adjunct of the Navy but I do not think aviation is at all. I think aviation has all but reached the point . . . of its becoming superior to the Navy as a fighting force."

"Of course, that might happen someday," Roosevelt said.

Wadsworth interrupted: "Do you really think that measures the future of aviation—as an adjunct?"

"It might conceivably even in the Navy become the principal factor," Roosevelt said. "I don't know whether the Chief of Operations will agree with me, but I might say that later on in the future aviation may make surface ships practically impossible to be used as an arm. That is possible."

"Isn't that practically agreeing with what General Mitchell says?" New asked.

"No. His intimation is that that is going to happen right away. I think that it is so far in the future that when it comes the Navy will automatically be transferred to the air, the whole Navy . . ."

New sounded a great deal like Mitchell: "I think, with all respect, that the Navy ought to adjust its binoculars and look searchingly into the future. I think they will discover, if they do . . . that something is coming, and it is almost here, and it is coming very rapidly, something for which we must make better provision than has yet been made by this government."

"I think probably, Senator," Roosevelt said, "I was unfortunate in my use of the word 'adjunct.' What I meant by 'adjunct' was that the Navy does not consider any one type of weapon as the principal weapon . . . It is conceivable that under certain conditions at the present time the naval aircraft branch might be more important than the battleship branch."

Roosevelt then took a sheaf of papers from the table and began his prepared attack on Mitchell. He read from Mitchell's previous testimony to the committee, quoting an exchange between the flier and the senators. When he read Mitchell's charge that naval aviation had been divided among six or seven branches, Roosevelt said: "Now, of course that testimony shows that General Mitchell knows absolutely nothing about the organization of the Navy Department. That is example number one. On the next page—"

Senator George Chamberlain broke in to ask in what way Mitchell's charge was wrong.

"It was wrong in this respect. He says the Navy Department stopped having a separate bureau for aviation. The Navy Department never had a separate bureau for aviation. It had an office of aviation under the Chief of Operations."

"Did you abandon that?"

"No, we still have that office."

"No change has been made in it?"

"No change has been made . . ." *

When Roosevelt had finished, an unanswered question hung in the air—either Mitchell or he was wrong. General Menoher called on Mitchell for proof and got a long memorandum: "It is believed that Mr. Roosevelt has been hoodwinked in his own office and that naval aviation has been disintegrated without his knowledge or consent . . . Mr. Roosevelt undoubtedly did not know that this order existed when he appeared before the committee." Mitchell sent Menoher a copy of Admiral Benson's order on "Discontinuance of Aviation Division," which opened: "In accordance with the policy of the Navy Department of merging aviation activities with those of other naval activities, the Aviation Division of this office will be abolished. As soon as practicable the transfer of the several activities of the department will be effected." As Senator New later told the committee, the order "does just exactly what General Mitchell said had been done."

Within the Army, hostility toward aviation was as great. Howard Coffin of the Crowell mission told the Senate Military Affairs Committee of the attitude of the General Staff: "They are not only not in favor of a progressive policy, but they have no appreciation of the value of it . . . There has never been a man on the General Staff who knew anything about the Air Service or cared whether he did."

It was about this time that the Army Reorganization Bill, sponsored by the General Staff, threatened to kill the already puny Air Service. Even Menoher was incensed, and joined Mitchell in protesting to Congress. When both said the bill would cripple aviation, the Army hastily called a board of officers to consider the matter, and in the end, with Pershing's aid, the Air Service managed to survive; the National Defense Act of 1920 gave it 1516 officers and 16,000 men, in an Army whose total strength was 280,000.

In the interim, however, Secretary Baker had ruled that all temporary officers must be discharged by the end of September

* Though Roosevelt was accurate in saying that no "bureau" of the Navy handled aviation, he was obviously wrong about the recent changes involving naval air, and his appearance before the committee left the impression that he chose a somewhat picayune defense, leaning on naval nomenclature.

1919, and that left only 232 air officers, the low point of the postwar Service. Six thousand fliers were discharged, many of them veterans of overseas duty. Congress cut the Air Service appropriation from Mitchell's requested $83 million to $25 million. (Within a short time, war-battered England was to vote about $350 million for the Royal Air Force.) Assistant Secretary Crowell resigned in protest, but his departure was hardly noticed.

In one of his interminable appearances before Congress (he was to address twenty-seven major hearings on Capitol Hill in his brief postwar career in uniform), Mitchell went to new lengths to incite the Navy traditionalists. He told the House Military Affairs Committee that if airmen were allowed to develop their techniques, they could "almost make navies useless on the surface of the water." He added casually: "The Navy General Board, I might say, agrees with me on that." He was probably thinking of the views of Admiral Winterhalter and Franklin Roosevelt.

Secretary of the Navy Josephus Daniels protested this statement to Secretary Baker, who looked over the report of the board's hearing and replied that Mitchell was "not justified in the conclusion." This letter was published, but as the Navy complained, drew little attention. It was impossible to catch up with Mitchell. A Navy historian put it rather plaintively: "Again and again he made the front page, whereas if a modification or even a flat refutation of what he said appeared in print, it formed a small item at the bottom of an inside column."

In May 1919, while Mitchell was fighting his early skirmishes, naval airmen had made a brilliant bid for world attention. Three new Curtiss seaplanes of the NC series, designed by Jerome Hunsaker, left from Newfoundland to cross the Atlantic. Two of them failed, but the NC-4, under Lieutenant Commander Albert C. Read, made it to the Azores—1380 miles—then went on to Portugal and England, to become the first transatlantic plane.

Spurred by this success, Mitchell planned a cross-country contest between seventy planes for the autumn. With Burdette Wright he laid out the route, one that was to mark the later path of commercial flights, a string of farm fields and tiny new municipal landing fields. As he started planes from the eastern end, on Long Island, Mitchell said the test would prove how fast he could mobilize the air forces in case of war. He pointed out that the planes would fly as far as the flight from New York to Constantinople, or from Berlin to Denver.

The first day brought five crashes and three deaths, with wrecks scattered from Port Deposit, New York, to Salt Lake City, the inevitable result of poor equipment. Hap Arnold, who was stationed at the western terminus, in Sacramento, looked back more than a generation later: "It was the foundation of commercial aviation in the United States." Regular airmail flights would follow these pioneers within a year.*

The aging planes flew by day, each making at least forty stops on each leg of the journey back and forth across the continent. Only ten planes finished the race, and the crashes and their casualties brought a roar from Congressman Fiorello La Guardia, a wartime flier. He protested the use of the old De Havillands which had killed most of the nine fliers lost: "The same gang that disregarded war in order to develop their own industries now sends boys across the continent with an obsolete, discarded machine in a vain hope to save their face."

Some editorials wondered if the contest had been worth the cost. It was called a Transcontinental Reliability Test, but the country followed it excitedly as a race. Libraries reported a surge of interest in books on aviation. A man in Philadelphia volunteered for the first flight to the moon. The Air Service had lost valuable men, including Townsend Dodd, and there was one death for each 180 hours flown, but there were dividends. Air routes had been laid; engines, propellers and other equipment had been tested; and improvements on the De Havillands were hastened—one thousand of these planes were modified.

Mitchell saw the end of American isolation in the cross-country sweeps, and said: "There can no longer be any doubt that complete control of the air by any nation means military control of the world."

. . .

* The test had several lively moments. When Major Carl Spaatz, an early leader, finished the first leg and someone asked him how he felt, he said: "I feel like a drink of whiskey!" and then: "The real lesson of this race is that aviators can read maps as accurately as a motorist." The winner, Lieutenant B. M. Maynard, a Baptist preacher from North Carolina, who flew with a police dog, told the press that the numerous crashes were due to "too much booze."

In December 1919 Mitchell made a docile appearance before a House committee. A few days earlier Hap Arnold had insisted that there must be a Cabinet officer for air, but Mitchell argued: "I believe at this time we should organize it as a department, but not with a Cabinet officer. On the other hand, I think its importance is such that it will be a Cabinet position eventually. I think its importance is coequal with that of the Army in the national defense scheme at present, and will soon be superior to that of the Navy."

In this early phase of the air-power struggle it was Ben Foulois who set off the fireworks, inviting court-martial in tones reminiscent of Patrick Henry. He spoke as strongly as Mitchell ever did in later years, and yet did not seem to draw the wrath of the high command. He made Mitchell's testimony in this hearing seem almost ladylike:

"The General Staff, either through lack of vision, lack of practical knowledge, or deliberate intention to subordinate the Air Service . . . has utterly failed to appreciate the full military value of this new weapon . . . I can frankly say that in my opinion the War Department has earned no right or title to claim future control over aviation or the aircraft industries of the United States. Is it any wonder that a few of us dare to risk the charge of insubordination . . . in order that our cause may be heard . . . If any of my statements can be construed as insubordinate . . . then I am ready to stand before any military court in the land . . . to take my chances of punishment in a cause which, in my opinion, will develop and go ahead in spite of every effort to impede its progress."

Long afterward, when he was aged and Mitchell had been dead for almost thirty years, Foulois looked back to this month of 1919 with an air of bafflement, as if he could not understand Mitchell's fame: "Mitchell very carefully avoided the controversial issues on this. I opened up all the way through on this stuff and they wanted to court-martial me. They could, all right, but I had the facts."

Mitchell was not ready to challenge the high command in open combat. This was made clearer when he told Fiorello La Guardia's subcommittee a few days later: "I want it definitely understood that insofar as the Army is concerned, no attempt from above has ever been made to influence our testimony . . . Our relations with the other branches of the Army, with the General Staff and the Secretary of War . . . are most cordial."

Mitchell did not cease his efforts, however. His magazine articles began to appear, the first one a résumé of the air strikes at St. Mihiel, in *World's Work.* But in the press, as before Congress, his tone was still respectful, as if he expected to win over the authorities with the logic of his message. He would wait for another day to challenge the solid ranks of the opposition—Pershing, Baker, Menoher and the General Staff, to say nothing of the Navy.

5

Give Us the Ships to Attack and Come Out and Watch It

Near the end of the first year of his campaign, denied at every turn, Mitchell changed his tactics. He talked more of defending the United States from attack and less of building an offensive force for the future. He saw the need of some arresting device to win public attention, some way in which air power could be dramatized with appealing simplicity. With the passing months his logical target became clearer—the Navy.

Mitchell was promoted to Assistant Chief of the Air Service, and he was restored to the rank of brigadier general. His office became even busier, and a stream of information and opinion, prepared articles and editorials went out to congressmen and newspaper editors.

By now he was working with several inventors. His collaboration with Seversky was well under way, though the work was still secret. The Russian was mysteriously involved in a small shop in Dayton, where Mitchell often went. He returned to Bolling Field after these visits looking "strangely bulgy," disgorging onto his desk a mound of papers and drawings, some scrawled on envelopes. Mitchell could never decipher the Russian script, and sent out a call for a neighborhood delicatessen dealer, the only man within reach who could translate Sasha's spidery notes. They were pushing a new bombsight to completion.

He corresponded more and more frequently with Colonel Thurman Bane, chief of his engineering section at McCook Field, revealing his wide range of interest in all details of aviation. In one letter Mitchell discussed the Liberty engine, which he accepted as the best then available, but he pressed Bane for a 700-horsepower engine: "It will be interesting to see how this scheme develops. I don't see why you shouldn't make a radial engine in banks of six cylinders all the way around eventually. If we stick to reciprocating engines, that is the only solution of high power." It was an accurate forecast of the next development in the field.

The pattern of Mitchell's daily life was still hectic. In the bitter weather of early 1920 he flew almost daily, went ice-skating, jumped his horses, lectured the Army's general officers on aviation, testified before Congress, went trapshooting, conferred with Goodyear officials on dirigibles, took the Postmaster General on a flight. On January 20 Caroline Mitchell gave birth to their last child, John Lendrum Mitchell, III, named for the general's brother who had been killed in France.

Mitchell left soon afterward to address the cadet corps at West Point, at the invitation of his friend Douglas MacArthur, the commandant. He spoke for an hour and a half and held the cadets spellbound with stories of war in the air in France and his forecasts of the future. He got a standing ovation from the corps, many of whom were to serve on Bataan with MacArthur, and some of whom were to lead distinguished careers: Maxwell Taylor as Chairman of the Joint Chiefs of Staff; Lyman Lemnitzer, Supreme Allied Commander, Europe; Hoyt Vandenberg, Air Force Chief of Staff; and Earl Blaik, the football coach.

His first direct challenge to the Navy came in a House hearing in early February, when he appeared with charts and diagrams to give a vivid picture of an invasion of the United States by hostile fleets. The congressmen, who had not thought of the problem beyond the Navy's traditional role of coastal defense, in which fleets met fleets, were transfixed by Mitchell's descriptions. He told of dirigibles finding the enemy, of dogfights raging for hundreds of miles over the American approaches, and then of a savage air assault on the enemy fleet, with survivors finished off by submarines.

Mitchell told the congressmen that a battleship, which events would soon prove almost worthless, cost as much as a thousand bombers, and said that a few of his fliers could destroy the most powerful fleet. "A ship at sea is much more easily picked out than an object on land." Neither detection nor destruction would be difficult, given an alert air force.

Nonflying officers, he said, could not be expected to handle aviation in this way—especially naval officers: "They look with abhorrence—all navies do—on a system of attack against their vessels by airplanes, because it will mean eventually the diminution or entire elimination of their strength on the water, and many think, therefore, that helping aviation will diminish naval strength." He gave the committee a challenge: "We would like very much to take the members of your committee down to Chesapeake Bay, to our airdrome there, and show you these things from the air, which we can do at any time, so that you can judge for yourselves." He had not yet demanded battleships as targets, but the Navy could see that as the next step.

Secretary Daniels reacted vigorously. He was a North Carolina newspaper editor who had been brought to Washington by Woodrow Wilson, an ardent temperance man who had banished the Navy's grog ration and won the sobriquet "the Grape Juice Admiral." * Excoriating Mitchell, Daniels wrote Secretary Baker that all of his testimony was misleading and inaccurate. Daniels seemed to resent such criticism, of whatever importance:

"It would seem most unfortunate that the efforts of the great majority of the officers of the Army and the Navy should be interfered with by an individual . . . It would seem particularly unhappy at this time when there is so much constructive work confronting both the Army and the Navy in aeronautical matters."

Baker gave Mitchell "a tongue-lashing" and ordered him to remain silent on naval affairs; the Secretary then told Daniels that he had nothing further to worry about from Mitchell.

It was too late. Mitchell was winning more attention in the press than ever. When the *New York Times* headlined one of his

* Another Daniels reform forbade use of the terms "port" and "starboard" in the Navy, substituting "left" and "right." The order was signed by Franklin Roosevelt.

speeches with "DECLARES AMERICA HELPLESS IN AIR WAR," Mitchell had found the theme he was to use throughout his fight with the Navy.

By September 1920 he had begun in earnest his effort to get a floating target. He wrote Menoher: "We must at all costs obtain the battleship to attack and the necessary bombs, planes and so on to make the test a thorough and complete one."

The idea of bombing warships, though it would soon be linked permanently with his name, was not original with Mitchell. Naval aviators had been clamoring for such a chance themselves, but until Mitchell created a stir in Congress and began to loom as a greater threat, the naval aviators were always refused. Only when the naval high command understood Mitchell's menace to the old Navy did it begin to encourage its own airmen as the lesser of two evils. The Navy would test its own bombing skill against warships.

The old U.S.S. *Indiana*, a veteran of the war with Spain, became a target, and in the fall of 1920, under secret conditions, she was subjected to a battering. Captain Chester Nimitz was in charge. In late October and early November, when the nation's attention was on Warren G. Harding's campaign for the Presidency, the old ship was attacked by the Navy. Unfortunately for its hopes of secrecy, Captain C. H. M. Roberts, a shrewd air armament specialist of the Ordnance Corps, took part in the test.

Planes attacked the old ship, but only with dummy bombs. Ordnance men set off underwater charges which broke the ship, parted her seams and settled her. Run aground, she was wrecked by bombs fixed to her deck. The Navy made meager announcements on the test and these were misleading, saying that the experiments proved the "improbability" that a modern battleship could be sunk from the air.

Captain Roberts learned a great deal about how to crush hulls underwater, below the torpedo bells, where battleships had thin skins; he was also already working on bombs large enough for the work, testing them in a wind tunnel.

The truth about the test slipped out in a strange and still unknown manner—two photographs of the maimed *Indiana* appeared in the London *Illustrated News*, with her upper works torn to steel shreds, the sort of picture the Navy had hoped the public would never see.

No one accused Mitchell of complicity in the leak, not publicly at least, but the secret was out. Even so, the Navy managed to keep the details so well concealed that few Americans knew of them until early January 1921, when Mitchell was called before a friendly congressional committee headed by Representative Daniel R. Anthony of Kansas. Mitchell came armed with drawings, photographs and charts from the *Indiana* test, given to him by Captain Roberts.

Mitchell told the committee flatly that he could "destroy or sink any ship in existence," and showed the congressmen how the Navy had attempted subterfuge with its *Indiana* test, hoping to stave off a showdown between plane and battleship. The congressmen had been completely misled by Navy releases, and for half an hour or more Mitchell tried gently to explain that the Navy had dropped no live bombs, that the damaging charges had been fired statically on the ship's deck. He also had to convince them that it was the Navy, not the Air Service, which had done the work.

He talked for hours, explaining charts of armor thicknesses on battleships, U.S. and foreign, of comparisons between cannon fire and aerial bombing as to cost, range and accuracy, and of bomber speeds and fuels.

Representative Bascom Slemp of Big Stone Gap, Virginia, who was soon to become secretary to President Calvin Coolidge, put Mitchell through a catechism, once he had brought him back to the point of the *Indiana* test and official resistance to change:

"Why is it, if your statements are true—and I'm not casting any doubt upon them at all—that you aren't able to convince the high-ranking officers of the Army who have the consideration of these problems? For example, General March told us that if some foreign power defeated our Navy, they could land any number of troops on our shores without reference at all to any air force we might have.

"If these statements of yours are true, why is it that these officers can't see the light? What is your explanation of that?"

Mitchell was prudence itself; the time had not yet come when he was willing to attack his superiors head-on. "We are presenting the situation to you, and we're ready to demonstrate this thing. If you allow no air force, not only will an opposing fleet land at will, but their aircraft will fly all over our country."

Slemp persisted: "What does that mean? They're intelligent individuals, and they want to get the best defense they can for their country."

Representative Louis Cramton of Michigan broke in: "Isn't it for the same reason that confronted Ericsson, in that after he had demonstrated the success of the *Monitor,* still he couldn't get the ear of the high-ranking officers of the War Department?"

Mitchell appeared to be grateful for the shifting of ground, making his targets unidentifiable: "We can show right straight down through the beginning how this thing has been held down. First in Professor Langley's time and then in the Wrights' time, but today it isn't quite as bad as it was—although it's almost as bad . . ."

He made an important disclaimer in the long exchange: "I want it to be distinctly understood that I do not consider that the air force is to be considered as in any means supplanting the Army. You have always got to come to manpower as the ultimate thing, but we do believe that the air force will control all communications, that it will have a very great effect on land troops and a decisive one against a navy." Later, in the heat of pitched battles over air power, and frustrated at every turn, Mitchell often made less complete or balanced statements of his position.

After a wrangle with Slemp, Mitchell conceded that the war had produced no examples of the superiority of planes over ships, and the Virginian seemed to be content: "Then this war was conducted for four or five years without airships demonstrating any usefulness outside of keeping other airships or other air vessels off, that is, so far as naval vessels are concerned."

Mitchell agreed and Slemp said: "And we have got to eliminate the experience of the past in considering the future, and go on theoretical possibilities?"

"It isn't theoretical, as our experience points directly to what I have said."

"They had their chance for four or five years and didn't do it."

"They didn't have the equipment to do it. The war in Europe was essentially one on land. It wasn't a naval war."

Slemp went on doggedly: "But at the same time Germany was controlling the air."

Mitchell lost patience: "No, sir. Germany was not . . . This same conservatism in the development of new methods of war is what has wrecked many nations before, and what has made every war we've had dangerous to our well-being and very expensive . . ."

They argued over the value of planes and submarines until Mitchell said: "We should demonstrate the matter conclusively . . . but we ought to avoid mistakes by not getting too far behind. Eventually you will find that, dollar for dollar, you will get more from an air force than from submarines, as an air force will both protect sea communications and destroy hostile vessels . . ."

Representative Thomas W. Sisson of Mississippi, in a more friendly vein, asked if the British example in carriers and a unified air force should serve as a model for the United States. "Yes, sir. We can easily lead at a comparatively small cost. We have the men, the material and the factories all within our own country. No other nation is so well placed."

Near the end Slemp said: "Your argument really leads up to the advocacy of a combined air service."

"There is no other efficient solution of the air problem," Mitchell said. "If you scatter the air force all around it leads to double overhead, and to a double system of command, and many other difficulties. It has been proved wrong everywhere."

Slemp said finally, in the manner of a man coming up for air: "It seems to me that the principal problem is to demonstrate the certainty of your conclusions." This was what Mitchell wanted to hear.

"Give us the warships to attack and come and watch it," he said.

"How much money would you need for demonstration purposes?"

"We need no money . . . All we want are the targets and to have you watch it."

It was an important day's work for Mitchell. Within two days two resolutions in Congress urged that the Navy give the Air Service battleships for targets—and other committees sought some of his exciting testimony. Mitchell wrote Thurman Bane at

McCook Field: "I believe I am to appear tomorrow . . . We will have some more fireworks. We are going to smoke these people out that do not believe in the air business and either make them 'fish or cut bait.' "

He tried "smoking them out" before the House Naval Affairs Committee, this time with two allies, the New York *Tribune* and a tart-tongued admiral, William S. Sims.

The newspaper published more pictures of the stricken *Indiana,* six weeks after their appearance in London, and the editors gave the admirals a lecture: the pictures proved, they said, that the battleship would have been put out of action, its crew eliminated. They ridiculed naval defenses and said that a $50,000 plane could outperform any number of $500,000 coastal guns. In summary: "The Navy should have solved this problem long ago."

Admiral Sims, who preceded Mitchell in this hearing, was a surprising witness. The handsome chief of the Naval War College bore many scars from fights with his high command. His campaign to improve U.S. gunnery had almost ruined his career (his claim that one British ship could outshoot four or five American ships inspired a House resolution barring him from U.S. soil). He had spurned the offer of a Distinguished Service Cross from Secretary Daniels on the grounds that the honor had been sullied by presentation to unworthy men.

Sims had belittled air power since 1910, when he thought the Wright brothers were justified in their prediction that missiles dropped from their planes would never hit a target. "That man Wright is right," Sims had said. He had changed his mind recently when, playing war games with ship models at the Naval War College, he had pitted an all-carrier force against a mixed fleet of battleships, cruisers and carriers. The plane-carrying fleet had made short work of its opponents, and Sims wrote Admiral Bradley Fiske: "We had a discussion with the entire staff over the whole matter, and it was easy to see that the question of the passing of the battleship was not an agreeable one to various members."

This committee, like that of the Senate, was ignorant about the *Indiana* test, and Sims exposed its secrets. He explained that only dummy bombs had been dropped, but that the bombing was so accurate that it would have destroyed the ship if the bombs had been live.

Two high naval officers were on hand to defend the test, one of whom, Admiral Charles Badger of the Navy General Board, said that Mitchell's charts of the bombing test were new to him; he implied that Mitchell had filched them. When Mitchell took the stand he was queried on the point: "You didn't push a door open to get this?"

"No, sir," Mitchell said, hurriedly leaving the subject. "It is our business to know about those things and get a true estimate of what they're worth . . . We have tried to get targets of actual ships . . . and for that reason we watched the experiment on the *Indiana* with great interest."

Sims was more fully convinced by this hearing, and wrote to Fiske: "If I had my way, I would arrest the building of great battleships and put money into the development of new devices and not wait to see what other countries are doing." Sims invited Mitchell to the War College, where they talked over new air theories and presumably spent time over the game board. Sims could foresee what a hard fight Mitchell faced: "It is a singular thing that you can present irrefutable arguments to officers on this subject and they will still defend the old methods and the old surface ships. I know, of course, something of the psychology of opinion, but this seems to me to go beyond the theories of psychological experts. Can it be that the Navy is reluctant to give up the big ships to live in?"

As such hearings drew wider attention the Navy was pressed to furnish warships as targets for planes. It was probably Senator William Borah of Idaho who forced Daniels' hand, with a resolution calling for a halt to naval construction until Congress could determine what constituted "a modern navy." Even so, the Navy insisted on its own terms for the testing of plane against ship. It would conduct the tests itself, and the Air Service would come as an invited guest. Navy and Army planes would alternate in attacks on old German warships.

The program would open with the bombing of a submarine, working upward through a destroyer and a cruiser to a battleship, the allegedly unsinkable *Ostfriesland.* As an additional problem the old U.S.S. *Iowa,* under radio control, would be the target for a search from the air. Later in the summer the Air Service would be given an old battleship of its own—this one was to be the U.S.S. *Alabama.*

Daniels was defiant in the months of waiting. The *Indiana* test, he told the press, had little meaning. He cited the report of his director of Naval Gunnery, Captain William D. Leahy (who was to become the personal Chief of Staff to Franklin D. Roosevelt and nominal Chairman of the Joint Chiefs of Staff in World War II):

"The entire experiment pointed to the improbability of a modern battleship being either destroyed or completely put out of action by aerial bombs." Leahy also said that the ship was not sunk by bombing alone, since many of its doors were not watertight.

Daniels then sent Mitchell a warning: "He will soon discover, if he ever tries laying bombs on the deck of a naval vessel, that he will be blown to atoms long before he is near enough to drop salt upon the tail of the Navy."

Editor Daniels seemed to be groping for colorful phrases that would express the issue in a way that the nation would not forget. He did so in early February 1921, calling a challenge which provoked laughter that would echo as long as the controversy was remembered. He was speaking of the use of the radio-controlled U.S.S. *Iowa* as a bombing target:

"I am so confident that neither Army nor Navy aviators can hit the *Iowa* when she is under way that I would be perfectly willing to be on board her when they bomb her, provided that they were kept at the altitude which they could be compelled to maintain in battle." *

Mitchell could have asked for no more. The country was fasci-

* The exact circumstances surrounding this familiar quotation are in doubt. The statement appeared in the *New York Times* on February 7, 1921, allegedly made by "one high naval official"; the next day other papers attributed it to Daniels, and he made no denial. His family, as of 1965, knew nothing of the origin of the challenge, and Daniels' papers appear to shed no light on this detail. Navy men still insist that Daniels was right, if fully and accurately quoted. They point out as supporting evidence the lack of success of most Army bombers at the battle of Midway against Japanese capital ships, including carriers.

nated by the vision of Daniels aboard a battleship, under heavy attack by Army planes. For the first time the man in the street appeared to grasp the issue. However, the final, clarifying provision of the statement by Daniels was omitted from all the comments that followed. Battle conditions and altitude were not allowed to complicate the personal duel between Daniels and Mitchell.

Reaction in the press was so immediate that it was almost as if the humorists had been waiting in the wings. A letter in the New York *Tribune* the next day called Daniels' offer "the most sensible and graceful suggestion that the admiral has made during the last eight years." It concluded: "The whole Navy will vociferously applaud this gallant act of Admiral Daniels in throwing himself as a sacrifice upon the altar of his country only 22 days before he is billed to retire to the simple life for which he longs."

Aviators assailed Mitchell with requests that there be real battle conditions, and that the Navy be permitted to fire back at the planes; there were dozens of volunteers for this war game. Mitchell, now confident of his target ships, wrote hurriedly to Bane, and their exchange revealed the gap between Mitchell's enthusiasms of the committee rooms and the facts of life within the tiny Air Service:

"This means, of course, that it is up to us to make the best demonstration possible . . . Now, what I wish you would do is have whatever armament that you think would be good ready to send here at any time for demonstration . . . Let me hear from you on these things as soon as you can, because we may be called upon to carry out this attack very quickly . . .

"I want you to be sure to have what bombardment ships you have ready to be used with their crews when the attack of warships takes place. This to my mind is the most important thing that we have before us."

Bane's calm reply revealed only between the lines the shock he had sustained:

"Your letter of January 31 is at hand. The first paragraph, in which you say you want me to have what bombardment ships we have ready to be used with their crews for the attack on warships, is a little perturbing. Of course, you know we have no crews assigned to ships. In fact, we have not a single officer who ever dropped a bomb with a bombsight or ever was instructed to drop bombs with the idea of hitting a target."

Bane did not yet realize that he was dealing with a man to whom such handicaps were as nothing, that Mitchell was determined to make history off the Virginia Capes on Chesapeake Bay, and that the lack of trained men, big planes, big bombs and all else were mere details, obstacles meant to be overcome in the course of events.

6

You Are Throwing the Navy into Convulsions

No warship had ever been sunk from the air, and but for Mitchell and his young men, few believed that a battleship could be destroyed by planes. Bombsights were primitive, the largest American bomb weighed 1100 pounds, and the attack planes were untested. Nearly all veteran bombardiers of war times were gone, and the Air Service had no trained crews. Army fliers lacked practice in overwater navigation.

In the face of all this Mitchell created the First Provisional Air Brigade, based at Langley Field, Virginia, near the small city of Hampton at the mouth of Chesapeake Bay. A start had been made. Lieutenant Clayton Bissell, a Pennsylvanian who had flown under the British and won their Distinguished Flying Cross, had proposed a tactical school at Langley, and Tom Milling was already directing it, with Bissell and a few other instructors teaching dive bombing and gunnery. Bissell was to become one of Mitchell's chief aides.

Mitchell ordered Milling to build the kind of striking force he had developed for St. Mihiel; he sent elaborate charts of operations, and diagrams as to approach, formation and angle of bomb drops of the squadrons. He tried to allay Thurman Bane's fears: "Do not worry about the plan of operations for the attack on battleships. We will take care of that . . . What I want to impress on you is that we do not want to waste time about this."

Langley was a sleepy post with seven instructors and eight or nine students when he began, but Mitchell quickly changed it. He literally stripped the Air Service of available pilots and planes at every post, flying them from as far as Texas, until he had about 1000 men and 250 planes at the base. Things moved with such speed that by early February 1921, crews were bombing a 600-foot outline target of a battleship in nearby salt marshes. This practice drew from Washington a reaction typical of harassments to come: "Attention is called to your violation of Supply Circular No. 62 . . . as well as instructions from this office in constructing one model battleship for target practice before funds were allotted." Practice went ahead without a break. Mitchell had steeled himself against sniping by Menoher, the Navy or anyone else; within or without regulations, he would bomb his ships. He went after the big bombs in the same spirit.

One day he called Captain C. H. M. Roberts of Ordnance into his office. "Do we have a bomb that will sink a battleship?"

"No, we don't."

"Can you make one?"

"Yes, sir."

Mitchell glared at the captain. As Roberts recalled it years later, the general's indignant manner posed an almost audible question: "Well, what're you sitting there wasting time for? We've got to sink a battleship in June."

"There are a couple of details," Roberts said. "First, we've got no money." (The Ordnance budget at the time was about $100,000 a year.)

"How much?"

"Half a million dollars."

"I'll have that for you tomorrow morning," Mitchell said.

"And I'll need a blank check as a government purchasing agent. I won't have time to wait for clearance; if I need steel I'll have to go to a yard and buy and give them a check."

Mitchell agreed. "What else?"

"I need a plane and a pilot at my disposal twenty-four hours a day, ready to fly anywhere."

Mitchell turned and pointed across the office to Burdette Wright: "That's your job, Burdy."

Roberts and Mitchell talked with General C. C. Williams, the chief of Ordnance, and the captain was given emergency powers to work at Frankford Arsenal, which had heavy machinery necessary to produce large bombs. Roberts already planned to build the largest bombs in the world, 2000- and 4000-pounders; he and his chief draftsman sat up all night to finish sketches. Within two days after they arrived in Philadelphia, fins for the missiles were being fabricated.

Mitchell somehow rode out the trouble he stirred with finance officers. Within a day or so, Ordnance was anxiously telling the Army Chief of Staff about requisitions from Mitchell, and asking to be advised "as to what extent it is intended to obligate funds for this purpose." The chief responded sharply, sending a special messenger to General Menoher: "The Secretary of War has not approved a program for such tests, and no obligation is authorized by any service until such a program is approved." He demanded details of Mitchell's needs, in advance. Only then did Mitchell send his Brigade requests through channels; in the end, he got the funds.

Mitchell next arrived unexpectedly at George Goddard's tiny photographic studio at McCook Field: "I'm going to bomb some ships and I've got to have a photography man who knows his stuff. I hate to move you so soon, but I want you to come to my office in Washington."

Goddard was soon installed in the Munitions Building, next door to Mitchell; on the other side was Lieutenant Oliver Echols, a specialist in radio communications, busily working out a network for the bombing fleet. Goddard found that he was to do more than direct his aerial photographers. "Most of all," Mitchell said, "I need you to handle the newsreel and movie people. They're temperamental, and we've got to get all we can out of them. I want newsreels of those sinking ships in every theater in the country, just as soon as we can get 'em there."

Goddard gathered the best cameramen from stations across the country, assembled eighteen De Havillands as photographic planes, and wheedled a small dirigible from Aberdeen Proving Ground.

To newspapermen, Langley seemed like a secret base on the eve of hostilities. Reporters who made their way there heard tinkering behind hangar doors, found mechanics unwilling to talk, and got only grins and shakes of the head from Mitchell. They wrote of black hangars along the two short runways, a furor of plane motors, of cars coming and going, people yelling, and planes almost beyond counting. "The Army," one Norfolk paper said, "thinks these are not Army at all, just fancy playthings used by reckless young men. The Navy agrees."

Cameramen took pictures of the planes, including the new-model Martin bomber with folding wings. In the background were rows of tents where many enlisted men lived. One headline said: "VEIL OF SECRECY OVER PREPARATIONS OF ARMY AIRMEN."

Majors Bill Hensley and Davenport ("Jam") Johnson, Milling's chief aides, gave reporters hints of the Brigade morale. "Our crews can hit a moving target fifty percent of the time in a thirty-five-mile gale," Hensley said. "With a little more practice we'll be able to pick the crow's-nest off any ship in Uncle Sam's Navy."

Johnson said: "Our men think bombs, talk bombs, and expect to make the Navy eat bombs. Our biggest trouble now is getting targets. My men are blowing them up so fast, the government is having trouble keeping us supplied."

When most of the men and planes had arrived, and Milling had formed these scatterings into squadrons, Mitchell flew down from Washington to give them a pep talk. He reminded them that they were on historic ground. Hampton was the oldest continually inhabited town in British America. Some fifteen miles away was Yorktown, where Cornwallis had surrendered and where George McClellan had dug in with Federal troops during the Civil War, using the first military aircraft—the balloons of Professor Thaddeus Lowe. Through the waters offshore the first English settlers had come to Jamestown, British and French fleets had fought in the Revolution, and the *Monitor* had overcome the *Merrimac*. He spoke of stubborn resistance to progress by admirals and generals in the past and challenged his young men to teach the critics of the Air Service a lesson. They cheered him and returned to work.

When the bombing crews had become proficient on land, Milling took them to the Bay where they hammered at the wreckage of the Navy's old target, the *Indiana*, and at a nearby hulk, the old U.S.S. *Texas*. Mitchell flew with them one hazy day, eight miles from the nearest land at Tangier Island: "We found ourselves with no horizon or point of reference by which to level our planes because everything was the same color, air, sky and water. It was very much as if we were on the inside of a sphere all painted the same hue. Many who had had this experience in overwater flying held that it was impossible for this reason to level an airplane so that good bombing could be done." He solved the problem with the aid of Lawrence Sperry and his gyroscope, putting the first artificial horizon into use, adding greatly to the confidence of his crews.

As they gained in skill, the bombardiers practiced with a moving target towed behind a barge, and Mitchell soon thought them ready: "Even the most doubting of our officers knew that whether hostile seacraft were at rest or moving no matter how fast, there would be no difficulty hitting them."

The crews also practiced at night, using their new radio telephones. The radio net had not been easy, for veteran pilots thought the radio only a toy and refused to wear the uncomfortable helmets with headphones. Many had returned from flights to report malfunctions of their sets but were sent back aloft until they reported progress. Soon all crews accepted the devices, and a radio operator accompanied each flight. Lieutenant Echols had brought in ten qualified radio operators, and continued to train the men until all crews could hold contact with other flights in the area. Mitchell established a radio net that stretched from Roanoke Island, North Carolina, into Delaware.

At first there was a shortage of everything—forms for daily reports, light bulbs, rollers for maps, landing lights, clocks, office fans, buzzer systems, batteries, pumps, motion picture film. Yet there was time for a band and a baseball team, morale builders for the green crews. Harassments continued. Menoher tried to reduce the number of radiomen, and Milling was forced to explain the need for them; a request for motion picture film was once held up for exhaustion of funds, and a telegram asked whether the amount was actually needed.

In the midst of training, the Army's Third Corps Area quartermaster dismissed the Langley fire department without warning, leaving only the chief and one truck driver; Mitchell warned Washington that the great stockpile of bombs made more firemen essential. A week later three of his best fliers were ordered back to McCook Field by Thurman Bane, and Mitchell saved them temporarily with an appeal to Menoher.

The shortage of money plagued him constantly, often when only pennies were involved. Thurman Bane had too little money in his budget to reply to Mitchell's telegrams by wire and was forced to write instead. Mitchell wanted Hap Arnold to help in the tests, but failed to get him for lack of funds for travel from California.

As practice flights increased, there were crashes. Milling could not persuade his superiors to allow him to cut a fringe of tall pines at one end of a runway, despite the danger to bomb-loaded planes. He radioed Menoher for authority to have this work done, and Menoher said the request had been sent on to the quartermaster of the Corps Area. Another urgent request was also in vain—and soon after, two cadets were killed when their plane grazed a treetop and burst into flames, exploding one bomb.

Major Hensley sent an angry message to Menoher: "Cadets Thompson and Bowen killed in airplane crash 2 P.M. taking off with four 100-pound bombs. Struck trees that we have been endeavoring for three months to have taken down . . . These trees have been the cause of four accidents within the past three months."

Daily bombing practice continued, with all squadrons showing improvement. (The best of the crews had begun with an accuracy of no more than 50 percent, but by June the heavy bombers were nearing perfection.) One day the 14th Heavy Bombardment Squadron put 30 of 36 bombs within a hundred feet of the bull's-eye and a few days later dropped all but twelve of 143 demolition bombs on target. The men of the First Pursuit Squadron, led by Captain C. V. Baucom, scored over 94 percent accuracy on a target 125 by 50 feet.

The big bombs in which Mitchell put his hopes were produced by the heroic efforts of ordnance men in three months—though the work would ordinarily have taken a year. Roberts ordered 150 of the 2000-pounders, though not all were ready for the test, and 75 of the giant 4000-pounders, to be delivered later.

Roberts ordered seamless steel tubes from a Pittsburgh steel plant, with the help of the Navy, which was using large dies in this plant to make its torpedoes. Steel noses and tails were fixed to the tubes—which were filled with TNT. The 1000 pounds of explosive was melted in steam-jacketed kettles and poured into the cylinders in small increments; no such quantity of TNT had been handled in this way before, and the process was unexpectedly slow. Since the explosive had to recrystallize, it must be cooled, and there was too little time to allow for the successive coolings in a normal way. Ice water and electric fans were used to hurry the process and get the bombs to Mitchell on time.

Roberts and his engineers designed a foolproof detonation system with a charge running the length of the cylinder, and set off ingeniously with a 12-gauge shotgun shell. After tests, they developed a delayed detonation which would explode the bombs thirty to forty feet beneath the surface of the water, just deep enough to cause maximum damage to ship hulls in case of near misses. The bombs were so sturdy that when dropped without a charge, they would penetrate a six-foot block of reinforced concrete and three feet of gravel beneath, without damage to the cylinders, which were used over and over in such tests.

When the first 2000-pounder was dropped live from a plane at Aberdeen, Roberts and Captain Norbert Carolin released it from what they thought a safe height, about 2000 feet, but when it struck, as Roberts remembered it, "a pipeline straight to hell opened up below us, like a volcanic eruption. The plane, a big old Handley Page, was flung high in the air, and the struts on the wings snapped all over the place. Carolin and I looked back to see if the tail was still there, and somehow, it was." They never dropped another from so low an altitude.

Bringing a naval observer, Commander P. N. Ballenger, Mitchell came up for the tests. He was delighted with the underwater explosions, which raised huge geysers of mud and water. The water-hammer effect was so great that the ordinary measuring devices were useless.

Roberts tried to convince Mitchell that this was the way to sink ships, and found him willing to listen. Other officers were not so receptive, Roberts recalled later: "I remember Bissell was especially hard to win over. He had been trained, and was training others, that the Air Service should always hit what it aimed at, the pickle-barrel mentality. I had to argue like the devil, for weeks. Others were more amenable than he was. I talked until I was blue in the face to all those bombardiers before the tests, trying to tell them that when they hit a ship, all they did was knock off the bric-a-brac and tear up their bomb, but when they hit within fifty feet, the expansion and contraction of gas from underwater explosions would tear those hulls apart." *

Captains Roberts and S. R. Stribling went to Langley as bombardiers, and the technicians from Aberdeen, Frederick V. Ludden, Joseph P. Collins, Charles Hilderbrand and George Bertram, went down for the exacting work of assembling the bombs, inserting fuses, inspecting, storing and loading them into the bomb racks. Major W. A. Borden, who was Roberts' superior as chief of the Armament Division, said later that these bombs were as large as any used in the first years of World War II, and almost as effective. "Mitchell made us establish designs, and all that followed were refinements only."

There were still uncertainties. The new Martin bombers were only now being finished in Cleveland, and testing began in May at Langley. In March, Mitchell had written Bane urgently: "I am anxious to see the actual tests of the lifting power of the Martin. I want again to impress upon you the necessity for getting those ships out and getting them to Langley in the *shortest possible time*. This is the most important thing there is today . . . *get those Martin airplanes*."

He was soon reporting glumly from his first tests: "We are having a lot of troubles. The one Martin at Langley can't make the motors turn up and apparently the ship won't lift the load it is designed to lift."

Suddenly the situation brightened. Mitchell went down from Washington to see a test of a Martin carrying 1700 pounds plus fuel and crew. The big ship made it, but barely, and the Langley log said dubiously: "The experiment proved that it is going to be possible to take off a Martin carrying a 1600-pound bomb, but that if there is very little wind it is going to require the entire length of the field in order to insure safe takeoff."

Only a few days later Carl Cover, a veteran test pilot, took a Martin up with a full load, barely skimming over the pine trees in which the young pilots had died. Milling and Hensley sent Mitchell a triumphant announcement by radio: "Martin bomber carrying 2512 pounds live weight this date in addition full gas, oil

* Major Alexander de Seversky later said that he, too, pressed the idea of the water hammer upon Mitchell, based on his experience with a transport in the Baltic which had been sunk in that manner during the war.

and water tank. Lt. Cover pilot. Stop. Believe ship will carry 500 pounds additional under more favorable conditions."

Final success seemed certain now. A band of meteorologists from the Signal Corps arrived and scattered along the coast, to train with Mitchell's radiomen, the last of his specialists.

Mitchell was even busier in Washington as the time for the tests drew near. Warren G. Harding had been inaugurated as President on March 4, and the Air Service had been led to expect better days. Just before taking office, Harding announced that his new Secretaries of War and Navy would be John W. Weeks of Massachusetts and Edwin Denby of Michigan, but the big news was that the new President had promised to abolish the two secretaryships and create a Ministry of Defense. Aviation would have equal rank with the Army and Navy. There was an ominous reminder in the announcement: the plan would also mean a congressional shake-up, with standing committees on military and naval affairs revamped or abolished. Seniority would be in jeopardy.

Within three weeks after Harding took office his enthusiasm for the reform began to cool, and Mitchell assumed that veteran congressmen and naval lobbyists had been at work. Unofficial word was passed that independence for the Air Service depended on the success of the bombing tests, but by June, Mitchell concluded that Harding would not carry out his promise, no matter what the outcome.

Yet he was unperturbed: "The system of education seems to be going successfully and the people on the 'Hill' are beginning to see the practical value of aviation." One piece of evidence was the introduction by Representative Charles F. Curry of California of a new bill calling for unification of all U.S. air forces. Mitchell sent copies of it to newspapers and men of influence. One of his notes went to Robert McCormick, the Chicago publisher:

"My Dear Bob: I am sending you herewith a copy of a bill by Mr. Curry for a department of aviation. This bill has been gone over by our people, by the Navy flying people and by the Marine flying people and it is the result of our combined deliberations. We believe it is an excellent act in every way and this is the one we are going to get behind."

Mitchell's first book, *Our Air Force,* had appeared during the spring, and was also sent to many congressmen and civilian leaders. The *New York Times* thought that his naval critics "might not like it," and said that the author was "either in advance of his time or misconceives and exaggerates the scope and value of aviation." In summary: "General Mitchell's treatment of the subject is by no means exhaustive. There are loose ends. The style might be better, but it is an honest book and penned in the spirit of patriotic service. He is a pioneer who blazes the way as a practical aviator as well as a thinker."

A good deal of Mitchell's pioneering in these months went unobserved by the public. He seemed to be alone among military men in his awareness of growing Japanese air power, and was so concerned that he investigated even the sensational charges of the Hearst press in its "yellow peril" campaign. He sent a clipping from the New York *American* to Major Melvin Hall, the air attaché in London, and asked him whether Japan was actually buying fleets of British planes, and if British officers were training a Japanese air force, as the newspaper alleged. Hall replied at length.

Though the article was inaccurate in detail, Japan was buying planes in significant numbers. The largest order in Britain had been for fifty planes, but "it is true that orders have been placed by Japan in both France and Italy and that the Japanese government is in fact embarking upon a very comprehensive program." A Colonel Sempill, formerly of the Air Ministry, led a mission of thirty from London to Japan to help establish an air force; these men had gone as civilians because the British feared a military mission might make "a bad impression on American public opinion."

Hall listed planes shipped to Japan, the most modern of which were Nieuport "Sparrow Hawks," able to take off from battleship turrets or aircraft carriers. "The Japanese navy is said to have one mother ship at the present time, but it is believed that some aircraft carriers are under construction."

Mitchell was insatiable in his thirst for information, and air attachés apparently heard more from him than from the Intelligence Section of the General Staff. Hall once sent him proofs of an article by the controversial British aviation authority, C. G. Grey:

"It is already fairly well known that Japan is preparing for war on a grand scale . . . The Japanese are not natural aviators. This raises the question . . . whether the Japanese can be taught to fly . . . Out of a people numbering over 70 million . . . it must be possible to find a few thousand who can fly, if only by the book, provided the Japanese government does not mind killing a few more thousand in finding them, and the Japanese have never in the past shown any particular objection to being killed . . .

"Everybody in Japan is convinced that a war with America must occur. Meantime [in America] pacifists, copperheads, pussy-foots and the rest will be resisting . . . every attempt even to maintain, let alone increase, American air power. And even the heads of the American Air Service have seemed none too sound in their ideas. If one may judge by his public utterances, Gen. Mitchell seems to think that he can sink battleships with bombs. American bombing may be very fine, but bombing battleships is just a waste of time when torpedoes can be used."

Mitchell built a file of such reports from abroad, and tried to spur American action. He urged Menoher to send a U.S. air mission to China, as an antidote to the growth of a Japanese air force. He also wrote to Bane at McCook: "You have got to watch this foreign development. The Japanese have got Type 30 Nieuports, the Breguet, with modern 450-horsepower motor for light bombardment, and the Farman bimotor for bombardment. These are very fine ships . . . Now, you are the bird that is charged with fixing these programs primarily. Of course, each year the system will get a little better unless we get so much system that nothing will work—the way it is apt to, in time of peace."

Mitchell kept up his usual round of horse shows, speeches, conferences and flights while inspecting progress at Langley Field and Aberdeen Proving Ground. His sister Harriet visited at Langley and flew with him several times, once to New York, where Mrs. Babe Ruth called for them at their hotel and took them to a baseball game where they met Babe and shared the attention of the crowd. As they passed over the Virginia countryside on these flights, Mitchell circled sites of Civil War battles they had visited with their father as children, and shouted explanations to Harriet. He took her to several dances at Langley, impressing her afresh with his "magnificent sense of humor and magnetic, dynamic personality; he was great fun to be with, always the center of attraction." She once saw an example of his aplomb during a formal inspection of the Brigade when, as he stooped to look at some piece of equipment, there was a sound of tearing cloth. Rather than end the inspection, Mitchell went to a hangar, called a sailmaker, and with breeches repaired soon completed his rounds of the troops.

A brief interruption in Brigade training took him to Charleston, West Virginia, where striking miners threatened an uprising in the state. Several of Mitchell's planes were sent into the hills in case they were needed to put down insurrection, and he spent a few hours there, a visit that provoked headlines. After an interview with Mitchell a reporter forecast the use of gas against the miners. Mitchell took no part in the resulting furor, but his officers insisted that he had been misquoted, and that he would never have urged the gassing of Americans.

He returned to Langley to discover a new squabble with the Navy in full swing. Films of the Air Service bombing the old *Indiana* hulk had been shown in newsreels, and the public was amused to see a bomb with "Regards to the Navy" painted by some enlisted man. Secretary Denby protested to Secretary Weeks that this was irresponsible; he sent captions of the Fox newsreel film, and intimated that Mitchell was to blame. Weeks agreed, and despite efforts by the Fox company to assume responsibility, insisted upon muzzling Mitchell. He reminded Menoher of the decree of the Joint Army-Navy Board that the experiments were to be secret, and said firmly: "The Secretary of War directs that all members of the Air Service be strictly instructed to refrain from making any public statements or from giving any information to the press or to any persons not members of the military or naval service regarding the bombing experiments."

Menoher's patience was further tried by Mitchell's public comments on a tragedy at the end of May, when a large Curtiss Eagle plane crashed in a thunderstorm on a flight from Langley to Washington, killing seven men. Mitchell flew around this storm, once encountering winds so strong that his plane was driven backward in a 120-mile-an-hour gale. He called a press conference in Washington. The loss of the Eagle, he said, should be a lesson to the country. If there had been weather reports and proper air routes, the plane might have been saved.

"This is an important thing. We must have a system of air routes and landing fields and regular weather reports . . . How far do you think the motorcar would have gone if motorists had done without roads or fuel stations?"

The only way to get improvement, he said, was through central control of aviation. General Menoher denounced him openly, saying that he had used the tragedy to advance his pet ideas for personal gain. The Navy took up this refrain.

Admiral William A. Moffett, who had been designated as the anti-Mitchell specialist of the Navy, and was soon to head the new Bureau of Naval Aeronautics, prepared a case against Mitchell for the Chief of Naval Operations, also charging that Mitchell "used the recent disaster which resulted in the deaths of five brother officers and two civilians as an argument in favor of a united air service . . . This disaster had nothing whatever to do with the united air service."

Moffett, a dapper little man in a faultlessly tailored uniform, was known to his staff as "the South Carolina Gamecock," and was as fearless and as colorful as Mitchell himself. He charged Mitchell with a list of past sins against the Navy, especially with trying to kill the Bureau of Naval Aeronautics: "It has been ascertained that General Mitchell has interfered, meddled and hampered the passage of the bill by instigating a member of the Senate to offer certain amendments." *

Herbert Corey, an Associated Newspapers writer who had been a well-known war correspondent, returned from a Navy training cruise and wrote Mitchell that he was galling the enemy: "You are throwing the Navy into convulsions. The entire fleet trembles with rage at the mention of your name."

In New York, Franklin D. Roosevelt, who had campaigned unsuccessfully as a vice-presidential candidate on the Democratic ticket with James Cox, reflected the Navy's view of the approach-

* This opened a long warfare between Mitchell and Moffett, both advocates of a strong air arm. Moffett fought for Navy control of its own aviation, but according to Eugene Wilson once said: "If the Navy doesn't hurry and build up its own air force, it will be obsolete, just as Mitchell claims. Without an air force, the fleet would be a sitting duck." Mitchell and Moffett were bitter antagonists until the admiral's death in the crash of the dirigible *Akron* in 1932.

ing bombing tests, without mentioning Mitchell's name. He told a Kiwanis Club: "It is highly unlikely that an airplane or a fleet of them could ever successfully attack a fleet of Navy vessels under battle conditions."

Moreover, official Navy protests, passed through Secretary Weeks to Menoher, made Mitchell's superior increasingly impatient. His daily conflicts with Mitchell during the bombing tests had worsened their already strained relationship. The mounting complaints were at last too much for the Chief of the Air Service. Just as Mitchell was becoming the most talked-about man in the country, and was within a week of starting the experiments which would make him famous, Menoher demanded that he be dismissed. He wrote to Weeks without warning:

"It is recommended and requested that Brigadier General William Mitchell be relieved of duty as Assistant Chief of the Air Service . . .

"He has given serious offense to the Navy Department by his public utterances and publicity . . .

"Unfortunate and undesirable publicity given to his individual exploits at the time immediately following the fatal accident of the Curtiss Eagle ambulance plane . . . has caused a very great revulsion of feelings . . ."

Menoher then revealed his pent-up personal resentment: "Persistent publicity in the daily press . . . [enhanced] his own prestige at the expense of and to the detriment of the prestige of his immediate commanding officer. This publicity, if not carried on by him personally, is at least known to him and subject to his control."

Menoher acknowledged Mitchell's value, but said "the effect of his activities has been so demoralizing to the personnel" that he was "a positive detriment."

In other words, Menoher or Mitchell must go.

Secretary Weeks wavered for a few days after receiving Menoher's letter. The press got wind of the showdown, and Weeks told the New York *Sun* that Army discipline and precedent would probably dictate that he side with Menoher and move Mitchell to another post. The *Sun* reported: "It is taken for certain that Mitchell will be removed, although his friends were asserting that it would not be long before Menoher would be shelved."

This trial balloon, if it was one, collapsed under fire from veterans' organizations, aerial clubs and the press. There was a rumor that the bombing tests would be canceled if Mitchell went out.

The Harding Administration had no trouble reading the public mind, and in response to the chorus of support for Mitchell, Weeks retreated. He called Mitchell and Menoher into a private conference and laid down new rules for Mitchell. He was to cease lobbying with Congress, baiting the Navy, and pressing for aviation reforms if they were counter to War Department policy. He ended with an admonition to Mitchell that had the ring of Knute Rockne's locker-room oratory: "In general, get into harness and pull with the team and in such a matter as an alleged line of cleavage between fliers and nonfliers, attempt to close the breach instead of widen it."

This was the first reprimand of any moment in Mitchell's career, and it was to mark a new phase of his campaign, a pattern of defiance to be repeated until the end. From now on, he became open in his challenge to authority where he thought the future of air power was at stake.

Weeks called in the press and said that Menoher had withdrawn his request that Mitchell be fired. The Secretary had made peace between the two, since he thought it would be "undesirable and unfortunate at this time" to lose Mitchell. The bombing show could go on, but Weeks pointed out that Menoher was not only the nominal head "but the actual head" of the Air Service. He said that Mitchell had agreed to abide by his new instructions.

The Detroit *Free Press* translated for the man in the street: "The Secretary has solemnly told General Mitchell not to do it again . . . he has declined to give Mitchell more than a small slap on the wrist. Menoher is advised to go way back and sit down, while Mitchell will get a chance to show whether a dreadnought is obsolete in the presence of a modern bombing plane."

Many messages of support came to Mitchell during the controversy, including one from his mother: "Am anxious to hear what prompted General Menoher in his action. Keep cool and use good judgment. Do not worry about the outcome of anything. Take care of your health."

To Representative Hubert Fisher of Tennessee, who expressed

his support and "extravagant admiration," Mitchell gave a dispassionate explanation of the squabble: "The controversy is merely the result of the older services not fully appreciating the powers, capabilities and necessities for an air force. I think we will be able to work it out to the best interests of the government all the way through. There is nothing personal in any matter between General Menoher and myself."

In May, as the tempo of training increased in the Brigade, Mitchell began to fear that he might not get his chance at the warships, after all. Whether the Navy actually planned to cancel the tests could not be determined, but Mitchell, at least, was concerned. He wrote to Colonel Bane: "The Navy are again trying to stop our obtaining a battleship. How far they will go I don't know, but they have attempted in every way to stop it."

Under the prodding of Representative Anthony, Secretary Weeks pressed the Navy and got fresh assurances that the tests would be held in June and July. The Navy then called Mitchell and his officers into conference, to establish regulations for the bombing. Army-Navy differences became apparent at once.

Captain Alfred Johnson, commander of the fleet air arm, spoke for the Navy. The mere sinking of ships, he said, was not the purpose of the tests. By careful inspection of decks, hulls, turrets, communications systems and fire rooms, the effects of bombs on warships could be measured. A boarding party must make an inspection after each hit; targets must not be destroyed before evidence could be examined.

Mitchell's purpose was a different matter indeed: could bombers destroy warships, especially battleships?

The Navy would not hear of testing without rigid controls. It feared the public reaction in case ships were sunk without regard to conditions. And public opinion, it realized, might determine future naval appropriations. Mitchell hoped to convince the public, if not the Navy, that American defense now rested upon air power, and that nothing should stand in the way of its development.

From these opposite poles, Johnson and Mitchell attempted to reach a compromise as they considered details.

Mitchell fought to have the target ships placed within easy

reach of his Langley squadrons; he suggested a point thirty miles east of Cape Hatteras off the North Carolina coast, which was the nearest 50-fathom depth, the minimum required by the Navy for sinking the old ships. The commander of the Atlantic Fleet refused. The ships would be anchored about seventy miles east of the Cape Charles Lightship—which would put them nearly a hundred miles from Langley Field and stretch the bombing runs to the limit. The Navy would not budge from this.

Mitchell warned the Navy: "This necessitates travel over approximately two hundred miles, which means that the targets must be clear upon the arrival of the planes." The fuel capacity, he said, would not permit them to circle and wait while observers were cleared from the target ships. But he was so eager to prove his assertions, and so sure of success, that he accepted almost all of the Navy's restrictions. He agreed to take orders from Captain Johnson, his junior in rank, but insisted that he alone would give orders to the Army squadrons.

Mitchell refused to join the search for the radio-controlled U.S.S. *Iowa* with his bombers, since they might have to fly four hundred miles over water while locating the ship. Further, he said, the Navy's plan to use dummy bombs was pointless, since damage could not be accurately assessed, and such practice might lead to false conclusions. When the Navy rejected his arguments, he said he would send only Army dirigibles into this hunt.

Mitchell also lost an attempt to have torpedoes used in the tests; when the Navy refused him, he tried, through Hap Arnold, to get information on naval torpedo development. Arnold was told by a naval officer that no information would be given the Army without a direct order from the Secretary of the Navy, since he believed "the information was being obtained to undermine the Navy."

In early June, at last, the bickering of committees came to an end and the old German warships were towed into position off the Virginia Capes. Mitchell and the First Provisional Air Brigade would be put to the test.

7

Kill, Lay Out and Bury This Great Ship

The naval transport *Henderson* dropped down the Potomac on June 20 with a party of notables, and the next day joined the fleet off the capes to watch the opening of the test. This was the Navy's day, won by the toss of a coin; later on, the Army and the Navy would attack on alternate days. Still, on Langley Field the bombers waited, loaded, in case the Navy did not sink its target.

Mitchell flew out with Captain Streett in his favorite plane, the *Osprey*. She was an elderly DH4B, sporting his private Air Service insignia, and flying a long blue command pennant at the tail for identification. She was painted blue and white, and was specially fitted; her engine was practically new. They joined the dozen or more planes and three dirigibles above the target.

The first act of the spectacle was over so quickly that it would be forgotten in the attacks that were to follow during the summer. The German submarine *U-117* was the smallest and most fragile of the targets, 267 feet long, about 1200 tons, but the Navy attacked her with enthusiasm. She had torpedoed nine ships during the war and caused the loss of at least a hundred Allied lives, largely by potting helpless fishing vessels off New England.

The anchored sub was to be bombed by three waves of Navy F-5-L planes with 165-pound bombs, and then, if necessary, by Navy Martins and Marine Corps De Havillands. Only if all these flights failed would the Air Service be called out.

It was over before the Marines came into sight. The first three planes straddled the target from 1000 feet and the next flight scored direct hits, broke her hull in two, and sank the submarine. Mitchell said: "None except the air people had expected such a rapid termination . . . These bombs tore her all to pieces . . . Some of the skeptics began to be convinced that there was something to air bombing."

But the Navy was not persuaded, and arguments raged on the *Henderson* as she returned to Washington; an unarmored sub, perhaps, was easily sunk, but not a heavy capital ship.

The Brigade had not wasted the day. George Goddard's movie film of the quick sinking was on its way to the newsreel theaters, and the public would soon see for itself what could be done from the air.

There was a lapse of more than a week before the next bombing, and Mitchell used every moment to complete training. The following day he lost Captain Howard T. Douglas and Lieutenant Plumb in a midair collision over the Chesapeake. Mitchell had flown with fifty-three planes and three airships to the wreck of the old U.S.S. *Texas,* where they dropped almost two hundred bombs. Douglas and Plumb crashed amid the circling flights and fell into the bay, the first casualties from overwater strikes during the exercise.

Mitchell led three flights of his SE-5 fighters to a memorial service the next morning, and with Milling and Streett, dropped flowers near the spot where his men had died. When the blooms were floating on Tangier Sound, the flights of SE-5's dropped salvos of 25-pound bombs in final salute. The Navy complained angrily, saying that Mitchell had deliberately dropped bombs near some of its working divers. Menoher called him to account once more, and Mitchell replied that the Navy had been notified of the ceremony and had all its personnel out of the water when the salute was fired, a mile and a half away.

When news of the crash appeared in the newspapers, Secretary Weeks wrote to Menoher: "I have been seriously disturbed and concerned over the succession of accidents . . . Most rigid instructions will be given by you for the purpose of preventing a repetition."

Menoher, as if air safety had never come to his attention from Langley, sent Mitchell a brusque message, asking for a report by radio of all orders he had issued as to safety precautions. Mitchell replied at length, saying that all personnel, planes, bombs and equipment were inspected before takeoff, that flight surgeons were always on duty, that mechanics and other technical men accompanied the flights, that the condition of the Brigade was excellent. He went so far as to report on supplies of earplugs and tongue depressors. He tried to reassure Menoher that there had been little trouble, considering the hurried operation: "Every precaution practicable is taken by the personnel whose own life depends on the proper function of this equipment."

Even this was not the most important matter to Menoher. While he kept the Langley staff busy otherwise, he was zealously guarding the secrecy of the bombing tests themselves. He sent new orders to every Air Service base, requiring officers to certify that they had received his orders on "Avoidance of Publicity in Connection with Bombing Experiments," and that they were being complied with. A small army of reporters and photographers would take news of every stage of the bombing tests to the public, but Menoher was determined not to be caught again by Mitchell's airing his own opinions.

On June 29 a second phase of the tests was staged at sea, the search for the U.S.S. *Iowa*, radio-controlled by the *Ohio,* steaming five miles to her rear. She was on the move somewhere between Cape Henlopen and Cape Hatteras, an area of 25,000 square miles. The old ship was well known to the Navy. In the war with Spain she had been the flagship of "Fighting Bob" Evans. "Give me the *Iowa,*" he had said, "and I will see that Spanish is the only language spoken in hell for the next twenty years."

At the last minute Mitchell changed his mind and offered to send nine bombers to join the Navy in this search, in addition to his dirigibles, but Admiral Hilary Jones refused: "However willing the general may be at this late hour to take a responsibility which he declined in May, the senior officer present cannot bring himself to permit now the entrance of personnel lacking the training necessary . . ."

Jones clung to this view despite the warning of Captain Alfred Johnson that the Navy faced a serious public relations problem with Mitchell, and that Jones should not "permit it to be stated that the Navy refused to allow the Army to participate." Jones was adamant; the only Army vessels allowed were the dirigibles.

To Mitchell's delight, the Navy's seaplanes droned back and forth for hours over an empty sea—and it was the Army blimps, after all, that spotted the *Iowa,* almost an hour ahead of the Navy planes. The Navy flying boats then gathered, and dropped dummy bombs on the target, with two hits in eighty tries. The Navy took this as evidence that Mitchell's bombing crews would fail when the time came to attack big ships.

The destroyer was next in the test series, two weeks later. She was the *G-102,* a long-range torpedo destroyer built for Argentina by Krupp's just before the war, and commandeered for the German Navy. She was a smaller target than the *Iowa,* 312 feet long and 30 feet abeam, but she was the Brigade's own. The Army airmen had permission to sink her themselves, without restrictions, using whatever tactics they might think necessary.

Mitchell's attack opened with eighteen pursuit planes in three flights, in position to meet enemy action at any altitude, and carrying machine guns and light bombs to clear the destroyer's decks. Behind them were the light bombers, De Havillands with 100-pounders, and last would come the Martin heavies, with 600-pounders. "It was the first time in aeronautical history," Mitchell said, "that an attack had been made in this way. Every element of a large force was there."

The SE-5's dived within 200 feet of the deck, dropping bombs at thirty-second intervals; they kept up a constant roar of explosions. Mitchell wrote: "The attack was beautiful to watch . . . Practically every bomb went where it was directed. The decks of the destroyer were punctured and swept from end to end."

So that the fighter pilots would have time to watch the sinking of the ship, Mitchell waved off the light bombers and brought in the Martins, led by Captain W. R. ("Tiny") Lawson. Within twenty minutes the destroyer was gone. As Mitchell saw it:

"In less time than it takes to tell, their bombs began churning the water around the destroyer. They hit close in front of it, behind it, opposite its side and directly in its center. Columns of water rose hundreds of feet into the air. For a few minutes the vessel looked as if it were on fire. Smoke came out of its funnels and vapors along its deck. Then it broke completely in two in the middle and sank out of sight . . . All our methods and systems of bombing had proved to be correct."

There were close calls as the planes returned to their base. One Martin barely made the coast. Lieutenant Dunlap had an engine failure at sea and limped home on one motor, slowly losing altitude. He cleared the surf and landed in sand, his engine so overheated that he could not cut if off. It roared on, whipping the bomber in circles and into the waves, where it fell apart.

Lieutenant Fonda B. Johnston, ran out of gas in his Morse pursuit and glided down near Dunlap's wreck. He was still thirty-five miles from Langley, so he swam to the ruined bomber, cut a gas tank from its wing, refueled and flew home.

Langley roared after dark. As Mitchell recalled it: "That night all our men had returned safely . . . after their first great experience in bombing. Their rejoicing was tremendous. They knew now that unless something most unusual happened it would be proved for all time that aircraft dominated seacraft."

Five days later the crews faced a more formidable target, the 5100-ton light cruiser *Frankfurt,* six years old, buoyed by many steel compartments and shielded by side armor. She was to be attacked by about sixty planes, in ten waves, with Army, Navy and Marines alternating. The first waves would carry 100-pound bombs, the next ones 250- and 300-pounders, and the last one 600-pounders. Mitchell thought the lighter bombs a waste of time, but the Navy insisted on all types so that inspection parties aboard the tender *Shawmut* could assess the damage between attacks.

Small bombs rained down during the morning, with long intervals between strikes while the boarding party climbed over the *Frankfurt.* Mitchell watched it from the *Osprey,* and this time his passenger was his sister Harriet, who was visiting at Langley. Mitchell thought the target was almost too beautiful to bomb: "As she lay in the water, she resembled a swan, so gracefully did she ride the waves. I hated to sink her, as she was far more attractive than any of the seacraft looking on."

Inspectors found no major damage from the light bombs. Goats and other small animals caged on the deck were dead, but the ship was sound below decks. "Imagine that baby under steam and able to fight 'em off," a naval officer said.

Mitchell's big bombers appeared at three-thirty—six Martins led by Lawson. They found the *Shawmut,* from which the tests were directed by radio, lying close by the target, and were forced to circle overhead for half an hour while Navy inspectors prowled the ship: they had decided that the cruiser was too stout to be sunk from the air, and ordered the *South Dakota,* of the observation fleet, to prepare a time bomb.

Lawson finally went to work after a prolonged delay. As Mitchell recorded it: "The bombs fell so fast that the attack could not be stopped before mortal damage had been done to the ship. The control vessel made the signal to cease as the good ship was toppling over . . . tremendous columns of water shot up. Some fell in tons on the deck of the ship, sweeping it clear. It was the first time we had used our 600-pound bombs and they worked splendidly . . . the cruiser . . . sank rapidly."

The *Frankfurt* hung on for several minutes after one bomb blew a huge hole in her forward compartments, and just before she sank, Mitchell skimmed a few feet above her with Harriet. His bombers turned toward Langley, low on gasoline. The *Frankfurt* disappeared behind them.

George Goddard's photographic planes, flying in relays, had been working to perfection. As soon as movie film of the sinking had come to Langley on the blimp, Goddard prepared to fly it to Bolling Field, where newsreel men would pick it up, hurry it to New York for development, and have it in big-city theaters the next day.

The only mishap of the day was caused by Mitchell's insistence that Goddard fly a large bag of fresh oysters to Senator Borah. Goddard's cockpit was already full of film and equipment, and he had a faulty camera tripod lashed to one wing, on its way to a repair shop. Mitchell said to him: "You've got one wing open, and we've got to keep Borah happy." Then he had the bag of oysters strapped to the other wing. Goddard eased the ship off the ground, but his overworked engine went dead on the way and he landed in a ditch, scattering film cans and oysters over the landscape. Goddard managed to get the film to Washington soon after daylight, following a wild night ride over bottomless country roads in a commandeered Model T Ford. Senator Borah's oysters, salvaged by a group of farm hands who had come to Goddard's rescue, were eaten on the spot.

Captain Roberts never forgot Mitchell's flying of that day: "Once, when Lawson's bombers were still working, dropping bombs intermittently, Mitchell flew right under them, just over the *Frankfurt,* but neither he nor Harriet nor the Lawson crews turned a hair, so far as anyone could see."

Mitchell was struck by another incident of the day's attack: "At the first direct hit of the bomb on the *Frankfurt's* deck, fragments of steel were thrown over the water for a mile. The crews of the observing ships had crowded to the rails to watch, but as the pieces of steel came nearer and nearer to them they rushed to the other side of the vessel for protection. It made one think what might happen in case a real attack was made."

Still, the Navy was cheerful: if a light cruiser could resist so tenaciously, a battleship would be safe. Mitchell's crews would find the *Ostfriesland* a far different matter.

The Brigade had one more day to prepare for the battleship, July 19, and that was spent in a review at Langley, where General Pershing, Secretary Weeks and a large official party inspected the planes, hangars and quarters. The crews put on an air show, with acrobatics, stunting over the bay and the fleet, and passing in attack formations. Mitchell went aloft with them, watching from the *Osprey.*

At the end of the show he took the long way home, swinging more than sixty-five miles to sea in the late afternoon for a final check on the *Ostfriesland.* He spotted her at sunset, visible from a great distance with red, white and blue target circles painted on her dull works. He admired her: ". . . like a grim old bulldog with the vicious scars of Jutland still on her, where the *Frankfurt* had looked like a swan. She was sullen and dark and we knew we had a tough nut to crack."

The *Ostfriesland,* the British had discovered after the Armistice, was more powerful than the Germans had admitted—27,000 tons rather than her rated 22,000. She had been built in 1911 but was still as formidable as any ship afloat, designed on the orders of Admiral von Tirpitz to be practically unsinkable. The captain who brought her to the United States had said: "She had four skins to protect her against mines and torpedoes . . . many watertight compartments . . . no matter how many holes were made in her hull, she would be able to get home." Her tight bulkheads had saved her at Jutland, where she took eighteen hits from big shells and struck a mine, yet made her way to port for repairs.

Mitchell knew that if he failed with the *Ostfriesland,* the early tests would be forgotten and "the development of air power might be arrested . . . We had to kill, lay out and bury this great ship."

As he flew home to prepare for the climax, a Navy inspection party had just left the *Ostfriesland.* Commander Alexander van Keuren, an expert in ship construction, had measured her draught at 28 feet, a foot more than she had drawn in the Brooklyn Navy Yard a few days earlier. The water was too rough for accurate measurement, but van Keuren thought the ship was taking water through the bottom—a report that was to become important later, when the Navy challenged Mitchell's work at sea.

The coming assault on the battleship had drawn about fifty reporters and hundreds of distinguished guests—three hundred of them on the transport *Henderson* alone. Three Cabinet members were on hand—Weeks, Denby and Wallace, Secretaries of War, Navy and Agriculture; Assistant Secretary of the Navy Theodore Roosevelt, Jr.; eight senators and a dozen congressmen. The *Pennsylvania,* flagship of the Atlantic Fleet, carried many ranking officers, among them Admiral William Fullam and Major General John Lejeune, Commandant of the Marine Corps.

One of Denby's special guests was General (later Marshal) Badoglio, with an Italian air mission. Among other foreign observers were Commodore Charlton and Captain S. R. Bailey, R.N., from England; and Captain Nagano, G. Katsuda of the House of Peers, and G. Shibuta of the Kobe Chamber of Commerce, from Japan. Others were from France, Spain, Portugal and Brazil.

In the American official party were, among others, Mitchell's companion on the *Aquitania,* naval constructor J. C. Hunsaker; Commander Richard E. Byrd; and Lieutenant Commander Zachary Lansdowne, an expert dirigible skipper. General Menoher represented the Air Service; General C. C. Williams, Ordnance; and General A. A. Fries, Chemical Warfare. Among the civilians was Glenn Martin, who had come to watch his bombers.

The last party of guests boarded the *Henderson* before dawn of July 20 and steamed out to join the fleet. It was an impressive armada of eight battleships, ranging from the new *Pennsylvania* to the antique *Olympia,* Dewey's flagship at Manila Bay; with destroyers and auxiliaries they formed a great circle about the *Ostfriesland,* about two miles from the target.

Daylight revealed a rough sea, with whitecaps running under a northeast wind gusting to 30 knots. The ceiling at eight o'clock was 1000 feet, but within an hour had lifted to 2000. The *Shawmut* bobbed around during the morning near the target, with the bombing schedule postponed from hour to hour. Mitchell, waiting at Langley, kept the radio busy, requesting information. At one o'clock, when his bombers still had not been called, he left the crews by their loaded planes and flew out with Streett to investigate. They were halted short of the target: "To our astonishment we saw the whole Atlantic Fleet making for the Chesapeake Bay . . . We found that since there was about a 20-knot wind blowing they determined an airplane could not act."

He was convinced that it was a Navy trick, to prove that planes were helpless in windy weather. "We then signaled that we wished to begin at once, whereupon the fleet returned to the targets." *

The Navy and Marine planes dropped 250-pound bombs until three o'clock, with little effect, and the *Shawmut*'s umpires were on the target when Captain Johnson got a surprise—the Martin bombers had left Langley without orders from the Navy and were coming to attack. The planes arrived, led by Clayton Bissell. Mitchell called the control ship as Bissell's flight circled: "Must attack in 40 minutes. Fuel limited." He was told to send the bombers back to base if they were short of gasoline but Mitchell refused, and they remained overhead until about three-thirty, when they were ordered to begin with their 600-pound bombs.

Mitchell recorded the next few minutes: "Lt. Bissell's flight of

* Mitchell was never shaken in his belief that the Navy conspired against him in the tests. Much later he wrote: "I believe to this day that the officer controlling the air attacks had orders from the Admiral not to let us sink the *Ostfriesland.*"

five planes deployed into column and fired five bombs in extremely rapid succession. It looked as if two or three bombs were in the air at the same time. Two hits alongside and three on the deck or on the side, causing terrific detonations, and serious damage . . . We felt the jolts and noise of the explosions in the air 3000 feet above." It was the end of the day's bombing. A storm was approaching, and the planes left for shore.

The Navy was content with the day's work. The Washington *Post* correspondent, Clinton Gilbert, who had watched from the *Henderson,* said that when Secretary Denby told them what little impression the bombs had made on the ship, "high naval officers sniggered cheerfully."

Reporters were taken to Norfolk on the fast destroyer *Leary* to file stories on the battleship's victory over the plane, basing them on the report of umpires that she was "absolutely intact and undamaged." The *New York Times* pictured the old ship "riding snugly at anchor on the high seas tonight."

Some of the observers had had enough, and there was seasickness on many ships. Two of the dignitaries, Secretary Weeks and General Pershing, went shoreward on the destroyer *Dahlgren* through the pelting rain and decided to spend the next day at Old Point Comfort, since it looked as if the ship would not be sunk.

Mitchell and his crews got back to Langley, but not without adventures. The dirigibles escaped to the north, in a roundabout route over Maryland, but Mitchell circled with other planes to the south, trying to escape the storm's center. The drenched fliers blamed the Navy for the day's failures of every kind—restrictions on the bombs, the long waits, even the weather. George Goddard charged: "The Navy weather boys knew that storm was on the way, and deliberately failed to tell us, hoping to catch the planes up there."

Mitchell and Streett landed in a North Carolina peanut field and only with the aid of a team of farm horses managed to find a level spot and take off again. They landed in rain at Langley, Mitchell's goggles running with water and the field's primitive landing lights glaring in his face. The experimental lighting cable had been damaged by salt water on the field, and the remaining lights were supplemented with flaming tin cans in which a mixture of gasoline and kerosene fed crude wicks made from woollen puttees. The big Martin bombers, loaded with 2000-pounders for the next day, lined one side of the field, and Mitchell skimmed over them, realizing that he would kill "every human being in the place" if he struck one. He was up late, welcoming the storm-tossed planes. Incredibly, there were no casualties. Captain Lawson, forced down near Norfolk, had broken a wheel on his bomber, but returned by car, train and ferry to report at one o'clock in the morning. One dirigible came in about five o'clock with Captain Roberts aboard, but George Goddard did not arrive until the next morning.

Flying the *Osprey* to the target and back that day, Mitchell and Streett had covered six hundred and sixty miles, and like his fliers, Mitchell was "terribly overstrained." As his sister Ruth wrote: "He . . . had been unable to eat a meal for five days, his orderly merely running around after him with cups of coffee." But his first day's failure against the *Ostfriesland* seemed only to spur him on. Ruth added: "Bill was mad clear through. Next morning, he decided, it was going to be 'kill or die trying.' "

By dawn on July 21 Mitchell was already busy at Langley, inspecting planes and crews, watching as Surgeon Strong checked men who would be in the air that day. It was a clear, mild morning, ideal for flying. Just before seven o'clock Mitchell took off with a flight of Martins led by Bissell, to watch the first round, the dropping of 1100-pound bombs. Navy planes were to join the early attack, but Mitchell called Navy headquarters by radio, reporting Bissell on the way, and asked curtly that "they not be interfered with by naval aircraft."

He circled the target while the bombers passed in review, the pilots dipping their wings in salute and Mitchell wagging the *Osprey* in reply, his long blue command pennant fluttering behind. It was not quite eight-thirty when the bombers began.

It was obvious that the target had settled during the night. Van Keuren's inspection party took her draught as 26 feet forward and 36 feet aft, but she was now without a list. The Navy had let in water so that she rode evenly, but she was down so far that portholes of her third deck were awash at the stern.

The Army moved to the attack the instant the *Shawmut* gave its "all clear" signal, a white canvas painted with a red cross. At eight-thirty-five Bissell himself dropped the first 1100-pounder, a direct hit on the forecastle—"sheer luck," Bissell thought. The next few moments produced a bitter wrangle. The *Shawmut* was about a mile from the target and the rest of Bissell's planes came on so quickly that by the time the *Shawmut* made frantic signals for the attack to stop, four bombs had already been dropped, two more of them hits. Navy observers thought that the removal of the "all clear" canvas, and the sudden puffs of heavy smoke from the *Shawmut's* stack as an emergency signal, should have halted Bissell's attack, but the lieutenant maintained that he could not possibly have halted the bombers in time. As it was, the last men in his flight had to turn back without dropping bombs, after their long months of training. They were, Bissell said, "mad as hornets."

Johnson was calling Mitchell by radio from the *Shawmut:* "Cease firing. Observers going aboard. Acknowledge." Mitchell's reply, so Navy sources said, was: "Martin bomber No. 23 will let you know when it's safe to board target." Johnson and the *Shawmut* were now within the 1000-foot danger zone. More than a generation later some Navy men maintained that Mitchell actually meant harm to the naval inspection team, in his anger over real or imagined Navy interference.

The first attack was soon over, and Bissell's planes, ordered back to base with seven 1100-pound bombs left, turned toward the shore. Bissell dropped his remaining bomb far from the fleet and ordered his pilots to drop their own, since they could not land on the rough Langley field with the bombs. The angry fliers took matters into their own hands. They spotted the line of destroyers, stationed at seven-mile intervals on the way home, and decided "to give the boys something to think about." The bombs fell within half a mile of some of these ships, and though the pilots gave no thought to potential damage, the water-hammer effect sent tons of salt water into the condenser systems of the destroyers.

The destroyers turned rapidly away from the returning flight. "They thought our crews had gone crazy," Bissell recalled, "but the fliers didn't even know what they'd done."

Umpires found so much wreckage aboard the *Ostfriesland* that they could not go below the third deck, but saw through bomb holes that water was two feet deep on the armored deck aft.

Inspectors agreed that the ship, though badly wounded, was "still in action" despite incoming water and wreckage above. The Navy was optimistic. "By Jove," Captain Johnson said, "we're not going to sink this ship!"

Mitchell was back at Langley and ready for the last chance by ten o'clock. Lawson was to lead six Martins and two Handley Pages, each carrying a 2000-pound bomb, the giants which were, as Hap Arnold later said, "in basic design the same we were to use against Germany and Japan in World War II." Mitchell was still briefing his pilots when Captain Johnson called him to the attack. There had been a change in the rules, Johnson said—an important one. The bombers would bring out no more than three of the big bombs.

Mitchell was infuriated: "This was the last straw. We had an agreement with the Navy in writing that we would be allowed to make at least two direct hits on deck with our heaviest bombs." He complained that this "narrowest interpretation" by the Navy might well end the test with the fleet's guns sinking the *Ostfriesland.*

He disregarded Johnson's final instructions, and the flight left with one bomb on each plane—a total of eight. His last order to the pilots was: "Try for near misses." He then waved Lawson down the runway and the eight big planes lumbered off, barely clearing the pine trees.

Mitchell radioed the Navy when he was in the air: "Martin bomber and Handley Page formation with 2000-pound bombs have taken off . . . In case of failure to secure two direct hits, subsequent attacks will be made until we have secured the two hits the Army is authorized to make." The Navy did not reply. Mitchell and Streett flew across the picket ships seaward. Visibility was fair, with a slight haze, and the wind was northeast, at 10 miles an hour. On the way out they saw a Handley Page land in the sea, going up on its nose. One of those aboard was Captain Roberts, who had saved the plane by cutting loose a 2000-pounder just before they struck the water. The crew paddled about in life jackets until a boat from a destroyer picked them up. When he saw that they were safe, Mitchell flew low, waving, and turned seaward.

Visibility was poorer near the target, with a haze creeping

from the southeast, and they had some brief trouble finding the fleet. They were hardly in place when the attack began, just after noon.

There was a shout from the watching ships, ending in laughter—instead of the expected monster bomb, a sand-loaded range-finding shell splashed 150 feet in front of the battleship's bow. When the first big bomb fell, reporters watched it as if the whole year's work rode with it.

It was much longer than the Navy bombs, dropped straight as an arrow and blazed in the sunshine. On impact there was a heavy water-hammer blow against the side of the *Henderson* and a dozen warships. Mitchell wrote: ". . . up came the spout of water, more than any geyser, more than any missile made by man had ever produced. Three thousand feet above we felt the rush of air as it 'bumped' the wings of our plane. Higher and higher mounted the great water . . . The noise of the discharge reached us through the whirr of the motor. The old bulldog winced at the shock . . ." He estimated that 30,000 tons of water had been thrown up by the bomb.

Mitchell shouted boyishly to Streett: "What do you think?"

"The crew would jump overboard."

"How about the captain?"

"He'd have to sink with her."

There was another miss, but at twenty-one minutes past noon a direct hit on the point of the bow was followed by billowing smoke and fire, and a gaping hole was torn in the forecastle. Five minutes later Lawson's crews got another hit in the water near the mainmast, which lifted the ship high and threw such a heavy fall of water across the deck that one reporter thought it looked "like a Niagara."

A minute later the fifth large bomb fell near the stern and another great sheet of water fell across the quarter-deck. The nose of the ship rose and she began slipping under by the stern. Two big guns of the afterturret, long since knocked out of alignment, were now out of sight. She was sinking rapidly. Eleven minutes after the first direct hit, the sixth bomb struck, less than fifty feet aft. The water boiled about the stern, which was already awash. The *World* reporter, Austin Parker, a veteran of the Lafayette

Escadrille, had the impression that "some unseen force had started the engineless propellers in a vain effort to escape the deadly missiles."

The bow pointed high, with dull paint exposed below the waterline and water gleaming over her barnacles. The *Ostfriesland* went over on her port side and down by the stern. As Parker saw it: "At 12:38 the *Ostfriesland* was on her beam ends. A minute later she had almost turned turtle . . ."

Observers on the *Henderson* were still talking of watertight compartments, and of badly damaged ships that had stayed afloat for days, when the rusty hulk turned over. Those with field glasses saw split seams and holes in her bottom. Parker wrote: "She rolled there like some immense, round, helpless sea animal."

In the *Osprey,* Streett became so excited that he stood in his cockpit, shouting: "She's gone!" Mitchell described the end: "In a minute more there was only the tip of her beak showing above the water. It looked as if her stern had touched the bottom of the sea as she stood there, straight up in a hundred fathoms of water, to bid a last farewell."

Aboard the *Henderson,* so Clinton Gilbert reported, "the chins of Navy officers . . . dropped. Their eyes seemed to be coming out of the ends of their marine glasses . . . seemed to be watching the end of an era which began when Rome crossed the high seas and smote Carthage."

Benedict Crowell saw admirals and captains dab their eyes with handkerchiefs, some of them sobbing openly. The Washington *Times* reporter followed a disconsolate group to the rail—two admirals, Secretary Denby and General Menoher: "Not a word was spoken by the men as the great rust-encrusted hulk took its final plunge. It seemed as though all in the little knot of onlookers were attending a funeral, as if one of their dearest friends was being buried, and they couldn't believe it."

As the battleship vanished, this group walked silently aft and there "looked expectantly at one another." Menoher said at last: "I guess maybe the Navy will get its airplane carriers."

One reporter who had kept his eye on Senator Poindexter recalled: "The senator looked as if he had been bombed."

To some, the bubbling and gushing of air from the sinking

Ostfriesland seemed like great sobs. A Handley Page now crossed the foaming vortex of her disappearance and dropped a final bomb precisely on target, helping to force her to the bottom. A sailor, evidently an air enthusiast at heart, blew the *Henderson*'s steam whistle so long that he had to be dragged away.

Mitchell swooped low over the ship's grave, and as he later confessed to his sister Ruth, he had tears in his eyes: "We wanted to destroy her from the air, but when it was actually accomplished it was a very serious and awesome sight . . . I watched her sink from a few feet above her. Then I flew my plane to the *Henderson,* where the people . . . were waving and cheering on the decks and in the rigging." The *Osprey* zoomed so near the transport that those aboard could see Mitchell's grin, his waves and his final salute before he turned shoreward. Ruth was sure it was the "high moment" of his life.

Reporters on the *Henderson* questioned Denby, who said: "I'm sorry. I can give no opinion in advance of the report of the board of observers." Under badgering he managed a statement which avoided controversy: "The plunge of the *Ostfriesland* when she sank after the terrific pounding of the last two days, ended one of the most remarkable and interesting series of tests ever conducted. They have been practically perfect in co-ordination between the two services, and have been characterized throughout by a fine spirit of comradeship. Scientific conclusions of the utmost value undoubtedly will result . . . One outstanding and most admirable feature has been the splendid courage and skill of the aviators. I congratulate them with all my heart." Secretary Weeks, ashore, echoed Denby: "I'm tremendously pleased with the way the fliers handled themselves; they seemed full of pep. I won't commit myself as to the plane against the battleship. I consider expert opinion more valuable than mine."

General Menoher posed as an old bombing enthusiast when cornered by the press, but in the end took a rather cautious view: "I have always contended that the bomb did constitute a grave menace to the capital ship . . . That's the whole story. I never claimed that the menace of the aerial bomb would drive the battleships from the sea. I don't think this shows that the battleships are doomed, but I fail to see how anyone can doubt that the aerial bomb does constitute a real menace . . ." He trailed off into generalities about training and discipline among airmen, the value of the Liberty motor, and the fine bombs and fuses.

Admiral Moffett was more positive: "The lesson is that we must put planes on battleships and get aircraft carriers quickly." He pointed out that Congress had been slow to see the wisdom of building carriers: "We should have a minimum of eight carriers. The Department has recommended only two. The House struck them out, the Senate restored them, and they came out again in a joint conference."

To Glenn Martin it seemed that the day's work had changed the course of world events: ". . . No fleet afloat is safe if it loses control of the air . . . an enemy by gaining control of the air can now carry his own peace terms into the heart of any country. The sinking of the *Ostfriesland* will be epoch-making."

Even at this moment there were nonbelievers. Senator Poindexter, throwing off his shock, managed to sound as if he had been personally offended: ". . . the sinking of the *Ostfriesland* was a matter of coast defense, and does not enter into the larger questions of naval warfare except as related to coast defense. Navies, of course, cannot be limited merely to offshore action such as this. The primal purpose of a navy is to carry the power of the nation onto the high seas and into foreign waters, if necessary, to back up our policies . . ."

Theodore Roosevelt, Jr., the Assistant Secretary of the Navy, reached back to his African safari days in a vain search for a relevant parallel for criticism: "I once saw a man kill a lion with a 30-30 caliber rifle under certain conditions, but that doesn't mean that a 30-30 rifle is a lion gun."

The Navy was going down fighting, if at all.

The only naval officer of high rank who spoke unequivocally for Mitchell was Admiral William Fullam, who had retired after a distinguished career of fighting for a modern navy. The former Pacific commander was arguing with an officer at the moment the old battleship went down: the younger man was insisting that the *Ostfriesland*'s protective deck would yet save her, when she slipped from sight. Fullam said: "Her protective deck is just now protecting just the amount of ocean bottom that it covers."

Of the comments gathered by reporters on the *Henderson* it

was a rather obvious one by General C. C. Williams that was to be remembered. The Ordnance chief said happily: "A bomb has been fired that will be heard around the world." Bystanders were so struck by the aptness of this remark that they repeated the ringing parody when they in turn were asked for comment.*

Mitchell returned to a celebration. He and Streett found the air filled with planes and airships as they neared Langley Field—everything that could fly had been sent up from the base to welcome them home. Cannon boomed below, and officers and men, mechanics and crewmen waved and shouted. A crude sign on a hangar wall preserved the memory of the *Ostfriesland* turning turtle and whirling down to her grave: "We don't sink battleships. We loop 'em."

The mob rushed the *Osprey* and pulled Mitchell from the plane before the propeller had stopped, pressing to shake his hands, slap his back or call greetings. Mitchell tore off his goggles, laughing with tears in his eyes. His words were drowned by the band, which was caught in the crush and almost silenced, with only the drummer left, pounding away in the lead as three men cleared a path to Mitchell's side. Men hoisted the general to their shoulders and carried him around the field. When he went to his quarters there was still an uproar. Bonfires burned during most of the night, the reassembled band endured and people danced about the fires.

An aide, Lieutenant Farewell Bragg, told of a brief speech Mitchell made that night: "'Well, lads, I guess we showed old Admiral Tubaguts today! . . . in the war to come, and you'll see it, God will be on the side of the heaviest air force. What we did to

* According to one source, the reactions of two Japanese observers were more realistic. Messrs. Katsuda and Shibuta had kept four cameras busy during the sinking, and as stated by Mitchell's biographers, Emile Gauvreau and Lester Cohen, Katsuda told the Hartford *Courant* correspondent, Daniel Bidwell: "Very great experiment, profoundly exciting. Our people will cheer your great Mitchell and, you may be sure, will study his experiments. There is much to learn here." Katsuda allegedly spoke of a Japanese-American war: "Should there be such a war America would have to fight it a long way from home . . . It would be gravely embarrassing to the American people if the ideas of your General Mitchell were more appreciated in Japan than in the United States. Gratitude is not one of the attributes of democracy." The writer was unable to locate other accounts of this Japanese reaction.

the *Frankfurt* and the *Ostfriesland* is what will happen to all warships in future wars. And don't you forget it. Keep your eye on the sky!' " Mitchell watched the celebrants from his window for a long time, saying fondly: "Damn those boys. But, by God, they did it!"

He hardly slept that night, watching people around the fires on the field. Ruth wrote: "He was exalted. They had done it. Now at last everyone, even the stupidest, must understand. And there would be no second world war."

There were still spontaneous snake dances around Langley Field two or three days later as officers and men, in exultation over the bombing tests, resumed their celebration.

8

The Biggest Man in the Country

Mitchell became a national hero and a figure of American folklore overnight. He no longer belonged to the Army, the Navy or congressional committees. Millions who watched the deaths of the warships on newsreel screens saw that Mitchell had been devastatingly right; the battleship was doomed, the plane was supreme. The public waited for no protracted study—and to the dismay of the Navy its own role in conducting the tests was largely ignored. Only Mitchell was remembered.

The *New York Times* described the tests as "an epoch-making performance." The New York *Tribune* said: "When the subject is calmly considered, the Navy will awake to the truth—we must have air forces and submarines not only to protect our surface fleet, but to enable it to assume the offensive in war." According to the Dayton (Ohio) *Journal,* "no single incident since the days of the *Monitor* and the *Merrimac* has had so revolutionary an effect upon warfare." However, there were some skeptical editors, including one on the Brooklyn *Eagle:* "The question as to what was proved by the demonstrations will be discussed by military and naval experts of the world for some time to come."

Mitchell was deluged with congratulations. Admiral Fullam wrote: "It is the greatest of all revolutions in warfare afloat and ashore. *Forts are gone and no nation that has good sense will lay the keel of another battleship of the present type.* Indeed it is difficult to outline the general features of future battleships—ships that can resist air and submarine attack. It seems impossible!"

Representative Curry wrote: "You have done more for America in time of peace than any soldier I know . . . Now we must fight harder than ever for a great American air force . . . It will be a hard fight but we will win it."

John O. LaGorce, an editor of the *National Geographic*, wrote: "I was on board the *Henderson* cheek by jowl with all the brass hats . . . and I saw a lot of admirals and captains . . . who used to parade around like a lot of big red bulls sitting quiet like and looking damn blue. You and yours wrote a new page in warfare, Mitchell, and . . . if you weren't blessed with that extra inch of guts it would not have been written in your day or mine."

Servicemen and civilians sent many telegrams: "If we don't make the Air Service our first line of defense, we will get a very hard lesson in the next war" . . . "The tests were convincing past words" . . . "We are all proud of the biggest man in the country." Captain Alfred Johnson sent congratulations from the Atlantic Fleet air forces.

Secretary Weeks and General Menoher both praised Mitchell, and though he replied warmly, he hinted that Menoher had failed to grasp the significance of the effort: "It is difficult for one to realize what a tremendous amount of work is necessary in the organization, administration and tactical handling of an air brigade." What could be seen from the *Henderson*, he said, was only "the apex of the cone of the whole work."

Mitchell sent his thanks to General Williams of the Ordnance Corps for "the finest bombs in the world," urging that he continue development: "We are on the right track." * He wrote several other men of his regrets that they had missed the sinkings. He told Colonel C. G. Hall at Ross Field, California: "The cards were stacked against us just about as much as they could be." And with a touch of nostalgia he wrote Captain John Curry in Hawaii: "I wish you had been with us . . . The First Provisional Air Brigade was the first real air organization we have ever had in this country. It seemed like one of our old outfits in Europe again."

His sudden popularity was world-wide. Among the magazines

* Ordnance did not remain on "the right track." Colonel C. H. M. Roberts, the chief developer of the big bombs, who returned to active duty to head ammunition development during World War II, found that U.S. bomb design had "deteriorated" since 1921.

bidding for Mitchell's writing was the *Gasschutz und Luftschutz,* in Berlin. He began the most prolific period of his career as a writer on aviation.

But Mitchell was not finished yet. On July 29 the heavy bombers flew in formation from Langley to New York. Mitchell led them down Broadway to the Battery at 8000 feet, picking as targets familiar landmarks—the Woolworth Building, the Treasury and the Customs House. In theory, his planes rained twenty-one tons of bombs on the city—enough, by Mitchell's estimate, to paralyze it.

He landed on Long Island and gave reporters a dramatic picture of the end of New York City. The morning papers did their best to give the public his message. The *Herald* headlined:

CITY IN THEORETICAL RUINS FROM AIR RAID

SURVIVORS FLEE STRICKEN ISLAND SEEKING SHELTER IN THE COUNTRY. GEN. MITCHELL SAYS SO.

The story gave graphic details: "The sun rose today on a city whose tallest tower lay scattered in crumbled bits of stone . . . Bridges did not exist . . .

"The sun saw, when its light penetrated the ruins, hordes of people on foot, working their way very slowly and painfully up the island. A few started with automobiles but the masses of stone buildings barricading the avenues soon halted their vehicles. Rich and poor alike, welded together in a real democracy of misery, headed northward. They carried babies, jewel cases, bits of furniture, bags, joints of meat and canned goods made into rough packs.

"Always they looked fearfully upward at the sky . . . bodies lay like revelers overcome in grotesque attitudes . . . The majority had died swiftly of poison gas . . . This is the picture painted by Brigadier General William Mitchell . . ."

While the city digested stories of its ruin, Mitchell led his planes against Philadelphia, where thousands saw his squadron come over William Penn's statue on City Hall, dropping its theoretical bombs. Evening newspapers pictured Philadelphia as a shambles, but the commandant of the local navy yard, though he declined to give details, said that if it had been a real raid, the defense would have been vigorous.

On their way south the planes flew over Wilmington, Baltimore and the Naval Academy at Annapolis, dropping gas bombs. By midafternoon Mitchell was describing his raid to reporters at Langley.

He had more surprises in store. One night in early August he led four pursuit planes against destroyers in Hampton Roads, using million-candlepower flares as he swooped to within 500 feet of the unsuspecting deck crews, blinding them with the glare. Mitchell theorized that the destroyers had been sunk, and announced to the press that navies were no longer safe in their own harbors by day or night.

A few days later Mitchell gave a party in Washington's Army and Navy Club which was to live long in the memories of airmen, a commemoration of the emergence of air power and a massive assault upon American sobriety. There were powerful and extemporaneous refreshments. Mitchell had ordered liquor from subterranean sources in New York, as was the custom in Prohibition days, but it was smashed in an accident on the eve of the party, so he called on George Goddard, who kept a supply of grain alcohol at Bolling Field for his photographic laboratory. Goddard delivered forty or fifty gallons and helped to mix the drinks—pure alcohol and Virginia Dare wine. "I never met anybody afterward," Goddard recalled later, "who knew a whole lot about what happened that night, except that it was a big one."

There were triumphant speeches from air and ordnance officers, and from two or three air-minded Navy officers who were in civilian garb; most speakers lambasted the Navy hierarchy, much in the vein of Horace Hickam, Mitchell's information chief, who wrote about this time: "It looks very much as though the naval board put all the obstacles possible in our way . . . We are all hoping that the Secretary will allow us to open up sooner or later. As it is the Navy has a free hand, but God knows they need it."

The Navy had no intention of accepting Mitchell's verdict on the bombing tests. Commander van Keuren, the inspector, filed a report in which it appeared that the *Ostfriesland* had sunk almost accidentally. He stated that she was down almost a foot lower in the water before a bomb was dropped, and aside from the effects of bombs, was slowly sinking throughout the test. If a crew had been aboard, it could "easily have kept the ship almost free of water"—even under the battering of 2000-pound bombs.

Captain Alfred Johnson reported that Mitchell's disregard of the rules had made it impossible for the Navy to gather data for protection of ships against bombs. Naval historians who wrote later agreed with him: "The effect of these violations of carefully drawn rules was to destroy the value of these tests to the Navy." *

The Navy's confidential report stressed the ideal conditions for attack, low altitude and lack of resistance, but conceded: "The fact remains that in every case of attack by bombs, the ships . . . were eventually sunk." It recommended improved defenses and carriers, but insisted that the capital ship was the chief naval weapon of the future.

Mitchell's hope of official approval for his theories lay with the Joint Board of Army and Navy officers, headed by General Pershing, which would make the only public statement on the tests. When the Joint Board released its findings in September, newspapermen unerringly found the major conclusion near the end of the document: "The battleship is still the backbone of the fleet and the bulwark of the nation's sea defense and will so remain so long as safe navigation of the sea for purposes of trade or transportation is vital to success in war."

Mitchell saw at once that Pershing had sided with the Navy. The involved report embodied several conflicting points, as if two independent opinions had been combined. On the one hand the summary acknowledged that "aircraft . . . have adequate offensive power to sink or seriously damage any naval vessel at present constructed . . ." but upheld the battleship's traditional role as "the backbone of the fleet."

There were some positive statements with which Mitchell could agree: "The aviation and ordnance experiments . . . proved that

* This Navy plaint lived on for many years. Admiral Moffett's publicist, Eugene Wilson, said that by preventing a "reasonable test" of the vulnerability of warships, Mitchell did great damage by closing the minds of naval officers to the possibilities of air strikes—and from this concluded that Mitchell, "as much as anybody else in this country, is responsible to a certain measure for the Pearl Harbor debacle."

it has become imperative as a matter of national defense to provide for the maximum possible development of aviation in both the Army and the Navy. They have also proved the necessity for aircraft carriers." *

Mitchell was so outraged by official refusal to accept the overwhelming evidence of the bombing tests that he was driven, for the first time, to a serious defiance of orders. He was obviously determined to get the truth, as he saw it, before the public. He was equally determined to challenge Menoher, to oust him from office and to become Chief himself. His first move was to file a long report with Menoher—his own detailed evaluation of the bombing tests:

"Aircraft now in existence can find and destroy all classes of sea craft under war conditions with a negligible loss . . . Aircraft acting from suitable floating airdromes can destroy any class of surface sea craft on the high seas . . .

"The problem of the destruction of seacraft by air forces has been solved and is finished. It is now necessary to provide an air organization and a method of defending not only our coast cities but our interior cities against the attack of hostile air forces."

This forthright report said that national defense must be revised at once, since no aerial defense was possible so long as aviation forces were buried in the Navy and Army. "There is no common head—except Congress—where matters relating to land defense, sea defense and air defense can be submitted on their own merits . . . An efficient solution . . . will not exist until a department of national defense is organized."

Menoher was shocked. He passed on the document to the Secretary of War with a terse endorsement: "Attention is invited especially to that part of the above memorandum . . . which recommends the creation of a 'Department of Aeronautics' . . . While there is need for further co-operation . . . I do not concur in the specific recommendation."

The report led to Menoher's departure as Air Chief. On its heels Mitchell submitted his resignation as Assistant Chief, on the

* The Navy's first carrier, *Langley*, was commissioned seven months later, in March 1922, a converted collier which was the only U.S. carrier for more than five years, until joined by the *Saratoga* and the *Lexington*. Mitchell helped spur this development; as early as January 1921 he had insisted to Congress that carriers were essential.

grounds that conditions in the War Department made his presence "a source of irritation." Secretary Weeks, as if he feared public reaction, asked him to remain until the final stage of the bomb tests was finished, against the old U.S.S. *Alabama*—and then, as Mitchell apparently anticipated, Menoher submitted his own resignation. Weeks did not hesitate, as he had in the spring, but sided with the popular hero. Menoher was given his transfer, to command troops in the field.

The War Department announced the sudden change with an other-worldly air: "Friction between General Menoher and General William Mitchell, which became openly manifest several months ago, had no connection with the request."

As Menoher departed, Mitchell's staff (perhaps with his knowledge) took matters into its own hands, determined to install Mitchell as the new Chief. A barrage of "news stories" was fired from the office.

To the Associated Press: "Air Service officers over the whole U.S. are unanimous in their demand for an officer in command who will fly with them . . . they fear that there will be much useless expenditure and loss of life if their new chief is selected from some other branch of the service and put over them."

Other stories, prepared for the *New York Times*, the *World* and the *Herald*, called for Mitchell in a chorus: "While General Menoher has been busy with this task, his very able assistant, General Mitchell, has been making exhaustive studies on the hundreds of problems of military aviation and leaving the problems of paperwork to his superior officer. He has gone out in his plane to tackle them for himself . . ."

Though this was Air Service propaganda, it reflected the truth. Hap Arnold wrote from the Coast: "According to newspaper dispatches there is a very good chance of your being made the next Chief . . . We out here on the Coast believe that you are the logical man for the job and wish you all the luck in the world . . . In every case you have produced the goods."

But it was not to be. Neither Weeks nor the General Staff considered Mitchell as a prospect. Even as his publicity campaign was growing in strength, General Pershing was calling his old West Point comrade, Mason Patrick, to come and quiet the wild airmen, as he had during the war. Mitchell got the news at

Langley, where he was preparing for the *Alabama* bombings. His friend William S. Jewett of the Washington *Times* wired: "The President sent the name of General Patrick to the Senate today to be Chief of the Air Service."

Mitchell gave no hint of his reaction in public, but his friends were outspoken. Eddie Rickenbacker said: "General Patrick is a capable soldier, but he knows nothing of the Air Service. His appointment is as sensible as making General Pershing Admiral of the Swiss Navy." But Hap Arnold saw the motive in the recall of Patrick: ". . . the new Chief's experience with air power was a secondary consideration . . . In the eyes of the General Staff, it was experience with General Mitchell that counted. If there was any officer in the Army who should . . . be able to control him, Patrick was the man."

Mitchell was to lose many battles in his campaign for American air power, but no one routed him so completely in a personal clash as Mason Patrick did. On the eve of the final bombing tests, late in September, they fought a brief duel for control of the Air Service; Patrick won almost effortlessly.

A day or so after the new Chief had taken office, Mitchell submitted a plan for reorganizing the Service. Patrick read it with rising anger. "Even a casual reading," he said later, "disclosed the fact that if it were put into effect he would practically have charge of most of the Air Service."

In rejecting the plan, Patrick told Mitchell: "I propose to be Chief in fact as well as in name. I want to keep you here as the principal assistant, and I'll be glad to consult with you on all matters. But I want it understood—you'll give no orders. The final decisions will be mine."

"I can't continue under those conditions," Mitchell said. "I'll resign."

Patrick forced the issue immediately by taking him into the office of General Harbord, who was now Deputy Chief of Staff, so that Mitchell could resign formally.

"General Mitchell finds it impossible to serve under me under the conditions I have set forth," Patrick said. "He has come to offer his resignation." He then explained Mitchell's plan for the Air Service.

Harbord turned to Mitchell. "Well, are you going to offer your resignation? If so, it will be accepted at once."

"I've thought it over," Mitchell said. "I've made up my mind that I don't care to resign. I'll assist General Patrick along the lines he has laid down."

Patrick had prepared for this confrontation; he handed Harbord a written summary of Mitchell's duties. Harbord read it aloud. "Do you thoroughly understand this?" he asked. Mitchell said that he did. The interview was over.

Even then Patrick did not leave matters to chance. He sent Mitchell a memorandum covering the lines of authority once more, reviewing Mitchell's suggestions (which he said he approved in general) and added: "I expect you to bring to my personal attention all matters which concern the efficiency of the Air Service without waiting for me to call upon you for recommendations."

There was a warning: "You will realize that to any organization there can be but one head and that all directions and instructions . . . must emanate from that source." He had Mitchell reply in writing that he understood the memorandum.

The truce was established, but neither party could have found it satisfactory. Mitchell had agreed to bow to the command of a superior who knew almost nothing about aviation, hopeful that he could find ways to by-pass Patrick and accomplish his aims. Patrick had no delusions about Mitchell; he knew that he was not likely to change his ways. He wrote of him: "Mitchell is very likeable and has ability; his ego is highly developed and he has an undoubted love for the limelight, a desire to be in the public eye. He is forceful, aggressive, spectacular. He has a better knowledge of the tactics of air fighting than any man in this country . . . I think I understood quite well his characteristics, the good in him—and there was much of it—and his faults."

As Hap Arnold said of his friend: "For once in his life, he backed down and agreed to Patrick's terms."

This uneasy peace at headquarters had just taken effect when Mitchell returned to the final act of the bombing tests of 1921, for which the old *Alabama* had been promised to the Air Service alone, as the target for any weapons it chose.

9

Sorrowfully We Broke Up This Splendid Little Air Force

The Navy clung to the old *Alabama* until the last moment, trying every possible delaying tactic to prevent another Mitchell triumph during 1921. As weeks passed without a sign that the ship would be delivered, Mitchell prodded Patrick, who prodded Secretary Weeks, who approached Secretary Denby.

In mid-August, Denby announced that the ship could not be delivered for six weeks. Weeks then asked for a definite date—and also demanded that the *Alabama* be handed over in operating condition so that his fliers could test new weapons against her. She should be under way for these attacks, with all systems in operation, and except for her crew, be in battle condition.

All that would be too expensive, Denby said. He could, of course, fill the requests if Weeks were prepared to pay the bills from his own budget. He estimated that it would cost $200,000 to put even obsolete ammunition aboard and to get the communications system, compasses and other gear in working order. He went into such details as the cost of coal for getting up steam, an estimated $22.44 per hour. Even if Weeks did pay for all this, Denby warned, Mitchell's project was worthless: "It would be ridiculous to assume that the damaging effect of large bombs . . . on an old vessel like the *Alabama* would be comparable with the effect on a modern capital ship."

Weeks gave up and agreed that Mitchell should not be given all he asked for. He wearily requested that the old ship be turned over "in such condition as the Secretary of Navy desires." He urged haste, since Mitchell's fliers must be sent back to their permanent stations as soon as possible; they had been at Langley for about five months now.

Denby had a final request before handing over the ship—Mitchell must not discuss the results of this test, either. There would be no reports of results or damages of any kind without Navy approval. Weeks told Mitchell: "No report of conclusions as to probable damage and no publicity shall be given to the opinions or conclusions . . ."

Just one day before he prepared to attack the *Alabama* in the lower Chesapeake, in the climax to a triumphant season of his campaign, Mitchell was stunned by a stern reprimand from Washington. He was charged with slipshod management of the Brigade during preparations for the bombing tests; the War Department seemed to find this matter far more important than the outcome of the tests themselves. The public was to know nothing of this harassment.

During the hectic scramble of the spring, when Langley Field was receiving its men and planes, and Milling's staff was desperate to get things into order, an enlisted man had complained to his congressman of his living conditions. Representative Martin Ansorge of New York wrote to Weeks, who called in the Inspector General. The crewman, whose name was withheld, was critical of the Brigade's housekeeping, especially the food, and as a result a long admonition was filed against Mitchell, charging irregularities at Langley. "It is clearly shown that because of the lack of advance preparation, the airdrome company was without proper officer supervision, and for nearly a month was not properly fed, or clothed, resulting in reduced morale, general discontent and many absences without leave. The primary responsibility for these conditions rests with Brigadier General William Mitchell, who . . . concerned himself solely with the tactical phase of the maneuver, neglected any study of the administrative and supply phases, and actually admits he never saw the orders directing the concentration of troops for the maneuver."

Mitchell had revolutionized modern warfare and captured the imagination of the country—and lost the battle on the mess line. The official commendations he had received were models of brevity by comparison with the documents inspired by the disgruntled young man on hangar duty.

Mitchell began the final phase of the year's bombing tests against the *Alabama* on September 23, a clear, mild day when the old ship could be seen for miles. She was tethered only 48 miles from Langley near Tangier Island in the Chesapeake, near the battered hulks of the *Indiana* and the *Texas*.

For several days the old ship was to be attacked with new weapons, smoke screens, phosphorus and tear-gas bombs; a night mission was planned to test experimental equipment on the bombers, and the target was to be sunk finally with conventional bombs. The crowd of observers was much smaller for this part of the bomb experiments, which seemed an anticlimax, but attitudes had not changed since the summer spectacle. Randolph Shaw of Universal News, coming down from Washington on a boat, heard an Army colonel berating Mitchell: "He didn't observe service etiquette, and never has. He should never do or say anything to discredit a sister service!"

The first day's attack on the *Alabama* was another blow to the Navy. This time Mitchell watched from the surface, with Admiral Fullam and a few reporters on the motor launch *Dodd*, the inspection vessel of the umpires.

One flight of Mitchell's planes laid a perfect smoke screen to the windward of the old battleship and within three minutes covered her from sight. Bombers attacked above the smoke. "Just imagine what crewmen would be thinking now," Fullam said. "There's nothing in war more demoralizing than waiting for an attack you can't defend against."

Small phosphorus bombs struck the ship, and flames swept the decks, with popping particles thrown far into the water. Fullam said: "That's the saddest sight of my career . . . That takes all the fun out of the Navy."

Tear-gas bombs then showered the *Alabama*, and inspectors who went aboard wore gas masks; some of these men were lost below deck for a while and had to be led out before bombers returned. When the inspectors went ashore for the night to temporary quarters in a farmhouse, gas still clung to their clothing and brought tears to the eyes of the girls who waited on the dinner tables.

The night attack, the first of its kind, was launched from Langley about ten-thirty under a half-moon. The crews now had lighted compasses to steer the familiar course. Mitchell's engineers had added modifications for use in night bombing: longer tailpipes on the exhausts concealed flames and muffled engines, and running lights were hooded so that they could not be seen from below. The new gyroscopic stabilizing devices would keep the planes level during bombing runs.

The lead planes spotted the *Alabama* at about eleven o'clock despite the darkness of the bay; she was a dark finger with a tiny collar of white at her prow, whipped by the running tide.

Mitchell wrote: "First can be heard the distant hum of an airplane engine, then another . . . they could not be seen and it was difficult to tell their directions. Suddenly a star shell dropped . . . Admiral Fullam is thunderstruck."

As the star shell lit the area and 300-pound bombs burst on the old ship and set her afire once more, Fullam did seem thunderstruck: "This test at night proves beyond all question that surface ships are menaced from the air more seriously than had been anticipated. General Mitchell's night attack marks a new era in air navigation. It demonstrates that a fleet cannot safely approach or remain near a hostile coast night or day."

The *Alabama* was finished off three days later by daylight, when the first of Captain Lawson's 2000-pound bombs hit alongside her from 2500 feet; she was on the bottom within thirty seconds, with her upper works above water. Later flights hammered her until she was hardly recognizable.

Fullam's report in the newspapers said that this revolution in military tactics had been staged by a handful of airmen with "old and inferior material, crude sights, and in spite of many obstacles and discouragements." He wrote as if he had the Navy high command in mind: "It is childish to attempt to discount this result by saying the *Alabama* is an old ship. No modern dreadnought could have survived this attack."

Mitchell tried to keep the remnants of the Brigade together for a few more days for other tests, but Washington refused: "Disapproval recommended. It is desired that the Provisional Air Brigade be disbanded and that the personnel return to their proper stations and normal functions without delay."

Mitchell said good-bye to the last of his men. "Sorrowfully we broke up this splendid little air force," he wrote. "Never again except after another war shall we have such experience and efficiency."

As if trying to forget, he flew to New York at the invitation of Christy Walsh, the sports promoter, for the opening game of the World Series.

Two weeks after the sinking of the *Alabama*, excerpts from Mitchell's confidential report on the project leaked out in a mysterious fashion. A brief summary of the report was published in Chicago, and within a day was headlined across the country. The *New York Times* said: "A sensational chapter has been added to the aircraft vs. capital ships discussion . . . General Mitchell in this report flatly contradicts the reports submitted to congressional committees that witnessed the bombing tests."

The War Department assumed that Mitchell had deliberately leaked the report. The Adjutant General wrote him: "It is now desired that you state if you showed or otherwise communicated your report . . . to any person outside the military service, and if so, to whom. Statement is desired from you as to your opinion of how this information . . . could have fallen into the hands of the press."

Mitchell replied that all officers of the Brigade had seen the report, that he did not consider it confidential, but that he had not authorized its publication, even in part. "Copies have undoubtedly found their way to our various flying fields and may have been seen by people outside the military service."

Patrick demanded an exact count of the copies Mitchell had made, and found that there were only six—one sent to headquarters, one kept by Mitchell, and the rest put into Langley files, eliminating the possibility of a leak from some distant airfield. Mitchell said that many people at Langley had seen the report and that its substance was "a matter of common knowledge among the personnel at Langley Field and doubtless throughout the Air Service."

There the matter was dropped, and the bombing tests ended in the atmosphere of a criminal investigation. Mitchell emerged from the final test under a cloud, so far as his superiors in Washington were concerned. The friends of Mitchell took a far different view: the Army and Navy had welcomed the coming of reporters and photographers to the opening of the test, expecting the Air Service to fail; the official suppression of Mitchell's report was solely because it clashed with the views of the Navy, as expressed by General Pershing.

Even after the partial publication of Mitchell's conclusions, the Army continued its strict secrecy. Congressmen tried to pry loose the report, and failed. Representative Earl C. Michener of Michigan wrote Secretary Weeks: "I am impressed with the thought that the public is entitled to know General Mitchell's views. The people from my section of the country have much faith in General Mitchell's judgment . . . only a compelling reason should deprive our citizenship of his views at this time."

Weeks refused. The Senate then ordered Weeks to send it Mitchell's report. Weeks called on the Administration for help and replied stiffly, defying the Senate: ". . . you are informed that I have been directed by the President to say that he considers the transmission of this report incompatible with the public interest."

Mitchell continued to drive the men of the dwindling Brigade as if there were no distractions. On September 19 Lieutenant Jimmy Doolittle, a daring flier who was to become famous, had left his squadron briefly to try life in Mitchell's headquarters. He looked back on it forty years later: "I was Mitchell's aide for one day, and on that one day, I've never moved as fast or covered as much country before or since. He was a veritable dynamo of energy. Everything he did, he did just as hard as he could."

Thurman Bane might have added to the testimony; he was harried by mail for better planes and equipment, since the engineers were Mitchell's chief hope of developing a more powerful striking force. The Mitchell-Bane correspondence of these days was full of urgent communications. For example, Mitchell once wrote: "There is something I have spoken to you about several times, but not very pointedly; that is the necessity for developing equipment and means of flying in rain, hail, snow, etc. This is extremely important." The "cloud board" for which he pressed made possible the first safe flying in bad weather; he had manufacturers at work on flight indicators and inclinometers.

He urged Bane in many directions: radio equipment, four-bladed propellers, gliders, better fuels, control of battery fumes, and especially engines. He insisted that the Thomas Morse pursuit plane be strengthened so that it could be used in dogfights. He pored over photographs of the first agricultural use of planes—a Jenny equipped with a hopper to sprinkle an Ohio orchard with insecticide. He inspected every invention which came to his office—wrenches and bomb sights, hydraulic transmissions, catapults for planes, rain-making schemes.

Once, when he insisted on speedier communication from McCook Field, Bane wrote testily that he could not reply by telegram since "we have not one cent at McCook for telegrams."

Mitchell also flew, almost daily, in practice bombing runs with his crews over the Chesapeake. He was named air adviser to the U.S. mission to the Limitation of Armaments Conference, then meeting in Washington. He was also faced with serious domestic troubles. His wife had been "somehow inveigled" into trying to halt the bombing tests, apparently through friends in the Army, and Mitchell "was never able to forgive her." Mrs. Mitchell had also learned of his plans to make a European tour to gather information on new aviation development, and had done everything possible to persuade the Army to keep him at home.

Mitchell seemed to find relief in even harder work. He bombarded Patrick with suggestions, as if the successful sinking of the *Alabama* left much to be desired. He asked for improved phosphorus bombs, torpedoes, aids for night flying. He called Alexander de Seversky to his office and offered him a place as consultant to the Air Service. The Russian was overjoyed. He had never worked with such a man: "He had a ready grasp of technical details which even trained engineers did not comprehend so swiftly."

Mitchell asked for a bombsight more accurate than any in service, and Seversky explained a crude sight he had designed for use against Germans in the Baltic: "I could design a better one, based on fire-control mechanism, like they use on battleships. But for great heights and great speed, it would have to be much more complex."

"That's what we've been looking for. Have you patented the sight?"

"No, sir."

Mitchell sent Seversky to Army lawyers who helped him file patents for his own protection, then to the Sperry gyroscope plant to develop a model. Mitchell overcame all obstacles, somehow providing the money, though each of the new sights cost $50,000, as against $2000 for the old models. When contract officers advised that the project be canceled as unrealistic, Mitchell overruled them: "An automatic bombsight is essential. I'd rather have one bomber that can hit the target than a whole flock that can't hit anything. Cut down on the number of planes and divert money into this project. The sight must be built."

Mitchell told the Russian: "I've stuck my neck out on this thing because I think you're on the right track. Go ahead and build the best damn bombsight you can. But God help you if it doesn't turn out the way you claim." Seversky and the Sperry engineers began their long task.

Despite his other interests, Mitchell found time for a favorite pursuit, the operation of a personal intelligence network in foreign capitals. The reports of military attachés abroad went to Army Intelligence, but Mitchell also corresponded with these men—and he seemed to be the only officer in the United States who thought their observations of real importance. Arthur Christie, who had flown in France, was now military attaché in Tokyo. He wrote in October: "I am still awaiting permission from the Japanese to visit their airdromes . . . The Japanese are trying to build planes and motors and I believe it will be only a question of time before they can turn out a decent number." Christie warned that the Japanese were taking aviation seriously "and working their heads off to be prepared." He also reported a meeting with a young Japanese naval officer who knew a great deal about U.S. aviation: "He mentioned your name and evidently was a great admirer of yours . . . A number of Army and Navy officers have mentioned your name many times and you are regarded here as the greatest authority on military aviation."

Without warning, Mitchell's domestic troubles reached a climax, an ironic finale to his triumph in the bombing tests, and a painful interlude in a crucial phase of his career. Mrs. Mitchell, complaining of his "recent erratic conduct," persuaded influential Army officers to intervene with Secretary Weeks, saying that Mitchell should not be permitted to go to Europe while he was "nervous and not himself." Weeks was easily persuaded, and at the first hint of Mitchell's alleged instability, sent him peremptory orders to cancel a flight to New York planned for that day, and to report to Walter Reed Hospital for psychiatric examination.

Mitchell fought his way through the unpleasant matter in characteristic fashion. He went to Weeks and convinced him that he should not be committed to the hospital in advance: "Why should I be stigmatized by being placed in a hospital under mental examination when I know I can convince any fair-minded person within a few minutes that there is nothing wrong with me?" The Secretary modified his order. Mitchell would be examined in his own quarters by Army doctors.

The doctors interviewed him several times, especially Major W. L. Sheep of the Medical Corps, and found Mitchell eminently sane. They discovered a typical case of marital difficulties.

Major Sheep's report revealed an energetic, controlled man of middle age: "The officer is oriented in all spheres . . . Admits that he likes to take a drink and when with a crowd of congenial companions at times imbibes too freely, but has never been 'down and out,' nor does alcohol make him unduly hilarious, irritable or depressed . . .

"Officer recalls dates of happenings in his early career. He discusses in detail with examiner characteristics of mutual acquaintances and gives in sequence the various details he has had during his service in the Army. He has quite a great amount of information . . . and can discuss fluently any subject . . . from the duties of a flight surgeon to the essential qualifications of a pursuit pilot. He is particularly adept at recalling statistics . . .

"Attention is easy to gain and to hold. No questions have to be repeated. There is no disorder of apprehension or apperception. Emotionally at time of examination patient appears neither depressed nor elated. He admits he is greatly worried over his domestic situation but he states that he cannot afford to let worry get the best of him, and that he has trained himself at all times to restrain his emotions and not give expression to them.

"Undoubtedly he holds himself and his abilities in no small esteem. He states that he has met many obstacles in his career, but that he has overcome them. He believes that he has done much toward the advancement of aviation and that he is one of the few whose foresight and aggressiveness have made possible a great future for the Army Air Service. Considering this officer's presumable ability and his rapid advancement in the service, such ideas are not inconsistent with the normal content of thought.

"From his explanation as regards his conduct related by his wife, no error of judgment stands out . . .

"The officer's conversation is free, relevant and coherent. There is no flight of ideas, no distractibility or other evidence of disturbance of the train of thought. No ideas which can be considered of a delusional nature are elicited, nor is there a history of any sense deceptions. Officer is agreeable and co-operative during examination. Manner is calm and collected and impression is obtained of above an average mental poise . . .

"No signs of acute or chronic alcoholism . . . no evidence of mental or physical disease. He is reported as fit for full military duty."

Weeks did not hesitate. He cleared Mitchell and ordered him to resume his plans for the European inspection tour.

Even during these unsettling interviews, Mitchell hardly slowed his hectic pace. The last day of November 1921 was typical: he worked early in his office, at eleven o'clock attended the first meeting of the aircraft committee of the Limitation of Armaments Conference, in the afternoon rode Home Again, his favorite horse, and saw Major Sheep soon afterward. The Limitation of Armaments Conference session brought another minor clash with the Navy.

Mitchell sat with the technical committee as aviation expert for the Army, and the Navy had sent Admiral William A. Moffett as his counterpart. Lieutenant Eugene Wilson of Moffett's staff long remembered the scene when they met.

Moffett entered the committee room, filled with representatives of England, Japan and the United States, to find Mitchell in the chair, presiding. "Since when," Moffett said, "does a brigadier general of Air Service rank a rear admiral of the Navy?" Moffett left, and there was at least an inference that he helped to oust

Mitchell from the conference committee, to be replaced by General Patrick.

The Navy had entered the conference in an uneasy mood, since Mitchell had so recently made the role of the battleship less important. The naval high command seemed to feel that Mitchell's presence was dangerous to its program, if not something of a sacrilege. The Navy may have hurried him on his tour of Europe.

On December 7 Mitchell made final preparations for his departure. He called on the Secretary of War, saw General Harbord and had lunch with General Pershing and a foreign military visitor. After flying at Bolling in the afternoon, he dined at the Shoreham, where Pershing was entertaining a Japanese general.

10

The Military Spirit of Germany Is By No Means Crushed

Mitchell sailed on the *Rotterdam,* and was on the captain's bridge as the ship passed through the Narrows. A squadron from Mitchel Field escorted the ship a few miles to sea, and his sister Ruth swooped low in a flying boat to drop a farewell message. The general's companion was his aide, Captain Clayton Bissell, who knew his methods intimately, was efficient in handling details, and a man of savoir-faire, expert in the ways of protocol.

They were to be followed by a brilliant young plane designer, Alfred Verville, whom Mitchell had literally abducted from McCook Field. When Colonel Thurman Bane refused to release Verville for the inspection trip because of his important work, Mitchell merely had Patrick order the designer to sail on the first Army transport to Europe and join the tour. Verville had no college education and was a correspondence-school graduate in electricity, but he had already designed planes for Glenn Curtiss and Thomas Morse and was now a leading expert for the Air Service. Mitchell expected him to evaluate European developments.

It was a mission smacking as much of adventure as of hard work. They were under official orders to "obtain complete and exhaustive information" on European aviation, and though they were to work openly and not as spies, they were to use every means of getting information, even on social occasions.

Patrick was uneasy about the mission and warned Mitchell to

be discreet in Europe lest he create an international squabble while the Limitation of Armaments Conference was in session. Above all, he must not criticize the Washington high command: "Your mission is primarily and exclusively the gathering of information and not the discussion of Air Service or aeronautical policies."

Mitchell obeyed. It was clear from the moment they docked at Plymouth that he took the mission seriously. Major Melvin Hall, the U.S. air attaché in London, met the ship, and he and Mitchell talked incessantly about British air-power developments until they reached Boulogne.

Lewis Brereton joined them in Paris, with plans for a full schedule. Marshal Foch was giving a formal dinner party to open a round of entertainment. By chance they arrived when French air officers were holding a conference in the city, and Mitchell was invited as a consulting expert. For two weeks or more he conferred with these officers, debating lessons from the Western Front and the future of war in the air. The French listened to Mitchell with respect and hailed him as the hero of the Battle of the Chesapeake, but he found his former Allies backward at first. He reported to Patrick:

"It took a great deal of discussion . . . since the French mind hadn't separated itself from the idea of armies locked along the Marne or the Meuse . . . However, by taking a map and playing a war game against possible adversaries, the future probabilities are very quickly brought out."

In the end he convinced French airmen, he thought, that mobile warfare, with air power as a dominant factor, was the warfare of the future.

When he was too busy in Paris, Verville and Bissell inspected flying fields, factories, gunnery and bombing ranges, and a wind tunnel; the French showed them everything and Verville collected hundreds of charts and diagrams.

Verville saw Mitchell as a striking figure in the midst of his social life in Paris: "There was something so strongly magnetic about him that he drew attention, no matter where he was. Especially women were attracted. They couldn't keep their eyes off him." Mitchell frequently entertained in self-defense, to return French hospitality at dinners and parties, but reported faithfully to Patrick. It was not only Gallic friendship or plane development that concerned him. He was observant of the French state of mind: "France is in abject terror of a future military Germany."

The French air service, he said, was handicapped by a universal problem—the active young officers were fliers, but they were commanded by older men, nonfliers who had no understanding of aviation potentials. Mitchell reported that the French had designed high-altitude bombers, made possible by new turbo-compressors which the United States should develop at once.

Mitchell declined a tempting offer to fire a transatlantic blast at his adversaries in Washington before he left Paris. A New York *Herald* reporter brought him a dispatch quoting Senator Borah, who was outraged over the issue of secrecy in the Virginia bombing tests. Borah threatened to go over President Harding's head and make public Mitchell's report. Surely Mitchell must have something to say. "Nothing now," he said. "I might talk when I get back home."

In early January 1922 they left for southern France and made a stop in Nice, Mitchell's birthplace. He took Verville to the handsome old building on Place Grimaldi, charmed the present tenants of the second-floor apartment, and looked about for a few minutes. He posed on a balcony for a photograph and spoke feelingly of his French birth. The building, which was later to bear a bronze plaque designating his birthplace, was then unmarked.

They stopped in Cuers where, in a cold hangar, they clambered through the shell of the huge dirigible *Dixmude,* which was soon to be lost over the Mediterranean. Verville noticed that Mitchell was fascinated by every detail of its construction. At the naval base in Toulon they saw two ships on which Mitchell reported at length, the experimental "carrier" *Berne,* with a small flight deck, and the old Austrian battleship *Prinz Eugen,* which the French had used as a bombing target.

The French took the *Berne* to sea for Mitchell, though its lower decks were still incomplete, and pilots took off and landed, using arresting gear of ropes weighted with sandbags. Mitchell was impressed by their skill in operating from the deck and found the French work "most sensible," but thought they were "far behind" in development, since the *Berne* seemed to comprise their entire naval air program. He found French officers dubious of the future value of carriers, because of their vulnerability to air attack.

The *Prinz Eugen* had been bombed, but only with dummy bombs; even these had pierced her steel decks and gone right through the bottom, so that she had to be towed back to port "in a sinking condition." Mitchell was not impressed by this bombing: "We are way ahead of them in this stuff because it is impossible for them to conduct it on the scale that we did."

They went next to Rome, where King Victor Emmanuel gave a dinner party for them and had Mitchell recount the story of the bombed warships off the Virginia coast. Verville retained a vivid impression of the animated talk between Mitchell and the tiny king, and their mutual fascination with air power. Mitchell liked the Italians and admired their mechanical ability, though he realized that they were unlikely to build a great air force. "I think we met more men of exceptional ability than we did in any other country," he wrote Patrick. The general became ill during the Italian tour, and inspections were largely carried out by Verville and Bissell.

When they passed through Paris on their way north, General Henry T. Allen, commander of the U.S. army of occupation in the Ruhr, provided transportation to Germany; Mitchell's condition became worse on the trip in the unheated Army cars, but he persisted to the end. Verville remembered the ride for many years: "We went by Verdun and Château-Thierry and Épernay and other fields, and Mitchell told us what had happened there during the war. He was marvelous, so eloquent and clear and persuasive. If we had only had a tape recorder then! We stopped in the cemetery at Thiaucourt, where his brother John and the famous flier Raoul Lufbery were buried. Dozens, hundreds of men in hip boots were working there, disinterring the pathetic remnants of the dead for removal, a terrible scene. It was the first time I ever saw Mitchell in tears. He cried while he put bronze wreaths on the two graves.

"Then we went by the spot where Lufbery had been killed, in a fall from his plane. He had struck a picket fence, and the pickets were still there. We met the farmer's daughter who had seen him fall."

By the time they reached Coblenz, Mitchell had influenza and went to bed, under protest. Bissell and Verville alternated in standing watch in his bedroom, to keep him indoors, but he soon escaped. He inspected the air detachment at Weissenthurm, and with Bissell and Major Frank Andrews gave the Germans a demonstration flight over the Moselle and the Rhine, flying down to Remagen and back at about 10 feet above the water. Afterward he lectured officers on the value of formation flying in war.

He inspected German villages and cities carefully, and made observations that would appear in his report: "The military spirit of Germany is by no means crushed. It could be seen in the attitude of all the boys on the streets of every town we visited, and these towns were full of boys who will attain their majorities within a few years . . . At the first opportunity, Germany may ally herself to any nation that is willing to help her . . . Some countries, such as Austria, are absolutely helpless for the future under present conditions . . . therefore, Austria will join under Germany at the first opportunity. A joining of all the Germanic people will give them 100 million population."

They went to Berlin, whose drab look reflected the ruinous inflation of the country's currency, the loss of colonies and resources, and the hostility of its neighbors. When Mitchell went to the Department of National Defense he stepped into a different world: "What few officers are left . . . are working diligently in the War Department building. The models of all their old battleships are in the halls . . . The German mind is still militaristic."

General Hans von Seeckt, the German Commander-in-Chief, complained to Mitchell that he was limited to small artillery pieces, was allowed only 100,000 men, and had no aviation—but Mitchell observed that a group of war pilots was in fact an air reserve, and that these aviators flew gliders when denied motored planes by the Allies.

The German Aero Club gave a luncheon for the Mitchell party, with several famous German fliers in the crowd, including the ace, Ernst Udet, Hermann Göring and Erhard Milch. Verville was surprised to see that Mitchell and Bissell got on so well with the German pilots, "like a bunch of boys, like opposing ball teams who had gotten together after a ball game in which one side had lost, one side had won." The fliers compared notes enthusiastically, scribbling diagrams of formations and dogfights on the tablecloths. "I was struck by their absolute letting down of their hair,"

Verville said. "There was a seeming admiration, an affable, amiable feeling on the part of these men toward Mitchell. They liked him. I could see that."

One morning Ben Foulois, who was now air attaché in Berlin, was at breakfast with the Mitchell party in its hotel. Mitchell began a new search.

"You know, these aircraft engines we're using now are all wrong. These pistons jiggling back and forth with cylinders, connecting rods, crankshafts and things whistling around. It's all out of balance." He turned to Foulois. "Ben, I'll bet you there's some long-haired German scientist working right now in a two-by-four shed of a laboratory, figuring out some new power plant for the next war, fifteen or twenty years from now. I want you to go out and find him for me."

"I don't know what you're talking about, General," Foulois said, "but I'll try."

Verville had a call from Foulois later in the day: "Tell the general I think I've found his man." On the outskirts of Berlin they were taken to a flimsy wooden building where a shabbily dressed German scientist was at work. Mitchell explained his theory of plane engines of the future and the scientist said: "You're quite right, General. It's quite unusual for a military man to have such far-sighted vision. Yes, fifteen to twenty years from now the Otto cycle engine will not be used in aircraft, or it will not be preeminent. It will be superseded by turbines."

These turbines, he said, would use kerosene or gas; he had not built such an engine, but was convinced that it was feasible. "Now it is up to the engineers to build one." *

The mission sought out all the leading figures of German aviation. Verville went to Friedrichshafen to see the Dornier plant, where planes of bold new design were being produced in the old

* This incident was not included in Mitchell's report, and Verville did not later recall the name of the scientist who impressed him so vividly. He said the German also told Mitchell of a flying bomb, or "rocket bomb" of the future, to use liquid oxygen and alcohol as fuel; an assistant brought a foaming beaker of liquid oxygen, Verville recalled, and showed Mitchell how it disintegrated an ordinary glass tumbler. Verville was as impressed by Mitchell's forecast as by the German: "Bissell and I were flabbergasted. Now, this was in 1922, and taking it right in the middle, 15 or 20 years later would make it 1940, just right for World War II. That's how Mitchell always was, looking ahead."

Zeppelin plant, using steel spars and duralumin covering. Mitchell reported this work as "very interesting" and predicted that Dornier would turn out large German bombers.

In Dessau he found "a great spirit" of German aviation, Dr. Hugo Junkers, who presided over a remarkable factory. Junkers manufactured stoves, boats, bathtubs, diesel and gasoline engines, tools and plumbing fixtures, but, as he told Mitchell, aviation was his love, and he turned all profits into its development. Mitchell inspected the plant with such thoroughness that Junkers said, "This place has never been gone over so carefully—not by anyone."

Mitchell was impressed by the largest plane he had ever seen, a four-engined monoplane without external bracing, its wings five feet thick. He thought Junkers "a great investigator and scientist . . . devoted to his work . . . a master of materials." He saw many large experimental engines in the plant, diesel and air-cooled gasoline models, some with fuel injection systems. He reported to Patrick: "We should keep in the closest touch with both Dornier and Dr. Junkers."

He found the Germans eager to share knowledge with him, and thought this attitude should be encouraged: "The Germans combine resourcefulness of design with practical ability to create aircraft which is second to none in the world."

It was in Holland that he found the most versatile plane builder in Europe, the plump Anthony Fokker, who drove the Mitchell party about in his World War-vintage Cadillac, constantly digging chocolates from his bulging pockets and popping them into his mouth. Fokker's services had been declined by England and France during the war, so he turned to Germany, for whom he built eight thousand fine planes. Fokker had made modern fighter planes possible by solving the problem of synchronizing machine-gun fire with propellers. He had fled Germany after the Armistice with three hundred carloads of parts and machinery, to open the Netherlands Aircraft Company.

Fokker sent Bissell up in a new torpedo plane he had just sold to the U.S. Navy. Bissell complained that it was sluggish in its tail controls, and Fokker said that could easily be remedied. The next morning, he simply had mechanics saw a three-foot section from the tail, welded the metal frame together, and the defect disappeared. Mitchell ordered several of his planes for the Air Service.

Fokker was talking of coming to America, and Mitchell urged him to do so, though he knew American manufacturers would be resentful, and the U.S. public would not forget that Fokker planes had shot down many American pilots. Mitchell recommended Fokker to Patrick: "This man has capabilities which are unlimited in the development of aircraft." *

In Holland, as in all other countries, Mitchell's visit drew official attention; the queen invited him to dinner, and much of his brief stay was devoted to social rounds.

In England, Mitchell reviewed cadets at the new Royal Air Force College at Cranwell, dined with Winston Churchill and was entertained at a formal dinner by his old friends Sir Hugh Trenchard and Freddie Guest, now Minister of Aviation. Trenchard and Mitchell exchanged complimentary speeches; the Briton led the praise of Mitchell's work in the recent bombing tests.

Mitchell flew R.A.F. fighters of great maneuverability and climbing power, but thought the British too slow in building all-metal planes; they were clinging to biplane models with thin, fabric-covered wings. He saw advanced work in guidance systems and landing devices for flying in fog and by night, and found British torpedoes superior. In general, he told Patrick, the British would make formidable foes in the air, because of their practicality.

One bright moment of another kind was provided by the Earl of Cavan, who called at the Hotel Cecil to greet Mitchell with three bottles of 1812 Napoleon Brandy. "My father left me eighty bottles," the Earl said, "and it's running low. But I want to share it with you, General."

As soon as they were back in Washington, in March 1922, Mitchell had Verville making the report of their tour—a closely detailed technical study of a thousand pages in four volumes, complete with photographs and drawings of planes, engines, airfields and factories, revealing speed, weight, armament, fuel

* Fokker later opened an aircraft plant at Hasbrouck Heights, New Jersey. His presence was not widely known until the success of his T-2, the first plane to cross the United States nonstop. Mitchell influenced Fokker's move to America.

consumption of planes found in each country. It was a summary of the aviation effort of western Europe that would have done credit to master spies. It was accompanied by more of Mitchell's urgent recommendations:

"All the great nations have assigned definite missions to their air forces, to their armies, and to their navies. In the United States we have not done this, and, at this time, if we should be attacked, no one can tell what the duties of these three arms are." The coastal defenses were divided between so many branches, he said, that "our hands would almost be tied in case we were attacked by a first-class power."

He suggested that a joint committee of Congress "investigate the whole question of our organization for national defense." The War Department was never to act on this study, and perhaps never saw it. Bissell, who later edited and rewrote the report, thought it unlikely that Patrick himself actually read the ten-pound work.

11

Air Power Doesn't Seem to Be Getting Anywhere

Mason Patrick was now a four-toupee general. He was learning to fly and indulged his vanity by wearing a tousled spare wig under his flying helmet (he rotated three dress wigs carefully, to create the illusion of his hair growing as the days passed, returning to a short wig under the pretext that he had a fresh haircut). He was taken about the country by veteran fliers, one of them Major Herbert Dargue, who lured Patrick into flying himself. Patrick began by handling controls under Dargue's eye and won his rating as a Junior Military Aviator—but never flew without another pilot aboard.

Headquarters officers were amused by Patrick's late-blooming career. The bewigged novice encountered a distressing problem familiar to open-cockpit fliers of the day, the difficulty of relieving kidneys, a need made acute in the cold air. Engineers experimented with a tiny pump device inserted in the rubber relief tube used by Patrick, but on one flight it somehow reversed itself and the Chief descended in fury, hurriedly stripping off a drenched flying suit. On another trip he remained painfully attached to the tube, unable to free himself, and flew cross-country for hours; he was in delicate condition when ground crewmen rescued him.

Mitchell found his work of plane development easier under the new Chief. Patrick was a forceful disciplinarian, but had a much keener appreciation of aviation than Menoher, and was willing to leave technical details to his assistant. He had quickly discovered that Mitchell's charges were true—the Air Service was handicapped by lack of equipment. Almost all planes were survivors of the war, and obsolete ships were scattered across the country, expensively maintained. He won Mitchell's admiration by his direct action. Patrick found twenty-two depots in whose sheds and hangars old planes and engines were piled, and ordered all but five of these stations abandoned and the worthless planes junked or sold.

Patrick soon became loyal to his new service; in his way he shared Mitchell's determination to build it into a powerful arm. "Little or nothing was known of what aircraft or airmen could or should do," Patrick wrote later. "This lack of understanding was most notable in the War Department itself, where a certain jealousy of the Air Service was markedly in evidence."

Ira Eaker, who was to command the 8th Air Force in World War II, was Patrick's executive officer during this period. He found the Chief "our most effective defender and supporter, a very brilliant man . . . as he learned the facts, he soon became the leading exponent of aviation." Eaker saw, however, that Patrick and Mitchell were often at odds. Patrick sometimes spoke to Mitchell severely and thought him "a sort of spoiled brat." Eaker said: "Patrick had great admiration for his objectives, but thought there were better ways to accomplish them . . . than taking them to the people."

After two or three months together in the Air Service office in the old Munitions Building, Patrick and Mitchell seemed to be coming to an understanding, both aware of the uneasy terms of their truce. From the beginning of this phase the tone of efficiency reports made on Mitchell began to change. They were still highly favorable, but there was a new note of insistent criticism. The report of June 1922 by Patrick said: "A more than usually able, forceful and energetic officer . . . He knows more of air force strategy and tactics than anyone else in this country. The results of the bombing experiments conducted by him in the fall of 1921 are important and far-reaching. He deserves credit for this work."

Patrick was candid about Mitchell's faults as he saw them: "He is impulsive and at times his opinions are colored by his prejudices. His judgment is not always sound. He is somewhat overbearing and dictatorial toward his subordinates. He himself is impatient of control and not always willing to subordinate his own views to accord with those of his superiors."

This impatience demanded of Mitchell the firm self-control that Major Sheep had admired. As usual, he found an outlet in work. Alfred Verville, for one, was soon deeply involved in his plans. The designer had hardly completed the technical report of their European tour when Mitchell called him to his office.

"Verville, I want you to design a racer for the Pulitzer Air Races this fall."

"General, that's in October—and here it is April already. It can't be done."

"There must be a way."

"Well, if I design it, and if we get a good, small plant to produce it where I can take my own draftsmen and be in full charge. Somebody like Sperry."

"Good. I'll be in Dayton in about ten days. Have drawings for me then."

Verville was stunned but willing. "Well, what kind of a plane do you have in mind, General?"

"I want you to design tomorrow's airplane today. I don't want a squirrel cage. You understand me—none of this old stuff." He wanted an end to struts and wires and protruding elements.

Working day and night at home, Verville produced drawings of a revolutionary small plane that marked the passing of the old-fashioned biplane fighters.

Thurman Bane stoutly opposed the project. "You shouldn't fool with Mitchell," he said. "He's crazy, and if you keep on with that retractable landing gear, you'll hang yourself. Who wants retractable wheels? Suppose they forget to let 'em down when they land?" Verville persisted, and when Mitchell arrived his work was done.

Mitchell glanced at the three-view drawings. He was delighted. "That's what I call an airplane! That's exactly what we need. Why didn't you design a ship like that years ago?"

"General, you never asked me to."

The drawings revealed a low-wing racer, an internally stressed monoplane without struts or bracing wires. A retractable landing gear folded into recesses under the wing, which had a tapered double camber of recent design.* The wings also housed the radiators of a Curtiss engine mounted on rubber-spool shock absorbers, the first of their kind. The small ship was built on Long Island by Sperry, with Verville and his draftsmen in the shop until it was complete.

The plane was a sensation at the Selfridge Field races, though it finished second to a Curtiss biplane of greater power; two years later, in 1924, the Verville-Sperry defeated all contestants for the trophy. This ship, a result of Mitchell's relentless prodding, was a joy to its designer:

"We were content with the first public flight demonstration of a low-wing aircraft with retractable gear, a prophetic design. General Mitchell's vision on this 'tomorrow's airplane' was fulfilled. This was a forerunner of the fighter types of ten to fifteen years later. In fact, it was the mother of the fighter types of World War II—including the Spitfire and the Zero."

Mitchell insisted that the advances featured in the design be used in American military aircraft immediately, but it was many years before this came to pass.

The Mitchells' domestic misfortunes passed their crisis in 1922. Mitchell had filed for divorce in Milwaukee when he returned from Europe, after a long period of separation. Mrs. Mitchell denied his charges in a countersuit and asked custody of their children. The court granted her the divorce.

Clayton Bissell was now called in as Mitchell's aide; his first duty was to get the general's clothing from the home of his estranged wife—a moment he remembered as the most trying of his service with Mitchell. There was another unusual duty. Mitchell bought a powerful Dusenberg car and drove it like the wind, with Bissell posted in the rear to guard against traffic cops on the high-speed runs to and from Bolling Field.

Mitchell was so upset by his divorce that he wrote Harriet in despair, but inadvertently addressed it to his elderly mother, who

* The waggish Jimmy Doolittle shocked Dayton with this plane. He had a false undercarriage mounted on top, and a cockpit painted on the bottom of the plane. He flew over the city with the gear retracted, as if upside down—with a dummy hanging from the false cockpit.

reacted instantly: "Harriet, we're leaving for Washington tonight. Willie needs us."

Mrs. Mitchell took over in the capital as if nothing had changed since the general's boyhood. Harriet found a house on Phelps Place and the two lived with him through a troubled time. Mitchell was outwardly carefree, frequently entertaining at home, and impressed Harriet anew with his "magnificent sense of humor and magnetic, dynamic personality." They were often invited to dances and parties and Harriet long remembered being "entertained lavishly and welcomed royally."

Mitchell refused to play card games and frowned on gambling, but despite endless rounds of activities found time to read. He kept several books under way at once, and had three pairs of reading glasses so that he would never be without them.

His mother still invariably called him Willie and ordered him about like a child. Once when she saw him in a gaudy pair of black-and-white riding breeches she called: "Willie, didn't I tell you never to wear those horrible breeches? Don't let me see them on you again." The general obediently did as he was told.

Harriet remembered a luncheon with their old friend from Milwaukee, Douglas MacArthur. She found him quite unlike the boy she had known, for he was now quite serious and reserved, no longer gay and full of fun, as he had been when he wrote a sonnet on Harriet's dance card so many years earlier.

Harriet and her mother remained with the general until Mrs. Mitchell's death in December 1922. She had contributed generously to his support, since he was still living beyond the means provided by his modest salary. She left him a life interest in an estate which yielded about $12,000 a year.

The young men of the Air Service got no hint of Mitchell's difficult personal life. He drove them with all his energies, as if the building of an air force were his only concern. Spurgeon Phillips, a nineteen-year-old North Carolina farm boy who became his personal mechanic, got a first-hand course in Mitchell's uncompromising methods.

Phillips was stationed at Bolling Field, a little nervously awaiting the appearance of his new chief, who was known in the hangars as a hard taskmaster. Mitchell arrived unexpectedly, slapping his hand absently with a swagger stick, carefully eying his new man and looking over his waiting plane. When Phillips started the engine, Mitchell grasped the tip of a wing and held tightly. "Gun her up now, slowly, as high as she'll go." The general held the wing until he was satisfied, from the vibrations, that the ship was airworthy and her engine in tune. Mitchell mystified the mechanic by taking a small rubber tube from a pocket, sticking one end into an ear and listening to the engine, much as a doctor might have used a stethoscope. Phillips found that the general's ear was uncanny, apparently able to detect slight malfunctions of valves, cams or pistons.

"He wasn't handy with tools," Phillips remembered, "but he knew his engines. He knew so much about planes that nobody could fool him."

Phillips found Mitchell fair and considerate, quick to praise good work; he often passed out five-dollar tips to mechanics and ground-crew men. His eye never missed even the most minute details. The old DH4's of the time had outer bracing wires fastened to a turnbuckle that was locked with copper wire. The wire was to be wrapped around the turnbuckle seven times, a detail Mitchell never overlooked. "If you had one of those wires turned around just six times, the general was sure to spot it," Phillips said.

Mitchell insisted on testing new and remodeled planes himself. Phillips watched him in amazement as he dived and rolled the planes: "He took chances, but they were always deliberate, and he wasn't reckless. He flew rings around those spurred West Point officers who came out there."

Mitchell and Phillips came near a rift over a sensitive piece of equipment, the compass. It was filled with alcohol and was fair game for thirsty enlisted men at every field. Phillips kept a close watch but was not infallible. Mitchell once found his compass dry on a flight into the West, too late to turn back, and made his way by familiar landmarks. "You never saw a madder man than he was when he came back," Phillips said. "But he never held a grudge. He'd bawl us out as quick as he'd look at us, but the next time he saw you, he'd slap you on the back and hand you a cigar. He never thought of anything but making a better air force, and no personalities stood in the way."

Young men at other fields got vivid impressions of Mitchell during this time. Auby Strickland, a student pilot at Kelly Field who later became a general, was in ranks one day when Mitchell flew in for an inspection. Officers had their men drawn up near a hangar at parade attention, and when Mitchell saw them he shouted: "My God, I've seen these fool things for twenty-five years! I don't want that. Let's see 'em in the air. No marching or any of that stuff."

He watched the squadrons perform, but was not satisfied. "I want some machine gunnery and bombing," he said. Dismayed officers explained that there was not a machine gun or a bomb rack at the field, so Mitchell ordered some flown in at once. Before the week was out, the students put on an attack show for him.

The inspection left nothing untouched. Mitchell prowled down the lines of planes, stopping to ask mechanics what their spark-plug clearance was. Strickland saw that this was not a pose: "He knew when they had it right. He knew the make and model and all the variants. He ate 'em up if they didn't know their stuff."

Navy men who met Mitchell in these days were not so favorably impressed. On one of his frequent flights to the Midwest, the Assistant Chief was invited to inspect the new naval training station for aviation mechanics at Great Lakes, Illinois. On the day of the inspection he called on Army headquarters in Chicago, and was still there at noon when he got an anxious telephone call from Lieutenant Eugene E. Wilson of the Great Lakes staff.

"General, you know we're to lunch at the commandant's house today, and we must be on time."

"Oh, I know all about that. I'll be there."

"But we're due at one o'clock. It takes an hour and a half to drive up from Chicago—and it's noon now."

"Don't worry about it," Mitchell said.

At about one o'clock a Stutz Bearcat swerved off the highway on a dirt lane leading to the Great Lakes station, and the waiting Lieutenant Wilson saw in astonishment that Mitchell was at the wheel, trailing a fishtail of dust high in the air, with an Army sergeant beside him holding on for dear life. Mitchell squealed to a halt and the sergeant was led to a mess hall; he told Navy men he was "a nervous wreck," that he was living on borrowed time. "That so-and-so is going to kill both of us," the sergeant said.

Lieutenant Wilson thought Mitchell's manner with the commandant was so casual as to be disrespectful, even arrogant, and the Navy hands were irritated by the way Mitchell snapped through his inspection "in the Continental manner, blustering around and criticizing" as he went through the vast machine shops, where hundreds of men worked at lathes.

Mitchell's final words left laughter behind in the Navy's guard of honor: "Well, Wilson, keep going. Maybe some day you can catch up with Chanute Field"—a tiny Air Service machine center that was dwarfed by Great Lakes.

Mitchell's Bearcat roared away with the sergeant still hanging on, and Wilson looked after him in wonder. "I thought to myself, 'What kind of a bird is that?' . . . He was a fine-looking man, who looked like a soldier ought to look."

During this summer of 1922 Mitchell met the girl who was to become his second wife, Elizabeth Trumbull Miller, the daughter of a prominent Detroit attorney, Sidney Miller, who lived in Grosse Pointe. He met her at a Detroit horse show where she was riding, a small, slender, blue-eyed young woman who knew so much about horses that she could hold her own with Mitchell; she had published articles about jumping. She was also a veteran of nursing service in France.

A few hours after their meeting he took her for her first plane ride, and they were at about 10,000 feet over Lake Huron when the motor failed and he was forced to glide through clouds to Selfridge Field. She denied that she was nervous, but when an officer came to the plane and saw her small pale face in the rear cockpit he said: "What's the matter with your mechanic, sir?" Indignation revived Betty: "I'm no mechanic!"

Mitchell became a familiar sight at airfields near Detroit while he was courting Betty Miller. His sister Ruth, who approved, said it was love at first sight for Billy. She thought Betty an ideal match for him, an accomplished hostess, gay and warm-hearted, and a crack shot as well as a horsewoman. Within six months they were engaged.

It was not always to see Betty that Mitchell went to the Midwest. On one inspection tour, accompanied by several of his officers, he saw one of his favorite fliers, Captain Tiny Lawson, glide into the Miami River, in Ohio, as his engine failed. Mitchell dashed to the scene, plunged into the water and made futile dives amid the wreckage, trying to save the pilot. Alfred Verville, who was on the river bank, remembered it as another of the occasions when he saw Mitchell cry. The general "wept like a child" at Lawson's funeral.

A Detroit visit in 1922 caused one of the rare ruptures between Mitchell and his younger officers when he captured the world's speed record in an Army Curtiss racer. One of his men, Lieutenant R. H. M. Maughan, flew the ship over the course first and was clocked at a new record of 248.5 miles per hour, but this mark was disallowed when it was discovered that no foreign judges were on the course. Mitchell then took up the plane, flew the same course at the slower speed of 224.38 miles an hour, but since foreign judges were then on hand with watches, he was awarded the new record. Some newspapers cried foul, and the Detroit *Free Press* spoke of "a new wrangle," under the headline: "DISSENSION BUZZES IN RANKS OF ARMY." Mitchell urged the National Aeronautical Association to arrange a new trial for Maughan immediately, and his own record was soon surpassed. He did not attempt another.

In the week of this furor, Mitchell flew East to address the National Geographic Society of Philadelphia, and a local newspaper account of his appearance did nothing to diminish his status as a national hero: "General Mitchell has speed written all over him. He talks, thinks and practices speed. His very person is streamlined in real-man fashion. Just short of six feet in height, weight about 180 pounds, looking about ten years younger than his actual 42, the most competent and intrepid pilot in America is as trim and fit as a college halfback . . . The most conspicuous officer in any armed branch of the government looked the part. His dark hair parted over a high brow, his strong stern face and compelling eye, his entire person had speed, intelligence and pride of race written all over it."

Friends found Mitchell changed after he met Betty Miller, calmer and more temperate, but Hap Arnold, on a visit in early 1923, thought him unusually pessimistic about the future of the Air Service, as if all the headlines and newsreels had been in vain. Arnold was worried: "He was down in the dumps."

The BILLY MITCHELL AFFAIR

Smithsonian Institution

Lt. Mitchell, 18 *(third from right)*, youngest Army officer, as Signal Corpsman in Spanish-American War.

Capt. Mitchell *(seated, second from right)* in Manchuria, 1911, on first "spy" mission. He forecast a Japanese-American war, 30 years before Pearl Harbor. His host, the war lord Chang Tso-Lin, is seated at left.

Library of Congress

Library of Congress

Maj. Mitchell in a French trench, 1917, the first U.S. officer under fire.

U.S. Air Force

Mitchell and Pershing in a happier moment, 1920, waiting to greet the Alaskan fliers.

Trophies of a French boar hunt.

Library of Congress

U. S. Air Force

Mitchell's staff, 1920, aides in the battle with Army and Navy conservatives. *Seated from left:* Maj. P. E. Van Nostrand, Lt. Col. W. C. Sherman, Mitchell, Lt. Col. Harold E. Hartney, Capt. Corliss C. Moseley. *Standing:* Lts. W. D. Wheeler and R. S. Olmstead, Capts. L. W. Miller and Burdette S. Wright, Lt. Phillip Schneeberger. (Note attack patterns on the wall.)

Clayton Bissell *(right)*, shown here with Mitchell in early 1920's, later helped direct the court-martial defense.

Library of Congress

Mitchell in his favorite De Havilland, the *Osprey*, directs attack on old battleships off Virginia coast in the sensational tests of 1921. The fluttering pennant and bold insignia identified him for bombing crews.

The 27,000 ton *Ostfriesland*, once pride of the Germany Navy, takes a direct hit and a near miss in climax of the tests.

U. S. Air Force

"It seemed as though all in the little knot of onlookers were attending a funeral, as if one of their dearest friends was being buried, and they couldn't believe it."

Wash. *Times*, July 21, 1921

U. S. Air Force

The *Ostfriesland* going...

U. S. Air Force

going...

U. S. Air Force

gone.

The first phosphorus bomb used against a military target makes spectacular hit on the old U.S.S. *Alabama*, September 1921.

U.S. Navy

U.S. Air Force

The *Alabama*'s deck after a pounding by Mitchell's bombers.

Three architects of American air power: Adm. W. F. Fullam, Orville Wright and Mitchell, at Detroit air races, 1922—in a Cadillac lent to Mitchell by the manufacturer and found to the general's liking, since he drove it at 90 m.p.h. with ease.

U.S. Air Force

Library of Congress

Pearl Harbor, during Mitchell's critical inspection, November 11, 1923; a plane is landing for the reviewing party. Here, on Ford Island, the Japanese struck in 1941 as he had so accurately predicted. Battleship Row is in the foreground. Mitchell detailed the probable method of the coming sneak assault: "Attack... to be made on Ford's Island at 7:30 A.M.... Group to move in column of flghts in V. Each ship will drop... projectiles on the target."

The wreck of the U.S.S. *Virginia (below)* two months earlier, an experiment whose results were not lost on the Japanese.

Smithsonian Institution

Capt. St. Clair ("Wingbone") Streett and the Verville-Sperry racer, prototype of World War II fighters, the first low-wing monoplane with retractable landing gear, winner of the national air race in 1924.

Smithsonian Institution

Mitchell in one of his flying creations, ready for the test of a newly equipped plane.

U. S. Air Force

Gen. Charles T. Menoher, Mitchell's adversary and first postwar chief.

Comdr. Zachary Lansdowne, Mitchell's frend and skipper of the ill-fated *Shenandoah*.

National Archives

U.S. Air Force

Mitchell in a Thomas Morse pursuit, a fast but unstable ship he ordered despite opposition of some pilots and engineers.

Adm. William A. Moffett, Asst. Navy Secretary Theodore Roosevelt, Jr., and Mitchell *(left)*, 1924, waiting to greet Round the World fliers.

Mitchell with his chief, the often difficult Gen. Mason M. Patrick, who took up flying in his sixties.

Will Rogers just before flight with Mitchell.

U.S. Air Force

Two of Mitchell's critics in a conspiratorial walk, Adm. Moffett and Gen. Patrick, 1922.

U. S. Navy

Part of the wreckage of the *Shenandoah,* near Sharon, Ohio, before crowds looted her for souvenirs. The disaster provoked Mitchell's final outburst against Army and Navy policy on aviation as "incompetency, criminal negligence... almost treasonable negligence." Thirteen men died in the crash.

Library of Congress

Mitchell and his wife flanked by aides, trapped by photographers before he went before the Morrow Aviation Board, September 29, 1925.

U. S. Air Force

Mitchell *(right)* faces his judges as charges are read. *Left to right:* Col. Herbert White, military defense counsel; defense assistant W. H. Webb; Frank Reid; Mitchell; Mrs. Mitchell; her father, Sidney Miller; Arthur Young; Mrs. Arthur Young (Mitchell's sister Ruth).

Library of Congress

Opening day at the Mitchell court-martial, with a block-long crowd seeking the hundred-odd seats for the spectacle.

Library of Congress

Gen. Charles P. Summerall, dismissed as president of the court because of his prejudice against Mitchell, leaves in a fury to denounce the defendant to the press: "We're enemies, Mitchell and I."

Library of Congress

The symbol of Army discipline, the unyielding face of the court president, Gen. Robert L. Howze

Library of Congress

Mrs. Lansdowne, widow of the *Shenandoah* skipper, before the Mitchell court. The generals are *(left to right):* Ewing E. Booth, Frank McCoy, Bert A. Poore, Douglas MacArthur.

Library of Congress

The Mitchells at Boxwood, in northern Virginia. Home at last, he spent the last years of his life with hi wife and young children, hunting and raising horses and dogs. In these years he gave no sign that he thought of himself as a martyr to air power. Picture was taken about 1934, two years before his deatl

Mitchell complained that "air power doesn't seem to be getting anywhere at all. The public's interested, but people in Washington who could do something about it aren't." He said that he was weary of the endless fight for funds, of fending off the Navy, the Army, "or some idiotic committee with an ax to grind." But Mitchell was to face greater odds now. President Harding's unexpected death after a trip to Alaska had made Calvin Coolidge President, and he was less friendly to aviation. Arnold thought that Mitchell seemed to irritate the President more than anyone else.

A current White House story had it that Coolidge, when lecturing some guests on the need for economy in government, burst out suddenly: "Now, take those aviators, for instance. They just like to run around and burn a lot of gasoline. There's that Mitchell fellow. Why, he thinks nothing of flying in a government plane to Michigan to visit the girl he's engaged to marry."

For almost two years Mitchell had tried to conduct further bombing tests against battleships. The Navy had delayed, despite promises, and despite sharp reminders from the Secretary of War. General Patrick at last appealed to General Pershing:

"Repeated requests have been made to the Navy . . . The Navy is simply stalling. I am now told that the Secretary of the Navy will not make these old vessels available until after the ratification of the disarmament treaty. This is simply and solely an excuse."

In late summer 1923 Pershing got action; the Navy surrendered the *Virginia* and the *New Jersey*, sister ships of 15,000 tons, almost twenty years old. They were to be anchored off Cape Hatteras, where the nearest 50-fathom depth was only twenty miles from shore, and Mitchell's planes could reach them easily. He began his preparations for the tests, to be held in early September, by building an airstrip in the sand dunes near Hatteras on the Outer Banks of North Carolina.

Mitchell asked that the ships be radio-controlled so that they could be bombed while in motion; he hoped to use his giant trimotor bomber, the Owl, to drop a 4000-pound bomb. He was refused. He must bomb the ships at anchor, and with conventional bombs left over from the tests of 1921.

Even worse, the trained pilots and bombardiers of the early

tests were no longer available, the planes older, and the Air Service was smaller and less skilled. Still, he was determined to sink the ships. Alexander de Seversky, who had now finished his automatic bombsight after two years of work in the Sperry plant, found Mitchell's enthusiasm undiminished. The one-legged Russian carried his model to McCook Field, where he built a miniature testing device in a hangar. The sight was mounted on an elevated platform, beneath which battleship models were moved about on the floor, by remote control. The bombsight, with the use of a computer, released tiny bombs at the ship models with great accuracy.

Mitchell appeared unexpectedly in the hangar one day, climbed onto the platform to act as bombardier, and scored a hit with each bomb: "That's the stuff, Seversky! Let's get it down to Langley and drop some live ones."

Mitchell was like a child with a new toy. Seversky remembered: "I have never seen anyone so boyishly excited, so enthusiastic. He . . . acted the role of bombardier, then the pilot; then he was on the floor maneuvering the 'battleship' to test the bombsight under every conceivable condition—all the while giving me valuable pointers for its future installation."

Within a few days the two were at Langley, to install the sight in the Martin bombers, but the sight was too large for the cockpit; the computer alone was about three cubic feet. Mitchell told the designer to modify the plane as he saw fit, and Seversky's direct approach won Mitchell's heart. The Russian used a hatchet and a hacksaw on the plane's nose until he had made a nest for the sight, squeezed in all the parts, and called Mitchell for an inspection.

Seversky called down from the narrow bombardier's space: "I hope you'll forgive me! I had to remove my wooden leg to get in at all."

"Don't let that bother you. If the sight works, we can remedy that easily enough. We'll amputate the right legs of all bombardiers!"

The two flew over an old battleship wreck in the Chesapeake for bombing tests and found the sight "one hundred percent satisfactory." A few weeks later, when he bought the Seversky sight for the Army, General Patrick wrote: "The Seversky sight is undoubtedly better than any in existence." This bombsight was the forerunner of American sights of World War II and afterward.*

Another of the inventors Mitchell had encouraged had finished his work during the summer, just in time; he was Sanford A. Moss, who built a supercharger to enable planes to climb to higher altitudes. Mitchell had one of these installed in a bomber, which made it possible for it to carry a large bomb load higher than the former 8000-foot ceiling. Only a handful of men in the Air Service knew that the supercharger existed.

The bombsight and supercharger, which had been developed primarily for future use, took Mitchell through the bombing tests of 1923. On August 31, just four days before the tests were to open, the Army notified him that the first bombing run must begin from an altitude of 10,000 feet, rather than the planned low-level sweeps. Mitchell complained to Patrick that only one plane in the world was capable of complying, but added at the end of his memorandum: "I shall make arrangements to comply with these instructions . . . notwithstanding the difficulties." His men worked on Sunday and Labor Day, installing superchargers furnished by Moss, transferring high-altitude sights and making practice bombing runs.

A naval transport, the *St. Mihiel,* came down from Washington with three hundred dignitaries, including Acting Secretary of War Dwight Davis, General Pershing, Vincent Astor, Glenn Curtiss and many foreign military attachés, congressmen and officers. Though it was an Air Service test, the ship swarmed with young naval officers who organized guests into small groups for indoctrination. The senior naval officer was Admiral William E. Shoemaker, known for his hostility to aviation (he thought the Navy needed a maximum of 750 pilots, and that flying pay should be cut to 10 percent of base pay). Reporters noted that Pershing and Shoemaker were cordial on the trip.

General Patrick called the press into the wardroom for a

* Seversky gave Mitchell much credit for this development: "Because of the relentless pressure from General Mitchell for greater accuracy and precision in the device, we at the Sperry plant had to improve the instrument's gyroscopes. This led to the development of the artificial horizon, the azimuth-gyro and other gyroscopic devices which are the mainstays of our present air navigation. As a result of the energy and foresight of this great man, Billy Mitchell, America today leads the world in instrument flying."

briefing, and was looking at his notes when Pershing came in quietly behind him, unnoticed by Patrick. "The differences between the Army and Navy on bombs versus battleships—" Patrick began. Pershing interrupted: "What General Patrick is telling you is that his Air Service is having some target practice." Patrick looked up, surprised, got to his feet and saluted. He stuffed the papers back in his pocket, and that, as reporter Samuel T. Moore noted, was the end of the interview.

The transport spent the night near the Diamond Shoals Lightship, waiting for the planes the next day. Two mine layers carrying reporters joined it during the evening.

Mitchell had gone to Hatteras the day before the bombing and found his temporary base a shambles: "The administrative and executive organization of the bombardment group went to pieces. I had expected this. It was necessary for me to take command . . . and issue detailed instructions in order to assure the success of the bombing." He relieved the Hatteras commander and took over himself, working in the radio shack until about midnight, giving orders to his crews back at Langley Field. He ordered Lieutenant Austin to take his supercharged planes from Langley to the target ships, timing his arrival for eight-twenty in the morning. Mitchell was up at four o'clock to check on the weather. He took off and circled the target ships for half an hour before Austin's flight appeared, a few minutes late, delayed by fog. Austin's planes flew over the *New Jersey* at 11,000 feet, scored some near misses with 600-pounders, and from 10,000 feet got a direct hit, the first of five. Aboard the *St. Mihiel,* Navy officers told Samuel Moore and other reporters, "Her paint hasn't been scratched." When someone pointed out that she was settling by the stern, the naval officer said, "the anti-aircraft fire would have driven off the planes by now."

The next flight, under Captain L. L. Harvey, carrying 2000-pound bombs, attacked from 6000 feet, but the fuses were improperly adjusted and failed to explode at the expected depths. The *New Jersey* seemed to be badly damaged, however, sinking still deeper, and Mitchell switched the attack to the *Virginia.* Naval officers on the *St. Mihiel* told Moore: "You civilians don't know how much punishment a battlewagon can take."

Lieutenant Harrison Crocker led the next attack, the day's

most effective, with several direct hits which blasted steel far over the water and sent smoke high into the air. Mitchell wrote: "At last an aircraft bomb had demonstrated the complete effect of demolition to the superstructure of a battleship." In less than twenty-six minutes the *Virginia* was gone, torn to bits by the blasts of fourteen bombs. The *New Jersey* was finished by 1100-pound bombs from 3000 feet.

The *St. Mihiel* left the scene at once, steaming back to Washington. Newspapermen who had come aboard were told that the ship's wireless was a government facility, and that individual newspapers could use it only by paying a fee—in advance, at the stiff rate of $170 per one thousand words. Only the *New York Times* reporter was able and willing to pay, and his was the only large newspaper to carry a special story on the successful bombings the next morning. Other papers were forced to run only the emasculated remarks of General Pershing, who had been persuaded to issue a statement approved by the Navy.

The tests off Hatteras, Pershing said, "mark another advance in the science of bombing," but the sinking of the ships was by no means the sole object of the maneuvers. The statement came to the Navy's point after several paragraphs, a rambling description of preparations for the tests, Mitchell's earlier flight of bombers from Langley to Bangor, Maine, and other assorted details:

"It may be stated that the watertight integrity of these older ships had been partially destroyed by the removal of watertight doors . . . These tests against obsolete battleships will not, I hope, be considered as conclusive evidence that similar bombs would sink modern types of battleships, particularly when manned, defended and able to take protective measures."

It was, in brief, a repetition of the rebuttal made by the Navy in 1921.

But there was more to come from the *St. Mihiel*. One writer aboard was Major Lester Gardner, publisher of *Aviation* magazine, who had come to prepare a radio program about the tests, in the form of a message from General Pershing. He had written his talk in outline form aboard ship, and had it approved by General Patrick and others. Pershing read it, but refused to commit himself until it had been approved by Admiral Shoemaker. A naval officer handed Gardner's pages to the admiral, who read

12

The Japanese Are Now Boiling Over

The bride and groom stood beneath an arch of white chrysanthemums which bore a large insignia of the Air Service, welcoming guests to the wedding reception. Blue and orange crepe streamers were draped over the garden. The celebrants shouted to make themselves heard over the roaring engines of a dozen planes from nearby Selfridge Field which circled overhead. The flight had drowned the words of the minister in the Grosse Pointe Presbyterian Church a few minutes earlier; the pilots were determined to honor the chief until they ran out of fuel.

Joseph E. Davies, the future ambassador to Russia, was Mitchell's best man; among the guests were Bill Larned, Bissell, Tom Milling and C. Bascom Slemp, President Coolidge's secretary. Detroit society reporters admired the charm of the bride and the grandeur of Mitchell in his new and bemedaled uniform, "the youngest man in the Legion of Honor since Napoleon," readers were told. Betty showed no effects of a recent fall from a horse in which she had narrowly escaped serious injury.

The couple left by train for San Francisco, where they had to wait for their Army transport, and as on his first honeymoon, Mitchell found time for military affairs. He watched maneuvers of West Coast air reserve squadrons and reported on them to Patrick, to whom he also wrote second thoughts on the Pacific tour: "In addition to the regular inspections I shall study the whole Pacific problem from both an offensive and a defense standpoint . . . It will comprise: the problem of destroying the enemy's armed forces . . . destruction of their power to make war . . . destruction of their morale, and I believe that we can arrive at a solution of the Pacific problem which will allow us to carry on an offensive campaign across the Pacific Ocean."

They sailed on the *Cambrai,* and while they were at sea Hawaii prepared a welcome. Patrick had written ahead to General Charles P. Summerall, commander of the Army's Hawaiian Department, that Mitchell would inspect the islands, that he had "a thorough knowledge of what we are trying to accomplish," and asked full co-operation. The day before they docked in Honolulu the Mitchells had a radio message of greetings from Summerall.

Eighteen planes circled their ship as they landed, and the press was waiting. The Mitchells were photographed and the reporters asked the general for some predictions; he said there would soon be a regular air service to California, with a twenty-hour flight—and that the next war would be fought in the air.

Within a few hours Mitchell was at work. He inspected Fort Shafter and wrote a memorandum for his report, looked for a bungalow, took Betty for a drive beyond Diamond Head, and rode a surfboard. At Schofield Barracks an honor guard received him as he called on his old adversary, General Menoher, now happily stationed there, far from Washington.

He inspected hangars, shops and barracks at Wheeler Field and had the squadrons fly in formation, sat in on a three-hour critique of recent maneuvers, exercises to train ground troops in the defense of Hawaii. He wrote in his journal that it had been "a very good exercise," but that he had reservations.

The maneuvers had included no planes, and he began to perceive the weaknesses of the island outpost: "The personnel, particularly the staff officers, are not familiar with the larger problem." One day, he predicted, there would be an attack on Oahu from the air, and ground maneuvers "are apt to lead to erroneous conclusions."

He told reporters that Wheeler Field was the best he had inspected for a long time and that Hawaii was already the most important air station in the Pacific. But in spare moments he was writing a hundred-page report to Patrick on the vulnerability of Hawaii. As he told a friend, Summerall was hopelessly unprepared for war: "Our defense is based on a land army, coast defense guns and battleships, all of which are unco-ordinated. A modern boy fifteen years old, who knows about air power and had a simple military training in high school, could work out a better system."

Betty went with him everywhere, happily involved in his rounds. His journal for early November hinted at the pace he set:

"Flew a De Havilland, a Thomas Morse and a Sopwith at Luke Field. Ordered white uniforms, worked in the office, had rifles repaired. Went to a reception. Rode horseback, went swimming. Tested rifles on the range. Flew another De Havilland. Inspected squadrons at Wheeler Field. Lunch at Engineers Club. Went swimming. Boat trip; lectured to officers aboard. Shooting and polo. Went to church. Saw Japanese wrestlers. Fished, went to races and a supper party. Played polo. Went surfing, climbed a mountain, shot pigs, pheasant, plover and wild sheep.* Played tennis, addressed officers' clubs, saw a prize fight." Despite all this, he visited every island in the group except Lehua, whose coast he sailed, studying the terrain through field glasses.

Mitchell had made the first inspection of the islands since the coming of air power and had sensed their importance in ways to which both Summerall and Patrick were blind.

By December 1 he sent a preliminary report to Patrick which made obvious the remarkable thoroughness of his six-week inspection of Hawaii. "I shall enlarge on this report a good deal in my final papers, but nearly everything is covered . . . Air power will certainly control the Pacific." He found the Army and Navy commanders at odds, "engaged in a controversy as to who was the superior in rank." He had given local reporters no indication of his official reaction to Wheeler Field: "There are only two little squadrons of pursuit aviation with a total of 23 Thomas Morse planes . . . even at war strength . . . these would be put out of business in one encounter." They had no machine guns, no reserve pilots; the fliers were untrained for combat and never fired at targets. The few bombers they had were equally ill equipped, and "hopelessly unable to ward off any decided attack."

The supply system was chaotic, the islands lacked airways,

* Mitchell was an accomplished huntsman, so accurate that he hunted quail with a small .410 shotgun. He is remembered at the Brandon plantation, in Virginia, for his interest in cuisine; he once shot a rare bird there and took it to the kitchen to instruct the cook—using a passage from the dietary laws of Leviticus which he pointed out in the family Bible.

weather-information system and listening posts. Anti-aircraft batteries and searchlights were not connected with headquarters or other commands. "In other words, there is no real organization of the air forces for war in the Hawaiian Department."

Summerall's concept of the strength of the position was outmoded, he said: "With the coming of air power this system of defense again needs revision; the mission of the ground forces should remain the same . . . for the air force, however, the mission must be to prevent landings on any islands and to destroy any force either in the air, on the water or under the water within the radius of their operations."

Summerall had seemed to be friendly during this inspection. The commander knew little of aviation, but Mitchell thought he had been willing to learn: "The spirit existing here toward the Air Service by the commanding general, General Summerall, is excellent in every way and he is fully alive to the necessity for developing our air power in this group."

As usual, Mitchell's criticism was open and impersonal. He took his report to headquarters at Schofield, went over it with staff officers and had friendly arguments with them about some shortcomings he had noted.

Just before they left Hawaii the Army reached Mitchell with a reprimand. Major General J. L. Hines, the acting Chief of Staff, sent a clipping from a Washington newspaper, a photograph of the honeymooners on tour in which Mitchell wore a comfortable jacket. The Secretary of War was "very much surprised" to find him in a uniform "which bears little resemblance to that of our Army." Mitchell was ordered to discard the uniform, and to explain without delay his reasons for wearing it. He returned the message with a casual explanation scrawled across it: "The costume . . . is used for flying and not as a uniform." The regulation uniform, he said, had been found unsafe by flight surgeons. "It is regretted that a photograph of this kind gained such circulation and caused this communication." *

Mitchell had postponed a medical examination until the last

* This flurry was caused by an anonymous note sent to the Army in Washington, penned in an accomplished feminine hand: "Why is this man permitted to wear a blouse like this? Is he in the English or the American Army?" The Army's swift response to the note indicated the high command's sensitivity where Mitchell was concerned.

moment, and only as he was about to leave for the Orient did he surrender to the Medical Corps. He flew over Luke Field, dived 7500 feet to a landing, and reported to Dr. David Myers. The doctor found numerous signs of old fractures and dislocations which were relics of a lifetime of riding, jumping and polo playing; there was also a punctured eardrum, a reminder of a swift plunge from high altitude in France. Blood pressure was slightly higher than normal, and Dr. Myers urged regular checkups during Mitchell's tour. He found one serious defect, "increased arterial tension." This tension may have been reflected in Mitchell's note to Patrick near his departure: "I have worked very hard here and have gotten a little tired, but will rest up while on my trip to the Philippines."

Mitchell had not only inspected during the six weeks; he had led the little air force in maneuvers; teaching formation flying and dive bombing. The men found him stimulating but hard to please. He had them prepare a final review for the day he and Betty sailed to the Orient on the Army transport *Thomas.* As the old ship picked up speed, Mitchell's war game opened. A surveillance plane shadowed her at high altitude, and while Mitchell watched from deck, eighteen planes appeared and dived on the ship from 4000 feet. Puzzled passengers gaped as the dive bombers roared down upon them and then soared away. Mitchell wrote in his journal: "This maneuver would have put . . . the *Thomas* out of business, as the attack would have been pushed home with the fire of .50-caliber machine guns and 25-pound bombs." But only perfection could satisfy him; he thought the planes had not dived as vertically as they should have, and some failed to take advantage of the sun: "An attack straight down the rays of a bright sun makes it practically impossible for persons on the water or ground to see the attacking plane."

Mitchell followed the bombers with field glasses back to Luke Field, some ten miles away—even there they were not safe from his critical eye: "It is a bad thing to disperse for a landing when it can be avoided. Landing should habitually be made in formation." But he found the progress of these pilots remarkable in the six weeks, and said that if they were well equipped and continued training, they would be "very hard to whip."

While the *Thomas* was at sea Summerall wrote Patrick in an

angry reaction to the Assistant Chief's inspection, saying that Mitchell's suggestions were based on "assumptions as to the action of the enemy" and were not sound. He denied that there was a lack of planning for air defense, and derided Mitchell's comments as "superficial impressions and academic discussions." Patrick tried to placate Summerall in a seven-page reply, a tactful apology for his impulsive assistant which explained that Mitchell's views, though theoretical, would "undoubtedly be of extreme value some 10 or 15 years hence." Patrick believed that air power must develop greatly before the United States should revise defenses along the lines Mitchell urged. In short, Patrick's support of Mitchell was half-hearted, and tended to confirm Summerall in his judgment that Hawaiian defenses needed no revision.

The Mitchells made the journey to Guam through calm seas, with passengers in a holiday mood. Only Betty was aware that one of them was busy day and night with war plans, as if the presumed enemy were real and imminently threatening. Mitchell worked even on Christmas Day. When they did not actually sight important islands on their route, he puzzled over his charts to estimate their strategic importance. He wrote Patrick about Wake Island though it was two hundred miles off his course; his sailing directory described it as a tiny brush-covered sandy islet, probably useless as an airdrome, radio station or observation point, but Mitchell was not content: "Before coming to this conclusion, a careful reconnaissance should be made of it. Wake Island lies about 300 miles north by west of Taongi Island of the Marshall group, which is now in the hands of the Japanese. From the vicinity of Wake Island westward our course everywhere lay within aircraft operation of Japanese islands."

He was already deep in a study of the Pacific basin in the air age, recalling early impressions of the Far East that he had expressed in his report of 1911. He had begun work on a dramatized version of a Japanese attack on Pearl Harbor that was complete even as to the time of day, a fusion of his working knowledge of air power and his imaginative vision. But the strategic concepts growing in his mind were new—applications of his air theories to the vast theater. He was making notes for an outline of a second world war which he foresaw in the Pacific; it was to prove astonishingly accurate and perceptive. His folders bulged with charts and diagrams; he tried to predict from his charts how the Japanese might approach Hawaii:

"The shortest routes are: Yokohama to Midway, 2340 miles. Midway to Niihau or Kauai, 1100 miles. Truk in the Carolines to Midway, 2340 miles. Truk to Guam, 1012 miles"—all routes that were to become familiar in World War II.

The ship entered the harbor at Apra on a sunny morning and two flying boats came out to meet it, the remnants of Guam's tiny air force, which had been decimated by typhoons. Mitchell went over the gun emplacements, saw that wharves and dry docks might be built, that rotting wood of the hangars should be replaced with concrete, and that the garrison of 650 Marines and sailors was inadequate. He thought that "the little dab" of aviation on Guam was useless, and that pilots should be given safe planes, though under the Three-Power Treaty the United States was prohibited from strengthening Guam. With an expanded air force and garrison, he said, Guam could defend itself: "If we ever use the southern line of operations against Japan, Guam is a point of tremendous importance. It has greater strength than our position in Manila, is as close to the heart of Japan, and has an uninterrupted line of small islands, stretching not only northward to Japan but southward to New Guinea and Australia, along which our air forces could operate."

He urged that Guam be developed as fully as possible as "a dominant factor in the military future of the western Pacific," and also pointed out the importance of the Mariana and Bonin island groups, under Japanese mandate, of whose development "practically nothing is known."

The ship left Guam and steamed westward toward the Philippines, and just after dawn on the last day of 1923 they sighted the island of Samar through a rainstorm. A few hours later as they passed into San Bernardino Strait an American plane circled over them, a crude sign painted on its fuselage: "Welcome General Mitchell."

As the newlyweds sailed past Corregidor they were greeted by bombers, flying boats and pursuit planes, and at the Manila dock were met by an official party, including Mitchell's old friend

General Douglas MacArthur, the Army commander of the islands, and his bride.* Mitchell started his two-week inspection of the Philippines immediately, moving so swiftly that a reporter covering his activities said he was "on the go most of the time, a strenuous pace." He flew over jungle country where he had fought with MacArthur's father many years before, and inspected virtually every man and plane in the Air Service detachments. He once took Emilio Aguinaldo aloft, the aging chief of the rebellion he had helped to put down. The old man went up bravely despite his distrust of planes, and when they flew over the village of his birth, Aguinaldo dropped a pack of his calling cards, one by one, to friends below.

Mitchell sent Patrick a sketch of the island tribes, their traits, customs and history, and pointed out that all but 2000 of the 12,000-man garrison force were natives, whose language and background were unknown to their officers. He also warned of a Japanese intrusion, an airway system reaching a point twenty miles from Luzon "within striking distance of Manila Bay, Clark Field, Cavite Naval Base . . . Corregidor."

The air units, he reported, were no better here than in Hawaii—the pursuit squadron of only sixteen Morse planes was just three months old, its men poorly trained and equipped. There was no definite system of command or operations. A so-called air group had only three officers and twenty-seven enlisted men, all in administrative work. An observation squadron on Corregidor had only five old flying boats, so underpowered that they could not rise from the water in rough weather. He sent Patrick a preliminary report on the Philippines, as he had on Hawaii, and promised a fuller account within a few weeks.

The Mitchells left for India on the *Franconia*, which was on a

* Mrs. MacArthur, the former Louise Cromwell Brooks, a charming, wealthy socialite, was the general's junior by sixteen years. Newspaper gossip had it that she had been "banished" to the Philippines with her bridegroom for her refusal to marry General Pershing. She was quoted as saying: "Jack wanted me to marry him, and when I wouldn't, he wanted me to marry one of his colonels. I wouldn't do that, so here I am." (Pershing told reporters this was "a lot of damned poppycock.") Out of boredom Mrs. MacArthur became a part-time policewoman in Manila; a few years later she divorced the general, leaving a memorable quotation: "Sir Galahad conducted his courtship as if he were reviewing a division of troops."

world cruise, and made stops in Java and Singapore. Mitchell paid the fares on this leg of their trip, though he inspected men and planes everywhere, and reported on them to Washington.*

In India, as guests of a maharajah, they went tiger hunting and bagged several animals, one of them killed by Betty; Mitchell sold an article on the hunt to the *National Geographic*. And even from India he sent notes to Patrick—the military operations of the British conquest, the contrasted abilities of various tribesmen as soldiers, charts of troop strength, air strength, depots and shops of the Indian army.

They found Siam "one of the pleasantest places" in the Far East, visited the king and inspected his air force of 260 planes. Mitchell flew some of them and thought them surprisingly good.

He went next into China, his first visit in thirteen years, and found it the most remarkable nation of the Pacific basin. He wrote of the people with an air of prophecy: "The Chinese themselves are extremely virile, democratic, industrious and very strong physically. Biologically they are undoubtedly superior to any people living. They are extremely intelligent and capable of carrying out any development that is desired."

For the benefit of staff officers back in Washington he outlined China's background, saying that though the nation was then undeveloped, it had resources to support a great modern power. He saw beyond poverty, anarchy and exploitation by foreigners to another day: "From being a nation that dominated everything around them, as was the case about a century ago, the Chinese have lost their military and political power and are an easy mark for the European nations and the Japanese . . . Commercially, however, and biologically their effect is tremendous and is being constantly extended, not only south to and across the equator, but north all the way to the Arctic Circle." Once China was organized, he predicted, her potential would be unlimited.

The Mitchells took the Blue Express from Shanghai to Peking

* Aboard the *Franconia* the popular Spanish novelist Blasco Ibáñez was impressed by Mitchell's correct Spanish and his vision of the future: "This warrior of the air explained to me with the sweet voice of a poet a series of 'expectations' that would amaze even the most lively imagination. Through him I learned how the airplane changed the war, how it will make war almost impossible, how one day it would be able to match the speed of the sun, with flying squadrons circling our planet without ever being overtaken by night."

for a few weeks' stay; the general told reporters on his arrival that there would soon be three-day flights from Peking to New York, which was headlined as "astounding prophecy." He found the Chinese air force insignificant, too weak for offensive use; the pilots were "pretty good," but had too little national spirit to take heavy losses in fighters. The mechanics, however, were "excellent, careful, painstaking, capable of a great deal of work." He wrote a summary of the country's crazy-quilt divisions, naming the war lords and leading White Russians, with an appraisal of their influence. He visited a friend of the 1911 tour, the war lord Chang Tso-lin, who now reigned at Mukden; Mitchell flew one of his planes and was given an officer as escort in the region.

Mitchell's real goal was an inspection tour of Japan, and his appetite was only whetted by a brief call at Kobe, where he had been asked to stop and negotiate for the passage of a Round the World flight of American planes through Japan later in the year. The call stretched into weeks, then months, for though the Foreign Office had agreed, the Japanese army and navy stubbornly resisted the proposed landing of the pioneering U.S. planes. Mitchell was frustrated by Japanese methods of diplomacy; his adversary was a fourteen-man committee headed by General Yatsumitsu, which led him through a series of interminable meetings, all marked by exquisite courtesy—and bland refusals to agree to Mitchell's requests.

In their first long encounter Yatsumitsu said that these great planes need not land in Japan, since they could fly two thousand miles nonstop; Mitchell explained that this report was an exaggeration, that he had ordered flights of no more than five hundred miles for the project. Then an interpreter simply told Mitchell that he would be advised when the next session was to be held. Through weekly meetings, all of which ended in futile arguments, Mitchell remained firm, insisting that if his pilots were not permitted to land every five hundred miles, the world flight could not come near Japan at all, and the generals must bear responsibility for the detour when it became news. The officers finally accepted his plan, but their restrictions were almost endless: no cameras on the American planes, no flights within five miles of land except on approaching and leaving Japan, and no flights within fifteen miles of a fortified place. When Mitchell agreed to those conditions, the Japanese added some more:

"We are sure your pilots will not intentionally fly over restricted areas. Still, there is the possibility . . . Therefore, it will be necessary for a Japanese pilot to fly with the leader's plane and guide the flight through Japan."

Mitchell replied that there was no room for another man and proposed that a Japanese plane lead the way. The committee dropped the subject, apparently because no such long-range planes were available to them. The suspicious officers succumbed to Mitchell after long bargaining and allowed him—but only when accompanied by Japanese officers—to visit the sites where planes would land.

Mitchell apparently made these visits during the winter of 1924; if so, it was with Japanese army and navy officers at his elbow. His experience with the committee led to an observation in his formal report: "Spies acquire the greatest merit in Japan. They are met everywhere in all sorts of guises and disguises. They are placed in the prospective enemy's service and left there for years to work up in it to positions of responsibility and trust . . . the most elaborate system of espionage is maintained by them, especially within the United States."

In contrast to stories of a friendly and picturesque people usually brought home by American tourists, Mitchell saw many signs of hostility toward the United States: "The Japanese are now boiling over in anti-American agitation in their press, which is really looked on with favor, if not gotten up by, the ruling classes. Its object is to see if America will be 'scared.' "

Japan felt "perfectly able" to fight a defensive war against America, but was not prepared to take the offensive. She was desperately seeking allies, "and an ally is a very difficult thing to obtain. She is trying . . . to find one in Europe . . . She thought for a while that Germany would be a ready listener . . ."

After their stay in Kobe the Mitchells went to Korea and then back to the Philippines once more. Mitchell had hoped to make a more leisurely tour of Japan before his return home, but was shaken by an anxious cable from Washington: "STATE DEPARTMENT ADVISES YOUR PRESENCE AT THIS TIME IN JAPAN OR

KOREA LIABLE TO MISCONSTRUCTION BY JAPANESE STOP DO NOT ATTEMPT TO VISIT EITHER JAPAN OR KOREA UNTIL WAR DEPARTMENT ADVISES SAME." *

But he was not to be stopped by nervous diplomats, and after an exchange of cables with the embassy in Tokyo, Mitchell got permission to go to Japan "as a tourist and unofficially on the way to transport at Nagasaki." He seized this opportunity, and as he and Betty passed through thriving Japanese cities, he interpreted all that he saw in military terms. Rural people were flocking to the cities and became skilled workers, and the mechanics were particularly good. He saw signs of progress in aviation, and translated these into a warning in his report to Washington:

"Her military effort is now centered on her air force, and everything else is secondary. Already this new air arm is rapidly approaching the second in size in the world, being exceeded in number only by France . . . She now has many more men, more machines and more factories working on her air force, yes three times over, than has the United States." He said that this air development was clothed with greater secrecy than her stealthy preparations before the Russo-Japanese war, which explained why such air progress had not been hinted at in previous dispatches to Washington.

Mitchell did not reveal his sources, but his report was full of details:

"The military arsenal of Tokorosawa has a splendid airplane factory on the grounds of a flying school . . . about nine miles outside Tokyo. Very well supplied with machine tools purchased largely in the U.S. Been employed heretofore in the manufacture of the Salmson 2A2 airplane and engine . . .

"The military arsenal Heika at Nagoya is not given over entirely to the manufacture of aircraft. It builds military automobiles and trucks as well.

* A precise reconstruction of the itinerary was impossible to obtain from documents found by the writer. Mitchell's correspondence reveals his presence in Kobe in February and March 1924; the cable from the General Staff forbidding his Japanese visit was sent to Manila and dated May 17. The assumption of this narrative is that the Mitchells made two visits to Japan while they were in the Far East, in winter and spring; it is obvious that the general spent more time in the country than his biographers have assumed.

"The military arsenal Tokyo, normal production artillery, has a small airplane factory.

"The military arsenal Kiki at Nagoya, heretofore specializing in manufacture of Salmson . . . engine. Has 500 men . . ."

He listed thirteen other arsenals by name, some of them making Sopwith two-seater observation planes, single-seater pursuits and torpedo planes.

Mitchell evolved his own theory of Japan's military thinking. He recalled that Japanese had witnessed his bombing of the old German warships off the Virginia Capes in 1921, had seen that battleships were doomed and that "a competition in naval construction would lead nowhere." He reasoned that Japan "kept quiet" and gave in to all the proposals at the Limitation of Armaments Conference of 1921, knowing that America and England had secretly agreed, and that "the cards were stacked against her." She was now building an air force as the way out of her dilemma, and though it had been belittled by American diplomatic observers and military attachés in general, Mitchell sounded an insistent warning:

"Japan knows what a tremendous change is coming in the conducting of oversea operations. Naval systems of the past will give way to the air systems of the future. She is ready from a naval standpoint, but is afraid of the air." He was making observations that no diplomat of his day could have made; even his military peers in Washington, including General Patrick, ignored the implications of his prophecies.

Mitchell realized that prejudices of the most absurd sort helped to obscure the truth about Japanese aviation: "One hears it often said that the Japanese cannot fly. Nothing is more fallacious than this. They can fly, are going to fly, and may end up by developing the greatest air power in the world . . . It takes no longer to teach Japanese than it does Anglo-Saxons."

He tried to explain why orthodox intelligence reports from Japan were inadequate: "In making estimates of the Japanese air power, care must be taken that it is not underestimated. According to our ordinary systems of gaining military information we only give credence to things of which we are absolutely sure. With the difficulty of gaining information about Japanese aviation it is almost impossible to be sure about anything." These warnings were in his formal report on his Pacific tour, but they might well have been written for Patrick alone, in the hope that they would be understood even by an inexperienced flier: "An estimate by people conversant with aeronautical systems, taking into consideration the problems that lie in front of the Japanese and the manner in which they can be met would be much more accurate."

The Japanese, he said, were buying planes and equipment everywhere: "They are getting the latest type of everything and are perfectly capable of manufacturing and handling . . . I believe there is no doubt that they have a striking force of at least 600 airplanes, half of which are pursuit and half bombardment."

The Mitchells arrived in Nagasaki in June, to sail for home on the *Thomas.* Anti-American demonstrations had broken out, and Mitchell saw signs that the Japanese feared a premature clash with the United States. He saw guards posted around the docks: "They were very nervous when the . . . *Thomas* called . . . for coal . . . Everything was watched, particularly the coal as it was passed in, for fear of explosives or chemical weapons being deposited in the bunkers. They were afraid that the mob might get out of control . . . and kill and savagely mutilate some Americans."

He got his last glimpse of Japan's growing power on June 17, 1924, an impressive view of the battle fleet in the harbor, just back from maneuvers. He noted two battleships, the *Nagato* and the *Mutsu;* two battle cruisers, the *Kongo* and the *Kirishima;* eighteen destroyers and eight submarines, with supply ships and a tender. The crews, he thought, were "in good shape, well-clothed and well-disciplined." He watched admiringly as the Japanese fleet moved back to sea in the foggy morning:

"The first intimation we had that the craft were moving out was the coming of two squadrons of Sopwith single-seater pursuit planes from the airdrome of Sasebo. These were followed by several two-seater observation planes. The submarines then moved out into the harbor, followed by the destroyers, light cruisers, battle cruisers, battleships and supply vessels. The whole thing struck me as being very well executed and smoothly done." *

* The modernized *Nagato* was Admiral Yamamoto's flagship during World War II. He was aboard her when he received word of Japanese triumph at Pearl Harbor, an action he had planned. All the other ships named here were at Midway in 1942, and the *Kirishima* was in the striking force at Pearl Harbor.

From Nagasaki the Mitchells sailed through fine weather for California. During these days the general began drafting the exhaustive report on the Pacific theater that was to be both a summary of the forces he had seen on his tour and a prophecy of war to come.

13

The Only Question Is How and When and Where

The report that Mitchell outlined on his homeward voyage was to be the masterpiece of his career, an all-encompassing, sometimes rambling study of the Pacific basin as he saw it, enhanced by observations made in his years of frustrating struggle for American air power. In the end he reduced his voluminous report to 323 pages. Somewhere inside was buried a glimpse of the opening moments of World War II in the Pacific:

"Japan . . . knows full well that the United States will probably enter the next war with the methods and weapons of the former war, and will, therefore, offer the enticing morsel which all nations that follow that system have done before.

"Japan also knows full well that the defense of the Hawaiian group is based on the island of Oahu and not on the defense of the whole group . . ."

Then he sketched the scene he thought was inevitable—the coming of a Japanese attack on Pearl Harbor:

"I believe, therefore, that should Japan decide upon the reduction or seizure of the Hawaiian Islands the following procedure would be adopted. Ten submarines would be loaded with six pursuit airplanes each * . . . Two airplane transports would be provided, each loaded with 50 bombardment planes. These ships could be equipped with a flying-off deck . . . These seacraft

* Though they did not use them at Pearl Harbor on December 7, 1941, the Japanese actually had plane-carrying submarines during World War II.

would be started so as to arrive at the islands of Niihau in Hawaii and Midway, respectively, on 'D' day . . .

"As soon as set up and tested, those ships would fly to Niihau and then be ready to attack Oahu immediately . . .

"The first attack would be arranged as follows: the Japanese pursuit, 60 ships organized into one group with three squadrons of 20 ships each; two squadrons to participate in combined attack with bombardment and one squadron remaining in reserve on alert . . .

"The Japanese bombardment, 100 ships organized into four squadrons of 25 ships each. The objectives for attack are 1) Ford Island [in the middle of Pearl Harbor], airdrome, hangars, storehouses, and ammunition dumps; 2) Navy fuel oil tanks; 3) water supply of Honolulu; 4) water supply of Schofield; 5) Schofield Barracks airdrome and troop establishments; 6) naval submarine station; 7) city and wharves of Honolulu.

"No attention will be paid to the naval dry dock because it can be used only for docking and repair of vessels. It is easier to sink these vessels than take time to destroy concrete work of dry dock . . .

"Attack will be launched as follows: bombardment, attack to be made on Ford Island at 7:30 A.M.* . . . Group to move in column of flights in V. Each ship will drop . . . projectiles on the targets . . .

"I have gone into attack by an enemy in some detail to show how easily it can be done by a determined and resourceful enemy . . . Actually nothing can stop it except air power . . .

"I have put in a landing on Midway to show that it can be done . . ."

He added, as if he expected staff officers in Washington to take him seriously: "Well may it be said, 'This sounds well, but what will our air force be doing in the meantime?' As things stand it would be almost useless. There are only two little squadrons of pur-

* Technically, Mitchell missed his prediction by twenty-five minutes, since the actual assault on Pearl Harbor began at 7:55 A.M.—but in fact, crewmen of the destroyer *Allen* saw Japanese planes circling overhead precisely at 7:30; they were waiting for slower torpedo planes to arrive. The date of his writing of this prediction cannot be fixed, but was between June and October 1924, more than seventeen years before the attack.

inflammable substances." The easiest advance against Japan would be from Alaska, down the Aleutian chain—a route that Japan would probably take in reverse if Washington did not seize the initiative.

Since aircraft could now cover almost any distance, American strategists should consider the northern Pacific as a vast triangle, with a base 11,000 miles long, running from the Panama Canal to the coast of Asia. The sides of his triangle were 7500 miles long, the eastern side dominated by the United States and a friendly Canada, "a homogeneous strategical entity complete in itself and menaced only from across the Pacific." The western side was dominated by Japan from Formosa to Kamchatka, for about 4000 miles. Since the Asian mainland was hostile to Japan, and her island empire was vulnerable from the air, Japan was seriously menaced from two directions.

Air forces were the hope of the United States in such a war, Mitchell said, since modern navies were not only at the mercy of air power (except for submarines), but were also becoming so complex, with their need for vast shore facilities, that they were less mobile. Air power, on the other hand, could base almost anywhere, more quickly and cheaply. He was so positive of the superiority of land bases and of the development of enormous fleets of planes that he could foresee only a minor, limited role for carriers against land forces: "There is nothing whatever to fear from so-called naval airplane carriers because not only can they not operate efficiently on the high seas, but even if they could, they cannot place sufficient aircraft in the air at one time to insure a concentrated operation. Consequently a hostile air force will seize land airdromes from which to launch its attacks against its intended victims." *

There was one way to prevent the kind of assault he had pictured against Pearl Harbor, he said, and he outlined it in detail for many pages—a repetition of the plans for Hawaii he had urged upon Patrick. There must be co-ordination of command, an airway system, radio, war training.

He was no less complete as to other phases of the coming war:

* Mitchell apparently had in mind here the relative value of carrier-based aircraft against land-based planes in great numbers; he had been, of course, an early disciple of U.S. carrier development.

how to carry the war to Japan, the best bombing targets there, the priorities among warships to be bombed . . . night fighting . . . signaling, rescue of men from the sea . . . training service units, even pamphlets of instruction.

Everything about the Japanese background seemed to him a part of the American problem; he reviewed Japan's use of French and then German military instructors and said that Japanese strategists were then divided as to how to fight America. One party wanted to wait until a great air force had been built, the other wanted to begin war at once by halting American imports, forcing Americans from Japanese possessions, "scaring them and otherwise mistreating them." America would react by enlarging her Navy and strengthening the Philippines. Japan would then declare that America had violated her treaties and would act to protect herself.

Both parties in Japan, however, wanted the "complete extermination" of American influence in the Far East: "They recognize that if the United States keeps on, sooner or later they will be made weaker in every way and that also sooner or later the United States will consider that the maintenance of a great military force by any Asiatic nation is a direct menace to the safety of the American nation and Anglo-Saxon destiny in the Pacific. Therefore sooner or later they must fight. The only question is how and when and where."

His pages were studded with stray facts from his reading of Asiatic history: "There is a feature about the Japanese that must be taken into serious account. They are of Malay extraction with many attributes of that race permanently implanted in them. They are apt to run amok at any time that their feelings are sufficiently wrought. This condition exists not only in the individual but in large bodies and also may extend to the whole state."

He added a warning that Japan was far from bankrupt, that she did not fear the United States, and that she was "perfectly able to make war in a very serious and dangerous manner."

He made no apologies for the fact that his theories might seem fantastic to most of his contemporaries. Instead, without a trace of self-consciousness, he told the War Department that his entire career and his recent tour of inspection had "given me greater insight into the various air forces than is the case with any other individual in any other service."

There were thirty-nine Conclusions for planners to consider, and a final plea—there must be an independent American air arm to face the hazards of future war.

Mitchell had the framework of this report completed when he and Betty docked in San Francisco in the first week of July 1924, and perhaps a draft of the final document. He carried it ashore as if he expected his old adversaries of the Army and Navy high commands to welcome his study and to put aside all other considerations in order to prepare the nation for the war which loomed before them.

A day or so after landing, he piloted a plane to sea to greet the British battle fleet, which was entering San Francisco Bay on a good-will tour. Two squadrons of U.S. pursuit planes took part in the welcome, but it was Mitchell who made the greeting official. He dived on the giant of the fleet, H.M.S. *Hood*, which was to play a role in the coming world war. He skimmed 20 feet above her superstructure, and as they passed the bridge, his passenger tossed out a floral wreath, a symbolic key to the city which struck like a well-aimed bomb.

After a ten-day leave in San Francisco on personal business Mitchell returned East with Betty, still absorbed in the completion of his Pacific study. They had been gone for nine months.

14

A Vehicle for Propaganda

The Pacific report may have been the most important achievement of Mitchell's career, a marvel of combined practical knowledge and intuitive vision, but it was received by the War Department with the enthusiasm of a green demolition team approaching an unexploded bomb.

The document was complete in October 1924, and at least one member of the General Staff, Major Gerald Brandt, saw it then. It was ignored or suppressed by the War Department, and not until two years later, in November 1926, did the Secretary of War ask his Chief of Staff for an opinion of it.

General Patrick himself, who was almost Mitchell's only hope within the hierarchy, was an important cause of delay. The Chief of the Air Service withheld comment until virtually forced to speak, after repeated requests from War Department officials, who seemed eager to have Patrick deal with this matter alone. When he wrote his first reaction, Patrick told his superiors that though the report from Mitchell was dated October 1924, he had not actually seen a copy until late January 1925 because he had been in the hospital. "I had no opportunity to examine it until February 2. It contains information of value and in due course would have been transmitted to the War Department."

Patrick stretched "due course" over more than a year, and not until April 1926, when Mitchell was out of uniform, did the Air Chief at last submit the opinions he had so stubbornly avoided putting to paper. To a second official reminder that he should report on Mitchell's observations—after sitting on them for fifteen months—Patrick replied: "This report is being studied, but due to the necessity of consideration of other matters, principally concerned with legislation . . . a reply will be delayed . . ."

The War Plans Division of the General Staff, which Mitchell's work concerned the most, did not react until mid-November 1925.

The integral divisions of the Army General Staff—Personnel (G-1), Intelligence (G-2), Operations (G-3) and Supply (G-4)—were asked to study Mitchell's report, and at length each division, after commenting that it was "worthy of consideration," proceeded to tear it to pieces. As a whole, the high command of the Army condemned or dismissed Mitchell's astonishing view of the future as an ill-assorted bag of old ideas, most of them propaganda for the Air Service. His detailed information was challenged, some of it as based upon false intelligence or drawn from the imagination.

It was to War Plans (a division directly answerable to Operations) that the opinions of these divisions eventually came, and the reaction of War Plans was enough to doom the report, even if others had been favorable. War Plans began by conceding that the study "contains much of value" and should be seen by the Chief of the Air Service and commanders in the Pacific, but then said: "Many of the opinions expressed and much of the discussion of national policy, strategy and the art of war are based upon the author's exaggerated ideas of the powers and importance of air power, and are therefore unsound . . ." Most of his conclusions, War Plans reported, were based on general ideas, and not on what Mitchell had seen in the Pacific.

"None of these so-called conclusions are new; all of them have been advanced by General Mitchell before and all of them have received or are receiving consideration by the War Department or other agency of the Government."

War Plans thought Mitchell's specific comments worthless: "Since he so notoriously overestimates what could be done with air power by the United States, it is not improbable that he has likewise grossly overestimated what Japan could do and would be able to accomplish with air power."

Mitchell's claims that the Hawaiian Department had no plans for war were "not true"; he obviously meant unit war plans—and General Summerall had given Washington assurance that there were unit plans in existence. But in the same paragraph, War Plans revealed that the Hawaiian situation was just as Mitchell pictured it: "Lack of unit plans was due to two causes, first, the Department plan had not been completed long enough . . . The other reason was that the personnel . . . was not familiar with the character of the plans . . ." The comment ended on a note of confusion.

Otherwise, this critique of Mitchell said, things in Hawaii were now improving. There was the beginning of an airway system, there was now "liaison" between the air and other services. There were, to be sure, some flaws—there was no money to provide communications between anti-aircraft batteries and searchlight batteries and other units.* And there was to be no weather service for the Army airmen, since that was the Navy's field.

Mitchell's comments on the Philippines were dealt with even more summarily.

War Plans was noncommittal as to Mitchell's analysis of how the United States should prepare for a Pacific war: "The discussion of the strategy of the Pacific and the influence of air power thereon is most interesting. It shows the modifications which General Mitchell believes should be made of the previous conception of strategy in the Pacific. . . . It is based on General Mitchell's fundamental contention that air power has entirely changed all previous theories of warfare and is now by far the dominating instrument for making war . . .

"Based upon this fundamental idea, and disregarding adverse conditions and the limitations of aircraft, while at the same time overestimating its power and importance, General Mitchell concludes that a war between the United States and Japan must be an 'air' war conducted along the northern route . . ."

Brigadier General Harry A. Smith, Assistant Chief of Staff, signed the War Plans Division's comment, and wrote:

"While General Mitchell's report purports to be a report upon his trip to the Pacific Ocean, it in reality covers a much broader field. The document has been used . . . as a vehicle for propaganda for a unified and separate Air Service, complete changes in

* Anti-aircraft batteries were largely ineffectual during the actual Japanese attack on Pearl Harbor; most of them lacked ammunition.

the organization of our national defenses, and a reconception of our doctrines of strategy and methods of conducting warfare."

This vast subject, he said, was the concern of Operations rather than of War Plans.

Operations (G-3) commented with vehemence:

"The report is so voluminous, and contains so many statements which indicate a misconception of the true role and proper employment of air units, a lack of any conception of the proper employment of the combined arms in warfare, and such an exaggerated idea of the powers of aviation . . . that detailed comment on this report is believed to be unnecessary."

General Malin Craig, Assistant Chief of Staff for G-3, said that Mitchell's plan for striking at Japan along the Aleutian Islands merely pointed out the shortest route over land areas, and ignored climatic conditions and the limited capacity of planes.

Craig then offered assurance to the high command: "The strategy of the Pacific is being continuously studied in connection with the Orange and Red Orange Plans by the Joint Board, and the power and development of aircraft is being given full consideration." (At the time he wrote, the United States had only one pursuit group in being, a total of about sixty modern planes.)

Operations took up Mitchell's points in detail only by commenting on General Patrick's belated reactions to the Pacific study, a form of criticism once removed. Though G-3 rejected most of Mitchell's proposals, it did concur in some important matters—the missions of the Army and Navy should be clearly defined, and in the Pacific islands, single commanders should direct combined defenses. Cities in the United States should also be protected against air attack, with plans worked out in peacetime. Otherwise, Operations found little to approve.

The Intelligence Division (G-2) grappled with Mitchell in specific cases. Its comments opened on a deceptively enthusiastic note: "As a whole, the report contains much valuable information. The discussion of the air defenses of the Hawaiian Islands seems especially timely . . ." But then: "That part . . . dealing with the Japanese air service has received special attention. General

Mitchell makes several statements which, in light of extended studies made in this division and by our military attachés in the Far East, do not seem to be borne out by the facts. For example, on page 276, 'she (Japan) now has more men, more machines, more factories working on her air force, yes three times more, than has the U.S.' "

Mitchell's estimate that Japan had six hundred or more planes, Intelligence said, was "a grossly erratic conclusion." *

The division warmed to its task. In commenting on Mitchell's estimate of Japan as the second air power in the world: "Since September 1924, all Japanese air battalions and schools have been inspected by the U.S. military attaché in Japan . . . The strength in personnel of the Japanese air service is very closely known, as is also the scope and quality of training. The G-2 data on air material cannot be far from correct also. The Japanese air service probably ranks fifth in the world today."

None of Mitchell's information on Japanese plane factories was to be trusted, G-2 said: "The members of the U.S. embassy at Tokyo have the opportunities for inspection and contact never accorded General Mitchell in his hasty tour of the Far East. The reliability of his 'most reliable and practically only source available' is, frankly, very much doubted. It is understood that General Mitchell made no inspections of air stations in Japan and it is not understood how he could have carefully checked the information of his reliable sources." **

Intelligence then went down the list of plane factories itemized by Mitchell, contrasting his information with its own, and picking flaws. For example:

Mitchell reported that the Tokorosawa arsenal, nine miles from Tokyo, using U.S. machine tools, had been making Salmson planes and engines.

G-2's challenge: "Tokorosawa is no longer an important

* It is difficult to obtain exact figures; even Japanese authorities disagree. But Japanese naval authorities estimated (in 1966) that about six hundred military planes were in service in Japan in 1925, a year after Mitchell's inspection.

** Mitchell had refrained from saying that diplomats were incapable of interpreting Japan's growing air power, though he strongly implied that. Intelligence evidently knew nothing of his negotiations with the Japanese army committee for the landing of Round the World flight planes, or of his conducted tour of landing sites by officers.

production center. Only a few planes are made here and these are largely for experimental purposes . . ."

An arsenal called Heika at Nagoya, Intelligence pointed out, was one of Mitchell's misnomers. *Heika* meant "arms," and the arsenal in question was the same as one called Kiki, also in Nagoya. Mitchell was correct as to the five hundred employees at Kiki, but Intelligence insisted that the plant made only six planes per month, rather than the twelve Mitchell reported; it made no motors, G-2 said, despite Mitchell's claim that it had produced 350.

The arsenal Tokyo, described by Mitchell as an artillery factory with a small airplane plant, was said by Intelligence to have a capacity of "only a small number of the obsolete Daimler engines," and to produce no planes.

Mitchell wrote of the naval arsenal of Yokusuka, where engines were overhauled, as making "a few hydroplanes," adding that it could be greatly expanded.

G-2's reply: "The Yokusuka type of plane is obsolete. The Yokusuka arsenal is devoted almost entirely to repairs."

The Aichi Tokei Kikai Works at Nagoya, an electrical and clock plant, had added a plane factory and was turning out eight seaplanes monthly.

G-2's comment: "The Aichi works at Nagoya is reported to have a capacity of 10 planes and no motors per month. It is of little importance."

Mitchell said that the Mitsubishi company, of Nagoya, made 10 Hispano engines each month, and could produce 40; it had also built 200 Sopwith planes. In Kobe, the same firm was building automobiles, submarines and diesel engines.

The comment by Intelligence: "The Mitsubishi company has a capacity of 25 planes and 20 motors per month. The motor is the Hispano-Suiza and the machines the Mitsubishi, Nieuport and Salmson. Employees number about 1500. The numbers produced mentioned by General Mitchell are believed to be too large."

Mitchell described the Kowasaki plant at Kobe, which worked for the War Ministry exclusively, as "very large and financially strong," with 1200 employees, turning out 18 Salmson engines monthly. G-2 corrected him: there were only 1000 employees, and the plant made 20 motors per month.

The Army's failure to grasp the import of Mitchell's warning was nowhere clearer than in its reception of his report on the Nakajima works at Ota, which he said was producing the highly maneuverable Nieuport-29 pursuit plane with a 300-horsepower Hispano engine: "Twelve of these are being turned out per month for the war department. Five hundred men are employed and excellent work done. It is to be noted that this is the best pursuit plane of the high-speed diving type with which any aviation is now equipped. It is at least the equal of our Thomas Morse."

G-2's comment was limited to details, as if the efficiency of the swift plane were of no moment, and no military threat were implied: "The Nakajima works makes *no motors*, as inferred by General Mitchell. The capacity is placed at 25 planes per month, usually of the Nieuport type."

Intelligence came closer to agreeing with Mitchell on smaller plants throughout Japan, subcontractors for the aviation industry. In fact, though Mitchell listed only six, G-2 said it had a list of thirty-three Japanese civilian firms making aircraft parts. It agreed that a Nagoya bicycle plant was making plane wheels, that a musical-instrument factory was making screws for planes (Mitchell said it also made propellers), that an electric-wire plant was producing balloons, a textile plant was producing linen for fuselage coverings, and so on.

Mitchell attached importance to the scattered plants in Japan which could be "quickly converted to aircraft use," but G-2 demurred: "It is believed there are comparatively few plants which could be converted to the successful manufacture of airplane motors. It is doubtful even today if there has been a complete machine (motor and plane) constructed in Japan from purely Japanese materials."

G-2 sent to the Chief of Staff a summary of its findings of Mitchell's errors:

	Mitchell	*G-2 data*
Motors, *present* production per month	102	15
Planes, *present* production per month	38	15
Capacity motors per month	175–350	60
Capacity planes per month	79–190	90

In short, G-2 and Mitchell spoke different languages.* However, Intelligence reflected the current official Army view of air power—its findings of inaccuracies in Mitchell's report were strictly numerical, and no estimate was made of the effect of Japanese plane production from the point of view of air power. Even when its own estimates of Japanese production exceeded Mitchell's, G-2 seemed to be oblivious to the potential threat from growing Japanese air power.

Mitchell's chapter on the tactical and strategical aspects of the Pacific drew the attention of G-1, probably because of statements like: "As the air covers the sea and the land in equal measure, there is no restriction on the application of air power as to location. Its sole limitation is in its radius of action." **

According to Personnel, this entire chapter was only "a recitation of the aspirations of the Air Service rather than a description of actualities . . . the chapter will not bear careful analysis." It was also in this chapter that Mitchell prophesied that the white and yellow races, competing in the Pacific, would come into conflict.

G-1 also spoke lightly of Mitchell's outline of a Japanese attack on Pearl Harbor, written, it said, "from the viewpoint of an Air Service officer. It gives an interesting description of an attack on Oahu from the air which can hardly be considered more than a possible employment of the Air Service in a raid."

The Supply Division, G-4, said that "so much discussion along imaginative lines" marked the report of this "technical enthusiast" that it could not be seriously considered. Supply was involved only with the money needed to put Mitchell's proposals into effect, and

* The writer found it impossible to judge whether Mitchell or G-2 was more nearly accurate, though general evidence would appear to be on Mitchell's side. As late as 1941, Army Intelligence placed Japanese plane production at 200 per month; actually, it was 426. G-2 also thought Japanese pilot training inferior to that of the United States, whereas it was much more thorough. Similar errors were made in underestimating speed and range of Japanese planes. The important point of the Mitchell—G-2 controversy was that the War Department rejected his findings *in toto,* blindly accepted its own sources—and evidently continued in this policy into World War II.

** The copy of this report in Mitchell's personal Army file (201) has "??????" penciled in the margin opposite this statement; it was perhaps used by the government in its prosecution of his court-martial.

"none of these can be seriously considered for a moment upon the basis of this report, even were the War Department carried away as is General Mitchell . . ." The report, G-4 said, needed review by field commanders "having a broader point of view" than Mitchell.

Thus the Army's four chief divisions agreed with War Plans that Mitchell's warnings had no real meaning for the nation. Their findings, with their baffling variety of grounds for disapproval, were made within the Army hierarchy over a long period. Hints of these reactions must have reached Mitchell, undoubtedly causing one of the great frustrations of his career, and when General Patrick, his last hope for firm support, finally made his comments, there was little to cheer Mitchell or his friends.

Mitchell's dramatic forecast of a Japanese attack on Pearl Harbor failed to impress Patrick: "This should be of value to the [Hawaiian] Department commander. No comments are necessary. And this is, of course, a suppositious enemy plan of operation, and in view of the known aerial strength of the enemy under consideration would not seem to be possible of execution at the present time."

Patrick said it was "of course an impossibility" to base 650 planes in Hawaii, as Mitchell urged. Mitchell had insisted that a 200-plane force in Hawaii was a minimum, and that fewer planes would be of no use at all. Patrick said: "This is certainly not a correct conclusion."

Patrick challenged Mitchell directly on many points:

As to the claim that Japan was the second-ranking air power, this was "not a correct statement."

As to Mitchell's assertion that the Japanese could fly: "There is a great difference of opinion as to the flying ability of the Japanese. Prior to this inspection the consensus of opinion was that the Japanese do not make good fliers but that they are steadily improving, and with their psychological attitude of mind toward sacrifice they would undoubtedly be dangerous opponents."

Mitchell's evaluation of Japanese plane factories drew a flat rejection: "The statements herein are at variance with those submitted by the military attaché."

Patrick challenged Mitchell's theory that air power had no restrictions: "The Air Service is undoubtedly restricted in its action, and any plans that are made should be based on the actual performance of present types."

The Chief also said Mitchell overestimated the ability of the Japanese to make modern war, saying that they lacked oil, for one thing.

Since Mitchell's inspection, he added, many of the faults noted had been rectified—and Patrick did agree that Guam should be considered as a U.S. base, that a single commander should direct all forces on island bases, and that the General Staff should study Mitchell's Triangular Plan of the Pacific.

In the end the Mitchell report came to naught after its route through the Army channels. Some parts of it were sent to Hawaii and the Philippines for the "information" of commanders. The new commander in Hawaii, succeeding Summerall, gave this opinion of the Mitchell report:

"It is considered unwise to reopen this controversial question. This report contains many excellent principles, helpful operations, training and war-preparations plans. On this count it has much value. The value is, however, harmfully affected by theories at present unpractical of solution."

The Hawaiian chief expressed regret that Mitchell found fault with the island defenses "without a statement of the reasons for the conditions criticized, which were well known"—most of the shortages, he implied, were due to a lack of funds, and not to the ineptness of local commanders or lack of appreciation for air power.

Thus, after a piecemeal assault upon his report by staff officers, Mitchell's work was cast aside. His critics were unanimously right on one point—his report was much more than a summary of his trip through the Pacific in the nine months of 1923 and 1924. It bore the fruit of his career, the lessons of the bombing tests, his European tour of inspection, his private "spy reports" from military attachés abroad, and his five years of incessant promotion of new aviation techniques.

As the first trained airman to inspect the American position in the Pacific he had found dangerous shortcomings; he had sounded the first alarm over Japan's rising air power; he became the most insistent prophet of the inevitable clash between Japan and the

United States. Even more important than the intuitive description of the opening of that war were his theories of how Japan would use her bases in the island chains she held under mandate, his warning of the dangers of an American advance through the South Pacific in the face of Japanese air power, and his insistence on the strategic importance of Alaska and the Aleutians.

Some details Mitchell had added were to become vital American concerns in the future—especially his comments on the Chinese military potential—but they drew little attention from the Army. He saw both Chinese and Japanese in a new light, and he believed that the Japanese visualized, as he did, the coming Pacific war and were preparing for it. He was one of perhaps half a dozen men of his day equipped to make such an estimate of this great theater and its future as an aerial strategist, and the only one who had done so.

For several reasons his contemporaries in Washington rejected his theories. Commanders with niggardly budgets felt only irritation when they were told that they could not meet the potential threat of the future; he had not paused to explain that it might take many years of slow, patient building before the United States would be able to cope with the military problems he outlined. Even if they had been disposed to act, the Pacific commanders were unable to follow his suggestions, and the War Department was unable to provide the means for major reforms.

The form of his work added to the dismay of brother officers, a long document that was by turns travelogue, engineering report, technical treatise, training manual, and a revision of past U.S. strategic concepts. It was eloquent, even flamboyant, but most of his theories had been buttressed in extended detail. He failed to win his audience, and in part the failure may have been due to his refusal to express himself in the orthodox lexicon of the infantryman or cavalryman who still thought of world conflict in terms of the war in France.

Staff officers of the War Department, already smarting from the effects of his long campaign, may have sensed that this report summarized his career as prophet and crusader. In any event, they saw within it, with few exceptions, only the distorted visions of a dreamer who had dreamt too long.

15

General Mitchell's Whole Course Has Been So Lawless

Mitchell returned to Washington in July of 1924 with a new sense of urgency, with the threat of Japanese air power so ominous to him that he could all but hear the crump of bombs on sleepy Pearl Harbor. The high command, as he knew so well, could not share his vision. The President, the Secretaries of War and Navy, the Army General Staff and the Navy General Board still adamantly opposed a unified air force and almost everything else he favored.

As he began the sixth year of his struggle—and his last in uniform—he determined to make Washington hear him, at whatever cost. He had not yet publicly expressed resentment of his superiors, but a hint of the growing frustrations he must have felt were reflected in the efficiency report put into his record by Patrick during this summer:

"He is impulsive, and in dealing with subordinates frequently shows evidence of temper and a tendency to use measures unnecessarily harsh. His recommendations frequently fail to take into account conditions actually existing and which must be, in a measure, controlling. He is erratic and his opinions on many matters are frequently biased."

There was no one on the General Staff to translate these complaints from an airman's point of view. Mitchell's insistence upon efficiency from his staff was growing with his increasing awareness of the drift toward world crisis. And as to "conditions actually existing," Patrick meant that there were simply no funds to build the air force of which Mitchell dreamed. Most baffling to Mitchell of all his problems, and one finally insoluble, was how to combat the ignorance of his profession, how to convince his brother officers of the vital role of the airplane in the nation's future security, without breaking the bonds of essential military discipline, the need for which he recognized and, fundamentally, respected throughout his career.

This year Mitchell had no such dramatic device to win attention as the bombing tests of 1921—and by now both the military and the public seemed to have forgotten that triumph. The nation's mood was such that Mitchell's warnings would have gone unheeded if he had cried them in the streets.

The Leopold-Loeb case had begun to unfold in Chicago. The Bonus Bill was passed, over the President's veto. The evangelist Billy Sunday stormed over the sawdust trail in an aura of brimstone. Rotogravure sections of Sunday newspapers pictured Pavlova, the Dolly Sisters, the Four Horsemen of Notre Dame, Johnny Weissmuller and Gertrude Ederle, Pearl White, Helen Wills, the eighty-six-year-old golfer, John D. Rockefeller—and the Navy dirigible *Shenandoah* on her first flight since a recent crash in a storm, with her smiling young skipper, Commander Zachary Lansdowne.

Lenin had died and Trotsky was in exile. Benito Mussolini had seized control in Rome and defied the Chamber of Deputies, Adolf Hitler drew a five-year prison sentence for an attempted revolt in Munich, and General Ludendorff was acquitted.

Washington was rocking to the Teapot Dome scandal, in which Harding's Ohio Gang had squandered Navy oil reserves; indictments or resignations had removed Attorney General Harry Daugherty, Secretary of the Interior Albert B. Fall and Navy Secretary Denby—the latter replaced by Chief Justice Dwight Wilbur of California.

Calvin Coolidge, with a new air of confidence, was running for a full term of his own, on a platform of economy and U.S. isolation. The income tax had been slashed by 25 percent; in four years, government spending had been reduced by almost 50 percent. The hapless Democrats had needed 103 ballots to nominate John W. Davis of West Virginia to challenge Coolidge. Mitchell's candidate was a forlorn hope, Senator Bob La Follette of Wisconsin. Coolidge was to receive the largest majority in American history, almost sixteen million votes.

Mitchell found that a familiar pattern had continued in Washington during his absence. Assistant Secretary of War Dwight Davis had announced plans for American mobilization and said that in case of war, industry would be ready to the last man and the last machine. The Washington *Post* was skeptical: "When the next war comes, how will it come? Will it arrive in familiar guise, giving full notice of its approach . . . or will it come in its own way, without regard for the plan so laboriously developed for the guidance of industry? War preparations of foreign powers are largely in the development of air forces . . . The attack will come from the air."

Mitchell was also joined by Admiral Fullam, who wrote to the *Post:* "Preparedness is vital, and conservatism may be fatal. The Army and Navy air forces are inadequate . . . if we continue to . . . depreciate the value of new weapons we will face inevitable and humiliating defeat in the next war on the sea."

Patrick had tried to fight the air battle in his own way while Mitchell was absent, and his failure strengthened Mitchell's conviction that the military hierarchy was hopelessly conservative. Patrick, working through Army channels with a restraint whose lack he deplored in Mitchell, urged the adoption of an Army-sponsored report by the Lassiter Board, a group of officers who believed that mass production of a large U.S. air force should begin immediately. Patrick got no more action with his gentle approach than Mitchell had by his defiance of authority.

In June, Patrick tried again with an appeal to the War Department: "The Air Service is practically demobilized and unable to play its part in any national emergency, or even to meet the many peacetime demands for service." The Army's response was the further reduction of air strength; during the year one air group was pared to almost nothing. Two squadrons, the 13th and 26th, were inactivated, and the 60th Squadron was reduced to forty-two men. Only ten officers were assigned to this entire group.

One of Mitchell's cherished projects got under way in the spring of 1924, the Round the World flight of four Douglas World Cruisers, two of which managed to complete the six-month trip around the globe. The flight had opened inauspiciously, with Secretary Weeks keeping the departing fliers waiting in an anteroom for almost an hour before he emerged to gape at them: "Who're these people?" When he was told of their mission, he shook hands quickly and said the flight was "a good idea." The aviators were then herded to the White House for an official farewell, and waited while parties of farmers and Indians went in to see Coolidge before them. The President had little time for fliers. A photographer lined them up in the garden, leaving a vacant place in the center for Coolidge, who at last trotted out to pose, saying, "Hurry up, hurry up," stood briefly in place, then disappeared.

Leslie Arnold, one of the men who completed the flight, retained bitter memories of the farewell: "When we got to Japan, the emperor had us out, and the people welcomed us in China. We saw the King of Siam—the king had a big picture of Mitchell in his study. Then we saw the Presidents of Turkey and France and the kings of Rumania and England. And all the time we were thinking of the miserable departure we had had out of our own government."

The fliers came back to Bolling Field on September 9, delayed in their schedule by bad weather. Coolidge and several Cabinet members plodded about in the rain, waiting for four hours.

Mitchell took off and flew out to meet the big planes, then conducted them—the *Chicago* and the *New Orleans*—to a landing on the bumpy Bolling runway. Their flying time was just under three hundred hours, an average of 74 miles an hour; they had lost one plane in an Alaskan crash and another after a motor failure in the North Sea, but they had made it, and were the first men to circle the planet by air. A French effort had ended with a crash in Shanghai, and the British had given up off the coast of Siberia. It was an American triumph, hailed by newspapers and followed by calls for the building of a great air force.

When the National Aeronautical Association met in Dayton in October, Coolidge sent Mitchell as his representative, and he used his prestige as presidential spokesman to make his first public utterance of his concept of strategic bombing, the use of planes against civilian targets and populations. It was familiar talk to his lieutenants, but no American had discussed the topic openly. He saw more wars as inevitable, and predicted that American planes attacking an enemy might "so smash up his means of production, supply and transportation . . . that there is a great probability that the armies will never come into contact on the field of battle." * He repeated forcefully his forecast that the true naval weapon of the future was the submarine, and that surface navies were obsolete.

Mitchell made his final official visit to McCook Field about this time. Almost as if he knew that it was a farewell, he told the officers and men in a lecture of what he had seen in the Pacific, and of the kinds of planes and armament the coming war would demand.

He then took another daring step. Since the leak of his report on the bombing tests of 1921, he had been under orders from Secretary Weeks to publish nothing without War Department clearance, and had obeyed. In October 1924, Thomas B. Costain, then a *Saturday Evening Post* editor, asked Mitchell to write a series of articles which would later be published as a book by George P. Putnam. The two made plans over a luncheon of brook trout at Mitchell's home, a meal that Costain remembered fondly for years. The editor also remembered Mitchell: "I can recall how quiet and modest Billy Mitchell seemed to me. There was something boyish about him. He had no feeling of his own importance, but he was burning with zeal."

Mitchell agreed to write the articles, provided that President Coolidge gave permission—he apparently saw this as a way to circumvent the order of Secretary Weeks. Mitchell left the only account of their meeting with Coolidge: "The President reiterated his great interest in aeronautics . . . and said he considered a series of articles on this subject to be beneficial, and that I should obtain the permission of my superior officer, the Chief of Air

* It is difficult to determine the extent of Mitchell's debt to Guilio Douhet, the Italian prophet of strategic bombing; his writings do not mention Douhet. He did correspond with Douhet's partner, the bomber manufacturer Gianni Caproni, during World War I, and possibly saw Douhet's book, *Il domino dell'aria*, soon after it appeared in 1921. A five-page extract from the book was in Air Service files by 1922, and a typed translation of the first one hundred pages was used by the Air Service Field Officers School at Langley Field the following year. The Italian air attaché, Guidoni, reported that Mitchell frequently discussed Douhet's ideas and was much impressed with them. It is logical to suppose that Mitchell's familiarity with Douhet's theories began during World War I.

Service." He added that when he told Patrick of the President's approval, Patrick also gave him permission. Weeks knew nothing of the arrangement.

What Mitchell failed to tell Patrick, even later, was that Coolidge, with a cautious second thought, had sent him a letter for the record:

"My Dear General Mitchell: Confirming my conversation with you this morning, I do not know of any objection to your preparing some articles so far as I am concerned, but of course I cannot speak for your superior officers. The matter should be taken up with them and their decision in relation to the articles followed."

When Mitchell got this letter he already had Patrick's permission to publish and was technically in the clear. It was only Weeks who had a surprise in store.*

The first article appeared just before Christmas, an expanded version of his Dayton speech on unrestricted aerial warfare. It was the first such publication most of his readers had seen: "In a trice, aircraft have set aside all ideas of frontiers. The whole country now becomes the frontier, and in case of war, one place is just as exposed to attack as another." In coming wars, fleets of hundreds of planes would devastate nations so that they could not rebuild in wartime. He defended this kind of war as less expensive and more humane, since it was briefer; it would be fought by a pampered warrior class "like the armored knights in the Middle Ages."

He wrote on commercial aviation: "The world itself will be made correspondingly smaller, because distance will be measured in hours and not in miles. The substantial and continued development of air power should be based on a sound commercial aviation. America is in a better position to develop commercial aviation than any other nation."

Mitchell's series of five articles ended in March 1925, with a

* When Weeks later demanded an explanation of the publication, Patrick insisted that Mitchell had deceived him by withholding the President's letter from him: "If I had known the President's permission . . . was contingent upon the approval of 'his superior officers' . . . I should certainly have taken the matter up with the War Department . . . and required Gen. Mitchell to submit copies of the articles to me." Mitchell's rejoinder was that he had permission from both Patrick and Coolidge, and that the Army could have halted the periodic and widely spaced articles if it had wished.

discussion of "How Should We Organize Our Air Power?" and repeated his theme of a single organization, under a single director. He urged that the matter be studied with care, "because air power has not only come to stay but is and will be a dominating factor in the world's development."

Mitchell said that the decision in any war must finally be won on the ground, but he attacked orthodox Army and Navy leaders who found their models in the dead past as "psychologically unfit" to judge the promise of aviation.

These magazine articles appeared while Mitchell and the Navy were squabbling over another bombing test against a battleship. The new hull of the U.S.S. *Washington*, scheduled to be scrapped under the Limitation of Armaments treaty, was battered by the Navy off the Virginia coast in a highly secret test. Mitchell was invited and watched with impatience as the Navy went through its experiments; he thought them pointless. Two sand-filled bombs were dropped from 4000 feet, their armor-piercing points striking the ship's deck. Underwater charges of TNT were set off at varying distances from the hull and opened holes in the ship. She was already sinking when a warship's guns sent her under. The press printed piecemeal reports of the Navy's version of the tests, saying that the *Washington* had withstood both bombs and depth charges, and had had to be sunk by naval gunfire.

Mitchell was spoiling to expose the facts. He got his chance before a House committee headed by Representative Julian Lampert of Michigan; he told the congressmen that "no bombs were used in any shape, form or fashion," that the Navy had attempted subterfuge and that it should be closely questioned.

Admiral Sims joined him. Sims said that the Navy had made ridiculous claims that wooden plugs could have stopped up the holes made by underwater charges in the *Washington*'s hull: "Now, if anybody knows anything about the double bottom of a battleship, he can imagine them crawling around in there looking for leaks and putting pine plugs in them . . . there isn't a pine tree growing in America today that would stop it up."

One friendly member of the Lampert committee was Representative Frank R. Reid of Illinois, who led Mitchell as if he were on a witness stand in court, and drew some striking phrases from him: "The Army and the Navy are the oldest institutions we have. They place everything on precedent. You can't do that in the air business. You've got to look ahead.

"I think if we plunged into war tomorrow," Mitchell continued, "it would take at least two years to get on a par with England or Japan . . . an air force could reduce our Philippine islands easily and we couldn't defend them with our present armament."

Reid said: "You say Japan could take the Philippines and Hawaii and we couldn't stop it?"

"Of course," Mitchell said. ". . . Alaska is far more important than the Philippines or Hawaii, and should be protected by air as well as on land."

Reid openly sided with Mitchell: "If you suffer any criticism, I think this committee will want to go on record to say that you have helped the country to be the greatest air republic in the world."

Committee appearances now demanded much of Mitchell's time, since Congress was investigating aviation on many fronts; he was always a star witness. He grew bolder in his testimony, as if deliberately inviting a challenge. He seemed to be enjoying himself. Admiral Sims thought that Mitchell "had the time of his life."

Hap Arnold, who was now in Patrick's office as director of information, feared that Mitchell was pressing too hard. "Billy, take it easy," Arnold said. "We need you. Don't throw away everything just to beat out some guy who doesn't understand. Air power is coming."

He asked Mitchell to put an assistant in his office as a "balance wheel," to help prepare less sensational testimony. Arnold thought the old-timers should be handled more gently: "Stop saying all these things about the independent air arm that are driving these old Army and Navy people crazy!"

Mitchell only smiled: "When senior officers won't see the facts, you've got to do something unorthodox, perhaps an explosion."

Then, as if he had made up his mind to take a new role in the struggle, he told Arnold: "I'm doing it for the good of the air force, for the future air force, for the good of you fellows. I can afford to do it. You can't."

Mitchell continued his familiar charges in Congress and the

uproar increased in the winter months of 1925. He was almost constantly in the headlines.

Outside the committee rooms Mitchell looked like anything but a crusading fanatic. Visitors to his office in the Munitions Building found it a carefree museum, where Mitchell sat behind a desk littered with papers, charts, photographs, sample plane parts, a steel fragment of a 2000-pound bomb. Instead of military splendor, Mitchell often wore a golf outfit with knickers and buckskin shoes. A pair of rubber fishing waders was draped over a hat rack. Model planes hung from the ceiling, twirling gently overhead. The walls were almost covered with pictures and souvenirs—the steering wheel of a Zeppelin shot down in France, the brass name plate of the U.S.S. *Alabama,* diagrams of air-attack schemes, water colors of planes. There was a huge, grinning tiger skull, from the largest man-eater ever killed in Siam, he told guests. A black book on his desk, marked "secret," bore the number and location of every Army plane, the only readiness record of its kind in the country.

By now Mitchell had added a new charge against his opposition; he said that critics were being silenced by high-ranking officers, and that air-minded men feared to speak. Many senior Army officers, he said, had probably falsified evidence "with the evident intent to confuse Congress." When these claims reached the headlines, Secretary Weeks, already smarting from the *Saturday Evening Post* incident, called in Patrick for a conference on Mitchell's future. The sorely tried Secretary reminded the general that Mitchell's four-year appointment as Assistant Chief of the Air Service would expire on March 26, and he asked: "Do you want him reappointed?"

"I do," Patrick said. He conceded that Mitchell was difficult, but said that he had "carried out in a fairly satisfactory manner his agreement to work with me."

For the first time Mitchell's tenuous position had been formally discussed. He might be removed as Assistant Chief at the pleasure of Patrick, Weeks or Coolidge, and if he was removed, would lose his temporary rank of brigadier general and revert to his permanent rank of colonel. Therefore, from the moment of the Patrick-Weeks conference, his banishment became a distinct possibility. Leaders of the anti-Mitchell faction within the War Department, especially the hostile infantryman General Hugh A. Drum, provided Weeks with frequent reminders of the possibility.

Mitchell refused to soften his testimony, and his attacks increased in vigor as they became more frequent.

On the same day that he told the Lampert committee that many officers were afraid to testify, Mitchell also charged that the United States had only nineteen planes "fit for war" (he later corrected this to mean pursuit planes only), that the War Department had ignored his Pacific report, and that they had failed to support him in his struggle with the Navy. He added that he expected to be punished for his statements. Chairman Lampert praised him for his courage and refreshing testimony, doing his duty even "with the expectation of discipline" being meted out to him.

The Navy greeted the occasion as a long-awaited opportunity. Admiral Hilary Jones urged punishment for Mitchell. He told the committee to "admonish all malcontents and agitators in the government service to attend strictly to business or get out of the service." Secretary of the Navy Wilbur replied angrily to Lampert, protesting the charge that naval officers had been cowed: "They have the freedom to express their opinions on any matter."

The Navy's reaction prompted Weeks to ask Mitchell for an explanation of his charges, and Mitchell replied with a long, almost defiant memorandum, affirming his charges, saying that he had advised younger officers to keep out of the debate and allow him to "assume all responsibilities because of possible consequences."

He then cited to Weeks many instances of testimony he thought misleading: Admiral Hilary Jones had been wrong about the British Royal Air Force as an "unsatisfactory" service; he attached documents as evidence. There were false reports on British war games involving bombing of battleships. There had been false reports on the U.S.S. *Washington* and *Iowa* tests, on the costs of planes and battleships. He especially challenged testimony of General Drum, who had claimed that the United States was a world leader in aviation. "The only way in which aviation in the U.S. is better," Mitchell said, "is in its unorganized resources."

Even now Patrick defended Mitchell as guilty of nothing more serious than "poor judgment," and said that he should merely be admonished. Weeks was not convinced. He began to feel out the possibility of ousting Mitchell. The *New York Times,* sniffing the rumors, printed the first gossip that Mitchell "may not only be demoted to a colonelcy, but perhaps charged with insubordination."

Representative Randolph Perkins of New Jersey, the chief examiner for the Lampert committee, said he had learned that both Mitchell and Admiral William Moffett were "going to be disciplined" for their testimony in support of air power. Reporters who asked Weeks and Wilbur about the rumor got vague replies; no final decision had been made, they said. The headlines reflected the truth: "FOES MAY FORCE MITCHELL OUT."

Weeks went before an executive session of the Senate Military Affairs Committee to explain his growing impatience with Mitchell. He said that the airman's claim that only nineteen U.S. planes were ready for war was absurd. As for the Pacific report on which Mitchell had charged inaction, Weeks had never seen a copy.

During his secret session with the senators, Weeks told them he had first tried to muzzle Mitchell after the bombing tests of 1921: "I was having a series of complaints, constant complaints, from the Navy Department that what General Mitchell was saying in the press did not cover the entire facts, and that it made an unreasonable reflection on the Navy Department, and we want to live in peace with other departments in the government . . . I thought I was warranted in saying to General Mitchell that I wanted to see what he published."

The *New York Times,* though it was not always strong in Mitchell's defense, thought that the time had come to defend him: "It may be that Gen. Mitchell sometimes talks indiscreetly, but he should have the credit of his admirable work in France . . . and for demonstrating that Army aviators could sink battleships with bombs. Gen. Mitchell has done more by example and initiative to advance military aviation than any other officer in either the Army or the Navy. . . .

"To get rid of him by demotion or exile would be a scandalous misuse of authority."

Patrick made a final effort to save Mitchell, suggesting to Weeks that he "be admonished by the War Department for his attitude and his methods," but Weeks had made up his mind. By March 1 Washington rumor had it that Mitchell would definitely not be reappointed.

The White House would say only that the President would appoint as Assistant Air Chief the man Weeks recommended. On March 3, the eve of Inauguration Day, Coolidge and Weeks conferred on the Mitchell problem, amid published reports that spies had been shadowing Mitchell, his favorite newspaper reporters and some naval aviators. Mitchell suspected the Navy. "They're welcome to shadow me," he said. "I have nothing to hide."

Newspapers also reported that both Weeks and Wilbur had warned Coolidge that he must choose between them and Mitchell—if he remained, both Secretaries would resign. Soon afterward Representative Fiorello La Guardia of New York introduced a bill that would protect any Army or Navy officer who was asked to testify before Congress, providing that he could not be transferred or demoted, no matter what his opinions. A joint resolution praised Mitchell's efforts to reveal the weakness of U.S. military aviation: ". . . Now, therefore, be it resolved . . . that we hereby compliment Brig. Gen. Mitchell and commend his position in this matter . . . and severely condemn the evident purpose of the national administration in its attempt to punish and discredit him. We believe in his courage and in his devotion to the nation . . ." This, like so many other attempts to aid Mitchell, died in committee.

Mitchell was the major figure in Washington in the eyes of society reporters, who looked anxiously for him in the crowd at the annual Army-Navy reception at the White House. They found him, "moving like a flagship" in the throng. One reporter sketched the scene: "General Billy Mitchell WAS there . . . with Mrs. Mitchell on his arm, he made a sort of triumphal progress through the drawing room, and was stopped every few feet by friends crowding in to shake his hand. He's a romantic sort of personage . . . with his swanky air and the rows on rows of decorations foreign and domestic pinned on his chest. Mrs. Mitchell looked like a bride, all in flowing white."

Mitchell was chairman of the floor committee for the inaugural ball, and caused a sensation when he announced, a few days before the event, that he must resign from the committee because of pressure of his duties. The rumors were that Weeks and Wilbur had forced him out, by refusing to attend if Mitchell remained in this important post. Mitchell's response to this was an appearance at a masked ball at the Italian embassy, wearing a costume that he had kept secret even from Betty and his sister Harriet—a sailor's uniform.

The noisy season of the Mitchell battle ended on March 5, 1925, when Weeks told Coolidge that he wanted to drop Mitchell as Assistant Chief of the Air Service. The particular reason he gave was the "false" testimony to the Lampert committee, in reporting only nineteen U.S. planes ready for war. Weeks said there were actually 1592 war-ready planes, 763 of them in storage; he did not add that most of these were left over from the World War, and that Mitchell thought them unsafe for flying, let alone for combat.

The real Air Service problem, Weeks told the President, was its failure to land the appropriation of $60,000,000 it had sought. He scolded Mitchell for his criticism of higher officers, including "those distinguished men who conducted operations on the other side which resulted in ever-lasting glory to American arms and the winning of the war." This, Weeks said, was an "unconscionable" attack.

He revealed the depths of his resentment in the final words of his request:

"General Mitchell's whole course has been so lawless, so contrary to the building up of an efficient organization, so lacking in reasonable team work, so indicative of a personal desire for publicity at the expense of everyone with whom he is associated, that his actions render him unfit for a high administrative position.

"I write this with great regret because he is a gallant officer, with an excellent war record. But his record since the war has been such that he has forfeited the good opinion of those who are familiar with the facts and who desire to promote the best interests of national defense."

Coolidge approved, and the next day Weeks chose what he thought the perfect moment to announce Mitchell's downfall.

The General Staff, eager to disprove Mitchell's claim that anti-aircraft fire was ineffective, had ordered tests for March 6 at Fort Monroe, Virginia. Mitchell went down to supervise three planes which were to tow targets for the guns. Through the Army grapevine he had learned that Weeks had requested his banishment, and before he left Washington he dictated a statement to be released when his demotion was announced:

"The question of my reappointment as Assistant Chief of the Air Service is a small matter. The question of reorganization of our system of national defense is a big matter . . .

"As soon as the sound of the cannon had ceased on the western front, the forces of retrogression began to work in our country. This was because our participation in the war had been of such short duration that the old, inefficient, bureaucratic system of handling our national defense had not yet been entirely eliminated and replaced by new and efficient systems and personnel as was the case in the countries of Europe and with us during the Civil War . . .

"Armies and navies are no longer capable of enunciating or putting into effect the complete military policy for a country. The voice of the air must be listened to in all councils with equal force." He called again for a department of defense, repeated his faith in the future of aviation, and pledged himself to keep up the fight.

At Fort Monroe, Mitchell's three planes flew slowly back and forth over the guns along a fixed course while artillerymen hammered away at the sleeve targets towed behind—targets ten feet long and four feet in diameter. Weeks and his General Staff experts were confident of success, and had invited many officers, congressmen and reporters, who saw the gunners fail. The coast artillery fired thirty-nine times without a hit, and when two planes dropped to 1000 feet and drifted the targets above massed machine guns, which fired many thousands of rounds, the targets showed only one hit.

Washington headlines paired Mitchell's downfall and the failure of the Army's anti-aircraft demonstration: "MITCHELL OUSTED . . . BLOW TO MITCHELL SHOCKS CONGRESS". . ."AIR TARGETS DEFY WEEKS' GUNNERS."

Mitchell asked Patrick to have him assigned to Chicago, where he could command a busy area and continue his leadership of the service by overseeing the work of engineers at McCook Field. The War Department denied this request and sentenced Mitchell to a lonely post at Fort Sam Houston, Texas, near San Antonio. He was replaced by an old companion, Lieutenant Colonel James E. Fechet, a spit-and-polish cavalryman who had been flying for eight years. Fechet was elevated to brigadier general.

About twenty-five of Mitchell's friends gathered for a surprise farewell luncheon at Bolling Field. Mitchell entered the room casually, as if he saw nothing unusual, and sat at the head of the table. As the others remained standing he looked quizzically about him. A spokesman said: "General, we're all going to apply for transfer to go with you. If they deny the applications, and of course they will, we're going to resign."

Mitchell was furious: "Sit down, every damned one of you. This is insurrection. Not one of you will resign. Not a one. And that's an order."

Then, as if it had occurred to him for the first time that he would give these men no more orders, he looked at them and said in a low voice: "Who will carry on . . . when I'm gone?"

There was a long silence. One officer remembers: "We obeyed him. We obeyed him the rest of our lives. And long after he was dead."

Hap Arnold gave him a farewell party at the Army and Navy Club, with both Patrick and Fechet in the crowd. Mitchell made a brief speech, looking back over twenty years of struggle to persuade the Army to adopt new methods: "It was with the greatest difficulty that the Army was made to adopt the telephone, the telegraph, the automobile and the radio. When all the people were illuminating their homes with kerosene, the Army continued to use candles. When the people used gas the Army used kerosene, and when all else used electricity the Army continued for years to stick to the old illuminants.

"In the Indian campaigns the savages were better armed than

our regular troops, as were the Spaniards in 1898, and as our opponents would have been in the World War had we not taken the weapons of our associates."

Arnold gave a barbecue party in the evening, an occasion marked by hilarity. Arnold had tried to invite Patrick, but was prevented by the general's irritating habit of interrupting his subordinates with his nervous rejoinder: "Yes, I know! . . . I know—I know!"

"Sir," Arnold said in Patrick's office, "we're having—"

"Yes, yes, yes, I know!"

"And we would like—"

"Yes, I know, I know," Patrick said, without listening.

"We would like, sir—"

"All right, I know, I know!" Arnold thought Patrick must have been invited by others, and left the office. The party was a great success, but Patrick did not appear. The next morning the Chief called Arnold to demand to know why he had not been invited, and when he could get a word in, Arnold began: "Sir—"

"Yes, yes, I know," Patrick said. And then, abruptly, as if it dawned on him how the misunderstanding had occurred, he halted, speechless, snatched a paperweight from his desk and hurled it at Arnold's head. Hap ducked out of the office.

The farewells of the Air Service were more in celebration of Mitchell's continued defiance than in sorrow over his banishment, since his friends expected him to return to Washington. And there were others who hailed him as he was ousted. Josephus Daniels came surprisingly to Mitchell's defense and said he would not have demoted him if he had been Secretary of War. "I don't think we can adequately protect our coastline without the airplane," Daniels said. "The thing today is the conquest of the air, and America is only playing with the idea when it ought to be leading."

The press was full of acclamations for the deposed rebel, as if he already lay in a hero's grave. The Cleveland *Press,* typical of many newspapers, said: "We may wait a hundred years for another such display of courage."

16

Almost Treasonable Administration

Mitchell's final public appearance before leaving Washington was with Will Rogers; he had promised to take him up on his first flight, a brief tour over the city. The humorist had drawn a crowd of reporters and photographers, and feigned fright as he entered the *Osprey*.

"Have you got cotton in your ears, Will?" Mitchell asked, and Rogers answered: "I just use that in the Senate gallery."

Photographers snapped pictures, and Rogers said he could envision them being used as the "Last Photograph of the Deceased." Rogers claimed that Mitchell flew so close to the Washington Monument that "if the thing had had handles on it he would have lost a passenger."

As they landed Mitchell told Rogers that he had just made his last flight as a brigadier and would revert to colonel at midnight, condemned to Texas. This piqued Rogers' curiosity, and they had a long talk about aviation and its future. It was the beginning of a friendship that ended only with the death of Rogers in a plane crash with Wiley Post. The humorist admired Mitchell: "He never squealed and he never whined. He knows that some day America will have to have a tremendous air force, but he can't understand why we aren't training it now . . . it does seem a strange way to repay a man who has fought for us through a war, and who has fought harder for us in peace, to be reprimanded for telling the truth . . ."

Rogers was soon joking about the problem, with his Ziegfeld

Follies audiences: "We ought to have the greatest air defense in the world. We've got more air . . . France gave Mitchell the Croix de Guerre, England the Order of the King, and the Republican Administration gave him the Order of the Tin Can . . . He is the only man ever connected with high-up aviation in Washington that used the air for anything but exhaling purposes."

Mitchell spent the next two months on furlough. Betty was due to bear their first child, and he left her with her parents in Detroit rather than expose her to the long journey and the isolation of his new post. He went for a few days to Milwaukee, where the old family home, Meadowmere, was being sold. Newspapers admired the mansion, its reception hall paneled in mahogany inlaid with brass, the rooms filled with Oriental curios, furniture of bamboo and teak inlaid with ivory, and fine rugs. The land was subdivided into small home sites, but the massive house was preserved for public use; it had cost $100,000 more than forty years before. Six carloads of furniture were shipped to Boxwood, Mitchell's home in Middleburg, Virginia.

The Wisconsin Legislature asked Mitchell to run for Congress; he declined, though his loyal sister Ruth thought he would have been elected unanimously. Reporters who found him in Milwaukee got spirited quotations from him: "I haven't even begun to fight . . . the job is now to jar the bureaucrats out of their swivel chairs."

He reached San Antonio in late June and was assigned to comfortable quarters on the Parade Ground. He had no troop command and his duties as Air Officer of the area were light, but correspondence poured in, and editors and publishers pursued him. His new secretary, Maydell Blackmon, was one of the busiest on the post.

Mitchell then flew to California in July, and inspected an aircraft plant in San Diego, and made a public speech in which he gave no sign of becoming more docile. The air force of the United States was "almost extinct," and the country was likely to learn, as usual, from "the disaster of war." The next war would be won by the nation which understood new weapons before war came. He urged a campaign to educate the people about air power.

He inspected some new Navy planes in San Diego, PN flying

boats with duralumin hulls, in which the Navy was planning an adventure. Three of the clumsy craft, with a top speed of 75 miles an hour, were to attempt to fly from California to Hawaii, which had never been done. With his customary thoroughness, Mitchell learned all he could about the planned flight.

Commander John Rodgers, an able young naval aviator, would lead the attempt, but control was in the hands of nonflying officers. Mitchell was convinced that the real mission of this hazardous flight was to gain publicity for naval aviation, as a counter to his own campaign, rather than to advance aviation itself. There were signs of impending disaster. The Navy fliers were not practiced navigators, and none had made very long flights over open water. The only practice runs of these planes over a course of comparable length had been up and down the Delaware River, where navigation was a simple problem.

The unwieldy planes would be heavily loaded, carrying five men each, and must buck prevailing westerly winds. Mitchell was skeptical of their refueling plans, which involved picket ships stationed in the Pacific at 200-mile intervals. The Navy's equipment seemed inadequate. The leader of the Army's Round the World flight, Lieutenant Lowell Smith, was in California, but the Navy had not asked his advice. Mitchell left the Coast with the feeling that these planes would not reach their goal and that the flight was just such a venture as would seem plausible only to inexperienced battleship officers who had turned to aviation as an antidote for Army triumphs.

Patrick kept a close eye on Mitchell from Washington during his Texas stay; the Chief seemed to fear that even in exile he would cause further trouble. When he read in newspapers of a flight of twenty-four planes flying from Kelly Field to the opening of a Dallas airport as an "honor guard" for Mitchell, Patrick sent a stiff reprimand to the field commander and demanded a report on every future flight in his area.

There was a rumor that Coolidge had offered Mitchell a choice before he left Washington: he could resign "for the good of the service" or go into isolation in Texas. The aviation writer Harry Bruno asked Mitchell if the story was true, and a strange, set look came over the colonel's face. "You know," he said, "when I was a kid I jumped off a barn roof with an umbrella for a chute. When I got back on my shaky pins, I had only myself to blame. And I'm still not ready to blame anyone but myself for where I land, or how." Bruno could get no more out of him.

In August the magazine *Liberty* published an article by Mitchell with a new jab at the Navy: "Exploding Disarmament Bunk: Why Have Treaties About Battleships When Airplanes Can Destroy Them?" He said once more that battleships, the most expensive of all war equipment, were near extinction: "What is keeping them up as much as anything else, and largely preventing open and free discussion of their uses, are the propaganda agencies maintained by navies . . ."

His daughter Lucy was born that month in Detroit, and Mitchell was there for a few days. He also saw his friend Henry Ford, as he often did, lunching with Ford, his son Edsel and Alfred Verville, the plane designer. Ford showed him a new plane engine he planned to produce, and it may have been at this time that Ford offered Mitchell a place as director of his aviation manufacturing. Verville saw that Mitchell was not tempted: "Well, you know, Mr. Ford, you and I would never get along. We're two forceful individuals. You'd want me to do something one way and I'd want to do it another. I'm not the man for the job. Furthermore, I have a big job to do—a big unfinished job, to carry on this fight to reorganize aviation and build up national defense."

He left familiar headlines in his wake in the Midwest, including a prediction that New York-to-Paris flights would soon become regular, and might be flown in 37 hours. He urged that the United States hurry to beat the French to the first crossings. (This was two years before Lindbergh's flight, which took 33 hours and 39 minutes.)

He was back in Texas when his new book *Winged Defense* appeared, comprised largely of his *Saturday Evening Post* articles. The censure on his writings was still in effect, but Mitchell had not submitted the book for approval. He said he had not disobeyed orders, but he sounded hopeful of trouble: "The truth of our deplorable situation is going to be put before the American people, come what may. If the War Department wants to start something, so much the better . . . then we will have a chance to remedy this unfortunate situation."

He was modest about *Winged Defense:* "This little book has

been thrown together hastily . . . from evidence that has been given before Congress, articles that have appeared in the public journals and from personal experiences. Its value lies in the ideas and theories . . . necessary for our people to consider very seriously in the development of our whole national system. The great countries of Europe have already acted along the lines indicated in this book. We are still backward."

The publisher described the book as "a bomb in the lap of American complacency." The endpapers displayed newspaper cartoons lampooning Secretary Weeks, who was now ill and on the point of resigning his office in favor of Dwight Davis, and the book was attacked as being in bad taste. Mitchell explained that the publisher had added the cartoons and that no offense was intended: "They appeared in the public press all over the country a number of months ago and I imagine they made Secretary Weeks laugh as much as anybody else. I think they made everybody laugh.

"Secretary Weeks is a graduate of the Naval Academy, and was a Navy officer and has many friends in the Navy, sees them frequently and this is bound to influence him as it would any other human being. But I want it distinctly understood that as far as I am personally concerned, I have the kindliest feelings for him individually."

On the last day of August, Mitchell almost lost his life in a plane crash. He was inspecting the old Remount Station at Fort Sam Houston, which was being made into a flying field; mule teams, trucks and workmen were everywhere. After his early-morning visit Mitchell took off with Harry Short, his mechanic, dog trainer and companion of many years. Many of the Corps Area staff officers watched as they left the runway.

The engine died at 80 feet and the plane, apparently doomed, hung briefly above trucks, mule teams, ditches, fences and a grove of trees. Mitchell had too little speed to turn back for the field, and too little altitude for maneuver; he turned the plane very slightly as he skimmed downward, narrowly missing animals and trucks, and put it into the only open space, in a fence corner. As the wheels struck a ditch the plane nosed forward and flopped over.

Mitchell crawled out, smiling and waving to those on the runway. "All in a day's work," he said, and went with Short to the post. His deft handling had saved him as it had in three or four other close calls in the air.

At the beginning of September two naval air mishaps caught the attention of the country, stirred Mitchell to new indignation, and finally led to the end of his Army career. The misfortunes were important in themselves; they also were of immediate moment in bringing Mitchell to court-martial.

News from the Navy's Pacific flight had been bad from the start. Of the three planes starting, one had failed to take off because of its heavy load, another had plopped into the sea not far offshore, and the third, carrying Captain Rodgers and four men, was in trouble. There had been a distress call from the plane by radio; it was running out of gas within three hundred miles of Hawaii. A change in the wind, poorly made plans or inept navigation had halted Rodgers as he neared his goal.

Late on September 1 there was news that the PN-9 was lost. Ships combed the area of its route, but as time passed without word it was clear that the plane was not on its proper course. The country kept a long vigil for the five fliers. Mitchell gave a radio broadcast from San Antonio the following night, when the search was more than thirty hours old, but he did not yet berate the Navy high command for its role in the mishap. He asked listeners to pray for the lost aviators: "They are just as much martyrs to the progress of civilization as Columbus would have been had he perished in his voyage to America."

While Mitchell was urging Texans to pray, a naval disaster was in the making to the north. The large dirigible *Shenandoah* left her hangar at Lakehurst, New Jersey, for a trip over state fairs in the Midwest—the Navy had discovered that people were thrilled by the sight of their great "battleship of the skies" when it floated over their homes, and now, despite uncertain weather and warnings from Commander Zachary Lansdowne, the Navy sent the ship out to be seen. Fall storms were raging over the Great Lakes.

Lansdowne was a popular young skipper, relaxed and laughing off duty, but coldly disciplined when aloft. He was experienced, able and fearless, presumably with some of the traits of a celebrated ancestor, John Knox, the Presbyterian reformer. Lansdowne's young wife had anxiously looked at the sky as he left Lakehurst, but he was reassuring. He would fly far to the south of the reported storms; she knew that he had protested the flight during the storm season, but had been overruled by the naval command. The *Shenandoah* was under peremptory orders to fly over the fairgrounds at Des Moines, Iowa, the next day, where taxpayers would be swarming by the thousands.

It was a warm, moonlit evening, and the ship went swiftly across Pennsylvania, over small towns beginning to light up at dusk, then over the Alleghenies, and by midnight had crossed the mountains into the safer flatlands beyond. There was no hint of trouble, the air was smooth despite a slight overcast, the engines lulled the crew of forty-three, most of them now asleep, and the gas cells of helium were at normal capacity, about 88 percent. The ship had shown no signs of weakness from storm damage of some months before, when she had been ripped from her mooring mast, tearing her nose section and two gas cells. Now she flew with many of her safety valves missing. Ten of the eighteen valves had been removed by the crew, for economy and convenience, and one of her engines had also been taken out. Her designer, Mitchell's naval critic Jerome Hunsaker, had protested these alterations, but on this flight no one gave them a thought. The *Shenandoah* was a veteran at the age of two.

About midnight the radio operator took a message into the control cabin reporting severe thunderstorms over the Lakes. Lieutenant Joseph Anderson plotted his weather map and took it to Lansdowne, who was peering through the gondola windows into the night. The skipper studied the map without comment, then went to his bunk. "Don't call me unless something unusual comes up," he said. "Talk it over with the officers in the control cabin first." This was scheduled to be Lansdowne's last flight in the ship, since he would be going on sea duty within two weeks.

Lansdowne was asleep at three o'clock when Bill Russell, a mechanic, saw the first lightning. When it began flickering in the sky both east and west, the skipper was called. The ship was now rolling a bit, bucking strong head winds at about 3000 feet. Lieutenant Anderson studied the weather reports once more and looked out at the storm clouds gathering about them. The south was the only open course. Lansdowne shook his head. He would push on westward. "That storm's still a long way off," he said. "We've been ordered to fly over a certain course, and I want to keep that course as long as I can."

By now the ship hung almost still, unable to move against the wind, even with engines turned up. They passed the city of Cambridge, Ohio, moving slowly. Lansdowne brought the ship down to 2000 feet and still could make little headway. Anderson pointed to the heavy lightning in clouds to the north. "The storm is backing up, sir. I don't understand it." Lansdowne refused to turn southward, out of its path. For a time the ship sailed easier, though she drifted slightly from her course in cross winds.

Two people in the dark countryside below looked up from their homes to see the great ship passing overhead and saw just above the *Shenandoah* a huge "boiling cloud" that looked as if "two storms had come together." The men of the *Shenandoah* sailed on over Ohio, unaware that a squall was forming above them.

By five o'clock there was occasional trouble with the engines; several of them missed fire when power was increased in an effort to hold the ship steady in the wind. A few minutes after five the crewman at the elevator controls called: "Captain, the ship's started to rise."

"Check her," Lansdowne said, but the elevatorman was helpless. He fought the wheel in vain. "She's rising two meters a second, sir. I can't check her." Lansdowne had engines speeded up once more, without effect. He saw that the nose of the ship was pointing downward as she rose. His crewmen in the car used all their controls, but still the tail rose at the dangerous angle. The ship began to roll, and the men in the bunks were shaken awake by the pitching motion.

Gas bags began distending as the ship rose; when they had reached 97 percent of capacity, crewmen uncovered the safety valves, ready to release excess gas. The ship kept rising, but in the gondola Lansdowne's low, steady voice reassured the men who struggled to control the *Shenandoah*. The safety valves were now bleeding off the gas and the ship steadied a bit; the cook was awake and about breakfast, cursing the navigators as he chased food and utensils falling about his galley. Somewhere in the ship two taut wires snapped; there was more engine trouble, and water lines were broken. The ship had risen to 5000 feet—1200 feet above the safe pressure level. From below, in the early daylight, people saw the ship "swinging like a pendulum" as her rise took her into a swift, dark cloud. The ship was entering the eye of a squall. She was now at 6000 feet, but rising so slowly that Lansdowne thought she was near the altitude limit. Preparing for a plunge, he had the men ready to release the fuel tanks in case of an emergency. The rise halted abruptly at 6300 feet and the ship plummeted, almost like a stone, and despite the release of water ballast, fell to 3200 feet in less than two minutes. One man noticed that the gas cell nearest him was so distended that it was in danger of bursting—the next one hung flabbily, its gas already gone.

In the midst of a gathering of clouds, Lansdowne finally ordered the ship turned south, and at five-thirty she started for an opening between two converging storms. She began to rise once more, faster than before.

Two engines were out, but Lansdowne ordered full speed in an effort to check the rise. The ship turned upward, rolling so that men were flung about; it was, some of them thought, like a plane in a spin. Then there was a tremendous vibration and she began to come apart at 6200 feet.

At five forty-five there was a crash far forward. The huge keel had snapped like a splinter, and a yawning hole was ripped in the bottom of the ship. Twisted girders screamed. Lansdowne, in his control car, said calmly: "Anybody who wants to can leave the car." Only two men returned to the hull. The ship was now torn almost in two, the parts bound together only by cables. Gasoline poured through the ship and there was the smell of burning cloth. Girders and wires flew wildly apart.

From below, several people watched the tail section float serenely away by itself, flapping pennants of torn fabric. The forward section, where most of the crew had slept, swooped swiftly toward the earth—and then, as the two engines tore away from below, it lifted upward and drifted, open at both ends. The first bodies plummeted to the ground. The mid-section drifted to earth with four survivors.

The tail section, with eighteen men, struck trees and finally came down in a small valley, with men leaping through the holes of its skin as they neared the earth; fifteen of them survived—and they still saw the torn bow section of the ship soaring above at 7000 feet (it had gone as high as 10,000 feet). The men in the bow, led by Charles Rosendahl, the navigator, slashed the gas cells and drifted downward in a vast circle, borne by the wind. Rosendahl and several others survived, but Lansdowne was dead, and a dozen more with him.

Within little more than an hour, hard on the heels of the rescue workers, looters and souvenir hunters were stripping the dirigible of all that could be carried away—fabric, instruments, logbooks, blankets—leaving the broken hull like a picked skeleton. Someone wrenched the Annapolis class ring from Lansdowne's finger.

Even the first reports of the tragedy hinted at the Navy's misuse of its airship on its nonmilitary mission, the controversy between Lansdowne and the Chief of Naval Operations over the weather, and the shortage of safety valves. In reply to criticism, Secretary Wilbur offered an unexpected interpretation of the wreck of the *Shenandoah* and the failure of the missing fliers in the Pacific—both incidents made him more confident than ever that no enemy could approach the United States by flying the oceans; there was no danger from aircraft.

Reporters began calling on Mitchell for a statement, and he went to work. His secretary, Maydell Blackmon, took his dictation as he slowly paced the office, seldom hesitating, sure of what he wanted to say and in command of his simple, direct and colorful phrasing. A few friends and lawyers were asked to look over the typed draft and a few changes were made. At five o'clock in the morning of September 5 he passed copies to reporters waiting in the office.

He read a few lines: "I have been asked from all parts of the country to give my opinion about the reasons for the frightful disasters that have occurred during the last few days.

"My opinion is as follows: These accidents are the result of the incompetency, the criminal negligence, and the almost treasonable negligence of our national defense by the Navy and War Departments."

He left the room and the reporters hurried away with their

carbon copies. One of them later discovered after a count that the full statement ran to 6080 words. It was full of incendiary charges, all of them, Mitchell said, set down after "mature deliberation" and after he had learned a little of what had happened in the twin disasters.

He charged that the Army and Navy had gone to absurd lengths in their efforts to prevent a separate air arm, that airmen were only "pawns in their hands," and that fliers were "bluffed and bulldozed" until they dared not tell the truth lest they be banished to "out-of-the-way places." Meanwhile, commanding officers "either distort facts or openly tell falsehoods about aviation to the people and Congress."

Further, Mitchell charged, both services had propaganda departments, and had become unions to perpetuate their own existence without regard for the public welfare. Their conduct of aviation had been "so disgusting as to make any self-respecting person ashamed of the cloth he wears." Only patriotism kept men flying. He charged that two racing pilots, Skeel and Pierson, were killed as a result of an Army-Navy agreement to divide the racing trophies evenly between them—the lack of competition had resulted in the use of old and inferior planes.

"We in the air fraternity," he said, "decided then and there to put the issue squarely up to Congress and the people." He told of the ill-starred bills for creating a separate air service, which would have passed by "a large majority" if they had reached the House floor. The attempted legislation showed that "the American people were awakening to the necessity for a change."

The Navy's recent maneuvers had been only "a Pacific parade," and the flight by the men of Rodgers was only "to fool the public." The Navy planes on the Hawaiian attempt were "untried . . . primitive, good-for-nothing big lumbering flying boats." They were overloaded, the picket vessels on their route were too widely spaced; the fleet should have helped in the flight, instead of "joy riding around the Antipodes." As for the brave men still afloat in the lost PN-9, he hoped that passing fishermen picked them up—as they had Lieutenant Leigh Wade of the Army's global flight when he went down in the North Sea.

The *Shenandoah* disaster, which killed Lansdowne, "the last of our really experienced airship captains, a splendid man," was a puzzle to Mitchell. "I don't know exactly what happened . . . She was an experimental ship . . . I believe she was about 50 percent overweight in her structure. She had broken away from her mooring mast . . . last spring and her whole structure was badly strained. I believe the number of valves in the gas bags containing the helium had been diminished." The trip had been used for propaganda: "What business had the Navy over the mountains, anyway?"

His criticism covered the familiar points he had been making for seven years, and as if determined to win the public now, though he had failed to convince the military conservatives, he went into great detail.

Of the need for meteorology he said: "The weather bureau is . . . organized to turn out reports affecting onions, cabbages and other crops. While this is very necessary, it is a complete failure as far as we're concerned. I say this after having flown across mountains and bucked their storms hundreds of times."

The state of American bombing was deplorable: "Not one heavy bomb has been dropped . . . in target practice for two years. Only about four or five modern sights are on hand . . . and today I, who know our personnel better than any other living man, can put my hand on only two perfectly capable bombardment crews . . . in case we are attacked."

Of the future Navy: ". . . a battleship . . . may cost from 50 to 70 million dollars. It has to be protected by submarines, destroyers, cruisers and aircraft, the total cost of which is around 100 million dollars . . . I believe a battleship today is a useless element in the national defensive armament of the United States. Suppose we had even one-half of the cost of a battleship to use in the development of our aircraft and submarines.

"What is our Navy for? Presumably it is to control lines of sea communication on the high seas. What is it actually? It is entirely and completely outpointed by Great Britain in the Atlantic. What can it do across the Pacific as at present organized? Nothing—against an insular Asiatic power whom you all know . . .

"To make a long story short, we utterly are disgusted with the conduct of our military affairs applying to aviation. Our pilots know they are going to be killed if they stay in service . . . in the old flaming coffins that we are still flying. Those that still remain have held on so long that if they got out they would starve . . . No finer body ever existed in the makeup of our country than these men."

He praised the able men of the Army and Navy, but said they were frustrated by bureaucracies that "have passed all bounds of national decency . . . deluding the public.

"This condition must be remedied. It is not in the field of partisan politics. It concerns us all. The American people must know the facts, and with their unfailing common sense and ability they will surely remedy it."

His final words: "As far as I am personally concerned, I am looking for no advancement . . . I have had the finest career that any man could in the armed service . . . from the Spanish War to the present and of commanding the greatest air forces ever brought together on the planet. I owe the government everything—the government owes me nothing. As a patriotic American citizen, I can stand by no longer and see these disgusting performances . . . at the expense of the lives of our people, and the delusion of the American public.

"The bodies of my former companions in the air molder under the soil in America and Asia, Europe and Africa, many, yes, a great many, sent there directly by official stupidity. We all may make mistakes but the criminal mistakes made by armies and navies, whenever they have been allowed to handle aeronautics, show their incompetence. We would not be keeping our trust with our departed comrades were we longer to conceal these facts.

"This, then, is what I have to say on the subject, and I hope that every American will hear."

Many of them did hear, for virtually every Sunday paper in the country headlined his message. In Washington, where few War Department officials were available over the weekend, there were only guarded comments. Newspapers quoted anonymous officialdom as saying that Mitchell had at last gone too far. There were only hints of disciplinary action until, a day or so later, Secretary of War Dwight Davis made it official. Mitchell would be disciplined; he did not say how or when. The inference was that a court-martial would be called.

Mitchell left San Antonio for a fishing trip and told a reporter before climbing into his plane: "I expect the War Department to arrest me, but I doubt they'll get to it before Monday. I'm going fishing today."

The press found him on the Gulf of Mexico, where he had gone with Horace Hickam and Harry Short. Mitchell wore a private's uniform without insignia, and apparently as a joke, wore a big sunflower on his chest in place of the usual ribbons. He had caught a large tarpon with light tackle, and said it gave him his "biggest thrill in many a day."

He was reluctant to talk of the crisis but answered a few questions. He would welcome a court-martial if it "stung the conscience" of the public: "The American people are not fools. They're going to demand this common-sense program . . . A few facts have been put before them, and they're going to hear many more." He shook a finger emphatically under a reporter's nose. "They know that it's true. Know that every word of that statement's true. That's why it's going to sting."

Newspaper reaction was overwhelmingly favorable to Mitchell, but there were hostile comments. The brother of the *Shenandoah* navigator, Rosendahl, wrote an open letter to the Houston *Chronicle* saying: "You have no place in the service of your country when you have so little respect for its authority."

The New York *World* said: "Permit this violent outburst to go unpunished and every private in the Army and enlisted man in the Navy will feel at liberty to denounce his superior officers. Armies and navies are not made that way."

The Los Angeles *Record* was more representative of the majority, supporting Mitchell and attacking the high command and the administration: "And what did President Coolidge say when he heard of the disaster? 'It is God's will.' God's will! Pious fiddlesticks. Sanctimonious drivel. We suggest rather than a court-martial, we might rather try our distinguished fellow townsman, the Secretary of Navy, for criminal stupidity."

In Boston, Mayor James Curley sent an American Legion convention into an uproar of applause as he praised Mitchell: "There is one man that is not lacking in courage. While other nations are gaining supremacy of the air with the finest planes and decent appropriations we are sending the bravest and best of our sons in rotten planes into the air."

17

America Will Endure As Long As There Are Mitchells

Mitchell forced the issue as if he feared that even now the War Department might back down. Almost as soon as he had seen his statement of September 5 in the hands of reporters he began negotiations with *Liberty* magazine and a newspaper syndicate for articles on his showdown with the Army. And four days later, on September 9, he gave reporters another statement—an even more inflammatory challenge, and one that could not be ignored.

"What I have said about the conditions in our national defense hurts the bureaucrats in Washington. It ought to hurt them, because it's the truth . . . I also note with amusement the question as to whether my statements are authentic. Whenever I make a statement it is authentic. I am always willing to back up every part of it."

The important thing, he said, was that the country should not lose sight of "the disgraceful condition" of aviation. The question of his insubordination should not obscure the issue.

He seemed to have no doubt that air-power enthusiasts would have their way: "Let every American know absolutely that we are going to better our national defense, that we are on the war path and we are going to stay there until conditions are remedied. The barking of the little dogs that follow the main pack should not delude any thinking person as to the subject of our chase."

He explained his apparent insubordination: "Discipline is a difficult thing to define. Some people call it the unhesitating obedience of a junior to a superior officer." But there were times when ignorant and incompetent superiors forfeited the good opinions of junior officers. There must be some means of criticizing such officers, for the nation's good.

He demanded a kind of supertrial, before the eyes of the country: "If an investigation is desired I am eager to have it. But it must be entirely public and all the evidence must be published for the people to know about. The board making it should be composed of representative Americans instead of members of the Army and Navy bureaucracy. Let its members be from the east and west, north and south, men from the fields and factories as well as from the counting houses. Then and only then will we begin to get at the actual facts involved and remove it from petty politics and bureaucratic suppression."

He said that his own fate was less important: "As far as I am personally concerned, it does not matter to me whether I am in the Army or not. If the bureaucracies wish to throw me out they probably have the machine for doing it, and it will be only one more evidence of the condition into which our national defense has drifted."

President Coolidge, on vacation in Swampscott, Massachusetts, still said nothing, though a staff member hinted that the President would take action. Secretary of War Dwight Davis, busy with the Davis Cup tennis matches in New York, said that he did not want to argue publicly with a subordinate, but intimated that Mitchell would not be kept long in suspense. Mitchell wrote Betty letters full of loneliness, warning her against overactivity so soon after the baby's birth: "You are something like me. If there is nothing to do you make something . . . They made the first move today of relieving me of duty as air officer. This is probably preparatory to my going to Washington to testify before the Select Committee. This is only a scheme of stalling for time and dropping a sop to the people, who want someone to be held responsible for the recent accident. They undoubtedly will come to a conclusion as to what to do before very long . . .

"I think they want to keep me away from the American Legion convention also. As matters now stand I believe you and I would be much better off out of the service. I hate to lose the retired pay, but that may not be necessary. Anyway, I can make enough to feed ourselves . . ." *

The newspapers were now full of the Mitchell affair, most of them fiercely partisan. The *New York Times* charged him with "insubordination and folly," and the *Herald Tribune* said he "shockingly violates military standards" and was "opinionative, arrogant and intolerant." The Kansas City *Star* was more dispassionate:

"How are you going to punish a man who wants nothing more than to be punished and is deliberately inviting court-martial? . . . Mitchell is a zealot, a fanatic, a one-idea man. He will go to any limit to make his case . . . But with all that, he sincerely believes in what he preaches.

"If a military court-martial is ordered, no one will be happier than Mitchell . . . If he is made a martyr in the process, no one knows better than Mitchell that there will be a wave of sympathy for him . . .

"Some day Mitchell's dream may come true. He may be a prophet without honor only because he came a decade or two decades ahead of time . . ."

Within less than a week after Mitchell's first attack, President Coolidge appointed an Aeronautical Board to investigate the whole field of aviation. He named as chairman Dwight Morrow, the Morgan banker and future father-in-law of Charles Lindbergh. The President had warned Morrow six months earlier that he might call on him to head such a group, and Morrow was ready with a blue-ribbon panel tailored to Coolidge's purpose, which was apparently to by-pass Congress and retain control of aviation development. The Morrow Board would take the spotlight off the crusading Mitchell, and in the event of a court-martial, the board's report might lessen the impact of the almost inevitable discipline

* Some of Mitchell's friends believed that he would not have issued the crucial statements from San Antonio if Betty had been there to restrain him. It is clear, however, that he meant to bring the long-fought issue to a climax. Maydell Blackmon doubted that Mrs. Mitchell would have prevented the statements, though she might have persuaded him to tone them down. Mrs. Hap Arnold said later: "We all felt, Billy felt, that unless you went overboard, you couldn't get the attention of this country . . . He got on the wrong track there someplace . . . He lost his perspective. We saw it going, and no one could stop him."

to be meted out to Mitchell. The Navy's concurrent court of inquiry into the *Shenandoah* crash would provide another diversion. Coolidge had no intention of allowing the master showman of the Air Service to hold the national stage alone.

The Morrow Board was not remotely like the tribunal Mitchell had in mind to investigate aviation or his own case, but he praised its creation: "I am confident of its integrity and ability and am most hopeful that much good will result from its inquiry and findings."

Morrow chose eight members: Federal Judge Arthur C. Denison; Dr. William F. Durand and Howard Coffin, who had been presidents of the American Society of Mechanical Engineers; Senator Hiram Bingham of the Military Affairs Committee; General James G. Harbord of Pershing's wartime staff, currently chairman of the board, Radio Corporation of America; Admiral Frank F. Fletcher, retired; and Congressmen Carl Vinson of Georgia and James F. Parker of New York.

Mitchell knew that the board was unlikely to find in his favor. Morrow was a lifelong friend of the President's; the retired officers were predictably conservative on aviation; Dr. Durand was a "Big Navy" man; Representative Vinson of the Naval Affairs Committee was an intimate friend of Admiral Moffett's.

On September 10 Commander John Rodgers and his crew were rescued near Hawaii, after drifting and sailing their flying boat for nine days at sea; the Navy's hapless adventure was over. Admiral Moffett chose that moment for a counterblast at Mitchell; he was chafing under restraint by his superiors, and had been silenced since Mitchell's banishment to Texas.

Moffett gave newspapers a statement attacking Mitchell without so much as reading it. His publicist, Lieutenant Commander Eugene Wilson, prepared the blast, but could not persuade his chief to look it over. There was a strong final paragraph in reply to Mitchell's San Antonio charges: "I am at a loss to understand these charges, vilifications and utter untruths . . . unless this man is suffering from delusions of grandeur or mental aberrations."

The resulting headlines drew little attention. Eugene Wilson said: "It had no effect whatever. Mitchell had already created this utterly false image and there was nothing that could change it."

. . .

The War Department sent an officer to San Antonio to investigate Mitchell's newspaper statements, but Mitchell promptly acknowledged that he was the guilty author. Within a few days he was summoned to Washington to appear before the Morrow Board—he did not yet know when he would face court-martial, but there was now no doubt that one would be called.

He shipped eight hundred pounds of documents to Washington, left San Antonio by car, and when a cloudburst halted him, took a train from Muskogee, Oklahoma. Reporters who hung about him there during a four-hour stop found him unexpectedly taciturn. "I've nothing to say. I've said most of it already."

"Are you afraid to appear before the committee, General?"

"Piffle," he said.

Betty met him in St. Louis for the ride to Washington. Four days before they arrived, the Morrow Board had begun its hearings. It would sit for five weeks before the Army called Mitchell to his court-martial.

Mitchell returned to a riotous welcome. Two American Legion posts and an estimated ten thousand spectators waited at Union Station on the evening of September 25. Hap Arnold came aboard the train to warn the Mitchells of an ordeal in store, but the general hopped out confidently and strode toward the crowd. He was tossed to the shoulders of five or six men and borne through a melee.

A drum and bugle corps played despite a ban on music in the station. Betty was almost knocked down in the commotion, but followed smiling, and was applauded: "Three cheers for the woman who stuck by her husband!" Mitchell waved a big sombrero with a snake band, and reached down to shake hands with men below until he seemed on the point of toppling to the pavement.

There were shouts of "Put it there, General. We're for you!" "We fought once. We'll fight for you now." "Tell 'em what's wrong with America!"

Photographers and police quarreled during the final moments of the demonstration; Arnold at last got the Mitchells into his car and drove them to their hotel. The *New York Times* thought Mitchell "fit for his ordeal, cheerful, with an air of determination."

The Washington *Post* said: "Colonel Mitchell was as usual a picturesque character. He wore a soft gray collar, a gray suit much in need of pressing, somewhat soiled by the long journey. The stoop to his shoulders, accentuated by many weary hours of flying, was a trifle more noticeable than usual, but that was all."

The Legionnaires abducted him again the next afternoon for a barbecue on the outskirts of the city, and he held court in an open carriage on Pennsylvania Avenue near the District Building before the procession began. He wore a pale blue poilu cap and blouse, grinning at a curious crowd. When the parade began, a drum and bugle corps marched ahead and men bore placards around the carriage:

WE'RE FOR GENERAL MITCHELL
AMERICAN FIGHTER UNAFRAID

WE DEMAND JUSTICE FOR MITCHELL—
WHO DOES NOT FEAR TO TELL THE
TRUTH ABOUT DEFENSELESS AMERICA

He made a brief, noncommittal speech at the barbecue and escaped. He spent the weekend in Virginia, resting, to prepare for his appearance before the Morrow Board.

A humorist on the editorial staff of the Washington *Post* made daily jokes at Mitchell's expense: "Colonel Billy Mitchell is willing to come to Washington to tell all even at the risk of getting his name in the papers," and "Colonel Mitchell's testimony will be somewhat delayed as it is understood that all arrangements for the movie rights have not been completed."

Just before Mitchell appeared before the Morrow Board the Army had announced that he would be tried by court-martial while he was in Washington, rather than at his post in Texas. It was apparent that a big show was being prepared.

The Mitchells arrived at the House Office Building late in the morning of September 29 and found an overflow crowd, with people on chairs and tiptoe peering through windows. Benny Foulois was testifying inside.

They pushed past a picket line of photographers and through a crowded hall. Foulois was speaking in a loud, aggressive voice before the board: "Yes, I was one of the first men to fly a plane for the Army, in 1908. I remember that in 1910 I was allowed only

$150 to keep our one plane going—and I had to spend $300 out of my own pocket to do it. I begged, borrowed and stole from the Quartermaster Corps . . . I say our lack of team work today is due to the utter ignorance of the General Staff of 90 percent of the Air Service problems . . ."

The crowd interrupted with applause as it caught sight of Mitchell. Several men shook hands with the newcomer and Foulois turned in his chair to greet him. Mitchell waited for almost an hour as Foulois continued his attacks, and was then called to the stand. He asked to be sworn, but Dwight Morrow said that was unnecessary. The board wanted him to speak informally, in his own way.

Mitchell called for a large globe, which was placed by the witness chair. After Senator Bingham had questioned him about his military career, Mitchell said: "Now I would like to read my statement without interruption, if I may. I would like to finish without questions." Morrow agreed.

"My statement is in nine parts," Mitchell said. "One of them is destructive, and I won't give that."

"Don't hold anything back," Morrow said. "We want to hear everything."

Mitchell then gave one of the rare dull public performances of his career. He appeared to suffer from physical or nervous exhaustion, and was perhaps determined to save his ammunition for the court-martial a few weeks later. He began reading from a sheaf of pages and had droned for ten minutes when Senator Bingham quietly left the room. He returned with a copy of Mitchell's book, *Winged Defense,* thumbed through it for a moment and began following the witness as he read. Clinton Gilbert of the Washington *Post* wrote: "The witness does not look you in the eye, his face is down . . . the unexpected never happens . . . you count the pages to see when he will be through."

Bingham interrupted: "We have a copy of your new book right here. In view of the fact that we've all read it . . ."

"Senator, I'm trying to make a point," Mitchell said, and read on.

Bea Arnold was distressed: "He read in a sing-song voice, on and on. Betty got fidgety. Everybody got nervous. You could feel the coldness go through the board. We were just sunk."

Hap Arnold tried mental telepathy: "We squirmed, wanting to yell: 'Come on, Billy, put down that damned book! Answer their questions and step down. That'll show them.' "

Now and then Mitchell paused to point to the globe in illustration of his argument, and there was an occasional aside, delivered with "a smiling kind of pugnacity," but there was nothing new, and there was little evidence of the familiar Mitchell charm today:

"Air matters must be handled by airmen who know their business. You can't have admirals and generals selected on the basis of 'Tag, you're it. Go and talk to Congress about aviation.' . . .

"The reserves are a myth. They're getting old. We have no corps of observers. No ready machine gunners. Our so-called mechanics are recruited by the Army system . . .

"We've got 12 pursuit ships and 22 bombers ready for war. The rest are DH4's with Liberty motors—neither fish nor fowl . . .

"The Army is nothing but a constabulary. All it can do is support the Constitution and quell insurrections."

The audience applauded him at the luncheon recess, despite his long and tedious delivery. In the afternoon he paused once again to say that he would read only eight of the nine sections of his testimony, and to avoid controversy would withhold the explosive ninth. Morrow was ready for him. He read a statement to Mitchell:

"As the board is not familiar with the facts of this special part of your testimony it is obviously not in position to assume the responsibility of advising you whether you should read it and have it made a part of the testimony. It is proper, however, to say that the board was appointed by the President to find facts . . . any fact that contributes to that purpose . . . Upon that assumption the board's position is quite clear. Put everything in."

Mitchell said that he might do so, and resumed his reading. The room drowsed until he interrupted himself and asked Morrow: "Getting tired of all this stuff?"

"Not at all," Morrow said. "Go right along."

The reading of familiar charges from the book continued. Clinton Gilbert described the effect: "No one felt that he was a sorehead or a crank. Of course he had nothing new to say. A man who has talked so much and written so much as he has in the last couple of years becomes an old story . . . It was impossible that he could be the star witness unless he had some new evidence in reserve, and Colonel Mitchell is not the kind of man to have anything in reserve."

General Harbord and Admiral Fletcher requested a night session so that Mitchell could be kept on the stand. The witness agreed, but near six o'clock said he was too tired to continue, and the board adjourned until the next day.

Newspaper headlines summarized his day in court: "U.S. Is AT MERCY OF ENEMY PLANES, MITCHELL DECLARES." In the same newspapers were stories competing for the attention of an America deep in peaceful isolation: "CHINA FEARS RED FIREBRAND"—an account by Roy Howard of the forecast by a Chinese war lord that creeping Bolshevism would take Asia while the Western world slept . . . Young Bob La Follette of Wisconsin had won a Senate seat by a landslide. Hope was waning for the crew of the submarine *S-51*, lost off New London. Jack Dempsey had signed to fight Wills.

Mitchell testified again the next day, and before he was through, there were a few lively moments. Once when he was talking of the Army's muzzling of junior officers who went before Congress he paused: "The War Department has a reporter in this room today, right now."

"Does this interfere with your testimony?" Representative Vinson asked.

"It doesn't bother me, but it tends to retard the flow of testimony from junior officers."

Judge Denison pressed the question: "Do you think this has any effect on the testimony if the Army General Staff has a stenographer here?"

Mitchell grinned. "It has the effect that you immediately get a letter asking for all the facts and data on your statement."

Spectators were intrigued when they noticed a young officer busily taking down in shorthand all that was said.*

* The Morrow Board was so casually assembled that it sometimes lacked stenographic help of its own. Before hearings opened, typists went on strike because there was no money to pay them. The White House replied candidly. Coolidge realized that no funds were on hand for the board, but since committeemen were "all sufficiently prosperous not to be handicapped seriously by the question of finances," he had provided none.

Representative Vinson challenged Mitchell's theory that the Navy lacked authority to send the dirigible *Shenandoah* on an overland trip. "What provisions of the law were violated in sending the dirigible westward?"

"The section which restricts Navy air activities to sea."

"Don't you think you're putting a far-fetched interpretation on the law?"

"I do not. The *Shenandoah* was sent on a propaganda mission. The law was evaded, not exactly disobeyed. The orders for the trip were from nonflying officers. The inquiry will bring that out."

Mitchell's appearance before the Morrow Board was so unimpressive that the Kansas City *Star* said: "It appeared almost as if the board were making a studied effort to have the Mitchell testimony appear as only an incident of the probe—not the central spot." Mitchell had talked himself out in a day and a half of seldom interrupted testimony.

Mitchell spent the first weeks of October in hectic preparation for his court-martial. He ignored a suggestion that he hire the famous defense lawyer, Clarence Darrow, then fresh from his spectacular performance in the Scopes Trial in Dayton, Tennessee. Mitchell chose instead Frank R. Reid, a freshman congressman from Illinois who had practiced with Darrow. Reid was forty-six, just Mitchell's age, and was one of a dozen children of an Irish immigrant; he had worked his way through the University of Chicago and law school after an apprenticeship in railroad shops. He was a tall, rangy man with a wicked, sometimes outlandish sense of humor, whose innocent expression and dimpled smile concealed the keen intelligence of an able courtroom lawyer. He was an ardent advocate of air power and had befriended Mitchell before congressional committees. Reid volunteered his services without charge.

Mitchell had not forgotten Reid's aid during the past spring's hearings. Once, when Captain Alfred Johnson of the Navy was testifying, an anonymous civilian was coaching him as he answered questions. Reid barked: "Who're you?"

"I happen to be the Assistant Secretary of the Navy, T. Douglas Robinson."

"I object to anyone not a member of the committee butting in here," Reid said. "You're not running this committee, and I'm objecting."

"Go ahead and object, but I can speak to him."

"No. Don't tell him in this committee what to say," Reid said. "You may run him outside, but you're not running him here."

Reid accompanied Mitchell to the *Shenandoah* inquiry in the old Navy Building, where the airship disaster was being aired. Sensational testimony had preceded Mitchell's appearance; the naval high command had ignored Commander Lansdowne's warnings that the flight would be dangerous, insisting that crowds at Midwestern state fairs should see the ship in any event. Newspapers were demanding the resignation of Secretary Wilbur, since he had tried to coerce witnesses and was attempting to whitewash the affair just as Mitchell had predicted. Captain Paul Foley, the court's Judge Advocate, was filing suit against the Hearst newspapers because of a cartoon depicting him as the agent of the whitewash.

Reid precipitated a noisy wrangle before the *Shenandoah* court. The president of the court was Admiral Hilary Jones, another of Mitchell's adversaries from the bombing tests of 1921. When Jones held forth a Bible so that Mitchell could be sworn, Reid objected.

"No subpoena has been issued for him, and he cannot be required to testify under oath."

Captain Foley said that since the Army had ordered Mitchell to appear, no subpoena was necessary.

"Will the court kindly allow the witness to read a statement explaining why he refuses to be sworn?" Reid asked.

Jones ordered the court closed and its members went into executive session. A few minutes later Captain Foley came out with a subpoena to serve on Mitchell. On Reid's advice, Mitchell refused to accept it and the two left the hearing. Mitchell gave a statement to reporters: "I am advised by my counsel that it would be inconsistent with my legal rights and might jeopardize my case, should I be required to testify before the naval court on matters likely to be the subject of inquiry in possible court-martial proceedings."

Reporters who asked Secretary Wilbur how he would punish the defiant Mitchell found him subdued: "I'm not interested in it.

That's up to Admiral Jones." The episode passed from the headlines within a day or two, lost among other sensations of the *Shenandoah* case.

Newspapers discovered that the Navy had refused to pay funeral expenses of the men killed in the crash, since regulations provided only $150 for burial of a man who lost his life on duty—and this amount had been spent at the scene of the tragedy, preparing bodies for shipment to Lakehurst.

One body arrived at a family home clad in underwear, in a crude casket packed with excelsior. Families who sent funeral bills to the Navy had them returned. The Miami *Herald* joined a press chorus to scold the Navy: "It is asking for six million dollars to construct another Zeppelin. Its failure to find the money to bury the dead navigators is likely to influence Congress when the appropriation for another huge dirigible is voted on."

Liberty magazine chose this time to award Mitchell a prize of $1000 for his courage in battling for air power. He turned the money over to the widow of Commander Lansdowne, to be distributed among the families of the airship's victims.

The American Legion, a powerful political force, was holding a convention in Omaha at the time, and played a brief role in the jockeying for position between Reid and the Administration. The Legion asked that Mitchell be permitted to address the convention, but the Army, evidently fearing a resounding resolution in his support, called him to appear before the Inspector General in the preliminary moves of court-martial proceedings. He was put under technical arrest and forbidden to leave the city without written permission. Since Mitchell was being disciplined, the Army told the Legion, "personal arrangements of officers could not be in the way of an investigation."

Coolidge spoke in Omaha and attacked Mitchell: "Any organization of men in the military service bent on inflaming the public mind for the purpose of forcing government action through the pressure of public opinion is an exceedingly dangerous undertaking . . . Peace and security are more likely to result from fair and honorable dealings and by mutual agreements for limitation of arms than by any attempt at competition in squadrons and battalions."

He was greeted with polite applause. In contrast, a telegram from Mitchell, read to the veterans, drew an ovation.

Back in Washington, Coolidge convened Mitchell's court-martial on October 20, and set its opening for eight days later. Twelve high-ranking generals would sit.

Mitchell told reporters: "I demand to be tried by a court of flying officers. No man should sit in judgment on me who doesn't know flying . . . Why, they're reverting to the medieval practice of coercion. It's like the old trials of heretics. Those charges have been so worded as to give me no chance to prove the truth. I think I'll insist on an open trial. The American people are interested in the truth."

Reporters found him willing to talk up to the eve of the trial. He once said, pounding a table: "I'm not afraid of what the court will do to me. I'll fight on to get a real department of national defense, no matter what happens." *

The Navy, with a fine sense of timing, chose the week before the court-martial to release a new recruiting film, *The Eyes of the Fleet*, showing planes at work. Every bomb dropped in the film missed its target. Charles Parmer of Universal News Service saw the film with a newsreel cameraman, J. B. Bockhurst. On the screen a Martin bomber struck at the U.S.S. *Alabama.* "Watch this," Bockhurst said. The bombs missed by a wide margin. Bockhurst protested. "I made those pictures. My plane was flying within a hundred feet of the water, and the concussion was so great from the hits that it blew the plane upward when the ship's superstructure was knocked off. Why don't they show the hits?"

Bockhurst took Parmer to his office to see the complete films, including sections deleted by the Navy: "In the second scene a salvo of four two-thousand-pound bombs struck the *Alabama* and she keeled over until her starboard deck was awash . . . Then the *Alabama* keeled over, a total wreck."

Excitement grew in Washington as the time for the court-martial approached, stimulated by newspaper speculation on every phase of the case. It was reported that the Army would hire

* Mitchell wrote Patrick about this time to deny rumors that he wanted to become Chief himself. "I want to see you continue as Chief . . . I hope that any rumors you may have heard . . . will have no effect . . . I wish again to express my appreciation and esteem for the . . . stand you have taken."

a hall, perhaps the large auditorium of the Department of the Interior. Secretary Davis retorted irritably: "This is serious War Department business. It isn't a vaudeville show—or an advertising scheme." The setting he chose for the drama would minimize its importance—the Emory Building, an empty warehouse which had once housed the Census Bureau. It had been vacant for two years, a low brick building at First and B streets, diagonally across from the Capitol.

Secretary Davis announced the site a few days before the court was to open, and Mitchell and Reid went there with two officers of the prosecution staff, Trial Judge Advocate Colonel Sherman Moreland and his assistant, Colonel Joseph McMullen. Reporters followed them.

Mitchell led the way over a pool of stagnant water at the foot of stairs leading to the trial room. The party clambered over a three-foot barrier, stooped beneath a dangling timber and entered the courtroom. One reporter wrote: "Little short of impossible, without heat, full of trash . . . small and dark . . . The floor is worn and splinters jab at people's shoes. The walls look as if they were lined with cardboard . . . there are posts in it."

Colonel Moreland jumped on the floor and frowned as it sagged. "Didn't you try to get the House caucus room?" Reid asked. Moreland said the War Department had left him no choice; the purpose seemed to be to limit the number of spectators and reporters.

Four workmen knocked about, building a dais for the judges. Mitchell and his party huddled in overcoats to watch. A reporter thought it would take a furnace two weeks to clear out the damp cold.

A few days later the Army announced that the building had been shored up, but that no standing spectators would be allowed for fear the floor would collapse.

At Mitchell's request, Clayton Bissell had been assigned as an assistant defense counsel, the expert on aviation matters, and he went now with Mitchell and Reid to the congressman's small office in the House Office Building, where a dozen stenographers and a flow of defense witnesses had begun work. Bissell remembered the first session: "We quickly decided that Mitchell was guilty as charged, with insubordination and conduct prejudicial to the service. We even convinced him that he would be found guilty. Reid asked what point we wanted to make, in that event—and we agreed that the trial had to be used to educate the American people on aviation, to make national defense mean something. It was the only way left. To do that we knew we had to stay on the front pages of newspapers. If we slipped off for a day, we'd have to find a way back, something spectacular, new stuff every day. We knew it would be a job."

Reid knew nothing of the evidence Bissell could produce to help Mitchell, and little of military law. Joseph E. Davies came to advise, and quickly had a wrangle with Reid. "You ought to plead guilty," Davies told Mitchell. "You are guilty, you know they'll find against you, and it would save time and sharpen the issue if you entered the plea."

"Nothing doing," Reid said. "So long as I'm in the case he'll defend himself. If they'll let us prove that he's been telling the truth, and that finally he got to the point where nobody would listen to him, so that he had to go to the people, then we've got a chance."

Reid brought in a young lawyer from a House committee staff, William H. Webb, who became the defense expert in finding legal precedent to back up Mitchell's position. He and Reid and Bissell spread Mitchell's long San Antonio statements on tables, cut them into pieces, numbered each statement of fact as charged by Mitchell, and assigned members of the staff to find documents and witnesses to bolster each charge.

Mitchell rented two floors of the Anchorage Apartments, known as the Flatiron Building, where he lived on one floor with Betty, and the Clayton Bissells shared the other with hundreds of boxes of documents.

Many of Mitchell's old friends came, but though all were quizzed by Reid before stenographers, many were turned away; Reid wanted to be sure that each one understood the matter thoroughly, and could handle himself well on the stand. Tom Milling, for one, was freed, since it seemed that he could do little more than offer testimony as a character witness. Expenses mounted rapidly, with the travel of witnesses and the extended work of stenographers. Betty Mitchell's father, Sidney Miller, a Packard

Motor Company lawyer, wrote checks for everything, and gave them to Webb to pay the costs, as he did throughout the trial.

The *Shenandoah* court of inquiry was still in session as Mitchell's trial drew near. The Morrow Board completed its hearings and retired to write its report for President Coolidge.

Sunday newspapers on the eve of the court-martial gave a sample of the eloquence with which Reid was tuning up. He said that Mitchell's plea would be based on freedom of speech. The military had often been criticized, he said, and Mitchell's charges had been mild when compared with those of Generals Hooker and McClellan during the Civil War, and with those of Colonel Theodore Roosevelt and Admiral Sims in more recent times—and none of these had been disciplined.

Reid asked reporters: "Could there be a greater contrast than is afforded by the wisdom of Presidents Lincoln and McKinley and Roosevelt and the actions of martinets in time of peace who would punish a faithful officer for timely and judicious advice on public matters of great importance?

"Rome endured as long as there were Romans. America will endure as long as there are Mitchells."

18

The Most August Tribunal . . . Since the Magna Carta

At nine o'clock on the morning of October 28 Mitchell answered a knock at his apartment door to find Captain K. J. Fielder, the acting adjutant of the District, with a bundle of papers in a pocket. The Army had waited until the last minute with its summons.

"Hello, Bill."

"Well, hello there, Ken. Come in." They sat for a time over coffee, talking of cold weather that had come overnight, but did not mention the trial. Fielder felt his pocket hesitantly. "By the way, I've got those papers here. Court-martial papers, you know."

"Oh, sure, let's have 'em. Thanks." Mitchell thrust them into a pocket without a glance. After a while Fielder left, and Betty urged her husband to finish dressing.

They arrived at the Emory Building just before ten o'clock, to find a crowd circling half the block. Mitchell sprang from the car, immaculate in a new uniform with ribbons on his chest, and turned to help Betty, who wore a black coat with a gray fur collar and a black velvet tam. He waved his brief case to the crowd, and in response to the applause, Betty waved an embroidered bag. His sister Ruth and the lawyers followed, the two women hanging to Mitchell's belt as they pushed past spectators. A reporter thought Mitchell looked "like a small boy on a picnic. If his nonchalance was insincere, then Mitchell is a great actor."

Several women in large automobiles came later and were

refused by guards, who said they would admit only a hundred or so of those nearest the door.

Mitchell went through the courtroom bowing to friends, swinging his malacca cane, and burst into the court's private anteroom to shake hands with the generals. "Hello, folks," he said. He put his arms around the shoulders of the old friends who were now his judges. This reunion was broken up promptly at ten o'clock by the bellow of an old sergeant from Fort Myer who clicked his heels and called: "Staaaand, hup!"

The judges filed to their places at the curved table, facing Mitchell and the lawyers. Betty and Harriet sat just behind the accused and to their rear were forty reporters and then the crowd, which jostled erect from rows of iron folding chairs. Uniformed soldiers stood guard along one wall. In the rear, news photographers were surrounded by standing spectators, who had somehow crowded in.

The court seemed perfectly cast for its role, a cadre of stern men from the army's inner circle who had helped to create the traditions assailed by Mitchell, the highest-ranking court ever assembled for an American military trial.

The major generals were Charles P. Summerall, now commander at Governors Island; Robert L. Howze, a stern cavalryman who had led the Fourth Division in France; Fred W. Sladen, the commandant at West Point; Douglas MacArthur, son of a prominent general and well on his way to a brilliant career; William S. Graves, 6th Corps Area commander, who had fought the Communists in Siberia; and Benjamin A. Poore. The brigadiers were Edward K. King, military aide to two Presidents; Albert L. Bowley; Frank R. McCoy; Edwin B. Winans, George L. Irwin, and Ewing E. Booth. The Law Member was Colonel Blanton Winship. The judges were infantrymen, cavalrymen or artillerymen; none was a flier.

Mitchell had known many of them well for more than twenty years. MacArthur was a boyhood friend from Milwaukee, Howze was a riding and hunting companion. (McCoy and Winship would become godfathers to his children and McCoy a pallbearer at his funeral.)

The court opened with introduction of counsel. For the defense—the civilians Frank Reid and Judge Frank G. Plain of

Aurora, Illinois, and the inevitable military attorney, appointed by the court, Colonel Herbert A. White. The Trial Judge Advocate—the prosecutor—was Colonel Sherman Moreland, a bespectacled, gruff-voiced regular in his early sixties.

Moreland questioned the judges until he was satisfied that they were impartial. "Has any member of the court a declared enmity against the accused?" he asked finally, and when they were silent he said that the government was content with the court.

Reid had other ideas. He challenged the right of General Bowley to sit, "on the ground of his prejudice, hostility and animosity." He read from a speech Bowley had made only a week earlier:

" 'The changing of our whole system of national defense should not be attempted without careful and mature consideration . . . should we put it aside for the visionary proposition of a National Defense Department? . . .

" 'A single air service? Do we want this? The backbone of every army is the infantry . . . there is no more reason for a single air service than there is for a single medical corps, or a single ordnance department . . . Pictures are painted, showing flocks of airplanes dropping bombs on New York City, with the skyscrapers toppling right and left. Stories of how the metropolis of the country can easily be destroyed appeal to the imagination of the public and they are prone to lose their balance . . .' "

Bowley was left alone by the court to face the photographers, and when the generals emerged from their anteroom, he was excused. The generals turned expectantly to Reid. The congressman paused for effect and looked at Summerall: "We wish to challenge the right of the president, General Summerall, to sit as a member of the court."

The crowd buzzed. Summerall chewed his lips and moved about in his high-backed chair. One reporter wrote: "Men who knew him as 'Oliver Cromwell in khaki' said they had never seen him so ruffled . . . His eyes blazed in indignation."

Reid quoted from Summerall's statements as examples of his prejudice:

" 'Aviation is a new arm. We all admire it. It is spectacular . . . but the public is being misled by fanciful and irresponsible talk emanating from a source either without experience or whose experience in war is limited to the very narrow field of aviation.' "

Reid then read a summary of Mitchell's report on Hawaiian defenses in Summerall's time as " 'inefficiently handled, badly organized, and ignorance of its application manifested by him and his staff. This . . . would lead to certain defeat in case of war.' "

Summerall nervously rubbed his forehead as Reid cited the shortages of planes, guns and equipment and the lack of airway routes, a radio net and a weather service. Reid told the court that Mitchell had discovered that squabbling Army and Navy commanders in Hawaii refused to attend the same social functions, and made co-operation of land and sea forces "practically impossible."

Reid also quoted from Summerall's reply to this criticism: " 'Superficial impressions and academic discussions may result in conclusions that are unfair to the command, whose officers and soldiers are laboring wholeheartedly . . .' "

Reid insisted that Summerall be dismissed from the court. The general's face flushed with resentment. He had made those statements, he said, but as to Mitchell: "I had regarded his inspection as friendly. I hadn't therefore conceived any personal prejudice toward him . . . although I regarded the report as untrue, unfair"—Summerall paused and glanced at Mitchell—"and ignorant."

A long "oooh" was heard from the audience.

"In view of the bitter personal hostility toward me by Colonel Mitchell," Summerall said, "I couldn't consent to sit as a member of this board and I shall ask the court to excuse me."

The others withdrew but returned after a few minutes, with General Howze in the lead. He announced in his Texas drawl that the challenge was sustained; he was now president. Robert Lee Howze was a hard-bitten plains trooper—"the best cavalryman who ever rode a horse," as the newspapers said. On the Mexican Border with Pershing he had become well-known for his motto: "Every man on a horse every day." Perhaps by coincidence, the army announced on the opening day of the court-martial that Howze had been awarded a Congressional Medal of Honor, somewhat belatedly, for an act of heroism in 1891 during an Indian fight in South Dakota.

Summerall left the room, trailed by a few reporters as he stalked to the War Department. When he reached his office he spoke to the press like a man wounded by a personal affront. "I have kept an open mind on Mitchell's case. I took him into my home as a friend when he came to Honolulu. I placed a private car at his disposal. I loaned him an airplane. Only ten minutes before court convened I shook hands with him. Now it's all over. We're enemies, Mitchell and I."

Summerall groped for words: "I don't recall having read a single line of his report . . . You know he was on his honeymoon tour . . . His charges are utterly ridiculous."

The reporters who had followed Summerall hurried back to court to find another judge missing—General Sladen, ousted by the defense. Sladen had taken it calmly, and "looked as if he welcomed the chance to get off the court." *

Then, as if content with the men who would decide Mitchell's fate, Reid began a plea for dismissal of the case. He said that the offense of which the colonel was accused was defined nowhere, neither in the Articles of War, nor in civilian or military law, nor in the Constitution, and "exists only in the mind of the accuser."

Mitchell had merely exercised the right of freedom of speech in his San Antonio statements, Reid said. Even Mitchell grinned when the lawyer said that "anyone who reads Colonel Mitchell's statement would recognize that it is a free play of words that really means nothing." If the First Amendment didn't apply to the Army, why didn't it say so? "Are soldiers people as defined in the Constitution?" Reid cited authorities, including President Coolidge in a recent address at Annapolis:

" 'The officers of the Navy are given the fullest latitude in expressing their views before their fellow citizens . . . It seems

* Senior officers realized how distasteful the judges found this duty. General Leonard Wood, who had been Chief of Staff when Mitchell was a captain on the General Staff, wrote to General McCoy: "I do not envy you your detail on the court. Mitchell has been a gallant, hard-fighting officer but always with a turn for overstating things."

(The judges ousted by the defense were not replaced; the Army required only six for a general court, and perhaps had foreseen that Reid would remove some for cause.)

to me perfectly proper for anyone upon any suitable occasion to advocate the maintenance of the Navy in keeping with the greatness and dignity of our country.' " Mitchell's demand for an adequate national defense should have met with the President's approval, Reid declared, "if he meant what he said in that speech."

Reid shifted to and fro in the narrow space behind his table as if he longed to be pacing before an Illinois jury. He seldom raised his voice, but its high, rather unpleasant tones reached every corner of the room. To one reporter he seemed like a small-town schoolteacher, though an unusual one, with a courtly manner and an ingratiating smile. He stretched his neck above his bow tie to peer at the court; black eyes glittered in his sallow face. His informality irritated the generals, who were unaccustomed to civilian lawyers. They were not "this august court" or "this honorable court," as they were to service lawyers—they were usually "you people." They smiled politely when Reid, fumbling for the proper designation for "Corps Areas," said "the whatchamacallums." Reid rose to occasional heights:

"I consider this the most august tribunal that has ever been called upon to act on any question since the Magna Carta. You have not only the rights of the individual here. You have the basis, the pillar of society here . . . the trial of this case goes to whether or not the republican form of government can last without the public and without the public's opinion as the basis for action by our congressional and other departments."

Congressman Reid said Mitchell had only done his duty by pointing out weaknesses in national defense: "Of course you people are very familiar with the history of our country and with the criticism of public officials, and we expect to be roasted right along. Of course you people aren't used to it yet. But the idea is . . . that not only the people who are immediately concerned should have this information, but that every citizen in the country may know about the condition of affairs . . .

"Your Commander-in-Chief said it is the duty of every officer to give their views to other public citizens and that is the only offense charged . . . and the only offense for which he can be charged. I thank you."

Moreland said he couldn't reply for the prosecution until he had studied the Coolidge speech quoted by Reid, and asked for an overnight adjournment. The court agreed gratefully. During the day the lengthy charges had been read until the generals were groggy. Mitchell's September 5 statement had been read six times, and that of September 9 three times—as often as they were mentioned in the charges.

Reid fought for three days to escape the jurisdiction of the court, and though there were a few exciting moments, the judges and the crowd seemed impatient with the fencing of the lawyers, eager to get on with the witnesses. Moreland opened the second day with a thrust at Reid, the civilian, who understood so little of their traditions: "I shall take but a moment of the time of military men to expose . . . one or two fundamental fallacies underlying the argument."

Every soldier had certain rights, he said, but must conform to "those things which military tradition, or military law . . . lay down upon him." He argued that when a man enlisted, he lost civilian status and gave up personal liberties. "If not, the Army of the United States would be left to rot on government soil."

Reid scorned Moreland's argument: "He didn't say there was any law covering this. He didn't say there was any common law covering this. Not a word. Here is the nearest he came to it: he says tradition . . . If his argument is right a military court is greater than God himself . . .

"Are you going to invoke the old Spartan system? . . . If they didn't like a person . . . if they didn't like his looks they would banish him. It's just the same idea as challenging a truth-teller."

The issue was put up to the court—did it have jurisdiction? The generals decided that it did.

Betty Mitchell was one of the most intent spectators. She twirled a white chrysanthemum in one hand during the early hours, and occasionally studied people in the room through her silver lorgnette, but soon began taking notes and remained furiously at this task, staring at the court and then scribbling in her notebook; she made the judges nervous. When the prosecution thundered loudest she put an arm about her husband's shoulders.

During recess the press followed her into the corridor, where she clung to Mitchell's arm: "Her talk is fast, nervous and has a ring of cheerfulness . . . She is difficult to interview. She talks of inconsequential things, for the talk is chosen deliberately. 'Ask William,' she will reply to questions. 'He does all the talking for this family.' But there is one definite statement she will make, 'Of course, William is right. He's always right.'" When a reporter asked why she had not brought her young daughter from Detroit, Betty said, "Oh, she has her father's big voice." At noon the Mitchells went with Mr. Miller and Ruth to the lunchroom at Union Station, to avoid crowds. Reid, Judge Plain, Bissell and Webb ate in the Senate Dining Room, with Henry Cabot Lodge, the reporter for the New York *Herald Tribune,* and Bill McAvoy of the Scripps-Howard newspapers.

In the afternoon Reid again challenged the court's legality: "I'm not arguing that the President couldn't call a court-martial . . . but I am arguing that the proceeding under the military law is a report from the commanding officer." He demanded dismissal of the charges, and when Moreland said it was an unusual case, brought by the President and not by a lower-ranking officer, Reid shouted: "I hesitate to believe what my ears convey to my mind. He does not mean to say that the President of the United States investigated these charges and started the machinery himself? He has not any comprehension of what this is about, if that is true . . ."

Reid complained bitterly: "I regret to find out here that the phrase 'necessity knows no law' comes here and spreads its power over everybody in the world. He has me in a peculiar position. I could not catch the offense, and now I cannot even catch the procedure. Why? Because of necessity it is an abnormal case."

The court refused him on all counts. At the end of the second day he came to the last of his major objections to the legality of the trial—that there was no bill of particulars, and that he could prepare no defense against such vague charges. "We ask as a matter of simple justice that they point out what is a violation of each specification."

Moreland agreed to do just that, but the next morning the Trial Judge Advocate said the government could not cite chapter and verse of Mitchell's violations. The document was too long, for one thing; for another, the court lacked authority to proceed in that way.

Reid said, "It is rather peculiar that, within the short space of twenty-four hours, there should be shorn from this court every power in the world. And when we start out this morning you haven't as much power as the Trial Judge Advocate contended you had yesterday . . .

"The Trial Judge Advocate was going ahead last night to pick out the facts so as to comply with this simple, ordinary and just request. What has happened? Has the midnight oil burned so badly they have not been able to discover a way to grant this bill of particulars? . . ."

When Reid ridiculed Moreland's claim that the 52-page charges were too long for particulars, Moreland lumbered to his feet to ask: "Whose fault is it that those statements are so long? Is it mine? Is it the court's? . . . By what right does counsel for the defense stand up here and ask me to correct the voluminosity of the statements of his own client?"

"May not the terrible length of the statement be due to the terrible state of our national defense?" Reid said. "That doesn't mean that . . . we must go on trial on a whole basket of things upon which you base your charges."

When Reid had been overruled on all his other objections, Mitchell was told to stand and state his plea to the general issue. He rose and called so loudly that spectators were startled: "Not guilty!"

As he was asked the same question on each of eight specifications, Mitchell replied in the same ringing voice, speaking before the questions were completed. The charges were:

1. That Colonel Mitchell, in his statement of September 5, conducted himself "to the prejudice of good order and military discipline";

2. That his statement was "insubordinate";

3. That his statement was "highly contemptuous and disrespectful" and intended to discredit the War Department;

4. The same specifications as those cited, but referring to the Navy Department.

The last four specifications repeated the first four, but applied to the statement of September 9.

When Mitchell returned to his seat, Betty held his hand for a few minutes.

The 96th Article of War was then read, as the basis for the

trial, the "Mother Hubbard" article under which, as Mitchell had said, officers were tried "for kicking a horse." It gave the Army almost unlimited authority:

"Though not mentioned in these Articles, all disorders and neglects to the prejudice of good order and military discipline, all conduct of a nature to bring discredit upon the military service . . . shall be taken cognizance of by a . . . court-martial and punished at the discretion of such court."

The prosecution had only to show that Mitchell had discredited the services in those broad terms, and he would be guilty as charged, without regard to motives, loyalty or overriding concern for the defense of his country.

Court adjourned for the weekend at the request of the lawyers. Moreland wanted to interview his first witnesses, who had come up from Texas, and Reid asked a respite from the wearing ordeal of the courtroom. Howze granted an adjournment but growled prophetically: "Don't worry about the physical endurance of this court."

19

This Ain't a Vaudeville Show

Newspapers that had forecast a trial of three or four days said rather ruefully, as the *New York Times* did with the opening of the second week, "the whole situation has changed." Mitchell's prolonged defense would force the government to bring dozens of witnesses, and the trial might drag on for weeks.

Half a dozen Texas reporters came to the stand to prove what Mitchell had already conceded—that he was the author of the San Antonio statements. The reporters said they had been given the fateful releases by the colonel and that they had published them the following day.

Reid then demanded that the government give him more documents and help assemble witnesses. The prosecution complained that only that morning Reid had offered "a partial list" of seventy-one defense witnesses from as far away as Hawaii and Texas, asked for hundreds of documents, and subpoenas for the Secretaries of War, Navy and Agriculture, Dwight Morrow and Everett Sanders, President Coolidge's secretary. It was unheard-of to summon such dignitaries, Moreland said.

Reid's opening statement took the court by surprise: "Of course a nation is adorned by good citizenship, the body by beauty, the soul by wisdom, acts by virtue and speech by truthfulness. But the opposites of these virtues are a disgrace. Man and woman, word and deed, department and government, we ought to praise if praiseworthy, and blame if blameworthy, for it is equally wrong and stupid to censure what is commendable and to commend what is censurable." He smiled at the long faces before him. "Don't get excited. I'm not going to make a speech. I'm coming to the facts."

He outlined points he would prove: That Mitchell had been beseeched by the press for a statement on the *Shenandoah* disaster and the hapless Hawaiian flight. "His heart was sad due to the distresses of his brave brethren and the thought of his companions who had passed one by one into the Great Beyond, and feeling it his overwhelming duty to do so he issued the statements of September 5, in the hope that it would arouse the conscience of the American people, and that they would . . . through their representatives, cause the evils to be corrected";

That Mitchell's charges of "incompetency, criminal negligence and almost treasonable administration" were true;

That the *Shenandoah,* lost during a "publicity stunt" carried out under protest by Commander Lansdowne, had been overweight and unsafe—and had been ordered to her doom by men ignorant of aviation;

That the Army and Navy had "propaganda agencies" and were little more than "unions" to perpetuate their own existence;

That the Hawaiian flight of the Navy, also a publicity stunt, was badly planned and executed.

The list covered all aspects of Mitchell's charges. Reid then came to the major theme:

"That Colonel Mitchell, after exhausting every usual means to safeguard the aerial defense of the United States, without result, took the only way possible that would cause a study of true conditions of the national defense to be made." It was a clear warning that the defense intended to air the whole question of military aviation in America, and that the matter of Mitchell's guilt or innocence might become incidental to the broader issue. (This strategy of the defense helped to perpetuate the image of Mitchell as a conscious martyr to the cause of air power. His own writings during the trial lent weight to this impression. One of his syndicated articles spoke of the court as "a necessary cog in the wheel of progress, a requisite step in the modernization and rehabilitation of the national defense." But a study of the record and of Mitchell's personality strongly indicates that he never conceived of himself as a martyr.) *

Reid called off a long list of recommendations Mitchell had made in vain, and followed that with a dismal inventory of U.S. air power. "This, then, is a fair statement of what we expect to prove and we are now ready to offer proof . . . May we have a recess for fifteen minutes, Mr. President, in order that I may recover my voice?"

One of the first defense witnesses was Major Carl ("Tooey") Spaatz, the thirty-five-year-old tactical chief of the Air Service, who wore the Distinguished Service Cross, had shot down three German planes and commanded a training school in France. In World War II he was to become commander of the U.S. Strategic Air Forces in Europe and the Pacific. Spaatz told the court of a pathetically small air force, short of men and planes and almost at a standstill in training.

All told, there were 1820 planes, but 1300 of these were obsolete—and only 400 were "standard." Of these 400, more than half were left over from the war. Only 26 bombers and 39 observation planes were rated as standard, and Spaatz insisted that only 59 planes in the United States were modern and fit for duty. As for properly equipped pursuit planes, with oxygen tanks, synchronized guns, radios and bomb racks, there were none.

By dragging all administrative officers from their desks at his post, Spaatz said, he could put 15 pursuit planes into the air: "It is very disheartening to attempt to train or do work under such circumstances."

Reid asked him if he thought aviation was being retarded by the War Department. The prosecution objected, since that called for a conclusion by the witness, but Spaatz managed to shout: "I do!" The crowd applauded.

* Mitchell's conscious martyrdom is a legend. Ira Eaker thought he invited trial to dramatize air power and that he "accomplished his purpose." Jerome Hunsaker said he "really expected to be hailed as a prophet." Mitchell told S.L.A. Marshall, then city editor of the El Paso *Herald*, that he would deliberately provoke a court-martial. Marshall protested: "Don't you see that if you compromise your position, they will drop you at once?" But Mitchell was positive of victory. Years later he told Marshall that he rued his false estimate of his chances.

"Would the recommendations made by Colonel Mitchell have improved the Air Service in the technical and other divisions?"

Moreland objected that Spaatz couldn't answer, since hearsay evidence would be involved, and Reid withdrew the question. Spaatz was then forbidden to say whether fliers were sufficiently well trained in gunnery to be ready for war.

When the lawyers had finished, Howze grilled Spaatz, and inadvertently exposed a view of a neglected air force. As the questions went on and the replies became more positive, Howze's tone grew brusque.

Who was to blame for these shortcomings? Spaatz said that where gunnery was involved, squadron commanders were responsible.

"Is there anybody higher up than the commander of this unit who is responsible for the gunnery work which—"

Spaatz broke in: "Well, in the case of the First Pursuit Group the commander of the Sixth Corps Area has charge of it."

The Sixth Corps Area commander was Graves, who sat at Howze's elbow, now more erect and impatient to question the witness. He interrupted a moment later to ask whether his office had ever denied help to the air squadrons.

Spaatz replied that he had once tried to find a field for gunnery practice, and that the people of the small town of Oscoda, Michigan, had offered a field for a nominal rental. He had trouble in persuading the War Department to pay. The rent demanded by the town: one dollar a year. The crowd's laughter drowned out the witness and Howze called for order.

Spaatz said that training of his pursuit group had been long delayed. Graves doggedly continued the matter as if the Army's honor were at stake: "Can you state definitely where this time was taken up—in what particular office?" The court seemed relieved when Spaatz could not fix the blame.

When the major had left the stand, Howze complained to Reid that the trial was going too slowly, and proposed longer hours and night sessions. Reid resisted. The backstage work of the defense was too burdensome: "I'm willing to go into almost any Herculean task. We have had six expert stenographers going and three or four men lugging in evidence and carrying it out, and I've got to examine witnesses tonight to go on tomorrow. I think we have expedited this matter more than any human beings . . ."

"Do you consider, Mr. Reid, that the hours we are following are too strenuous for you?"

"Ten to twelve-thirty and from two to four-thirty is about as much as anyone should stand. I'm different from you people. I have to learn this stuff anew each time I go into it."

Howze abandoned his attempted speed-up and adjourned court for the day.

At the end of each session Mitchell and his sister Harriet went horseback riding in Rock Creek Park, cantering in the dark along trails Mitchell had known for many years. He spent most evenings in the apartment in planning sessions. Hap Arnold and his wife were often there, and Bert Dargue and Commodore Charlton of the Royal Air Force, and sometimes Clayton Bissell. Tooey Spaatz and Ira Eaker came, and dozens of others passed through weekly. Reid was seldom there, since he met with Judge Plain and other lawyers in his room at the Willard Hotel. This activity seemed to keep Mitchell in high spirits, to the dismay of some friends.*

Many airmen spoke in Mitchell's defense, but there were absentees among his old friends. There was speculation that General Pershing, off on a long good-will visit to Chile, might have chosen this time to avoid an embarrassing appearance at the court-martial. Pershing did not speak publicly on the case, but wrote to a friend, General William M. Wright, that the airman's conduct was an example of a "Bolshevik bug" rife in the Army which must be exterminated.

The procession of air officers to the stand, unanimous in support of Mitchell, seemed to arouse the court's indignation. General Graves especially was hostile, and continually mumbled to other judges about Reid's conduct of the trial in the manner of a civilian lawyer; Reid heard him frequently over the voices of

* Mrs. Arnold later recalled: "Hap tried to keep Billy down. You couldn't do it . . . and his lawyer was a big mistake—a very brilliant man, but he didn't know the service . . . I don't think he knew how to handle Billy, either. Hap and Bert Dargue and this Englishman and this lawyer, they would all talk things over, getting ready for the next day, and they would tell Billy, 'For goodness' sake, this is a serious thing!' Billy couldn't believe it was serious."

Bissell, whose relationship with Mitchell was more intimate during these weeks, thought Mrs. Arnold misinterpreted the dogged air of optimism Mitchell affected.

witnesses and frowned at him, but Graves was not to be quieted so easily.

The fliers presented a damaging case against the enemies of aviation. Major Hap Arnold made a convincing appearance, with forthright answers and an air of being unafraid of retribution. He said that U.S. air strength was about half that of France or England. Reid quoted from a congressional report: " 'It is evident from these figures, from a flying-personnel viewpoint, the U.S. is well off and compares favorably with all foreign powers.' " Arnold identified the statement as from testimony of General Hugh A. Drum.

Moreland pounced on that in cross-examination, to ask Arnold if he meant to charge Drum with inaccuracy.

"I mean that he gives the impression that our air service compares favorably with other large powers' air service, and I mean to say that it doesn't compare favorably," Arnold said.

"And that is your opinion about his accuracy?"

"It will have to be accepted as more than opinion because the figures show that whereas we have only eight pursuit squadrons, England has thirteen, France has thirty and Italy has twenty-two."

"Now, then, did you take into consideration the relative positions, geographically, of the U.S. and England or France and Italy?"

"Yes, all that is considered."

"You consider, then, that in order to be as well off as England is, the U.S. must have just as many airships and personnel as England? . . . And you took into consideration also the fact that France is close to a power that has just spent all its energies upon trying to conquer?"

Arnold tried gamely to show that air power had deprived America of its traditional advantage of ocean barriers: "I think that makes no difference in an aerial war, where distance is annihilated by a few hours."

"Is three thousand five hundred miles of salt water annihilated?"

"Yes, sir. It is today."

"In what respect?"

"Airships have crossed the Atlantic and Pacific."

Moreland and Arnold quarreled over the significance of these crossings. Arnold insisted that though the planes bore no weapons, they might well have done so.

There were increasingly heated shouting matches between Reid and Moreland, most of them won by the defense, but even Judge Plain's daughter Eleanor, partial to Mitchell's cause, was distressed to see Moreland "so at a disadvantage in the give and take."

Some of the court's questions reflected the lasting resentment of the wartime doughboy toward aviators: "Do you consider duty in the Air Service more dangerous than serving in the line in the infantry, in wartime?"

Arnold cited General Staff figures showing 23 percent replacements for the Air Service and only 7 percent for the infantry. The judges were not satisfied.

"You have no data to show the percentages of the actually killed pilots in the Air Service during the war as compared to that of infantry officers' actual deaths?"

"Not with me, no, sir."

"Have you any data on that subject?"

"We have data . . . but every time we try to get something concrete, we find three or four sets of figures on casualties, as issued by the General Staff, and we didn't know what to use." *

Another witness was W. G. Schauffler, who had commanded a squadron at St. Mihiel, had left the service in disgust, but was still a reserve officer. He bore out Mitchell's criticism of the air reserve. Schauffler said he commanded six squadrons of reservists based in Washington; Baltimore and Oxford, Maryland; and Jeanette, Pennsylvania.

* Arnold, the future general of the Air Force, who was "banished" soon after the trial and spent many years away from Washington, thought he was punished by the Army for his role in the defense. Ira Eaker, another of the team gathering support for Mitchell, recalled: "We talked over how taking part in Mitchell's trial would jeopardize our careers and decided to go ahead anyhow. Arnold was the inspirational leader in that decision by this little group."

Many others who offered to testify for Mitchell were not put on the stand, and in some cases, officers called by the Army were so strong in support of Mitchell that their testimony was not used. Thurman Bane was one example; though he had often opposed Mitchell, when he was called out of retirement by the Army as a court-martial witness, he backed Mitchell so firmly that the Army dismissed him. Mitchell accepted Bane's apology for past criticism with a casual "Forget it. All that's water over the dam. We've got to work together now, and save air power."

"Did you ever have your squadrons together?" Reid asked.

"Never . . . I never saw but two of the commanding officers, and those unofficially." He said that the squadrons had been assembled once, for a parade.

"Did you ever have an airplane assigned to you?"

"Never."

"Are you a paper organization?"

"We are."

A general asked Schauffler what duties he had performed, and then wanted to know: "But haven't you otherwise extended your influence beyond the local situation—the local officers?"

"How could I?"

"Will you answer my questions? . . . I'm asking the questions and I want to know the reasons . . . What contact and influence do you have with the officers in your group?"

"I have none."

"Then why do you remain in the position you're in?"

"God knows, I don't."

The court turned to Schauffler's wartime flying to probe Mitchell's claims that anti-aircraft fire was ineffective.

"What altitude did you fly . . . at St. Mihiel, for instance?"

"From treetop height up . . . about five hundred feet."

"Were you in command of a group and allowed to fly that low?"

"We had to."

"Under what orders and instructions?"

"Common sense."

"Without entering into the record now, Colonel, we were all in Europe and I never saw a plane fly as low as five hundred feet."

"You must have been in the dugout, sir."

"No, I was not there, either. Why did you fly at such low altitude?"

"To find the infantry."

"Of the enemy?"

"Of our own troops."

Armistice Day, the seventh since the end of the war, brought no pause in the trial. An American Legion post in New York City had besieged President Coolidge to free Mitchell for a few hours so that he could attend its holiday banquet. The plea became a public issue; the post finally wired the White House: "PRESS REPORTS YOU HAVE NOT RECEIVED OUR TELEGRAM REQUESTING RELEASE OF COLONEL MITCHELL AS GUEST FOR OUR DINNER. TELEGRAM WAS SENT MONDAY MORNING BY POSTAL TELEGRAPH . . . WANT COL. MITCHELL AS GUEST OF HONOR . . ."

The Army replied that the accused could not leave Washington; the Legion's speech in New York that night was delivered by Benny Foulois, who was lukewarm in his defense of Mitchell (Foulois did not testify at the court-martial, and later said he would have both blamed and praised Mitchell if he had been summoned).

The court made a concession that day, as if mellowed by war memories. The generals agreed to a new trial procedure—the defense would be allowed to present evidence in mitigation of Mitchell's offense. If he could prove that he had proper basis for his charges, then he would be exonerated. Newspaper headlines hailed this as a victory for the defense.

To support Mitchell's claims that American defenses in the Pacific were weak, Reid put officers on the stand who had seen the Hawaiian maneuvers of the year before. The first of these, Major Gerald Brandt of the Air Service, who was on the General Staff, spent much of Armistice Day testifying. Reid used him to show that the War Department had smothered Mitchell's sensational report on the Pacific for more than a year—and seemed to have taken no note of it at all until the opening of the court-martial.

"Did General Mitchell make a report on the Hawaiian Islands?"

"He made a report on the conditions in the Pacific which included the Hawaiian Islands, in October, 1924."

"When did this report reach you through channels?"

"Saturday."

"Do you mean last Saturday?"

"Yes, sir."

Brandt said the War Plans Division had commented on this report: "It stated that these recommendations were based on General Mitchell's personal opinions and therefore no consideration need be given them."

Reid asked Brandt if he could bring the document into court;

the witness said he probably could not, since it dealt with strategy.*

Brandt then described the roundabout passage of orders in the Hawaiian maneuvers, when the Navy refused to submit to a unified air command. Each move of a plan, Brandt said, first had to be approved by Army operations, G-3, which took the order to the commanding general: "Then, that would be transmitted again down to the chief of staff of the 14th Naval District, who would take it in and explain it to the commanding officer, and having gotten his decision, it would be transmitted to the naval commander of the aircraft squadrons of the scouting fleet, Captain Yarnell."

Howze interrupted and called the courtroom to attention: "Mr. Reid, it is now about three minutes of eleven. The court is in a state of recess." The general read a brief speech:

"Seven years ago there came to an end the greatest war the world has ever seen; and I am sure that all persons in this room agree with me that we should pay tribute to the heroic dead of both the military and naval forces of the United States who gave their lives to their country and thereby joined the choir invisible—those immortal dead who live again in minds which are made better by their presence. I ask you to face to the east, which is to my right hand, and stand silently for two minutes."

The noise of traffic came through the windows while the crowd stood with its vivid memories of one war, waiting to hear more of the hapless preparations for the next in the remote Pacific islands.

"The court will come to order," Howze said. Reid resumed.

"What made necessary this circuitous route that you have just described?"

"The lack of a unified command," Brandt said. He explained that the attacking Blue force had seized an air base on the island

* At this stage of the trial the Army developed a sudden concern for the security of the Mitchell report. All known copies were located by telegram. For example, Patrick wired Col. C. C. Culver, commanding at Kelly Field, ordering him to report whether a copy of the report was safe at Kelly: "THIS IS SECRET DOCUMENT AND WILL BE MARKED SECRET UNDER PROVISIONS ARMY REGULATIONS 330–5 AS COPY NO. 3." Culver replied that the report was safe, and marked "secret." The sequence of events suggests that the Army was more concerned with publicity relating to the court-martial than with the national security. The copy of the report in Mitchell's Army file was declassified in 1958, when it was thirty-four years old.

of Molokai, seventy miles from Pearl Harbor, but that despite his pleas, the Navy had refused to join an attack on this base. Brandt said the Air Service was deteriorating, that the best pilots were leaving and the flying fields built during the war were getting run-down.

It was then that Mitchell saw the first sign of reinforcements sent into the courtroom by the Army and Navy high command, which had decided that the trial was going badly and that Moreland needed help. Mitchell was whispering advice to Reid, as he often did, when he saw a familiar face at the prosecution table a few feet away. Reid addressed the court: "May I ask who the gentlemen are, sitting as counsel at the table with the Trial Judge Advocate?" He was referring to two men in civilian clothes.

"They're from the Navy Department," Moreland said.

"I should like to know their names for the record."

Moreland announced what most people in the room already knew, that one of them was Captain Alfred Johnson, who had commanded Navy aviation during the 1921 bombing tests. Reid asked that Johnson be barred from the prosecution table, since he might be called as a defense witness. Johnson disappeared after the next recess.

Mitchell soon nudged Reid once more and the lawyer called to Moreland: "By the way, I see you have another Navy man. Can we find out who he is?"

"He's in the Army."

"What's his name?"

"Wilby . . . the War Department, General Staff."

Wilby's presence made a new man of Colonel Moreland, who began bobbing like a puppet during the testimony. Wilby whispered advice into his ear and the chief prosecutor rose to shout his objections as if on command. Howze lost patience: "Sit down, Colonel, sit down. Then you can get what they have to say and get the answers in a hurry."

The courtroom echoed with laughter and a guard rapped on the wall. "Don't go off so loud. This ain't a vaudeville show." Major Francis Wilby was only the first of the General Staff specialists sent to help Moreland save the day. Other reinforcements were on the way.

A new defense witness was Major Roycroft Walsh of the Air

Service, who had commanded Army planes during maneuvers in Panama, and had worked so well with naval air officers that he had taken plans of co-ordinated attack to the maneuvers in Hawaii. The prosecution was determined to hear as little as possible from Walsh. Moreland and Wilby beat back Reid's efforts to have Walsh recite such well-known figures as the total Army and Navy appropriations. Reid argued hotly that these could not be secret, since they had been published in newspapers, and then demanded a decision on the issue of "confidential" matters, insisting that the government unfairly barred his path with such claims. The court was cleared. Reid spotted two other men in civilian clothes with Moreland and was told they were Navy officers.

President Howze, as if to even the score, looked inquiringly over the group sitting with Mitchell and Reid, especially at Joseph E. Davies, and asked if everyone at the defense table belonged there.

Major White assured him that though they had not been introduced, they had been conferring with the defense, and he identified Davies. Howze closed the court, warning Davies and others not to divulge any secrets they might overhear. Even while court was closed the prosecution argued that Major Walsh could not tell certain details of the Hawaiian maneuvers, since they were confidential. Reid reminded the court that at least one hundred reporters had accompanied the Navy during the exercise and had written freely about it, but it was in vain.

When court was opened once more and the spectators had returned, Reid protested these tactics: "I want to call attention to the very foolish thing we were put to this morning in closing the court." He held up a copy of the aviation hearings of the Select Committee of the House. "Here is absolutely everything that was presented this morning . . . published in these reports. That is the point I make. Somebody ought to determine at some time whether what we have is or is not confidential."

"No harm has been done one way or the other," Moreland said blandly, "if the statement he made this morning is the same as that which he made at a public hearing," as if unaware that he had taken unfair advantage of the defense. These tactics were carried to such lengths that Reid was denied the right to introduce newspaper reports on the Hawaiian exercises as evidence, though he threatened to subpoena reporters and publishers.

A final version of these maneuvers came from Lieutenant H. W. Sheridan of the Air Service, who had sailed on the makeshift carrier *Langley*, the converted coal ship. When he told of the fleet of 150 ships leaving San Francisco against an imaginary enemy, Moreland asked if this was confidential.

"There's nothing in my testimony that should be considered secret," Sheridan said, "unless we want to suppress information regarding the condition of aviation in the Navy."

Moreland moved that the remark be stricken from the record "as a matter of plain decency," but he failed to slow Sheridan. The lieutenant told Reid of the clumsy movement of ships from the harbor: "There was . . . a mix-up of ships . . . They finally did get out of the harbor."

"And nearly destroyed the aircraft carrier on the way out?"

"We came within five feet of a collision with the *West Virginia*."

A new assistant prosecutor jumped up to object. He was Major Allen W. Gullion, a well-known courtroom brawler from Kentucky who had once taught military science and tactics at the University of Kentucky. He was in striking contrast to the plump, slow, rather pompous Moreland, a pale, lanky young man with long hair and a broad, mobile mouth, which he often licked with his tongue. He was to play a leading role as bully and villain in the court-martial, and from the first was loud and arrogant, playing to the crowd, ready with pocketsful of press releases of his speeches. He seemed to revel in his assignment, especially in heckling defense witnesses; defense counsel thought when they first saw him that he had been imported for the purpose of attacking Mitchell when he took the stand.*

Reid looked calmly from Wilby to Gullion, who were both on their feet. "Are you going to object, too? I object to tandem objections."

Sheridan said the fleet took twelve days to reach Hawaii because the *Langley* was so slow. He said that a few planes took off from the carrier's deck during the exercise, sometimes disastrously. "When they landed back on the *Langley* they smashed

* Gullion later became Adjutant General of the Army.

four planes." The Navy's planes were not combat planes and few fliers had been through combat training.

Gullion attacked Sheridan with such biting sarcasm that spectators were soon openly siding with the young airman: "Frankly, this witness doesn't know what he's talking about . . . He's not an expert . . . You testified with a great deal of confidence, Mr. Sheridan, about what you call the near collision between the *Langley* and the *West Virginia* . . . What is the draught of a battleship?"

Sheridan said he thought it was about 30 feet.

"Do you know the depth of the channel where that sortie was being made?"

"I'm not familiar with the underwater contours of San Francisco Bay." The crowd giggled.

"As I understand it, then, the only thing you are familiar with is naval tactics—is that so?"

"That is not so."

"Are you a graduate of the Naval War College?"

"I am not."

"Do you know that . . . no one can be a worthwhile commander of a ship or hold high command unless he is a graduate of the Naval War College?"

"I have no high command, sir."

"Do you think one capable of criticizing high command who is not capable of exercising it?"

"I'm capable of exercising air command, yes, sir." The crowd cheered.

Gullion pressed Sheridan so hard that Reid once protested the "Kentucky phrases" of the new prosecutor. When Sheridan admitted that he had been on the *Langley* only twelve days, Gullion asked: "You still believe yourself qualified as a critic of fleet maneuvers and tactics?"

"I can certainly tell when I am about to be collided with."

"Have you ever landed on the deck of an aircraft carrier?"

"No, sir."

"In view of the fact that you've never landed on one, do you feel justified in criticizing the performance of a pilot landing an airplane on the deck of a ship, especially in a seaway and pitch? Do you understand what I mean by seaway and pitch?"

"I think I understand it. If you can understand it, I can. I'm not critical of those naval pilots on the *Langley*. I think they are the finest young men we have in the service today."

"Very good."

Gullion moved to have Sheridan's testimony stricken, but Reid protested that it was "clean, direct" and detailed, and not critical of naval personnel.

Armistice Day ended with celebrations in most American cities. The New York Legionnaires who had sought Mitchell cheered a telegram of regrets from him, hissed and booed another from the War Department, and composed a message to the accused from their banquet table:

"GREETINGS FROM YOUR BUDDIES. AMERICA LOVES A MAN WITH GUTS. 1892 YEARS AGO A PACKED COURT-MARTIAL CONDEMNED A COURAGEOUS SOLDIER FOR TELLING THE TRUTH SO DON'T WORRY. WE ARE ALL WITH YOU AND WE DON'T MEAN MAYBE."

Fiorello La Guardia was one of the signers.

The next day Reid called several combat fliers to the stand, one of them the much-decorated Reed Chambers, who had left the pursuit command given him by Mitchell for commercial aviation. He said he had flown 208 hours in combat in France without being hit, and had "absolute contempt" for fire from the ground.

"You have had a great deal of combat experience in flying," Wilby said.

"I believe that, next to one man, I have had more than anyone else in the American Army."

Wilby cited the records of U.S. anti-aircraft batteries in battle, insisting that they were more deadly than the aviators claimed: "Are you aware that they averaged seventeen planes shot down with 10,273 shots, or an average of 605 shots per plane?"

Chambers said that was news to him, and Wilby projected his calculations in a single arithmetical leap to prove that with modern rapid-fire guns, a battery would shoot down a plane every ten minutes.

Chambers said that it was impossible to accept such figures.

Reid next called the war hero Eddie Rickenbacker, who had risen rapidly to fame after Mitchell had rescued him from his chauffeur's job and helped him become a superb pilot. Rickenbacker was now a manufacturer of automobiles and planes. He gave quick, assured replies.

"Are you a flier?"

"I am."

"And you have the title of 'Ace of Aces,' have you not?"

"I do."

"And for what was that?"

"The greatest number of enemy planes shot down by any American pilot . . . twenty-six—balloons and planes."

"Approximately how many hours were you in the air over there?"

"Approximately three hundred."

"How many hours over enemy lines?"

"Approximately three hundred."

"How many hours exposed to enemy anti-aircraft fire?"

"Approximately three hundred," Rickenbacker replied and added that the fire was never effective.

He said the United States was weak in air reserves, that it was "suicide" to send men aloft without parachutes. As to wartime planes and their continued use: "It is dangerous to have them on hand. The graveyards throughout the United States show that, located or attached to the flying fields."

The prosecution had the remark about graveyards stricken from the record.

Rickenbacker said the United States stood eighth among world powers in air power, and Major Wilby then cross-examined him.

"Did you ever hear of a German ace by the name of Baron von Richthofen?"

"He was exceptionally good—their best."

"How did he come to his death?"

"My understanding is that he was brought down by machine-gun fire from the ground in trench strafing during the advance on Paris."

"He wasn't as fortunate as you in avoiding machine-gun fire?"

"No, sir."

"Are you aware that our twenty-third Anti-aircraft Battery . . . in less than four months brought down officially nine planes with only 5092 shots?"

"Were all those German or some American?" Rickenbacker asked.

He said that bombers had flown as low as 5000 feet during the war, since they were unable to climb higher with their heavy loads.

"You would be very much surprised if the official records of the A.E.F. showed it was above ten thousand feet?"

"I wouldn't be surprised at anything the records show."

20

Nothing More Than Prediction and Prophecy

When the war veterans had left the stand, spectators were amused by the testimony on the summer's highly publicized anti-aircraft tests of the Army, which had been a fiasco. Mitchell's estimate that anti-aircraft guns were worthless against fleets of planes seemed conservative when the witnesses were through.

Lieutenant Harold L. George (who became chief of the Air Transport Command in World War II) told of towing a target back and forth, taking evasive action in an effort to avoid fire from guns below. "I did it for about an hour and came down and asked how things were going along. And the colonel who was running this anti-aircraft gun told me that he had quit long before . . . He said to operate the gun was like trying to pat his head with one hand and rub his stomach with the other." The crowd roared.

Captain Willis Hale, whose squadron had towed targets all summer, described how hits were scored by a man perched precariously on a bomber, with a small grid through which hits were sighted, holding a pencil, stopwatch and score card: ". . . we found it necessary for him to ride on top of the plane itself. He couldn't ride in a seat because he couldn't see the target, so he was lying down against one part of the fuselage with one arm wrapped around a strut . . . glancing back at the target, which was about two thousand feet behind." There had been few hits. After the tests, Hale said, the overworked bomber crews were so worn that they were sent on sick leave.

The court's discipline had slowly sagged and an air of merriment had come over the trial. One reporter wrote: "The court started it all . . . spectators shocked at the first outburst of laughter on the part of the court gradually ventured to let loose a snicker or two themselves. As the days passed the snickers blossomed out into guffaws . . . it is expected that stamping will be in order before the trial is over."

In the courtroom there was no indication that the future security of the United States might be at stake. General MacArthur was especially inattentive. He and his wife were like newlyweds, exchanging meaningful glances—Mrs. MacArthur smiling over a bunch of violets which she carried each day; her husband could hardly keep his eyes off her.

Mrs. Mitchell was busy reading mail and telegrams during many of the sessions, leafing through large bags of correspondence from well-wishers which were piled before the colonel each morning. The generals now strolled in late, bowing and speaking to Mitchell. They lolled in their chairs and stifled yawns as witnesses droned away. The case passed to the inner pages of newspapers and one editorial humorist wrote: "If the court-martial stays off the front page another two days it's feared Col. Billy Mitchell's going to lose interest in these proceedings."

General Howze, the legendary disciplinarian, had at first been sitting bolt upright, intoning after each opinion offered by Colonel Winship: "There being no objection, under the Thirty-first Article of War the ruling of the law member is made the ruling of the court and shall so stand." Now Howze slumped in his chair, feet stretched far under the table, mumbling: "Ruling of the court."

Things went so far that in mid-November Reid once halted and said; "If the court please, there's so much noise in the room that I can't marshal my thoughts." By now even the armed soldiers around the walls were joining each outbreak of laughter. Howze directed their commander to obtain order. The lieutenant told reporters: "Stop rattling those papers. This isn't a reading room." The lieutenant bruised his knuckles during the afternoon trying to quell outbursts of laughter.

Despite the hilarity there was so little public interest in the trial for a few days that one Washington paper sent a feature writer to discover what had become of it. He described the place as lacking in dignity, and the crowd chiefly "women whose domestic duties do not call upon them for time." Outside an open window behind General Howze was a clothesline with some family's wash flapping in the breeze. The *Star* reported: "The judges present an impressive array of medals, campaign stripes, division and officers' insignia, leather puttees and square jaws, and they pencil notes, whisper to each other and drum with their fingers on the curved table."

General King, however, kept the spectators on the edges of their seats. He played with a rubber band, chewed on it, held one end between his teeth and stretched it far in front of his face until spectators were tensely expectant, then eased his hand back and chewed the band once more. "If that band ever breaks," the *Star* reporter said, "many will quit going to the trial."

He found that Mitchell was still the focus of interest in the room: "Right in the center of the fight, with the battle raging all about him . . . gazing straight at the president of the court, right across the stenographer's table which bears the records of his amazing trial. Next to him sits Mrs. Mitchell, small and confident, and a little defiant. . . .

"Reid hurls sharp invective over his head and the prosecution roars back over his head at Reid, and at times Colonel Bill stretches, yawns and gazes out of the window at the flapping clothesline. Perhaps he is thinking of his laundry."

Reporters noted that Reid had worn the same mouse-colored suit, red bow tie and derby every day. When Reid was asked why he didn't wear a different tie, the lawyer responded: "If I put on another one, somebody would accuse me of taking a fee." Reid took his role as a volunteer seriously and returned a check for "several thousand dollars" offered by Mrs. Mitchell's father. When Mitchell presented him with a fine gold watch at the end of the trial, Reid returned that, too, because, he said, he believed in the justice of the cause and wanted no remuneration of any kind.

There were no complaints as to lack of variety in Mitchell's attire. One day he would wear slacks with his new Air Service blouse, and on the next, riding breeches with boots and spurs.

The parading witnesses usually made Mitchell the focus of their testimony. Occasionally, as when Colonel O. C. Pierce, a personnel officer, took the stand, this recognition was direct.

Pierce reported on the several pilot ratings, and said that only about thirty in the Air Service were rated as superior. He was asked to classify these as to type.

"One attack, twenty-one pursuit, five bombardment, and one unclassified."

"What is the unclassified one?"

"He flies anything."

"What is his name? Have you got anybody in that list?"

"General Mitchell is the unclassified one."

The *Shenandoah* case brought the court-martial back to life with a new sensation. The Navy's court of inquiry had been going on during the Mitchell trial, and Margaret Ross Lansdowne, the attractive widow of the airship's commander, had appeared as a witness. Her testimony was routine and drew little attention.

Mrs. Lansdowne was a friend of the Mitchells', and soon after her appearance before the Navy board, she told Mitchell of a Navy conspiracy to have her render false testimony. A naval officer, she said, had tried to persuade her to parrot a statement that would have been "an insult to the memory" of her husband. Here was a substantiation of Mitchell's forecast that the Navy would try to gloss over the *Shenandoah* disaster.

The widow agreed to help Mitchell by testifying before his court-martial. Reid announced her forthcoming appearance several times, and hinted that she would tell a story of a perjury attempt by the Navy. Moreland protested in vain that Reid was trying the case in the newspapers.

She came at last in mid-November, a beautiful, self-possessed woman of twenty-three, in black, with dark bobbed hair and long lashes about her blue-gray eyes; her fair skin was lightly freckled. The court rose as she entered and Howze bowed: "Good morning, Mrs. Lansdowne." She testified coolly, in a clear voice, smiling except when she mentioned her husband. She began by telling Reid that she had been before the Navy board a month earlier.

"Was there a communication delivered to you purporting to come from Captain Foley, the Judge Advocate of the *Shenandoah* court of inquiry?"

"It was delivered to me the day before the court."

"Have you a copy of this communication?"

"I have not . . . I tore it up."

When Reid asked Mrs. Lansdowne what was in the note, Moreland shouted objections. This was "incompetent, immaterial, inadmissible." Reid won his point: "Colonel Mitchell in his statement charged that the Navy would proceed to whitewash the *Shenandoah* accident . . . We expect to show that they did absolutely that by trying to get this witness to give false testimony . . . there couldn't be anything plainer."

"The statement of the accused consisted of nothing more than prediction and prophecy," Moreland said, "and is not the subject of confirmation . . ."

"It is the subject of trial here," Reid retorted.

When this skirmish subsided, Mrs. Lansdowne described the statement Foley had asked her to sign: "It began with the remark that when I first accepted the invitation to appear at the *Shenandoah* court and testify in my husband's behalf, I had done so with the idea that my husband was in need of defense, but . . . my opinion had been changed . . . and that I thought the court was absolutely capable of handling the entire situation, and I was entirely willing to leave it in their hands."

She said the statement offered by Foley also said that though her husband disapproved of "political flights" of his ship, he was willing to take it anywhere, regardless of conditions, for military purposes.

"Was that statement false?" Reid asked.

"False."

"Who sent you this letter?"

"Captain Paul Foley."

The court allowed this startling testimony to remain on the record, but when Reid attempted to add some evidence that she had given to the *Shenandoah* inquiry, he was overruled. He read from the widow's testimony before the Navy probe:

" 'My husband was very much opposed to this flight and protested as vigorously as any officer is allowed to do to his superiors. Everyone knows that in the military or naval services, orders are given to be obeyed and no officer cares to earn the stigma of cowardice or insubordination . . .' "

Reid asked: "Did you give that testimony?"

"I did."

The court sustained Moreland's objection and ruled that the testimony be excluded from the record, over Reid's protest that "it has been printed in every newspaper in the world."

When Moreland started his cross-examination he succeeded only in adding to the controversy. He led Mrs. Lansdowne to tell of the Navy prosecutor's visit to her before he sent the message:

"Captain Foley sought to impress me with the importance of the court and told me that the court had all the powers of any federal court and that the solemnity of my appearance was very great and that I should be sure to tell the truth . . . He then asked me what I was going to say and I answered him that I preferred to make my own statement to the court.

"He asserted that he wanted to find out what I had on my mind, and please to get it off, and said, 'Let's rehearse the statement you are going to make to the court. Tell me the entire thing you are going to say,' and I answered again that I did not want to make my statement.

"He told me that I had no right to say that the flight was a political flight, as the taxpayers in the Middle West had a perfect right to see their property, to which I answered that in the case of a battleship you wouldn't take it out to the Great Lakes and interest the taxpayers in their property, to which he answered that it couldn't be done—and I said that it couldn't in the case of the *Shenandoah,* but they were so stupid it had to be proven to them."

Mrs. Lansdowne left the stand to the grinding of movie cameras and the buzzing of spectators. She had convinced the country of the Navy's guilt, and many newspapers called for Secretary Wilbur's resignation; there were angry editorials about Foley's tactics.

Mrs. Lansdowne's appearance was followed by another, though lesser, sensation. Captain Foley himself came into court, and Moreland asked that the accused Navy prosecutor be heard in rebuttal to the widow. Reid would have none of it, saying that Foley's cause was not being tried there. The court declined to hear the captain and returned to its routine.*

* Foley returned to the Navy court, resigned as prosecutor, testified in his own behalf and was exonerated. Mrs. Lansdowne was called back by subpoena and stirred a new furor by taking Joseph E. Davies as counsel; the court barred civilian counsel, and a Marine guard twice hauled Davies from the room, once as the lawyer shouted: "A witness has those rights in any ordinary tribunal except in

Reid used other witnesses to show that the loss of the *Shenandoah* was due to ignorance of airship handling and inflexible Navy administration. The first of these men was Anton Heinen, a former Zeppelin worker who said that the big airship was based on plans of a German dirigible captured during the war, the L-49.

In halting English, Heinen told of how the *Shenandoah* had been damaged in an earlier accident, and of the failure of the Americans to take instructions from German dirigible crews. He said he did not realize the *Shenandoah*'s valves had been reduced until after the accident: "If I had known this before, everybody might rest assured I would have kicked up a small row."

In the end Heinen was a puzzling, erratic witness, for after having condemned the change in the airship's valves as dangerous, he said that no one could give the exact cause of the ship's loss: "Nobody has any knowledge of what caused the wreck . . . it is a question that nobody in this world can answer." Others were to disagree with the German, but he could not be budged.

The court was once more interrupted by the Navy's *Shenandoah* court of inquiry—a messenger called for Major Frank Kennedy, an airship expert who was waiting to testify for Mitchell. Reid said: "I'm surprised at the nerve of the people running that court down there," and demanded that President Coolidge be asked to halt the Navy's interference. Howze had someone telephone the Navy court to say that Kennedy would arrive shortly, after he had testified at the court-martial.

On the stand, Kennedy said that he had flown to the scene of the *Shenandoah* accident from McCook Field, arriving about three hours after the crash, to find the ship lying in five sections, its gas cells ripped apart. He said that the sleeves leading from the gas manifold had been tied off, which would have prevented the escape of helium. The court would not permit him to testify as to what survivors had told him, and he was dismissed.

Another airship commander, Captain Charles P. Clark, said that "something would have to go" if a dirigible had too few safety valves and went to high altitude. He also said that parachutes were essential; he was not allowed to say whether the absence of

---

Russia." This court fixed no blame for the *Shenandoah*'s loss, except for natural cause—she was ruled the victim of storm, not Navy negligence.

any 'chutes on the *Shenandoah* constituted "criminal negligence."

Lieutenant Colonel John Paegelow, the airship commander at Scott Field, said he would "try any man for disobedience of orders if he didn't carry parachutes."

Gullion asked if a falling airship wouldn't fall faster than a man on a parachute, and crush him. "The man had better be out of the ship when it commences to fall," Paegelow said.

"If he were under it, would he be killed?"

"He wouldn't be under it . . . if he has any sense." Paegelow said that crews of airships had often parachuted to safety in France.

After other airship men had testified, Reid called Earnest Sheehan, a reporter from Cambridge, Ohio, who said that he had reached the broken *Shenandoah* an hour after her crash and that survivors had talked freely with him until after the arrival of a Commander Klein of the Navy: "He requested me not to write the cause of the wreck—what I had determined as far as I had made my investigation . . . Klein knew what I had because I had told him . . . He asked me not to mix in it."

"You don't mean to say, do you, that Commander Klein intended you to permanently suppress any facts?"

"That was the impression I got."

When Sheehan said that neither he nor eyewitnesses had been called to testify before the Navy's inquiry, Gullion quickly excused him.

The court-martial took another turn with the appearance of Admiral William S. Sims, the aging Navy rebel, still vigorous and alert, his hair and imperial now white.

Reid asked Sims to describe the Navy's policy of handling aircraft.

"As I understand it, the Navy Department hasn't any defined policy. It is going along from day to day, more or less in a higgledy-piggledy way."

Were Navy officers afraid to speak their convictions?

Sims told of an officer who agreed with him on air power but feared to speak out before a group of Navy men who were discussing aviation. When Sims questioned him about it, this officer had said: "I can look around this assemblage and see half a dozen people who would probably beat me at the next selection, and I have a wife and two children."

"That's the trouble," Sims said.

As to the *Shenandoah*'s last trip over fairgrounds, he said the "motive behind the thing is wrong."

Sims described the role of the Naval War College in developing combat officers, who went there to learn techniques of handling fleets in war: "They are tested out on a game board in a room as big as this floor, divided into little squares, and the fleets are represented with small models. They have chart maneuvers that precede this and tactical maneuvers, and are given an indication of what it means.

"It is very interesting to see a fine officer come there with twenty-five years' experience, with a good reputation in the Navy, but not a student in any sense—to see him start in with the maneuvers and see the lack of knowledge he has of the proper tactics and strategy, because there is no place in the Navy where it is taught except in the War College, and then to see the man develop through years in the practice and see finally what we call a time maneuver, where two fleets are given to the different commanders and both fleets are surrounded by screens representing a fog . . ."

When the screens were raised, he said, the adjoining fleets were pushed swiftly together, so that in twenty to forty-five seconds the officers must make decisions involving entire fleets. With senators watching the game, the officers were under pressure to do their best. It was the training ground for war at sea.

"The Navy gives lip service to the War College," Sims said, "but they never have used its products in the selection of the three chief officers of the Navy—the Commander-in-Chief of the Fleet, the Chief of Naval Operations and the Superintendent of the Naval Academy—and that is what is the matter with the Navy today."

He quoted Admiral Mahan's dictum that the function of the War College was to find the men who should command the fleet and operations, but said the Navy did not agree. "Those are good men and friends of mine and honest men, but they are uneducated men and they are working all the working day and part of the night, principally attending to someone else's business because they do not understand the first principle of command. That is what we're kicking about all the time."

Major Gullion asked: "Don't you regard it as entirely possible for an officer of great native ability and combat experience to so equip himself by his own energies and study that he is fitted to command?"

"Just about as much as a man who makes a thorough study of all the books he can find on golf and never takes a golf club in his hand."

Gullion called out a list of high-ranking officers, including Admiral Edward Eberle, the Chief of Naval Operations, and Sims identified only seven as graduates of the War College.

"You think it affects the service, that the other men—that the other men headed by Admiral Eberle—do you consider that they are hidebound uneducated men?"

"I certainly do."

Gullion went back to 1919 to read Navy policy statements on aviation, but Sims said he couldn't remember them: "I think there are plenty of papers, but it's the active policy that I'm referring to." Sims said he did not agree with Mitchell's view of a separate air force, but he left no doubt of his opinion that the Navy was making little effective use of air power.

A day later, after another parade of aviators to the stand, Reid had finished his case and said he would present no more witnesses. Mitchell would take the stand on the following Monday, November 23.

The newspapers had built the trial toward a climax for Mitchell's appearance. One day the Washington *Star* ran the headline: "CAPITAL'S LONGING FOR A HERO FILLED PERFECTLY BY MITCHELL"; the paper said that there was a demonstration every time he appeared in public, and that he and Betty were wined and dined when they were out of court "as if he were some visiting prince or potentate."

21

This Factless Statement

Mitchell was pale and tense as he took the stand. One newspaper sketched him admiringly: "Head erect, shoulders thrown back, finely chiseled chin aloft, the very embodiment of defiance and the damnation of all traitors."

Colonel Winship explained to Mitchell that his legal rights permitted him to remain silent, or to testify under oath and face cross-examination, or merely to make a statement, and advised him to consult his lawyer.

"I've already consulted with the accused," Reid said, "and notwithstanding the fact we think we have proved every material fact one hundred percent, we tender the witness . . . and submit him for a full cross-examination by anybody and everybody in the world in this case."

Reid asked Mitchell to give a summary of his military career and to describe the opening of his crusade for air power in 1919 when he returned from the war: ". . . Before coming back I went into the interior of France and consulted with my companions in the air service of various countries . . . with a view to determining what the future use of air power would be in . . . any other war. I then went over to England and did the same thing . . .

"The result was . . . an absolute unanimity of opinion . . . that a future contest between nations would be preceded by two things: intensive action of submarines across the seas, and air attack on the nerve centers of the hostile states so as to eliminate the will to fight . . . that the future war would see an elimination probably of the cannon-fodder systems of the nations in arms as it has been practiced for the last two or three hundred years."

German cities along the Rhine had been bombed at the end of the war, he said, and larger planes were being built. Reid asked him to explain why he campaigned so noisily for aviation.

"When I returned to America it was problematical whether the war had really been finished or not; that is, whether we might be plunged into a contest at any time either east or west of us . . . I lost no time in presenting studies to those in authority which would show them . . . our specific needs."

Then, for more than an hour, Reid drew from him a summary of recommendations he had made, virtually none of them adopted:

In 1918, that the Army and Navy combine their supply systems and experiment stations;

That overseas air units be kept at war strength;

That carriers be built with a capacity of one hundred bombers or one hundred pursuit planes each, and hydrogen dirigibles as carriers of aircraft or aerial torpedoes.

Reid said: "Before we get away from the subject, I wish you would tell about the development in aerial torpedoes."

Mitchell said the weapon was an American invention, "an instrument that goes through the air . . . similar to the way a water torpedo goes through the water, that is, an airplane with gyroscopic controls and can be controlled by radio, with the object of hitting targets at a long distance . . . Every nation is working hard on that . . ."

Mitchell also described the "gliding bomb," which he said could be launched from planes at a distance of ten miles or more from targets in large cities—a winged bomb with accurate controls.

"What is necessary to protect cities like New York and Washington?"

Mitchell spoke as if his vision ranged fifteen years ahead and he were describing English plans for the Battle of Britain: "It involves co-ordinating and making every element work together . . . first, you must have listening posts . . . far enough out to enable our own forces to get into the air at any altitude, both by day and night, and meet the attack . . . they must be from one to two hundred miles out from the nucleus . . .

"These posts must be connected to a central control board . . . by wire lines, radio and every means, so as to distribute the information promptly . . . the scheme must be completely worked out for day and night attack because an attack is not made simply by a ship just flying over a place. Feint after feint is made and everything is done to confuse the defense . . . provision must be made for handling the civilian population . . . alarms . . . places of rendezvous, either underground or getting them completely out of the city . . . medical assistance, feeding these people . . . must be worked out ahead of time. Otherwise, no defense is possible.

"You might say we have never been able to get a study made of a thing like that in this country."

The World War veterans who had commanded in the mud trenches only seven years before stared blankly at him.

He continued with the familiar recommendations he had made: a grade of aviation mechanic, to improve ground crews; a radio network; a meteorological service. "Up to about 1920, as I remember it, we were allowed to telephone from place to place to find out what the weather was . . . those funds were cut off at that time, which I think was a very short-sighted thing."

He had asked for machines to load big bombs, without result. The list went on: amphibious planes for rescue work, floating packets of medical and food supplies, floating rafts . . . German Fokkers to replace De Havillands . . . Night-flying practice over water, all-metal bombers. Airways through the United States and the hemisphere, through Alaska and Asia and around the world . . . Air units in Alaska, a strategic point in Pacific defense . . . Skids and skis for planes . . . Four-engined bombers . . . Variable-pitch and reversible propellers for use at varying altitudes.

He had urged self-starters for planes: "The present method of starting is very inefficient and very dangerous. The men have to pull the propellers and if for any reason there is a back fire, or if the engine fires prematurely, the men are either killed or maimed."

New planes should be built for the annual speed races, to develop faster models . . . A new policy of Pacific defense . . . A revision of war plans so that a single air commander would direct the first phase of defense against attack . . . Closer liaison between the Air Service and other branches.

He said that fog-flying instruments, often recommended and still lacking, were an acute need, but could be provided with two years of development. He had asked for a bomber with a cruising range of "many thousands of miles" and an observation plane with a ceiling of 30,000 feet and a 1500-mile range. Neither existed, though engineers said the observation plane could be built promptly.

"Would they be useful?"

"They would be useful particularly in the Pacific. That's the kind of observation ship the future will require."

Mitchell described the first cross-country flights which had led to airway development, his Pacific trip of inspection, his speed record of 1922. Reid broke in: "Have you ever asked any man . . . to perform duties that you were not ready to undertake first yourself?"

"None that I know of."

Reid ran out of questions after almost an hour and a half. He at last asked Mitchell to name the major engagements of the war in which he had taken part. "With the American Army . . . Cambrai, the Somme Defensive, the Champagne-Marne, the Aisne-Marne, the Oise-Marne, St. Mihiel, Meuse-Argonne, the Defensive Sector."

"Now, with the French?"

"Mont Sans Nomme, Mont Cornouillet, Mort Homme, Champagne . . . Verdun." The list went on in Mitchell's fluent French, ending with the British battles at Bullecourt and Ypres. As the musical roll of the old battles ended, Reid turned him over to the eager Gullion.

Their first confrontation woke up the courtroom.

"Colonel Mitchell, have you any idea of the estimated wealth of the United States?" The crowd laughed at the unexpected opening.

"No."

Gullion fished the figure from the latest *World Almanac*—$302,803,862,000. "Now, I would be much obliged to you if you would keep that figure in solution, and the relevancy of the question will appear later. Now, I will repeat it again—"

"I object to that," Reid said, "to his holding anything in solution, and I ask that the question be passed on."

"It was only for Colonel Mitchell's benefit that I wanted to repeat the figure. I doubt now if Mr. Reid can repeat it."

"No, but I object to your repeating it."

After this squabble Gullion attacked Mitchell's criticism of Pacific Fleet maneuvers. He quoted Mitchell: " 'Suppose that we had been at war with a Pacific power and this fleet of surface vessels had been in San Francisco Harbor. Instantly the Pacific power's submarines would have planted all entrances to the harbor with mines.' Would you mind telling us what Pacific power you had in mind?"

"Japan."

When he was asked for an example of a ship sunk by a mine during the war, Mitchell replied: "The *Audacious*."

"Are you familiar with Corbett?"

"Jim Corbett?"

"No, not Jim Corbett. Don't think I'm trying to make a hippodrome out of this. I certainly didn't mean Jim Corbett. I have reference to the naval authority Corbett."

"No."

"In his book *Naval Operations of the World War* he says that the *Audacious* was not sunk that way."

"I have heard others say she was."

"Then you take what you have heard people say over what is laid down in serious history, do you?"

"I have heard people as serious as anybody could be say that."

When Mitchell clung to his opinion that mines would threaten a fleet leaving San Francisco in wartime, Gullion read further from the statement: " 'If the surface vessels ever got through these, the whole Pacific Ocean would be districted off into squares and to each of these districts submarines would be assigned for the purpose of tracking the surface ships and attacking them.' Didn't that create a false impression in the mind of the average reader?"

"No, I don't think so," Mitchell said. "I don't think it would create half the impression as if we had a war."

"Your statement . . . appears, from the kindliest interpretation, slightly exaggerated, doesn't it, Colonel?"

"No, it does not."

Gullion tried to pin Mitchell down on Japanese submarine tactics: "Do you think any . . . would be ordered to guard more than nine hundred miles?" Mitchell said he didn't know.

Gullion built a set of theoretical figures—the Pacific area involved, he said, was more than ten million square miles. He concluded from his own calculations that Mitchell's warning meant that the Japanese must send 2500 submarines to sea. "Now, I'll give you a pencil and paper to figure that out, if you want to."

"That's a foolish question as far as I'm concerned," Mitchell said.

Gullion said a submarine cost $5,000,000, and since no more than 10 percent of a submarine fleet could be kept at sea during war, Japan must have at least 124,946 submarines to become such a threat as Mitchell had "heralded to the world." And those vessels, he said, would cost almost $625 billion. He then came to the point of the long preamble: "Now, I believe we stated, for your edification and instruction, that the wealth of the U.S. was $302,803,862,000. It would cost, then, to carry out your plan, $624,730,000,000—over twice the wealth of the U.S.?"

Mitchell only smiled and said he would like to have his own plans financed on such a basis.

Gullion returned to Mitchell's statement, adding a few lines: " 'These ships would be under constant attack by gunfire from submarines that can carry any size cannon, and use projectiles containing gas, high-explosive or armor-piercing. They use underwater torpedoes which not only will hit the sides of the ships but will hit their bottoms, and can produce gas clouds which will completely envelop any fleet.' "

"I'd like to have that put into the record," Mitchell said, "because that is exactly what would happen."

When Mitchell said he couldn't predict how large the guns on Japanese submarines might be, Gullion asked: "Then, if you don't know, why did you say in your statement . . . that they could carry any size?"

"I say that was my opinion."

"That is your opinion now?"

"Yes."

"Then, any statement—there is no statement of fact in your whole paper?"

"The paper is an expression of opinion."

"There is no statement of fact in the whole paper?"

"No."

"Any statement of fact in your whole paper?"

"No."

Gullion asked for details of the torpedoes Mitchell had described, and was told they were being worked on abroad.

"You don't know whether any have been put into service?"

"I don't know. I've never been allowed to use torpedoes in the Air Service."

"Do you know of any torpedo that can produce a gas cloud which can completely envelop a fleet?"

"You don't produce gas clouds with torpedoes." *

". . . Now, in order to differentiate between opinion and imagination, I should like to know what was the source of your information."

"The source of my information was the studies I have made practically all over the northern hemisphere and what I have seen and what I believe is the case, looking forward into the future so as to render an adequate national defense to this country. That's it."

Occasionally Mitchell tried to divert Gullion in his literal pursuit of details by suggesting a broader view of national defense. To Gullion's question, "Can you cite a single instance where a submarine attacked a fleet by gunfire?" Mitchell replied: "The more we look back onto weapons that are obsolete, the less we will be prepared in the future."

* The Navy kept a close eye on Mitchell during the trial, and the director of its War Plans Division got a report from Captain M. G. Cook on this exchange: "It is not apparent . . . that the accused contradicts himself on any material point. It will be noted that the accused when obliged to confess his ignorance of details . . . usually took refuge in the statement that the whole of his statements at San Antonio were based on matters of opinion." As to the torpedoes: "On cross-examination the accused stated that you do not produce gas clouds with torpedoes. The Assistant Trial Judge Advocate claimed that this was a contradiction . . . In fairness to the accused it might be alleged that his statement is susceptible to another interpretation."

Gullion demanded more specific answers. "Is your idea of a submarine attacking a fleet by gunfire imagination?"

"No."

"Is it a fact?"

"No."

"Now, in your statement of September fifth, 1925—that is, this factless statement—"

"I object," Reid said.

"You want to stop that, Mr. Judge Advocate," Winship said. "That's merely an interjection that doesn't ask a question and that is a conclusion on your part."

"I withdraw that," Gullion said, "and I'm very sorry." He read the Mitchell statement again, this time including remarks about the movements of the Pacific Fleet and the cost of the maneuvers.

"Then, if you were not aware of the training motives in these exercises . . . how do you justify your statement?"

"From what I saw in the newspapers."

"Is that your usual source of information?"

"Usually, respecting the Navy, because I can't get statements from the Navy."

Mitchell conceded that the United States might have assembled the largest submarine fleet in history for the maneuvers. As to the naval aircraft, he didn't know.

"Are you aware of the fact that the number of . . . aircraft assembled in the Pacific . . . was greater than the number . . . assembled for the bombing tests off the Capes of the Chesapeake in 1921?"

"Yes, sir. And much more worthless than those assembled at Langley in 1921."

"The numbers were greater?"

"Numbers mean nothing, in the air. It is excellence."

"Excellence?"

"Yes, sir. Excellence in material and personnel . . ."

"Do you believe in training combatant forces in peace, in order to perform their functions in war?"

"Yes, sir. But it must not lead to a false conception or conclusions of conditions in war."

The duel had lasted for an hour, and though Mitchell finished stronger than when he began, he had disappointed the defense in his first clash with Gullion—especially in saying that his statements were not factual, when his whole defense was built on the claim that he had always spoken the truth. After a rest at lunch Mitchell returned, more like himself.

Gullion read from Mitchell's criticism: " 'Officers and agents sent by the War and Navy Departments to Congress have almost always given incomplete, misleading or false information about aeronautics.' "

"That is a fact and not opinion," Mitchell said.

"You made the statement? That is the question."

"Yes, and I wished to call attention to these things."

Reid cautioned him: "Wait a minute. Just answer his question."

"I don't want to precipitate a quarrel between Mr. Reid and the accused," Gullion said.

"There won't be any quarrel," Reid said, "not the slightest."

Gullion read another of Mitchell's statements: "I will ask you whether it is yours or not: 'In the development of air power one has to look ahead and not backward and figure out what is going to happen, not too much what has happened. That is why the older services have been psychologically unfit to develop this new arm to the fullest extent . . .' Isn't it a fact that air officers in the development of air power look backward for lessons to guide them?"

"They have so little to go on in looking backward, they have to look forward in order to meet the conditions in air arms."

Gullion turned to Mitchell's criticism of the Navy's Hawaiian flight: "Do you still regard the PN-9 as a really good-for-nothing big, lumbering flying boat?"

"For the purpose of flying from the Pacific Coast to Honolulu, I do." Mitchell described his visit to the Navy hangar at San Diego before the PN-9 left, and added: "I was perfectly certain then the ship could not make the trip."

"Do you offer yourself, speaking from San Antonio on September fifth, as a better critic of that flight than Commander Rodgers, who knows every detail of it, participated in it, and commanded the PN-9?"

"I do."

"In view of the fact that . . . they were able to navigate their ship and live through those seas for a period of nine days . . . knowing their position at all times—do you consider that the structural design was insufficient to properly protect personnel?"

"I don't know how heavy the seas were and I don't think they navigated entirely. I think they were carried by the current and I think it was a terrible thing to subject themselves to, under the circumstances."

"Did you know they had radio communication . . . with Pearl Harbor, a distance of over eight hundred miles?"

"That might be the case."

"Would you call that an inadequate transmitting set for a patrol of this type?"

"Entirely, because they couldn't transmit when they got down on the water."

Gullion read an opening sentence from Mitchell's statement: " 'These accidents are the direct result of incompetency, criminal negligence and almost treasonable administration of the national defense by the War and Navy Departments.' Well, what is treason?"

"May I refer to my sheet here where I have the definition written down? . . . There are two definitions of treason, one is that contained in the Constitution. That is, levying war against the United States, or giving aid and comfort to its enemies. The other is to give up or betray; betraying of any trust or confidence; perfidy or breach of faith. I believe that the departments, the system, is almost treasonable in that it does not give a proper place to air power in organizing the defenses of the country, which is vital as an element. That is what I believe. It is a question of the system, and not the individuals, entirely."

Gullion read on: " 'The conduct of affairs by these two departments, as far as aviation is concerned, has been so disgusting in the last few years as to make any self-respecting person ashamed of the cloth he wears.' Do you mean that to be taken literally?"

". . . Yes . . . I think officers in the Air Service who are subjected to the command of people who know absolutely nothing about aviation, who come and inspect their outfits without knowing anything about them whatever and ask foolish questions—"

"Please answer the question."

"I think that is repugnant in every way to a man who has given up his life to this duty and is constantly exposed to danger in the air in that way. It is the worst example of that sort of command I have ever known in aviation."

Gullion attacked Mitchell's remarks on aviation in the Navy and its only carrier, the *Langley,* the converted collier. "Do you know how the *Langley* ranks in size as compared with the carriers existing in the world?"

"I can give you all that data from looking at it. She is useless as a carrier."

"You can't give us an approximate idea?"

"No, except that she is almost worthless as a carrier."

"That is an opinion, is it?"

"That is a fact."

"Then you have found a fact, all right."

Reid objected and asked that the remark be stricken.

Gullion said: "Do you actually know of any aircraft carriers under construction by any nation which will possess as much speed and carry as many guns and aircraft as the *Lexington* and *Saratoga*?"

"I doubt if any other nation will construct any according to the present system of aircraft carriers."

Gullion tried to show that Mitchell advocated a new and dreadful form of war, directed against civilian populations. "You stated this morning that . . . the soldier in war will no longer be cannon fodder? Will bombing attacks on women and children in another war be more humane simply because they are destroyed in that way instead of by cannon?"

"I can't answer that question."

Gullion read a passage from Mitchell's book *Winged Defense:* " 'To gain a lasting factor in war, the hostile nation's power to make war must be destroyed. This means manufacturing, communications, food products and even bombs and fuel and oil and places where people live and carry on their daily lives.' Is that your statement?"

"Yes, that's correct."

Then, as if this had revealed Mitchell as the sole advocate of this concept of air war, the prosecutor probed the airman's invasion of the Navy's domain: "Did you recommend that the Army build . . . carriers?"

"I don't care who built them just so the United States had them. They ought to have had them five years ago."

Gullion turned to Mitchell's report on the military menace of Japan: "Upon what did you base that report?"

"The best information available in the world today about them."

"What is that?"

"I would like to give that in secret . . . It is very definite and very excellent and I have got it." Gullion dropped the matter and court was not closed to hear the secrets.

The *Shenandoah* and dirigibles came next. Gullion paused once to complain about the witness: "I don't like to make the objection, but most of my questions are 'yes' or 'no' questions, and I don't think the accused should be permitted to get the signal from his counsel."

Mitchell rose halfway out of his chair, shaking a finger angrily under Gullion's nose. Reid jumped up: "You're liable to encounter considerable trouble if you make that accusation. I want to object to any statement of that kind. I have made no signals to the witness and do not intend to and do not have to. I merely want him to keep within the rules . . ."

Gullion tried to show that Mitchell was not an expert on dirigibles. "Have you had any experience in the design or construction of rigid airships?"

Mitchell said he had studied their designs in Germany, France and Italy. "I don't consider myself a technical man at all, but I have studied them as far as I could."

By late afternoon the strain seemed to affect Mitchell. The New York *World* man, Arthur Chamberlin, described him as "extremely nervous" at the end of the day, with twitching jaw muscles, his eyes somewhat sunken; he had often been sitting with his chin lowered to his chest during the grilling, "yet every now and then his old-time defiance would flash forth." *

* William Webb of the defense thought Mitchell was tense because he suddenly realized that the whole burden of his case was upon him, and that Gullion would use every trick to confuse him. When he saw that he was doing

. . .

The largest gallery of the trial appeared the next morning, so that guards were forced to use ropes to control the crowd. Many congressmen and other notables came, and there was pushing and shoving all day, especially during the lively afternoon session. Mitchell seemed to be cheered by this show of interest. The *New York Times* said he had regained control and was alert and bright-eyed, without nervousness in his quick, sure replies to Gullion. The Kentuckian kept him on the stand all morning and for an hour in the afternoon. He began with air accidents. Mitchell could give no specific figures, but Gullion furnished them. "Do you know that the number of flying hours per fatality . . . increased from 934 in 1921 to 5269 in 1925?"

"I don't know without referring to my notes. It's a very misleading statement."

Gullion said that it was almost twice as safe to fly in the American as in the British air service, but when Reid asked to see his proof, the prosecutor said the figures were confidential and couldn't be shown unless court was closed.

"Show them to him," Colonel Winship said.

"Just slip them to me," Reid said. "Will you just whisper them to me?"

Gullion was not amused. He continued, saying that American military aviation was 50 percent safer than the French, four times as safe as the Italian. Mitchell said the figures were meaningless.

"Is your personal observation a safer guide than the statistics actually gathered and published?" Gullion asked.

"Yes, sir. Because the statistics don't show that our fliers are restricted to airdromes and never get away from them and never take the risks of cross-country runs. You can twist statistics . . ."

Gullion read the findings of several boards on plane crashes, detailing the deaths of pilots, and though the boards had fixed no blame, Mitchell said that each time faulty equipment had caused the accident.

---

badly, Webb thought, Mitchell "froze"; his lawyers did not coach him during the recess, but he came back refreshed, with a new grip on himself. Thereafter, he was much more impressive.

Ruth Mitchell said that the general's heart troubled him during his testimony, but that despite Reid's pleas, he refused to ask for a delay in the trial.

The prosecutor took up Mitchell's charge that "the airmen themselves are bluffed and bulldozed so that they dare not tell the truth," and asked what officers he had in mind.

"I refer to myself principally."

"You dare not tell the truth?"

"Not that I dare not tell the truth, but that I am bluffed and bulldozed."

"You speak in the plural—'the airmen themselves are bluffed and bulldozed.' "

"Yes."

"Do you consider yourself in the plural habitually?"

Reid objected and had Gullion read the entire paragraph from which he had quoted: " 'The airmen themselves . . . dare not tell the truth in a majority of cases, knowing full well if they do they will be deprived of their future career and sent to the most out-of-the-way places to prevent their telling the truth and deprive them of any chance for advancement unless they subscribe to the dictates of their nonflying bureaucratic superiors.' Do you feel that you were sent to an out-of-the-way place?"

"I certainly was."

"Do you consider San Antonio a most out-of-the-way place to which an officer can be sent?"

"I certainly consider it an out-of-the-way place so far as influencing air service development is concerned."

"How about as far as publicity is concerned?"

"That's a question."

Gullion's next move was to charge Mitchell with plagiarism. Again he read from *Winged Defense:* " 'Existing records show that during the war the Germans maintained only about thirty submarines at sea. They started the war with a total of about forty submarines, counting all sizes. That was a small number but they had a good start in their design and development work.' "

Offering in evidence a document confidential until then, he said: "It is a lecture delivered at the General Staff College by Captain Hart, United States Navy." *

"What are you trying to do?" Reid asked.

"I'm going to show that the accused cribbed page after page of this book from which he is making money."

* Thomas N. Hart, later an admiral, and commander of the Asiatic Fleet at the outbreak of World War II.

"Oh, that's it?"

"Yes."

The crowd hissed.

"That's fine, and material to the issue in this case," Reid said, "and shows how much you know what this case is about."

"We want it in evidence," Gullion said, ". . . and we will put it in in deadly parallel if the accused wants it."

"Nothing is deadly except in your mind. I object to it because it's not proper in this case. If you want to try a copyright suit or a libel suit, that's a different thing."

When the court asked the purpose of injecting the Hart matter, Gullion said: "Mr. Reid, when he introduced the accused, said, 'There is the witness. I don't care if you or anybody under the sun cross-examines him on his statements.' Now, the accused says in this statement, 'I have written this book,' and I am cross-examining him to show he didn't write the book."

Reid said: "Now, that's fine . . . You're trying to bring in another case. I didn't know you were practicing law on the outside. I object to it."

The Hart pamphlet was ruled inadmissible by the court, but Gullion kept trying: "Colonel Mitchell, did you write all the other pages of this book?"

"That book is under my signature."

When Gullion asked if Mitchell had given credit to his sources by footnotes, Reid objected: "I don't think it is proper evidence. I'm willing to have the court read it."

"And let the court pay $2.50 each for it?" Gullion asked.

The crowd hissed again.

Howze intervened: "Gentlemen, confine yourselves to the issue in the case."

"Colonel, you feel, do you not, that all of the committee recommendations you have made during the past seven years were sound and should have been adopted?"

"I feel they were the best made at the time they were made. Those things vary from year to year. As science develops, national defense methods improve and our position among the nations changes."

Mitchell defended his purchase of an experimental model of the large bomber, the Owl, as the only giant U.S. bomber of its day. He also said his purchase of three hundred Wright engines for over $2,000,000 was sound, since they were the only pursuit motors in the country at the time.

Gullion summed up the orders: "Do you realize that the above recommendations of yours, which were carried out, cost the nation $6,299,278.35?"

"It insured our developing our pursuit aviation, which couldn't have been done in any other way . . . I don't remember what the amount was . . . it was money well spent."

Gullion's tone became more derisive as he tweaked Mitchell about one of his phrases in the San Antonio release: "Now, Colonel Mitchell, in one of your statements you speak of 'we in the air fraternity'—do you recall the expression?"

"Yes."

"Is this 'we in the air fraternity' an incorporated organization?"

"Unquestionably, it is not."

"What does this air fraternity consist of?"

"It means the people who fly in the air."

"Is there an organized air fraternity?"

"No. Just a community of spirit and a community of interest."

"Has this community of spirit and community of interest been recognized by anybody as an official organization?"

"No."

"Who are the leaders of this air fraternity?"

"Everybody that flies has an equal voice in it."

". . . How are the funds raised to support this air fraternity?"

"There are no funds raised."

"Who is this 'we' you refer to in the air fraternity that 'then and there decided to put the issue squarely up to Congress and the people'?"

"We talked it over and discussed what had gone on and decided we would stand that sort of stuff no longer."

The probe turned to Mitchell's claim that aviation policies were set by nonflying officers, and that airmen were "pawns in their hands."

Gullion showed that four of the six men on the Aeronautical Board qualified as fliers or observers, but Mitchell said: "You can qualify a man with a trick course any time you want to, but that doesn't make him a flying officer knowing his business." He said that there was "no aircraft policy," and when Gullion showed him an Army order concerning aviation, he scoffed. "Yes. This is it, unfortunately . . . It's not worth the paper it's written on. That is one of the most dangerous orders we have ever had for national defense."

Gullion read from Mitchell's charges on the *Shenandoah:* " 'Her survivors are muzzled by the Navy Department, pending a whitewash board. Are these things so, or are they not? I'm down here in Texas and have not all the data at hand, but I'm sure the facts are practically as stated.' "

"Are you still sure the facts are practically as stated?"

"More so than ever. I know they are now."

The examination turned to the Army's "propaganda service": "Did you ever give any information to the press, while Assistant Chief of the Air Service?"

"Often. There was no other way of getting the truth out, I found."

Gullion wanted the reply stricken from the record as "not responsive." The court overruled him. As he neared the end, Gullion reminded Mitchell that in 1913 he had opposed separation of the Air Service from the Signal Corps. "Did you make that statement?"

Mitchell took no refuge in the qualifications he had made in his early pronouncement on air power. "Yes," he said, "and I never made a worse statement." The crowd laughed and Mitchell smiled.

Gullion then said, unexpectedly: "We are through with the witness." *

* Though Major Gullion carried the prosecution's burden in the trial, the Navy furnished him much of his material. The extent of the Navy's aid was noted during World War II by naval lieutenants in a Philadelphia warehouse, where they discovered a filing cabinet of Navy documents, position papers used in the Mitchell court-martial. They included questions to be put to Mitchell and others, some of them personal in nature, hostile, and evidently designed to destroy Mitchell's credibility. In the officer group were James Michener, the future novelist, and Gibson McCabe, the future president of *Newsweek*. Michener, who tried to pursue his reading of the papers for a second day, was incensed to find that another officer on duty had burned all of the papers overnight, on the theory that they reflected discredit upon the Navy.

Outside the courtroom Betty found his spirits still unflagging. When she despaired, he tried to cheer her: "Suppose they do find me guilty? Guilty of what? I've committed no crime. Suppose I am dismissed? Well, I've always wanted to hunt big game in Africa. Disgrace? What's the disgrace?"

At other times she found him so distracted by the strain of the trial that she concluded that he had put all other thoughts from his mind. Her birthday came during the trial, and when the day passed without a sign that he had taken note of it, she thought he had forgotten. That evening he came home late, urged her to dress hurriedly for dinner, and led her down the elevator to another floor. When the door opened she found herself in the midst of a celebration, a champagne party for scores of their friends, which Mitchell had arranged long in advance.

22

Damned Rot!

After Mitchell had left the stand, the trial entered its hectic final phase. The defense created fresh sensations almost daily, and the courtroom was so electric with tension that the least bit of humor brought hysterical laughter from the crowd. One attraction was Fiorello La Guardia, who had been warned by Mitchell that he might be called on for help.

Bissell telephoned The Little Flower, who was in New York; the future mayor of New York City, a war pilot and an ardent air-power advocate, was in his fourth term in Congress. "It's not convenient for me to come," he said, "but I'll be there." Bissell agreed to meet his train at four-thirty the next morning and take him to a hotel; he also followed La Guardia's orders and staged a press conference in the hotel room before court opened. La Guardia appeared with lathered face, in pajamas, ordered breakfast for the reporters, and regaled them with an attack on the Mitchell court: "Why, he's not being tried by his peers, but by dogrobbers of the General Staff!" The Washington newsmen ran out to file their story, and soon an extra edition was on the streets.

When La Guardia took the witness stand, the judges had already seen a copy of the paper. The witness entertained the crowd with a tale of the anti-aircraft tests at Fort Tilden, New York, gesturing with his arms as if flying. No targets had been hit, he said, no information given out, nothing accomplished; New York City would be helpless in an air attack. The crowd was still chuckling when Gullion took over the cross-examination.

"Mr. La Guardia, the newspapers recently . . . quoted you as saying . . . : 'Billy Mitchell isn't being tried by a jury of his peers, but by nine beribboned dogrobbers of the General Staff.' Were you correctly quoted?"

"I didn't say beribboned."

The laughter in the courtroom delayed the proceedings for several minutes. Howze broke in: "The court would like to have you explain what was meant by your characterization of this court."

"I don't think I'm called upon to do that, but I'll be glad to do it."

"This is a question sent in to me by the court," Howze said. "If you don't care to answer it, you needn't do so."

"From my experience as a member of Congress and from my contact with the General Staff, I'm convinced that the training, the background, the experience and the attitude of officers of high rank of the Army are conducive to carrying out the wishes and desires of the General Staff." La Guardia had an afterthought: "I want to say that at that time I didn't know General MacArthur was on this court."

The spectators burst into laughter once more, joined by the judges.*

"How high in rank does an officer have to get," Howze asked, "before he comes within your characterization?"

"General, it all depends on whether he wants to stay in the Army. There's no difference in the Army from what it is in real political circles. There's no difference. There is that same discipline. There is that same desire to carry out the wishes of those who control."

Soon after La Guardia's departure two officers, Brigadier General Leroy Eltinge and Major Jarvis Bain, tried to discredit Mitchell's views on the Hawaiian defenses by describing recent war games in the islands as a wonderland in which "imaginary Army troops on imaginary transport" fought one another to an

* This was the only moment during the trial when MacArthur drew official attention. He was otherwise uncharacteristically silent for the seven weeks. Mitchell described MacArthur as sitting in the court with "his features as cold as carved stone."

undetermined conclusion. Eltinge, former Assistant Chief of Staff for War Plans, also explained why there could never be an independent air arm: "The Army is organized primarily for and trained for duty on land, the Navy primarily for duty in the water. These two overlap at the shoreline. An additional service [air] which overlapped both of them completely would make co-operation absolutely impossible."

Reid asked Eltinge about the war games: "If there had been one command for the Army and Navy, would it have been better?"

"My opinion is that it would not have made any difference."

"Then why did you say that a third one would have made a big difference, if two wouldn't make any difference?"

"Because the line of demarcation between the two is very narrow, but the Air Service would overlap the entire two."

"Do you know any degrees of failure in war?"

"Oh, yes."

"You do?"

"Yes."

"Bad failure, poor failure and worse failure?"

"Yes."

The staff officer also denied that the Hawaiian maneuvers had shown serious defects in U.S. military training and defense.

"They did fail in this maneuver, didn't they, in their mission?"

"Not entirely."

"Well, how much did they fail—ninety percent, or seventy-five percent?"

"Oh, I would say about ten percent."

"You don't mean that, do you?" Reid barked—but he could move Eltinge no further. The staff officer left an impression of an indistinct, unexplored no man's land lying between the Army and Navy in the Pacific.* When he was defending the Army's plans for

* This general question of joint, or unified, command was one of the most vital aired in the trial, though it was unrecognized as such by many, including the court. It was an issue the United States was slow to face, in Pacific commands great and small. After World War II, Douglas MacArthur was complaining bitterly: "Of all the faulty decisions of the war, perhaps the most unexplainable one was the failure to unify the command in the Pacific . . . It resulted in divided effort . . . waste . . . duplication . . . added casualties and cost."

Pacific defense, Eltinge said he had one incomplete copy with him, but would not permit Reid to see it—the papers were passed down the row of generals of the court as proof that it existed, but they were not to read it either.

Major Bain heightened the impression left by Eltinge. He explained that Army-Navy co-operation worked on the principle of "paramount interest"—the Army commanding in the case of a land problem, and the Navy assuming control at or near the waterline. The service with the lesser interest, Major Bain explained, would co-operate voluntarily. This could not be forced—the Navy might, as it did in the Hawaiian maneuvers, decline to obey Army commands.

Reid asked Bain if he would have invoked "paramount interest," had he been commanding during the Hawaiian war games.

"Not if it was against the law."

"Is it against the law?"

"There's no provision for it so far as I know."

Reid tried to lead Bain to concede that Army-Navy co-operation was vital: "Is it considered against common sense even by military and naval men?"

"There's a difference of opinion about that."

Reid sensed that the heart of the defense problems Mitchell had attacked was here, and he fenced with Bain at length in an effort to prove that Army-Navy co-operation in the field amounted to anarchy. The court became impatient when he used the quick, sharp tactics of civilian lawyers in his cross-examination; Reid's questions often came so rapidly that the expert stenographers could not keep pace.

At one point he asked Bain: "Then there is no hope for the Joint Board ever promulgating a pamphlet which will give the command to the 'paramount interest' at any time?"

Bain said that Reid had confused "paramount interest" with "unity of command."

"No, I'm not confused on either. You said it was against the law for any Navy man to direct Army planes—is that correct?"

"As their commander."

"As their director—do you distinguish between a commander and a director?"

"There could be a distinction—yes, sir."

The frustrated Reid, pressing for an admission on the point, finally asked: "What is the correct thing?"

"That the Navy, having the paramount interest, should have co-ordinated their activities with the Army, but there is another question—"

General King could bear Reid's pursuit of Bain no longer. He turned angrily to his neighbor on the bench and exclaimed: "Damned rot!"

Reid whirled on him: "I object to that. This is not damned rot in your mind or anybody else's, and I object to it."

"I was talking to General—"

"I know, but I heard it."

"Go ahead with your questions," Colonel Winship said. The law member was obviously uneasy about the squabble between judge and defense counsel.

"I have kept within every rule in regard to this proceeding," Reid said, "and I certainly don't want any member of the court making such a remark."

"I'm sorry, Mr. Reid," King said.

"This may be a little tedious to you, but I have a mission to perform in my cross-examination of this witness and it is not being unnecessarily prolonged."

He turned back to Bain, but got little more from him, other than the opinion that joint Army-Navy air command would never become a fact in the U.S. service.

Another familiar figure who came to the stand was Captain Alfred Johnson, Mitchell's adversary of the 1921 bombing tests. Reid used him to give a glimpse of the Navy's methods of anti-Mitchell propaganda.

"Will you please state to the court—if you know—what the purpose of the Navy Department was in preparing and issuing a motion picture film called *Eyes of the Fleet*, showing only pictures of misses from bombs dropped by airplanes on battleships?"

Johnson said he didn't know, but he did produce a copy of a memorandum on the film, from which Reid quoted: ". . . it is suggested that when this film is assembled, a representative of the Recruiting Bureau go over the material available in the bureau so that parts of it as are appropriate may be cut . . ."

Reid also found a penciled note on the document: " 'The object of this is to combat the effect of General Mitchell's testimony and to belittle the value of the airplanes. It is to be developed by Naval Recruiting Service, probably this summer and fall, before Congress meets.' " Johnson said he couldn't recall this note, nor could he remember whether he had ever seen films of the bombs missing the battleship targets.

When Gullion objected, the reading and the testimony of Johnson were ordered stricken from the record.

A last-minute discovery gave the defense new evidence that the Army was propagandizing the Mitchell affair, even while the court-martial was in session. James T. Williams, an editor of the Boston *American,* appeared with some Army releases which he had been asked to publish.

Issued early in the trial, one release read: "This trial has been in progress for four days, during which not one iota of evidence has been presented; the fault, if any, cannot fairly be charged to the prosecution. This was the natural result of the attempts by the defense to make of the court-martial a general inquiry into the ramifications of the air service of the Army and Navy . . ."

Reid's defense was criticized as "an endless procession of objections" with the "object of evading the issue, that of the innocence or guilt of the defendant on the 96th Article of War."

Major Wilby protested for the government that this was not a press release but an Army information sheet, since the word "release" appeared nowhere on its pages. He asked that it be ruled out as irrelevant.

"He forgets what the subject is," Reid said. "The subject is propaganda. We don't care what you call it, press release, love letter . . . It has the same effect."

When Wilby said this was not propaganda from the War Department itself, Reid asked: "Who is it . . . the ladies' aid society?"

The court couldn't make up its mind and would rule the releases neither in nor out, but held them under advisement.

The defense ended its case by reading into the record the exhaustive findings of the Lassiter Board, whose urgent calls for stronger aviation had been ignored for almost three years. It was a basic document, bristling with statistics and interminable technical problems; the Washington *Star* found the session "tiresome in the extreme."

As court adjourned for the day, General King called to Reid: "I'm very sorry about that, and I again apologize. I'll keep my remarks to myself hereafter." The general was smiling pleasantly, trying to make amends. Reporters, crowding close to overhear the exchange, could not make out Reid's unsmiling reply. The defense counsel told reporters he would not seek a mistrial based on General King's attitude, "though you all know that if this was a civilian court, this case would be thrown out immediately."

King's outburst was not the only sign of fatigue among the judges. One of them told the press: "It's costing us each about twenty dollars a day to stay in Washington. The trial has already lasted thirty days, which means we have spent about six hundred dollars each to stay here—while we all have to keep up our establishments at home." The most demanding sacrifice asked of the judges, he said, was "sitting here, thinking that our commands meanwhile may be going to hell." General McCoy had been forced to find new accommodations in Washington, since he had worn out his welcome with friends who had taken him in, expecting a short trial.

This was the last weekend of November. Mitchell had asked permission to leave the city until Monday so that he could see his infant daughter Lucy, but the Army denied his request and Betty had to go to Detroit alone. The court was more lenient with other principals of the cast and declared a holiday because of the Army-Navy football game in New York. Worrying about the impatient remark of General King, the legal-staff members who were left behind spent long hours at the War Department, looking up precedents in military law for declaring mistrials. The Army decided to go ahead as if nothing had happened.

Army defeated Navy by a forward pass, leading to jokes about a unified air service on the field. The Sunday papers carried other news—the Morrow Board had chosen this moment for its report, perfectly timed to divert attention from Mitchell's recently completed defense. The board called for a comprehensive air program, but its report was full of compromises, rejected Mitchell's views and gave comfort to the court-martial prosecution. The Morrow Board concluded:

America was in no danger of air attack.

Army aviation should remain separate from that of the Navy, and should be known henceforth as the Air Corps, a semi-autonomous arm.

Assistant Secretaries of War, Navy and Commerce should be named to direct aviation development.

A swift build-up of air power such as Mitchell and the Lassiter Board urged was too costly; a less ambitious five-year program would make the nation secure. To encourage civilian plane production, planes should be sold to foreign powers (including future enemies) "so as to lessen the number of planes which the government must order to keep the industry in a strong position." *

The court returned to Washington with one vivid passage of the report fresh in mind: "The next war may well start in the air, but in all probability it will wind up as the last one did, in the mud." Coolidge said that the report was "reassuring to the country, gratifying to the service, and satisfactory to the Congress." Best of all, it would be far less costly than Mitchell's plans.

After the holiday Reid asked the court to expunge the unpleasant exchange with General King, and the prosecution agreed. The *New York Times*, which had decorously reported King's remark as "darned rot" and glossed over the incident, was obliged to explain and to expose its sheltered readers to one phrase in the news whose fitness for print was questionable.

Reid pursued Commander John Rodgers, the leader of the ill-fated Hawaiian flight, as if he held the key to the case. Rodgers told the story of the flight, of navigating the slow seaplane accurately past eight picket ships, approaching Hawaii, and then running out of fuel and drifting for nine harrowing days at sea before being rescued by a submarine. His story was in striking contrast to the spectacular Round the World flight by the Army Air

* Mitchell and his friends regarded the Morrow report as a disaster, but it did offer a basis for the first peacetime air program in the United States, and in early 1926 the Air Corps Act and a five-year building program went into effect. Civilian aviation also began its growth in the Morrow program, especially in air-mail service.

Service. Rodgers admitted that he had not followed the techniques used by the Army fliers because "I was trying to do my own navigating and not depend on outside assistance."

Reid tried to show that the flight was undertaken as a propaganda mission, ordered by Secretary Wilbur to counter Army successes: "What navigational value would a nonstop flight have from San Francisco to Honolulu?"

"It was an opportunity to practice navigation, which is the greatest immediate need of aviation in the Navy . . ."

"What was the object of the flight?"

"Well . . . primarily to test the practicability of sending planes from the West Coast to the Hawaiian Islands, with a view to transporting them in that way in time of war."

"Can you tell the court what the hurry was that you had to make it in one jump?"

". . . The longer you have to go, the more exercise you get at navigation." Rodgers added that navigators were not properly trained until they could make twenty-eight-hour trips over water.

"Then you haven't a single qualified aviator in the Navy?"

"I don't know whether we have or not."

"Have you ever flown twenty-eight hours?"

"Oh, I see what you mean. That's what we're trying to do—qualify ourselves." Rodgers conceded that no Navy flier had ever flown far enough to prove himself at navigation; Mitchell's criticism was borne out.

The government's rebuttal to charges of backwardness in aircraft-carrier development was made by Lieutenant Commander T. W. Pennoyer, chief of the Carrier Section, who had been on the *Langley* for three years. In cross-examination Reid managed to show how right Mitchell had been; the Navy's carrier men were valiant and loyal, but poorly trained and equipped.

In a long exchange Reid established the carrier's inferiority to foreign carriers, and then probed Japanese aviation. Pennoyer said the Japanese did not use American methods of carrier landing.

"They resort to trick aerodynamic methods."

"Is that bad?"

"Yes, sir. It limits the top speed and limits also the heaviest type of plane they can land."

"Hasn't the Navy furnished Japan with the plans of a certain ship?"

"No, sir."

"Have we ever been furnished with plans of the Japanese ships?"

Reid ran afoul the favorite tactic of the prosecution once more. Pennoyer said: "You're encroaching on confidential matter, sir."

"But you use encroachment to protect your answers."

Gullion broke in: "I submit that isn't fair. I never heard more straightforward testimony than this."

"You never did, and that is what hurts you," Reid retorted.

Gullion demanded that Reid apologize to Pennoyer. The defense lawyer was infuriated. "I say it is absolutely so, and I will not apologize to anybody."

"I'm not surprised," Gullion said. "I move that the remark of Mr. Reid be stricken from the record, that the witness has made an attempt to protect himself by pleading confidentiality."

Reid answered: "I move that it be framed and sent to the Navy Department."

The parting exchange with this witness gave Reid all he wanted when Pennoyer said that the *Langley* was meant only for development work and not for battle duty, and that she was to prepare men for the *Saratoga* and the *Lexington*.

"Then the United States has not now, nor has ever had, any aircraft carriers?" Reid asked.

"Not an effective aircraft carrier designed to operate with the fleet."

"That is all," Reid said.

Soon afterward, when he was cross-examining Captain H. E. Yarnell, the naval air commander of the Hawaiian maneuvers, Reid once more provoked the court. This time it was General Graves who exploded.

Reid was coaxing Yarnell to reveal the reasons for his failure to aid Army fliers in the exercise and used ridicule to move the stubborn witness: "The reason you did not join Major Brandt in this exercise was to show that you were co-operating with him—is that correct?"

Gullion interrupted: "I suggest he did not say such a thing. He's putting words into the witness' mouth."

"I'm putting words into his ear and not his mouth," Reid snapped.

General Graves called out to Winship, demanding that the counsel be restrained. Reid turned to the general: "Now, I say that I have a right to conduct this cross-examination as I see fit and I object to your saying it should be stopped."

"Mr. President," Graves said, "I ask that counsel for the accused be directed to stop. I do not acknowledge he has a right to lecture me as to my duty on this court."

"And I want the record to show," Reid said, "that during my cross-examination I was interrupted and interfered with by General Graves so that I was unable to continue my cross-examination on account of his remarks to the law member of the court. We will have a showdown on this."

Gullion read from the *Courts-Martial Manual:* no witness could be subjected to irrelevant, insulting or improper questions.

"You can cross-examine all you want," Reid said. "Everybody is for you, but when I attempt to bring the truth out of the witness, certain members of the court interfere with me."

"I again object," Graves said, "and I say I was not interfering with you."

Reid moved to oust Graves: "I hereby challenge General Graves' right to sit longer as a member of this court for the reasons that his actions while on this court show that he is not impartial and that he has repeatedly interfered by his conduct with my examination of witnesses. And in justice and fairness to the accused, General Graves should no longer be permitted to sit . . ."

To make peace, Howze read an official version of the remark by Graves that Reid found so offensive: "This wrangling between the opposing counsel is disgraceful and should be stopped." Howze said this referred "impartially" to both sides and should not be taken personally by Reid, but Reid would have none of it: "Day after day here, General Graves, every time I would attempt to bring out a certain line of argument from a witness, would immediately begin to talk, either to General King on one side or . . . the law member on the other side . . . he has interfered with me time and time again . . . and I say, in fairness to the accused and in fairness to the court, I cannot tolerate it any longer." *

The court was cleared again and the officers retired, leaving Graves alone on the bench, but they were soon back, to deny Reid's challenge. Graves would continue to sit. The examination of Yarnell went on lamely for a few minutes.

The government then called Lieutenant Commander Richard E. Byrd, to testify about an Arctic expedition criticized by Mitchell. Gullion asked: "Are you a descendant of the Byrd who settled or founded Richmond, Virginia?"

"Yes, sir."

Reid stood up: "I object to these anthropological questions."

"I submit," Gullion said, "this is an introductory question, and it will serve to qualify this witness just as much as bringing out the fact that the accused is the son of a U.S. senator, which was a question asked by Mr. Reid." **

Byrd told of the MacMillan Arctic expedition, financed by the National Geographic Society, commanded by a naval reservist, Donald MacMillan, and accompanied by the president of the Zenith Radio Corporation. He resisted Reid's attempts to show that the expedition was staged to sell magazines and radios. He said that the Loening amphibian plane, criticized by Mitchell, had flown six thousand miles in the Arctic, though it had certain defects (for one thing, leaky pontoons had to be bailed out daily). Reid made the foray look like a hapless adventure.

"Did you find the Pole?"

"We weren't looking for the Pole."

"What were you looking for?"

* Some observers found Reid remarkably patient. The *Aero Digest* said: "The verdict already has been rendered, so far as public opinion is concerned, upon a court who, impatient with the weak prosecution, brazenly brushed it aside and constituted themselves a court of inquisition. Rarely in any court, civil or military, have witnesses been subjected to such brutal bulldozing from a plainly prejudiced bench."

** After her husband's death, Betty Mitchell married the brother of Richard E. Byrd, Thomas Bolling Byrd, of the durable Virginia dynasty.

". . . Land in the Polar Sea, and we were looking over unexplored regions up there."

"All right, now, did you fail in your mission on the Arctic flight?"

"We failed in the main mission."

During a recess Mitchell displayed an enormous lemon to reporters, a gift from the chamber of commerce of Phoenix, Arizona. "They sent it for me to give to Gullion," he said, "but I'm going to use it myself. I've caught a fresh cold."

The next day—it was now December 2, the fifth week of the trial—Mitchell's old friend Commander Kenneth Whiting took the stand. The naval officer had worked with the Air Service behind the scenes in the days of preparation for the bombing test of 1921, and Mitchell knew from experience that Whiting shared many of his ideas but could not support him publicly. Whiting had learned to fly with the Wright brothers in 1911, had commanded the Pensacola flying school, briefly directed naval aviation in France, served with the Royal Air Force and helped Moffett set up the Bureau of Naval Aeronautics.

Whiting reviewed early Navy efforts to take planes to sea in 1911, when Eugene Ely had landed on a wooden platform on the cruiser *Pennsylvania.* He denied that Mitchell had always been ahead of the Navy; four years before Mitchell called for two big carriers, Whiting said, the Navy General Board had recommended similar ships. He added that though it now had only the *Langley* in service, the United States led the world in naval aviation.

Whiting had taken part in tests on the U.S.S. *Washington,* and described the underwater blasts which that ship had survived, then the 1600-pound shell, loaded with sand, which had been dropped on her deck. He and Reid then had another round about the Navy's policy of secrecy.

Whiting gave the reason why the dummy bomb was used: "We didn't care anything about the explosive. We wanted to find the penetration of the bomb into the deck of the ship."

"Did it penetrate the deck?"

"That is a secret."

"It is?"

"Yes, sir."

Reid picked up a copy of the printed report of the hearings before the Select Committee and read an exchange between Representative Prall of New York and Admiral Hilary Jones about this bomb drop:

"Prall: 'What happened?'

"Jones: 'It did not go through.'

" 'What happened to the deck?'

" 'What is technically called dished it. The point didn't go through.' "

Reid again asked Whiting if the bomb had damaged the ship and the commander replied doggedly: "As far as I'm concerned, I have told you it was a secret." Whiting admitted he had been in the public hearing when Jones revealed the facts to the committee, but the commander obeyed his orders—so far as the court-martial went, the test was still secret. The Navy's control of officer-witnesses had never been made more obvious.

After about an hour of grilling, Reid began to expose Whiting's personal convictions on air power. Only the intervention of the court saved the Navy from a rout: "Is the present policy of the Navy suited to bring out the best possible work by the personnel in aviation?"

"In my opinion, no."

"How many naval aviators with whom you have personally conferred are in favor of retaining the present system of separate air forces without change?"

Gullion was not quick enough to halt a reply.

"Very few."

". . . All the rest want a change?"

"Yes."

Reid asked if the Navy's role in the future might be to carry planes across the seas. The court refused to allow the officer to answer. Reid smiled wearily and took up another printed report from a public hearing. He read from testimony by Whiting: " 'We feel that maybe fifteen or twenty years from now the major work of the Navy may be the handling of air forces. The surface craft will merely be the means of transporting them across the ocean.' Did you ever make that statement?"

Still the court would not allow Whiting to reply.

Reid tried once more: "Now, have you any opinion as to the

future work of the main battle fleet of the American Navy?"

The court ordered Whiting to make no reply, so Reid gave up and turned to another sensitive spot: "Have you ever talked with any officers of the Navy with regard to their reluctance to go before the committees of Congress and advocate policies which are not in accord with the policies of the Navy Department?"

The court said the witness should not reply.

Reid then read from Whiting's published testimony before the Morrow Board: " 'I think many of them are reluctant to come before committees in Congress and advocate policies which are not in accordance with the policies of the Navy Department.'

"Now," Reid said, "with that in mind, do you still say that the United States leads in the methods of handling aviation of all the countries in the world?"

The court did not halt Whiting this time and he replied: "I made no statement about the methods of handling aviation. I compared naval aviation in this country with naval aviation in France and England and other countries. I said nothing about the methods of handling it. I said as we stand today our naval aviation is . . . better than aviation in any other country."

". . . Notwithstanding the men in the Navy are discontented with the system in use in the Navy Department, you still insist that the United States leads?"

"Yes, in spite of the system, we still lead."

Once more Gullion turned the attention of the court to the *Shenandoah,* offering half a dozen prosecution witnesses to counter Mitchell's claims of the Navy's mishandling of the airship. Her builder, Commander R. D. Weyerbacher, took the blame for lack of parachutes on the unlucky ship. He said that he had taken them from the crew because he thought it was safer to go down with the ship than in parachutes.

When it was Reid's turn, he pulled other facts from Weyerbacher: the *Shenandoah* was about 30 percent less buoyant when filled with helium instead of hydrogen, for which she was designed; she had been altered since Weyerbacher left her—one of the six engines had been removed and a heavy water-ballast recovery system added.

The *Shenandoah*'s designer, Jerome Hunsaker, he said, was

now assistant naval attaché in London, beyond the reach of the court.

"When did he go?" Reid asked.

"I think he sailed last week." The Navy had whisked him away just in time to prevent his appearance in court.

Lieutenant Commander C. E. Rosendahl, the senior survivor, gave his story of the fatal flight. He told of being aroused for his watch and climbing down to the control car at three-thirty while the huge ship lurched over the Ohio countryside. The courtroom was unusually quiet as he spoke:

"Captain Lansdowne was watching the weather and particularly the storm that the ship had just avoided. The moon showed itself occasionally with a rather dull light. During my drift observations, taken out of the central car window, I observed on the starboard bow a streaky cloud forming, and although it didn't seem to be threatening, I turned to call Lieutenant Anderson's attention to it . . . Shortly thereafter the captain came over to the starboard side and it was apparent to him that this new cloud was either coming toward us or building up very rapidly. About this time the elevatorman called out that the ship was rising.

"He was told to check her and put on sufficient elevator to check her. However, he kept reporting that the ship was rising and that he couldn't check her . . ."

When Gullion asked him the cause of the crash, Rosendahl said: "The *Shenandoah* was destroyed by the aerodynamic stresses imposed upon it by the vertical currents of a line squall . . ."

Reid cross-examined him carefully: "What time was the first time you found the ship was in danger?"

"Four thirty-five."

"And you landed at five forty-five—so it was one hour and ten minutes . . . Would it have been possible for anybody to have put a parachute on if they had been there, in the hour and ten minutes?"

"Certainly." Rosendahl maintained, however, that parachutes would not have helped.

"Did you see the gas valves at any time . . . at any time after you found there was danger?"

"I didn't see the gas valves themselves." Rosendahl was certain that the gas valves had opened, though he had not seen them. "I feel absolutely certain . . . of course, the only way to be absolutely certain would be to be present right at the valve."

"Then in your opinion whether the valves actually let out gas or not is merely an opinion."

"It is a well-founded opinion."

The defense theory that the ship had burst from increased gas pressure was still tenable.

Reid spoke of Lansdowne's reluctance to fly over the Midwestern fairs, and read from a letter the skipper had written to the Navy Department:

" 'It is pointed out that should the Department desire to make this flight . . . such a course is reasonably safe later in the season after the thunderstorm period . . . provided freedom of action with respect to the exact date the flight is scheduled is permitted.' "

Rosendahl said that this letter applied only to an earlier flight, planned for June.

Reid then read part of Admiral Moffett's endorsement on this letter: " 'While the Bureau has great respect for the judgment of the commanding officer of the U.S.S. *Shenandoah,* yet an analysis of his letter shows it to be based largely upon worry over contingencies—running out of fuel due to bad weather, head winds, high temperatures, thunderstorms . . .' "

Reid asked Rosendahl: "And still you say he never made any protest about taking this trip?"

Rosendahl stuck to his story that Lansdowne had not protested the actual flight on which the ship was lost in September.

Another witness was Colonel C. G. Hall of the Air Service, one of the survivors. He was ludicrously reluctant to commit himself, but under Reid's prodding he told a story of an uncontrollable airship. Hall insisted that it was only at the last moment before the breakup that he realized the ship was in danger:

"The ship was under control until fifteen seconds before she broke up."

"The ship was under control? How high did she go?"

"About sixty-one hundred feet."

"Was she under control when she went up?"

"Yes, sir."

"And when she came down?"

"Yes."

"Why didn't they keep her down, then?"

"Because they couldn't prevent the upward trend."

"Did they want to go up and down? Is that what you mean to tell the court—that they had it under control when they went up and down—is that correct?"

"They did not control that feature of it."

In an effort to show that Lansdowne had been sent on a routine mission, with his full consent, the government put on two high-ranking, nonflying officers—Captain G. S. Lincoln, director of Ships' Movements, and Admiral Edward W. Eberle, Chief of Naval Operations.

Lincoln traced the orders to the *Shenandoah:* Lansdowne had asked that his flight be postponed until the second week in September, largely because a mooring mast was not ready in Detroit. When Rosendahl, the mooring officer, inspected the mast and reported it in order, the Navy denied Lansdowne's request: "The reasons stated by him for his recommendations . . . found no longer to exist, the recommendations were not approved."

Lansdowne's letter of protest had said: ". . . the length of this flight is approximately 3000 statute miles . . . includes a mountain range requiring a minimum altitude of 3500 feet, so that in leaving Lakehurst the ship should be only 98 percent full [the gas bags expanded as altitude increased] . . . a flight toward the westward will probably be made against head winds . . ."

Admiral Eberle refused to postpone the *Shenandoah*'s flight until the second week in September. Lansdowne was ordered to pass over five cities during State Fair Week, from September 3 to 6: Columbus, Des Moines, Minneapolis, Milwaukee and Detroit. He was to pass over these cities by day so that the ship could be seen by crowds. He was given discretion to change his schedule, but Eberle had admonished him rather sternly to remember that "this route will be published in the press and that many will be disappointed should the *Shenandoah* fail to follow the approved schedule."

"Tell the court what naval mission the *Shenandoah* had to

perform at the state fair at Des Moines, Iowa, on September fourth," Reid said.

"The naval mission for the flight was training and development of the ship," Lincoln said.

Admiral Eberle, the Navy's senior officer, next took the stand, and though he was difficult and occasionally defiant, Reid used him to show the inadequacies of the Navy's tiny airship program.

"Was the *Shenandoah*'s crew badly in need of training?"

"It was. They had been in the hangar for about four months."

"What was the matter with the *Shenandoah* that she had been in the hangar for four months?"

"They had no helium."

"Where was there helium?"

"In the *Los Angeles*."

"Do you mean you have got two rigid airships in this country and only one set of helium?"

"I regret to say that is the case."

"And they have got to borrow helium from each other whenever you want to use one of them?"

"That is the situation now and has been for the last two years."

Eberle explained why the *Shenandoah* had been sent over the state fairs: "We always tried to pass over cities she had never visited before."

"What for?"

"Because millions of people have requested to see the ship that belonged to the government—to see an airship—requests from chambers of commerce, from governors, from members of Congress . . ."

"All right; do I understand you to state that this flight was taken to satisfy the curiosity of the American people, then?"

"No, I did not. I told you what the flight was undertaken for, and, incidentally, we like to fly over as many places as possible to let the people see it."

"What was the object of satisfying the curiosity of the people?"

"I suppose the people have an interest in their Navy as well as in the Army," Eberle said testily.

"Captain Lansdowne would be alive today if he hadn't gone on the trip, wouldn't he, under your direction?"

"I don't care to answer any such question."

The court took over, as if it were itself the prosecution, even to leading the witness: was this flight made in response to public requests? Eberle said it was.

"Is the *Shenandoah* a part of the Navy?"

"She is."

"To whom does the Navy belong?"

"The people of the United States is my understanding."

"In your judgment, have the people of the United States a right to see the *Shenandoah* in flight, whether it is a training flight or otherwise?"

"I think they have."

Reid outlasted the admiral (who now and then said he would answer questions "any way I like") and at the end elicited a glimpse of the Navy's decision-making process under Eberle:

"Are you a flying officer?"

"No."

". . . And you have to take the opinions of other people in regard to aviation matters that come under your supervision?"

"I do, in a great measure."

"Do you always take them?"

"I do if they are within reason."

"Do you finally determine whether they are within reason or not?"

"Yes."

Reid next had a bout with the Navy's chief of information, Commander John Stapler, who denied that he operated a propaganda mill of the kind described by Mitchell, or that he tried to sway public opinion. Reid soon led him afar.

Had the information office opposed the Mitchell plan for a unified air service?

"It has only taken part in issuing statements in regard to facts that are not in accordance with the facts as we know them . . . We have argued against the united air force . . . We send out information, correct information, to try to correct misinformation when we see it."

"And all these statements you send out are in regard to some inaccurate statement made against the Navy by someone?"

"That is the purpose . . ."

"And your object is to kill off the united air service or any opportunity of its being established?"

"Our object is to prevent the country from making the serious error of taking up an organization that is not in its best interests from the standpoint of national defense."

". . . And if the Army, in its wisdom, saw fit to have a united air force, do you still think the country was going on the rocks?"

"As long as they left the Navy out of it, that would be their interests . . ."

". . . Now, if the President and Congress should decide that a united air force was the proper thing, would you still think our national defense had suffered a severe blow?"

"We cannot prevent individuals having their own opinion . . . we would loyally go ahead and carry on in the most efficient way we could, if that is the decision, which I do not believe it will be."

23

Why, These Men Are My Friends!

As the end drew near, the prosecution called General Summerall to the stand, a stiff, proud figure unable to conceal his animosity for Mitchell. The deposed president of the court gave summaries of the airman's inspection of Hawaiian defenses and challenged his report; he spoke at length of the anti-aircraft tests of the past summer ridiculed by Mitchell. Reid at last opened the subject for which the courtroom was waiting: "Are you friendly with the accused?"

Summerall sat in silence and after a long wait Reid continued: "All right. Did you make this statement: 'From now on, Mitchell and I are enemies,' after you were challenged as president of this court?"

Summerall denied what the press had written of his angry reaction: "I have no recollection of ever having made that statement, and I am quite sure I never made that statement."

"Weren't you interviewed by certain newspaper reporters after being removed as president of this court on October 28?"

"I had some conversation in one of the offices of the War Department and some newspaper reporters were present."

"Now, I ask you again, did you ever make this statement to anybody: 'From now on, Mitchell and I are enemies'?"

"I do not recall making that statement."

"Are you now friendly with the accused?"

"I am indifferent toward the accused."

Summerall said he had seen Mitchell only three or four times during his six-week inspection of Hawaii. He also said that aviation in his command there was reported on regularly to General Patrick in Washington. A number of these reports, read in the courtroom, revealed a tiny, hopelessly unprepared force, its officers repeating month after month their futile requisitions for bombs, bomb racks, guns and gun mounts. Summerall refused to discuss the letter he had written to Patrick about Mitchell's report, saying that it was "secret," even if it had not been marked so when it was sent.

When Summerall left the stand, or soon after, he coined a memorable phrase that became a part of the trial's folklore: "Mitchell is one of that damned kind of soldier who's wonderful in war and terrible in peace."

An even more hostile witness was Major General Hugh A. Drum, the new Assistant Chief of Staff, G-3, and leader of the anti-aviation clique in the War Department. He gave positive opinions on every question:

Bombers could fly no higher than 12,500 feet—he rejected Air Service reports that even the old De Havillands had been flown to 17,000 feet. Planes would never be able to fly so high that they could not be seen through a telescope, and when they flew high, could not bomb effectively. Given a dozen anti-aircraft guns, he could keep any bombing squadron from its objectives. If he were firing at a single plane, he said, he could hit it eighteen times while it was within range, and cited tests to prove his claim.

Drum and Reid almost came to blows when the general baited the lawyer, hinting that he had been a wartime draft dodger.

"Did you ever hear of any bomber being sent out to perform any mission over an important area?" Reid asked.

"No. I don't remember any specific case—do you, Mr. Reid?"

"Certainly."

There was a studied insult in Drum's tone: "Will you tell me what your war experience was, and we can judge."

"Sure," Reid said. "My war experience is just as much in my line as yours in yours. I wasn't chief clerk of the General Staff, and I wasn't a handyboy, either."

McMullen, the assistant prosecutor, broke in: "Now, if the court please—"

"He has no business to say that," Reid said, "and is liable to get a personal affront if he brings those things in again."

Howze said: "The court will come to order. The court hopes that these proceedings will be continued with proper decorum, and that such instances . . . will not arise again."

Drum admitted that he and Major Wilby had written a letter for the signature of Secretary Weeks, opposing a unified air force—and left a strong impression that he had helped to write the acidulous letter from Weeks to Coolidge, excoriating Mitchell and urging that he be dropped as Assistant Chief of the Air Service. Drum could not be quieted, and when Reid asked a question he went on for several minutes despite the lawyer's attempts to halt him. Reid finally said: "In view of the condition of the witness and his refusal to answer the questions I have propounded to him, I refuse to examine him further." *

Another of the Army's high command who came to the stand was Lieutenant Colonel Lesley J. McNair of the General Staff, who had been in Hawaii during Mitchell's visit. He complained that Mitchell's inspection had been unorthodox; for one thing, he refused to tell the staff just what he wanted to see, and prowled about alone, prying into everything. McNair was reluctant to give details on Hawaiian defenses in open court. When Reid asked how many Navy planes had been there two years earlier, McNair wrote the answer on a slip of paper and passed it to the judges.

"All right," Reid said, "we've had it in the record at least half a dozen times . . . Of course, Pearl Harbor was the particular thing to be protected there?"

"Precisely."

"And that is where the oil tanks are located . . . And those tanks are vulnerable to bombardment, aren't they?"

"If unprotected, although they are very cleverly constructed, having in mind the possibility of aerial attack."

"And oil is combustible, and bombing planes can drop incendiary bombs, can they?"

"Yes, but that is provided for in the construction of the tanks."

* Drum had told the Morrow Board that a separate air force "will mean aid and assistance for our enemies, instead of their destruction and downfall. It will mean defeat in war instead of victory."

"Would you say that they are noncombustible?"

"I can explain that but I would prefer not to."

"Well, I don't care to have you explain it, then."

But the staff officer now seemed determined to detail secrets of the defense which would make Hawaii virtually invulnerable to attack: "The oil in those tanks wouldn't burn if bombed."

"You mean it is nonburnable oil?"

"Not burnable if they don't want it to burn."

McNair said that Mitchell had brought his report to headquarters before leaving Hawaii and discussed it with staff officers, "just generally went over his report rather rapidly, explaining it as he went." It was a picture of a candid critic, offering his observations without animus.

McNair remembered that he had challenged Mitchell on one point—a plan for aerial reconnaissance of the islands, saying that the Navy was assigned to that work.

"The accused replied that the Navy was no good; that they wouldn't do the reconnaissance properly if the time came, and we had to do it anyway." This recommendation was not put into effect, McNair said, because a 1920 pamphlet on Army-Navy co-operation forbade such a mission by the Army.

McNair also belittled Mitchell's warning of an attack on Pearl Harbor, and said it was not original with the airman; it had been drawn from a few lines in the 1920 pamphlet, McNair said, quoting: " 'There are some places in the Hawaiian Islands from which an enemy might launch a surprise attack on Pearl Harbor, and there are many places not covered by gunfire . . .' " From this germ, McNair told the court, Mitchell's detailed forecast of a Japanese attack on Pearl Harbor had grown.

According to McNair, the General Staff had paid no attention to Mitchell's suggestions for improving Hawaiian defenses, since his report had "brought up no essential plan which could be accepted by the Department"—and, he added inscrutably, in any event, most of Mitchell's proposals had been in effect long before he arrived.

McNair conceded, under pressure from Reid, that the defenses of Hawaii were planned and not actually in being; they would not be put into effect until war came. There was, for example, a liaison system for the Air Service: "One was planned, but it did not exist in time of peace."

When he was asked about Mitchell's observation that there was friction between Army and Navy commanders, McNair said the report was false. The two services frequently exchanged favors. Moreover, he said: "I have several very close personal friends among the Navy officials." *

That afternoon spectators enjoyed a break in the trial's routine. Will Rogers slipped into the courtroom, slumping far down in a seat to avoid recognition, but people were soon craning their necks to catch a glimpse of him, whispering until they drew the attention of the court.

Mitchell turned, smiled and winked at the humorist. Rogers nodded and returned his wink. General Howze stood: "Won't you come down, Mr. Rogers?" The famous cowboy crouched lower in his seat. "Now I know they're going to hang me," he said.

An aide escorted him to the judges' table to the laughter of the crowd, and Howze called a recess. The president and the actor walked into the anteroom with locked arms, and for a few minutes the court laughed and talked with Rogers. When they returned, he took a seat with the lawyers and the trial went on.

The annual Gridiron Club dinner staged its traditional lampooning of political figures that weekend, with President Coolidge and Vice-President Dawes in the audience. Mitchell had been invited, and there was much joking about his court-martial. In one of the acts several men posed as marionettes, controlled by "political strings." One of them shouted: "What's a ventriloquist?"

"Not General Mitchell. He can't control his voice."

There was a mock "world court-martial," to decide whether Mitchell or the War Department was on trial. The judges appeared in scarlet jackets beneath black robes, and found Mitchell guilty of violating the 96th Article of War: "Parking overtime in the newspapers." The case was then ordered back to the court of original

* McNair later rose to prominence in the Army, and in World War II was commanding general of Army Ground Forces. He was killed at St. Lô on an inspection trip seven weeks after D-Day, when B-24's accidentally dropped their bombs short of their assigned target.

jurisdiction—the newspapers themselves. Mitchell seemed to laugh harder than anyone else in the crowded hall.

The speaker of the evening was the noted humorist George Ade. His audience included a couple of elderly congressmen who were Civil War veterans, for whom the ban played "Dixie" and "Yankee Doodle." Several well-known men were in the crowd: Laurence Stallings, the author of *What Price Glory?*, John Rodgers and Richard E. Byrd of the Navy, Irving Berlin, Charles Dana Gibson, William Green of the American Federation of Labor, Bob La Follette, Dwight Morrow, Harry Byrd, Jimmy Walker, and Prince Otto von Bismarck, grandson of the German chancellor.

When court resumed on the following Monday, the last of the Army's high-ranking witnesses appeared against Mitchell, among them Major General Hanson Ely, commander of the War College, and General Patrick.

Ely talked at length of his troubles as an infantry commander in Europe in trying to control aviators: "The airman . . . has a great deal of independence of action. If he wants to beat it, he can beat it. He can say something is the matter with his plane and nobody can check him. The difficulty I found with him is that they are a little too independent of the commander."

Ely said planes usually brought back information, but that a commander never knew when they would return. He was positive about one thing—aviation was not a decisive military weapon: "I don't believe any air force, no matter what strength, can frighten the kind of people we are into throwing their hands up before they are materially injured . . . an air force cannot hit and hold. You have to hold what you get . . . They can injure morale and destroy ammunition dumps and factories . . . but not to the extent of winning a war."

"They can't win the war?" Reid asked.

"No, no, no . . . My solemn judgment is that an air force cannot now or in the future—and that is the consolidated judgment of scientific men—win a war by itself of any magnitude where the forces are anything near equal."

Reid cited a quotation to Ely, reading aloud: " 'The potentialities of aircraft attack on a large scale are almost incalculable, but it is clear that such an attack, owing to its crushing moral effect on a nation, may impress public opinion to the point of disarming the government and thus become decisive.' Do you believe that?"

"No."

"That was by Marshal Foch. Was he formerly well informed on military tactics?"

"Yes, but it might be that all men have dreams and visions."

Reid quoted another opinion: "'The development of aircraft indicates that our national defense must be supplemented by, if not dominated by, aviation.'"

Ely said he could not agree.

"You think it is absolutely absurd?"

"Yes."

"That is the statement of President Coolidge."

"I don't care what it is."

The court ordered the remarks about Coolidge stricken from the record.*

General Patrick took the stand to deny many of Mitchell's charges about the Air Service: the planes were reasonably safe, as safe as those of other nations; Mitchell had approved all purchases, and the only major problem was lack of money. The United States ranked third in the world in air power, and in technical matters was the leader.

But when he was forced to give details in cross-examination, the familiar picture emerged once more: Bombers did not practice in peacetime with full equipment. No big bombs had been dropped in recent years because of the expense (fifty cents a pound). New planes were scarce because they cost $16,000 each—as against $1800 for remodeling wartime De Havillands.

Reid asked Patrick: "Has the United States any real air force at this time?"

"Yes."

"What is it?"

* Ely's conception of Mitchell's claims for air power exists today in military circles. General Howze's sons, for example, both of whom led distinguished Army careers, believed that the United States would have come to disaster in World War II if it had followed Mitchell's recommendations. His partisans, on the other hand, contend that a large air force, built when Mitchell urged it, might have prevented war by deterring Axis aggression.

"A very small one. We have one pursuit group and one bombardment group in this country . . . and two small attack squadrons."

Patrick said there were twenty modern pursuit planes and twenty obsolete bombers.

"How about your attack?"

"We have no attack planes, and we are using merely planes of other types."

"Have you any real air policy, military or commercial, in this country?"

"It is very difficult to say whether there is any . . ."

In brief, Patrick conceded that all Mitchell had said was evidently true. As to the manner of his saying it . . .

On December 17, when the trial was seven weeks old and Reid had spent himself pouring out evidence to substantiate the truth of his client's charges, Mitchell challenged the court for having broken its promise to the defense. It had declined to rule on whether Mitchell had proved that he was speaking the truth in San Antonio. Thus, when General Howze called for arguments to sum up the case, Mitchell asked Reid to remain silent. Howze turned quizzically to Reid, but it was Mitchell who rose instead, with a surprise statement:

"My trial before this court-martial is the culmination of the efforts of the General Staff of the Army and the General Board of the Navy to depreciate the value of air power and keep it in auxiliary position, which absolutely compromises the whole system of national defense.

"These efforts . . . were begun as soon as the sound of the cannon had ceased on the Western Front in 1918. When we sank the battleships off the Virginia Capes in 1921, and again in 1923, and proved to the world that air power had revolutionized all schemes of national defense, these efforts were redoubled and have continued to this day.

"The truth of every statement which I have made has been proved by good and sufficient evidence before this court, not by men who gained their knowledge of aviation by staying on the ground and having their statements prepared by numerous staff . . . but by actual fliers . . . To proceed with the case would serve no useful purpose. I have therefore directed my counsel to entirely close out our part of the proceeding without argument."

When Mitchell returned to his seat after this statement, the spectators rose and stood briefly in silence.

Colonel Moreland said that since the defense would make no argument, the government should waive its own, but Major Gullion could not be restrained. When Howze said the court wanted to hear him, the young Kentuckian began an oration. He all but fawned upon the judges:

"You have been the Gamaliels at whose feet I have sat in acquiring what knowledge of my profession I now possess. As a cadet I was under the command of your brilliant youngest member [MacArthur]. As a platoon leader I learned the principles of modern tactics and my teacher was he who later so superbly commanded our army in Siberia [Graves]. As a regimental commander I served in a division whose chief of staff was that scholarly soldier who now sits as president of this court. It was from him that I learned the simple but all-important principles of command. Your law member, almost the dean of my own corps, and its pride and ornament, knows more law than I shall ever know. The careers of all of you are known in every club and barracks in the service, inspiring your juniors and forever forming part of the cherished records of our glorious Army . . ."

Then, with the air of a comrade denouncing a common enemy, Gullion led the court through a résumé of the Mitchell case that had become "a cause célèbre, exciting a widespread interest unparalleled in our annals of military jurisprudence." He scorned witnesses for the defense, hinting that many had committed perjury. Admiral Sims was "narrow-minded" and "egomaniacal."

"Then there is the congressional expert, Honorable F. H. La Guardia, with 'fifteen or twenty hours in the air.' He is beyond my powers of description. Thank heaven, he is *sui generis* . . .

"Finally, there is the Major Gerald Brandt type—the gay, gallant, lovable type. I have known and liked Gerry Brandt for twenty-five years. I still like him. I know he would lose his right arm before he would tell a lie. I think, though, that an evil influence has insidiously corrupted his opinions and, I fear, his loyalty . . .

"This casualness to fact which characterizes so many of the gallant Air Service witnesses springs not from dishonesty, but from temperament and habits of thought."

All these airmen, he said, had been infected by Mitchell's "grandiose schemes" and promises of rapid promotion. The prosecution witnesses, by contrast, were scholarly, patriotic, cautious men of common sense.

When he began to speak of Mitchell, Gullion's voice rose: "Is such a man a safe guide? Is he a constructive person or is he a loose-talking imaginative megalomaniac, cheered by the adulation of his juniors, who see promotion under his banner, and intoxicated by the ephemeral applause of the people whose fancy he has for the moment caught?

"Is this man a Moses, fitted to lead the people out of a wilderness which is his creation, only? Is he of the George Washington type, as counsel would have you believe? Is he not rather of the all-too-familiar charlatan and demagogue type—like Alcibiades, Catiline, and except for a decided difference in poise and mental powers in Burr's favor, like Aaron Burr?

"He is a good flier, a fair rider, a good shot, flamboyant, self-advertising, wildly imaginative, destructive, never constructive except in wild nonfeasible schemes, and never overly careful as to the ethics of his methods."

Gullion's final plea became strident: "Sirs, we ask the dismissal of the accused for the sake of the Army whose discipline he has endangered and whose fair name he has attempted to discredit . . . for the sake of those young officers of the Army Air Service whose ideals he has shadowed and whose loyalty he has corrupted . . . Finally we ask it in the name of the American people, whose fears he has played upon, whose hysteria he has fomented . . ."

The courtroom was quiet when Gullion sat down. Will Rogers hurried to Mitchell and put an arm around him. "The people are with you, Billy. Keep punching. You'll rope 'em yet." Mitchell was moved, and said years later: "It was a moment of tenderness—the one moment of all that nightmare which I'll never forget."

Gullion gave mimeographed copies of his speech to the press, and after noon recess, encouraged by the court's reaction to Gullion, Moreland made a speech in the same vein, saying that Mitchell had a "mad desire" for publicity, that he wanted to destroy the Army and Navy and all responsible officers and make them "beggars upon the street."

The Air Service, Moreland said, was the world's finest, and Mitchell unfairly compared it to those of Europe: "They don't take into consideration our breadth of land . . . our wealth . . . our isolation . . . the bravery of our sons and daughters . . . the fact that we all pull together. There is no foreign nation in the world that . . . can put an airplane on any part of the United States of America . . ."

He defended the De Havilland plane, indignant that it should be branded as a "flaming coffin." "Why, the DH plane is known, and might well be called, if you please, the Cadillac of the skies." There was a burst of laughter, but Moreland hardly paused: "I want to say, in closing, two things. The first one is that for every moment since the war we have had the ablest and most brilliant General Staff in the world as far as I can read history . . . and the second thing I want to say is this: How is Colonel Mitchell going to be left in the Army? Upon what possible theory?

"I do not believe that this court has any right to send out into the Army again an officer about whom there can be any question as to loyalty, as to subordination, as to his complete dedication to the best interests of the service, and, if the court itself does not feel that that would be the proper thing to do, then it has only one thing left for it to do, and, if the court please . . . nothing can be permanently helpful to any people except the spirit that is in their own hearts, when dedicated by their love for their native land. That is what makes a patriot; that is what makes an Army officer and that is what will expel from your midst every man who does not meet these requirements."

Moreland ceased, and it was over at last. Howze looked about as if he could not believe it and asked once more if the defense had no argument to present. Reid said that Mitchell's morning statement was final. The president, as if at a loss in the silence, turned back to Moreland, who said: "If the court please, the prosecution has concluded its case."

"And therefore rests?"

"The prosecution rests."

Howze asked Reid once more if the defense had no further statement. "None," Reid said.

Howze called a five-minute recess, then led the court into its anteroom to begin deliberating Mitchell's fate. They retired at three-forty, but within half an hour had made up their minds. They reappeared at twelve minutes past four, to ask Moreland if Mitchell had any previous convictions on his record. Moreland began a speech but Howze cut him short: "Please answer directly. We merely wish to know about previous convictions."

Moreland said there had been none, and the court went back to its room. The implication was clear—Mitchell had been found guilty, and the sentence was under debate. Reporters watched as he sat with Betty and her parents, a slight smile playing about his mouth. The *New York Times* later said: "If Colonel Mitchell was nervous he concealed it well . . . he appeared to be in the best of humor."

Waiting Army and Navy officers were "plainly elated." It grew dark, and lights went on under the high ceilings. The Mitchells and Millers talked in low tones and finally, after six o'clock, Mitchell persuaded Betty's parents to go to their hotel for dinner. Betty remained with him, and they were together a few minutes later when the generals came in with their verdict.

Howze warned the crowd to make no demonstration and then, in a terse staccato voice, read while Mitchell stood before him:

"The court finds the accused:

"Of Specification One—guilty."

Betty pressed a hand tightly against her lips.

"Of Specification Two—guilty . . ." He went through the eight specifications and the general charge, calling "Guilty" after each one.

Howze then said: "The court upon secret written ballot, two-thirds of the members present concurring, sentences the accused to be suspended from rank, command and duty with the forfeiture of all pay and allowances for five years."

There was no sound in the room until Howze continued: "The court is thus lenient because of the military record of the accused during the World War . . . The court is adjourned."

Mitchell listened throughout with a slight oblique smile, looking brightly at the court. Betty patted his hand when Howze's voice ceased and turned to whisper in his ear. He shook his head. Friends hurried to talk with him. He said over and over to reporters: "Nothing now. No. Nothing to say." One of them overheard him as he said in wonder, looking toward the court: "Why, those men are my friends!" He smiled at General MacArthur, who had a wan, pained look, and said: "MacArthur looks like he's been drawn through a knothole."

The *New York Times* reporter found Mitchell curiously calm: "Some thought he was actually disappointed at the lenient nature of the findings and regretted that he had not been dismissed."

Other reporters did not agree. Arthur Chamberlin of the New York *World* thought his face was bleak with chagrin and defeat.

As soon as he could force his way through the crowd, Mitchell went to the judges' table and shook hands with each of them; there seemed to be no embarrassment or rancor in the farewells.

The officers of the court had little to say to reporters. One or two admitted that the form of the sentence had come as a surprise. The generals themselves would not talk about how the verdict had been reached, or how any of the members had voted." *

* Seventeen years after the trial Fiorello La Guardia told Isaac Don Levine, a Mitchell biographer, that a slip of paper found in a courtroom wastebasket proved that MacArthur voted for dismissal; his handwriting had allegedly been recognized. Betty Mitchell said, however, that her husband never knew how any judge voted: "After all, he knew that his judges had their orders from the War Department to find him guilty of 'conduct prejudicial to the military service,' a charge, incidentally, of which he was guilty." General Howze later told the Mitchells that there had been a split verdict. "We never needed to know anything beyond that," Mrs. Mitchell said.

The Mitchells remained on intimate terms with several of the judges, including MacArthur. Nine years after Mitchell's death, in 1945, MacArthur wrote Senator Alexander Wiley of Wisconsin that he had cast the lone dissenting vote against Mitchell's conviction, that Mitchell knew it and had "never ceased to express his gratitude." MacArthur's memoirs said: "When the verdict was reached, many believed I had betrayed my friend . . . Nothing could be further from the truth. I did what I could in his behalf and I helped save him from dismissal. That he was wrong in the violence of his language is self-evident; that he was right in his thesis is equally true and incontrovertible . . . Had he lived through World War II he would have seen the fulfillment of many of his prophecies . . ."

MacArthur thought of himself as an ardent advocate of air power, but his

Two or three congressmen in the crowd came to shake Mitchell's hand and promised to introduce bills to have the verdict set aside. Mitchell told them: "This case is mighty far from closed, I'll tell you that . . . No, I won't have a thing to say until the President passes on this."

He finally led Betty out of the crowd and they went home.

The morning newspapers carried the verdict in large headlines, and there were predictions of a floor fight in Congress after the Christmas holidays, when the House and Senate were expected to take the Mitchell case into their own hands.

The papers bearing the verdict reflected a prosperous America in a mellow Christmas mood. Raccoon coats were advertised at $350 in New York; Ford touring cars were $290. A best-selling record was Rosa Ponselle singing "The Rosary" and "A Perfect Day." There were advertisements for Theodore Dreiser's first novel since 1915, in two volumes, *An American Tragedy.*

Rudolph Valentino was being sued for divorce, and said amiably that his wife's unreasonable attempts to isolate him from the women of the world was the cause. Harry Houdini had opened a new act in New York, including the Chinese Torture Trick. The New York Commission on Mental Defectives said that moviegoing weakened the mind.

Among the movies playing in the big city: Marilyn Miller in *Sunny,* Lon Chaney in *Phantom of the Opera,* The Marx Brothers in *Cocoanuts,* William S. Hart in *Tumbleweed.*

Weighing 226 pounds, Babe Ruth arrived in the city, saying that he needed no winter treatment at Hot Springs that year.

The United States Senate was fighting over the issue of the World Court. Abroad, the British had launched the new battle cruiser, *Rodney.* Explorers were finding new treasures in the tomb of King Tut in Egypt, dazzling the world with tales of gold and jewels. The Locarno Treaty was signed and, almost unnoticed, British troops were evacuating Cologne; the Rhineland was becoming German once more.

In Germany itself, Baron Manfred von Richthofen was lying in

---

conversion seems to have come with the blitzkrieg blows in 1939–40. He was adamant against the creation of an independent air arm before the war, including the period when he was Chief of Staff, 1930–35.

a new grave, after a bizarre journey from his wartime resting place in France. Dour French guards had left the unmarked railway car at the border, but a few miles beyond, the train stopped, carpenters and painters appeared, and the car was transformed into a baronial hearse. A German immortal began a triumphal procession through the Black Forest. At every stop men in wartime uniforms came aboard with flowers and gifts, until the car could hold no more. In Berlin, a boy carrying the plain iron cross which had marked the grave in France led the coffin to the Church of Mercy, and old soldiers holding torches escorted the master of the Flying Circus to a bier. Thousands came for a last look, before the body was borne away to burial. President von Hindenburg led the distinguished mourners to the new grave site.

Japanese troops had occupied another city in Manchuria—Mukden.

24

My Valves Are All Shot

Congressmen bellowed angrily over the verdict for a few days. Representative Thomas Blanton of Texas introduced a bill that would not only make Mitchell the Chief of Air Service and a brigadier general, but also take revenge on his tormentors: the outspoken Generals Graves and King would forfeit half their pay for five years, and Generals Drum and Dennis Nolan of the General Staff would be suspended for five years.

Fiorello La Guardia sent up a bill that would curtail the authority of a court-martial in cases involving the 96th Article of War; the maximum penalty would be a thirty-day suspension from the service.

On the House floor Representative John Tillman of Arkansas called the court "shameless and cruel, an insult to free America." Representative Loring M. Black, Jr., of New York called on Congress to reverse the verdict and restore Mitchell's rank and pay. Reporters predicted that Congress would investigate the General Staff and force it "to say flatly whether it regards aviation as an unknown quantity."

Reid told the press: "They may think they have silenced Mitchell, but his ideas will go marching on, and those who crucified him will be the first to put his aviation suggestions into practice. He is a 1925 John Brown."

The Washington *Post* forecast "a flood of bills and resolutions" in both houses when Mitchell's fate was finally decided, and veterans groups passed resolutions condemning the verdict.

Representative Sol Bloom of New York suggested to Mayor-elect Jimmy Walker that Mitchell would make an ideal chief of police for New York City. Newspapers noted that Mitchell declined all such offers, including many in private business. His mail was heavy with messages from people throughout the country.

But the furor diminished; Congress returned to normal without action, and for weeks Mitchell waited for the Board of Review to pass on the verdict. Reid finally asked the Adjutant General what had become of the case, and was told that the Army's legal chief was not "at liberty to answer your questions." Secretary of War Davis at last confirmed the popular suspicion: ". . . confidentially, the proceedings in this case are in the hands of the President."

The Washington *Post* said hopefully: "It is hardly conceivable that he [Coolidge] will approve of the sentence," adding that despite Mitchell's obvious guilt under the charge, the verdict should be set aside in light of the "unwise, illogical system" under which he was convicted. The paper expressed confidence that Coolidge would void the verdict.

"Silent Cal" spoke on January 26, approving the sentence:

". . . A duly constituted court-martial has determined that the accused has been guilty of highly censurable conduct. The country has every reason to expect that its officers, especially those who hold positions of high rank . . . will at all times be strictly obedient to the provisions of the law . . ."

As to Mitchell's charges after the *Shenandoah* disaster, he had taken "advantage of the horror-stricken state of the minds of the people." He had "violently assailed the War Department and the Navy Department." The President stressed the theory that Mitchell's course smacked of anarchy: "The theory of government implies that every official so long as he retains office shall deport himself with respect toward his superiors . . . Unless this rule is applied there could be no discipline in the Army and the Navy, without which those two forces would . . . become actually a menace to society. Discipline is the whole basis of military training."

Mitchell's base pay, the President noted, was $483.33 per month, plus a subsistence allowance of $156. He altered the court's verdict by granting him full subsistence and half pay, or $397.67 per month ($4760 per year), "during the pleasure of the President." Coolidge said he had done this out of consideration for Mitchell, since he would be unable to accept private employment while he was in uniform.

Mitchell's guarded comments began to appear on the same day in the press, attributed to "informants"; the general had no intention of accepting the "modified sentence" in order to live for five years as "an object of government charity."

Reid urged Mitchell to take time to consider his decision, especially since Congress now seemed on the point of action. La Guardia, Senator Borah and others promised retaliation.

But Mitchell had made up his mind. He immediately sent a note to the Adjutant General: "I hereby tender my resignation as an officer in the United States Army, to take effect February 1, 1926."

The acceptance by the War Department came back without delay: "The resignation by Colonel Mitchell, Air Service, as an officer in the Army to take effect February 1, 1926, is accepted by the President."

On the day of this acceptance former Secretary Weeks was in Los Angeles with his wife and friends, on his way to vacation in Hawaii. He told a reporter: "Mitchell wasn't sufficiently punished by the court. He's nothing but a publicity seeker, an advertiser for personal gain, and he knows as well as I know, and others in official position in Washington know, that what he says about the airplane situation is false."

The following day Mitchell gave a mimeographed statement to the press which summarized his twenty-eight-year career in the Army. It was not the farewell of a demoralized man:

"I look back upon this record with the greatest pride and with the satisfaction that I have done everything possible for my country. After all these years not one dark spot can be found on my record, and not one act which does not redound to the credit of the United States."

He repeated many of the now-familiar charges: "The military bureaucracy, resisting all innovations, has become such that it is impossible to secure any needed changes in the system. The reasons they give are veiled in mysteries and secrecies so as to confuse the public, whereas actually the conditions to be met are simple and public.

"This is one of the greatest menaces to our free institutions that has ever occurred. The bureaucratic party, as it might be called, in its inner workings in Washington, is more powerful than Democrats or Republicans . . ."

He argued for a Department of Defense, and added: "In our beloved America, the greatest of all countries, we must adopt a national defense policy founded on our particular needs, based on the abundance of our raw materials, the excellence of our industries, and the remarkable intelligence of our people."

He announced a continuing crusade: "From now on I feel I can better serve my country and the flag I love by bringing a realization of the true conditions of our national defense straight to the people than by remaining muzzled in the Army.

"I shall always be on hand in case of war or emergency, or wherever I am needed."

No one detected in him any signs of despair. One of his last acts in uniform had been to take thirty-seven flights in one day at Bolling, to run up the flight pay he had missed during the trial; after a delay while finance officers and Army lawyers shuffled the papers, he was paid.

As the Army began to settle affairs with him, it turned to the most picayune details. A shortage in his accounts was reported, and he was charged with "the following items of property":

"Two flags distinguishing Brigadier General's auto, $12.50; one each suit, flying, nutria-lined, half leather, experimental, $215; 2 each suits summer flying, size 40, $18.50; . . . 3 each protectors, face, $3; one each Kodak No. 1, with carrying case, lens, etc. . . ." The total ran to $353.92. Mitchell returned these items on request and some months later was reimbursed.

He was off almost immediately on a four-month lecture tour that would take him to the Pacific Coast and back, speaking almost nightly—and sometimes several times a day. His message was the necessity for air power, the dangers of the dead hand of the military past, and the urgency for an American awakening. He took along films of the Chesapeake bombings, the sinking ships and the clouds of smoke, gas and burning phosphorus over the old

Alabama. He traveled under the direction of the well-known agent James B. Pond, who had told him he could get $1000 for each appearance.

Mitchell opened to a small crowd in Carnegie Hall in mid-February in snowy weather; critics said his talk gave signs of hurried preparation, but the audience applauded him. His first lecture in New England occurred during a blizzard in Worcester, Massachusetts, and Pond could only get $500 of his guarantee from the box office. But Mitchell wrote Betty that the people assembled by the Veterans of Foreign Wars had been enthusiastic and "I gave them a very good talk, which was different from my last one."

He was a great success in Boston, where the Army had a spy in the audience; the report to Washington by Captain James C. Crockett said: "General Mitchell's appearance on the stage was the occasion of prolonged applause. He wore no decorations, had good stage presence but poor speaking voice and poor enunciation . . . the lecture was delivered in a tone of moderation without recourse to elocution."

Mitchell went on through Rochester and Buffalo, where he had $1500 guarantees, making more effective talks each night; he wrote Betty of his plans to build a United Air Force Association to enlighten the public "and show up any dirty work that the Army or Navy or other outfit was trying to put over."

He went westward, drawing bigger and bigger crowds. A mob of 75,000 met him in Altoona, Pennsylvania, and in Chicago the mayor and the City Council took him in hand and helped to swell the crowd for his lecture. In Detroit he felt the long arm of the White House. Coolidge's secretary, Everett Sanders, had wired prominent businessmen in the city in an effort to halt Mitchell's appearance. A newspaper headlined the story: "YAY, MITCHELL—BUT WHISPER IT," and he spoke to a half-empty house. A Detroit correspondent sent Sanders a clipping about the lecture and said: "No one of any consequence at all met Mr. Mitchell, nor did anyone of consequence hear his speech."

Mitchell did not lose heart. He spoke to 3500 in Cincinnati, and about as many in Toledo and in Columbus; he wrote Betty that he had earned $6000 in his last five appearances. A visit to McCook Field depressed him. He wrote to Betty: "McCook is pitiful. Practically nothing going on and everyone is way down in the mouth. I certainly am glad that we are out."

He was in Dayton when Congress rejected a bill for a unified air force, and the mayor, A. C. McDonald, used the occasion to launch a "Mitchell for President" drive which faded after a day in the newspapers. Mitchell spoke in Fort Wayne and Lansing to large crowds, and agreed to five interviews with the Hearst syndicate, for $3000. He enjoyed a hometown triumph in Milwaukee, where "I made the best speech I've made on the whole tour." He was urged to run for a Wisconsin Senate seat and thought seriously of running as a Republican, but told Betty: "Of course we won't go into it unless we can see a win pretty clearly."

In Minneapolis, where war veterans almost mobbed him at the train station, he told reporters: "I'll go on with this tour, a fighting tour, until I run out of breath—at the rate I'm going, about May first."

Through snowy weather he made St. Paul, Duluth and Hibbing, then turned south to Des Moines, where he complained to Betty that Pond was dealing with irresponsible people and adding "absurd" overhead costs. "This stuff is tiresome, going around the country," he wrote, "but I am sure it is the right thing." His letters were full of concern for the new project they were beginning in Middleburg, Virginia, the breeding of fine hunting horses. Between horses and writing and lecturing, he thought, he could support the family; he was writing articles for *Liberty* and *Collier's*, and had finished his newspaper work.

He used a new approach before a large audience in Omaha. He compared the Army General Staff to a board of directors: "And you know what a board is—long, narrow and wooden . . . The Army is run according to the book. If you look for something on page 14, column 3, and it isn't there, it cannot be. When a general who has seen an airplane from a dugout in France inspects our aviation, he looks at the kitchen and sees what kind of food the boys are having, sees if the grass is cut the proper length. He inspects the hobnails on ground-men's shoes, and if he looks at the airplane, all he inspects is the paint . . .

"Thousands of officers stationed in Washington spend their time writing novels to each other . . . The Navy does not like Alaska. Too many Eskimos. The social advantages are not so good as in Hawaii and San Diego . . . Our idea of protecting the Panama Canal is to go and sit on it instead of creating airplane bases to prevent an enemy approaching . . ."

From Sioux City he wrote Betty in a thoughtful mood: "As I look out my window over the old Missouri, just think, only a generation ago the pioneers were pushing across here with their ox teams over trackless prairies, under constant attack by the Indians . . . We had a nice talk. The place was packed. People had come from adjacent states, even some from Minnesota. You must keep a stiff upper lip, darling, this month and next until I get through running over the country. It is having a far-reaching effect."

Peoria, Rock Island and Indianapolis were also successes. In Springfield, Ohio, his audience "stood up and applauded for five minutes before he could make himself heard." He went down the Mississippi and into Texas, with a stop at Kelly Field, where he was entertained by his old friend General Frank McCoy, the first of his court-martial judges he had seen since the trial. He was more positive than ever that he was better off out of uniform: "My! Betty, but I'm glad we're out of the service. The everlasting humdrum existence that they lead . . . All the poor air people are perfectly despondent. They haven't a single ship that is really safe to fly. All single-seaters of all kinds have been condemned as unsafe. All would get out if they could get suitable positions . . ."

He tried to reassure her that though newspaper clippings made "it look as if I cussed the Army and Navy out all the time, that is not so."

In El Paso he encountered another court-martial judge, General Winans, whose attitude was anything but friendly. The American Legion post in the city had borrowed an old Army plane from Fort Bliss to park in San Jacinto Plaza as an advertisement of Mitchell's lecture—but this was canceled by Winans, who also forbade the posting of lecture notices on the post. The Legion post found a junked plane, propped up its sagging wings and repaired it for use in the plaza. "Judging from what Colonel Mitchell is saying now about Army planes," the local paper said, "he'll probably think the junked plane is as safe as some aviators are forced to use."

As he reached the West Coast he wrote Betty: "The Army and Navy have tried in all ways I think to keep this stuff down, but entirely without success . . . I'm glad this trip is drawing to a close. I have stayed with it from morning until night and the greatest trouble has been to fight shy of well-meaning friends."

He reported that he was making money rapidly, learning how to conduct his own lecturing and publishing affairs, and improving as a speaker: "I have learned a great deal in enunciation, delivery, not letting my voice drop, and so on." He spoke often in California, and was cheered by the San Diego reception: "Last night's lecture was a wonder. Here in this Navy town the place was packed. I never saw a more enthusiastic outfit. They just screamed and yelled. The fleet left yesterday afternoon so that the officers and men could not come."

On the way back he spoke in Denver, where fifteen planes circled the railroad station as he arrived, and he met the aging Mary Alexander, the Scottish governess of his youth, who told reporters that Mitchell had been "an awful boy." From Lincoln, Nebraska, near the end, he wrote to Betty: "The whole trip has been a tremendous success so far as getting our ideas scattered around the country." He said he had earned about $40,000 in the past year from speaking and writing, "done all by ourselves . . . and not in speculation or leaning on other parties or anything else." He was soon back in Middleburg with Betty, the "Angel Buddy Love Rat" of his increasingly ardent letters.

His career as a lecturer was over, except for sporadic appearances in the few years left to him. He settled happily at Boxwood, the fine country house which had been Betty's wedding gift from her parents, fox hunting with his neighbors, starring in horse shows, selling well-trained "hardmouthed" hunters which became famous among the Virginia gentry. He and Betty visited Russia and Germany in 1927, and he warned that the Russians were using German designers to help build a large air force. The Germans, he reported, were creating an army by finding new ways around the restrictions of the peace treaty. The U.S. military attaché, under orders from Washington, kept closer watch on Mitchell's movements than on any foreign agents, and noted his friendships with German aviation leaders as if he were an enemy.

Back at Boxwood, he taught his daughter Lucy to ride at a tender age, with a dedication and kindly firmness she never forgot. After a flurry of magazine articles, especially in *Liberty*, interest in his writing waned. He tried everything, even Civil War novels for boys, which were rejected by editors; from seventeen published articles in 1927, his output fell to five in 1930, the year his last book, *Skyways*, was published. The Great Depression diverted attention from Mitchell and air power, as it did from other concerns, and it was only with the coming of the New Deal of Franklin Roosevelt that Mitchell's popularity returned.

He campaigned for Roosevelt, and there was an exchange of warm letters with "Dear Franklin." Mitchell thought he was to become head of a new Defense Department in the Roosevelt regime, but if it had been promised, Roosevelt changed his mind. Mitchell seemed embittered by lack of attention from the incoming Administration, and this may have been reflected in his new outburst of prophetic writing, now centering largely on the threat of Japan ("Are We Ready for War With Japan?" and "Will Japan Try to Conquer the U.S.?").

He accumulated unpublished manuscripts: a World War diary called "From Start to Finish of Our Greatest War" (published in 1960 under the title *Memoirs of World War I*, in edited form); *America, Air Power and the Pacific; The Opening of Alaska;* and *General Greely*, which was published in the year of his death.*

Editors and the services might forget Mitchell, but the public and press did not. Mrs. Hap Arnold saw him one day in 1931 when she was in Washington for the dedication of a Potomac bridge. The Air Corps was out in force, and had come from its annual maneuvers with every available plane—about two hundred, of all ages and types. The Secretaries of War and Navy and many other Cabinet members were in the crowd. Mrs. Arnold saw an abrupt change in the scene:

"All of a sudden out of a car stepped Billy Mitchell, with a heavy coat on, and his hat on the side of his head, and a cane. In a

* Indicative of the scope of articles by and about Mitchell is the 1942 Library of Congress Mitchell bibliography of 33 pages, which lists 93 magazine articles by Mitchell, 29 of his appearances before government boards and committees, 146 books and articles about Mitchell—exclusive of hundreds of stories in the *New York Times*.

minute the newspapermen forgot all about these very important people and concentrated on Billy Mitchell. He was just the center of the whole thing, and people chased him wherever he went.

"He came over and hugged me."

As they watched a review of planes he turned to her: "Bea, some day there'll be thousands of planes in the air. Do you realize that?"

"Not while I live."

"Yes. Pretty soon. We're going to have lots of planes. The average person doesn't realize what's ahead of us."

She found his manner strangely detached, as if he were a bystander. "He didn't show any bitterness," she said.

Occasionally Mitchell came to the Army's attention in some way, and he was treated warily, as if he were a stranger whose motives were suspect. He had been flying in Army planes at Wright Field in Dayton from time to time as a passenger, and the chief of the Matériel Division became so concerned about the flights that he telephoned Washington. He talked with one of Mitchell's old officers, Major Kilner, who was obliged to take up the matter with General Fechet. The Army's policy on the aging prophet came back in an official dispatch:

"General Fechet has no objection to his being granted local flights as a passenger in planes . . . He further directs that General Mitchell be accorded the same privileges that would extend to any citizen of the U.S. This of course precludes divulging any confidential information, also precludes his being granted permission to see any secret or confidential developments."

Near the end of 1935 his friends in Washington got vague news from Middleburg that Mitchell was not well but that there was nothing alarming. In early February 1936, Alfred Verville had a call from Mitchell, his first word from him in over a month.

"I want to see you, Verveel," Mitchell said cheerily. "How about the Metropolitan Club Thursday evening?"

"Is something wrong, General? I heard you hadn't been well."

"Oh, nothing much. A heart condition, they say. They won't let me drive. You know how these doctors are. I'll be up with a chauffeur."

Mitchell was in a barber's chair when Verville found him at the Metropolitan Club: "He looked terrible, pasty, his flesh dropsical, his eye kind of dead. His eye still glistened, though, despite everything. You could see he had a spark."

Mitchell shook hands. "Well, you and Bissell ought to be happy now," he said. "I've just had nine ulcerated teeth taken out. Betty's been after me for years about them, thought they put poison into my system."

Mitchell called a waiter and ordered two brandies and soda. "General," Verville said, "I don't think you ought to have one."

"The doctor said it's quite all right for me to have brandy. It's good for me. I'll meet you in the library right away."

"Right then I could see something had happened to him," Verville recalled later. "He could move his head but he couldn't seem to roll his eyes as he did ordinarily. You could see that he was suffering, that there'd been a mortal blow to his system, that something had already happened." Verville waited in the library with tears in his eyes until Mitchell came in slowly and sank into a chair, breathing wearily.

"You know, Verveel, the doctors tell me my valves are all shot. I guess my bearings are gone, too. But you know I've lived three lives and all I wish is that I could stick around to finish up about three books I have in mind to write—and I want to be around for the next big show."

"What do you mean, General?"

"I mean the real air-power war, the real world war."

Verville asked him when and where he expected it to start.

"In the same place that it started last time, only this is going to be in everybody's backyard. It's going to be the air-power war, and I'd like to be around here to see the color of the faces of those who opposed our military aircraft program when they see the real role air power plays."

They talked for an hour or two, of work Verville was doing to help Mitchell in a libel suit brought against him by a manufacturing company he had charged with underhandedness in government contracts. They spoke of the men who Mitchell thought would lead the air-power war—Rickenbacker, Doolittle and Arnold.

Mitchell seemed reluctant to leave, as if it might be a confession of weakness to obey the doctor's orders and get home to bed early. Verville had a memory of their European tour in 1922, when Mitchell had come down with flu: "Oh, hell, Verveel, I don't need a doctor. I'll be all right. It's just the grippe. I'll take a little cognac. Give me cognac. It'll warm me up."

Verville never saw him again. A week later Betty took him to Doctors Hospital in New York, "merely for a rest," his doctor said. A heart specialist, Dr. Samuel Lambert, who was Betty's cousin, took over his case. Mitchell was placed in an oxygen tent, but he was not on the hospital's danger list. Harriet left her home in rural Wisconsin despite a devastating snowstorm which swept most of the country; she went a short distance in a sleigh drawn by two horses, but was forced to walk on snowshoes before she reached a streetcar in a Chicago suburb and was finally able to get to an airport and fly to New York. She found Mitchell happy and joking as usual; he insisted that Harriet get inside his oxygen tent with him.

A few days later the oxygen tent was removed and Mitchell seemed improved, though he slept often. Betty left him for a few hours, for the first time since his illness. Harriet stayed with him, and he talked with her about all his plans for the future. He seemed more like himself, Harriet thought, than he had since coming to New York. Betty returned to his room in the afternoon.

It was February 19, a still, bitterly cold day in New York. Mitchell, who had been walking about the room briefly, got back into bed and dozed off. He never awakened. Betty and Harriet sat on either side of his bed while he died, suddenly, quietly and without pain. Dr. Lambert attributed death to the complications of influenza, which Mitchell had so often scorned, and to "overwork," the strain of the "three lives" Mitchell said he had compressed into one during his fifty-six years.*

Betty and Harriet went to Pennsylvania Station with the coffin in a small procession led by Rickenbacker, with an honor guard of police and the American Legion. They rode through snow to Chicago, where the gray coffin was transferred to his grandfather's old railroad, the Milwaukee. Mitchell had asked to be buried in the family plot; there were radio reports, later branded as false, that the Army had denied him a place in Arlington Cemetery.

* Mitchell's estate was small: about $5,000 in personal effects, and an estimated total of $15,000.

A delegation of four congressmen came at last, after crashing in a plane on their first attempt. There was a simple funeral at St. Paul's Episcopal Church in Milwaukee, with only two hymns, "Lead, Kindly Light" and the general's favorite, "The Battle Hymn of the Republic." The hearse went to Forest Home Cemetery through head-high snowdrifts, and to the grave.

Among the pallbearers were three of Mitchell's nephews, one of his court-martial judges, General Frank McCoy—and McCoy's aide, Lt. Col. George Catlett Marshall. The only other military touches were furnished by an Army bugler who blew taps at the graveside, and a firing squad from Fort Sheridan which gave Mitchell a final salute in the frosty air.

He was buried on Washington's Birthday, which was celebrated elsewhere: in Berlin, the Nazi Party permitted the first offering of grace, in Washington's memory, at a ceremony attended by Ambassador William E. Dodd, Hitler's lieutenant Ernst F. S. ("Putzi") Hanfstaengl, Dr. Hjalmar Schacht and Dr. Hugo Eckener, the genius of the Zeppelins. In Fredericksburg, Virginia, the baseball hero, Walter Johnson, repeated Washington's legendary feat of flinging a silver dollar over the Rappahannock River. In Cambridge, Massachusetts, Franklin D. Roosevelt, visiting Harvard to see his son John initiated into the Fly Club, was booed by students, one of the first times the popular President had faced a hostile crowd.

The Nazi assault on Poland was little more than three years away.

Mitchell had been dead eight years when Franklin Roosevelt, on a wartime inspection of the Aleutians, paid the prophet one of the most eloquent, if unwitting, of tributes. The Presidential log showed in the entry of August 3, 1944, from Adak:

"If back in 1940 . . . I had said to the Chiefs of Staff of the Army and the Navy, 'Our next war is going to be in the Aleutians and down in the Southwest Pacific,' they would have all laughed at me. They are the experts at that sort of thing. I am not an expert. I am just an ordinary American. We can see now that Americans were caught unprepared because we were ordinary human beings, following the best advice we had at that time."

It was as if Mitchell had never lived.

. . .

In 1957 Mitchell's youngest child, William, Jr., asked the Air Force to set aside the court-martial verdict. The plea was based on a section of the U.S. Military Code permitting the Secretary of a military Department to "correct any military record . . . when he considers it necessary to correct an error or injustice."

Though hundreds of newspaper editorials urged that the request be granted, there were some thoughtful editors who advised that the facts of history be left as a sort of national monument. Mitchell's hometown paper, the Milwaukee *Journal*, said: "Time has proved how right Billy Mitchell was and how wrong were the smug generals who sat in judgment . . . but why attempt to reverse the findings of the 1925 court? The facts cannot be changed nor history rewritten. Neither can the true significance of the Mitchell court-martial be altered—that complacency and withdrawal into isolation cannot keep this nation strong or protected."

The Christian Science Monitor said: "A sure test of whether one is an adult is his willingness to accept the consequences of his own acts . . . Let Billy Mitchell remain in memory the adult he himself wanted to be."

The Air Force Board for Correction of Military Records (composed entirely of civilians) studied the application and the court-martial and agreed with the American majority—the rightness of Mitchell's cause should be admitted and the verdict of the court set aside. The board recommended approval of his son's plea to Secretary of the Air Force James H. Douglas.

The Secretary said:

"The history of recent years has shown that Colonel Mitchell's vision concerning the future of air power was amazingly accurate. He saw clearly the shape of things to come in the field of military aviation, and he forecast with precision the role of air power as it developed in World War II, and as we see it today. Our nation is deeply in his debt. . . . Colonel Mitchell's views have been vindicated. But while on active duty, and subject to the discipline of the military service, he characterized the administration of the War and Navy Departments as incompetent, criminally negligent and almost treasonable.

"Colonel Mitchell was free to resign his commission and to

seek to arouse the public in support of his strong views . . . He chose instead to remain on active duty while making his charges against his service superiors. In taking this course, he was bound to accept the consequences . . .

"The sole question in this case is whether an error or injustice has been committed . . . Although the Board . . . acting in its advisory capacity, has recommended the approval of the petition, I can find no ground for concluding at this time, more than thirty years after the President personally approved Colonel Mitchell's conviction, that the trial should not have taken place, or that the court-martial's finding that Colonel Mitchell was guilty of violating the 96th Article of War had no justification in fact.

"It is tragic that an officer who contributed so much to his country's welfare should have terminated his military career under such circumstances. Today, however, I am confident that his services to his country and his unique foresight as to the place of air power in the defense of our country are fully recognized by his countrymen. No more convincing or appropriate recognition could be given than was bestowed on Colonel Billy Mitchell on August 8, 1946, when the President signed a law posthumously bestowing upon him a Medal of Honor 'in recognition of his outstanding pioneer service and foresight in the field of American military aviation.' *

"The application is denied."

* The statement that Mitchell had been awarded the Congressional Medal of Honor was incorrect. Actually, a special medal was struck for him and presented to his sister Harriet.

Soon afterward, in the series of attempts to honor Mitchell posthumously, a bronze statue of the aviator was unveiled in the Smithsonian Institution. Nearby, among relics of his career, is a quotation from the dedication of the last book of his life: "My children in their lifetime will see aeronautics become the greatest and principal means of national defense and rapid transportation all over the world and possibly beyond our world into interstellar space."

Acknowledgments

The two major documentary sources for this book were the court-martial record itself, sealed since 1926 and never previously consulted by a writer, and Mitchell's personal military file, called the 201 file, also previously closed.

Unlike most 201 files, Mitchell's contains far more than the customary medical and duty records, confidential fitness reports, reprimands, and the like. It is one of the most voluminous in Army records, and includes such a variety of papers as his sensational (and suppressed) Pacific Report of 1924, as well as official reactions to it; papers and charges relating to his divorce; a lengthy psychiatrist's report; correspondence documenting the bitter quarrels between Mitchell and his superior officers; charges of Mitchell's mishandling of minor details during one of his great accomplishments, the bombing tests of 1921; and even such documents as an anonymous accusation that Mitchell demeaned the Army by appearing in a nonregulation and avant-garde uniform.

The file consists of fifteen parts, of varying length, and in total fills a large filing drawer. Since Mitchell's death it has been under the control of the Army except for a brief period in the hands of the Air Force. It is now stored in the U.S. Army Records Administration Center, St. Louis, Missouri.

Also of importance as sources were the Mitchell Papers in the Library of Congress, consisting of some 19,000 items; the Oral History Collection of Columbia University, which includes an aviation project; papers owned by William Mitchell, Jr.; and recollections of relatives, friends and other contemporaries of Mitchell.

I am grateful to members of the Mitchell family for granting access to the 201 file and the court-martial record. Permission was granted by Mitchell's children, Mrs. Lucy M. Gilpin and William Mitchell, Jr., of Boyce, Virginia; Mrs. Harriet M. Anderson of Arlington, Va.; and Miss Elizabeth Mitchell of Dublin, Ireland; and by his widows, now deceased, Mrs. Caroline S. Korell and Mrs. Elizabeth M. Mitchell.

I am grateful to Mrs. Henry H. Arnold of Sonoma, Calif., for permission to use the Mitchell papers in the Arnold Collection of the Oral History Project of Columbia University (hereafter OHP); to Mitchell's former secretaries, Mrs. P. E. Van Nostrand of Hampton, Va., and Mrs. Maydell McDarment of Austin, Tex., and to scores of others who knew or worked with Mitchell and aided in this work by correspondence or interviews—most of these are identified in the chapter notes.

Among Mitchell's own writings these books were of chief value: *Our Air Force* (1921); *Winged Defense* (1925); *Skyways* (1930); and *Memoirs of World War I* (N.Y., 1960). The last item refers to an edited version of a manuscript in Libr. Congr., Mitchell Papers, entitled *From Start to Finish of Our Greatest War,* from which a series of articles was written for *Liberty* magazine (hereafter *Memoirs*).

Also useful were the Mitchell biographies: *Billy Mitchell: Crusader for Air Power,* by Alfred Hurley (1964); *Billy Mitchell,* by Arch Whitehouse (1962); *General Billy Mitchell: Champion of Air Defense,* by Roger Burlingame (1953); *My Brother Bill,* by Ruth Mitchell (1952); *Mitchell: Pioneer of Air Power,* by Isaac Don Levine (1943); *Billy Mitchell: Founder of Our Air Force and Prophet Without Honor,* by Emile Gauvreau and Lester Cohen (1942). Levine's book is the most extensive and detailed narrative; Hurley's, the first critical study of Mitchell, is especially valuable on his campaign for air power; and the colorful sketch by Ruth Mitchell helps to reveal Mitchell's personality.

Other documents consulted were the Old Army Records (especially File RG 94) and Old Navy Records (especially RG 72 and RG 80) in the National Archives, where John E. Taylor was of invaluable aid. Also helpful were the archives of the Aerospace Studies Institute, Maxwell AFB, Alabama, where Miss Margot Kennedy and Dr. Albert F. Simpson aided greatly in the search for materials.

Also consulted: The Calvin Coolidge Papers and the John J. Pershing Papers, Libr. Congr.; the published diaries of Josephus Daniels, Secretary of the Navy; and published personal correspondence of Franklin D. Roosevelt.

Through the courtesy of Mrs. H. M. Baumhofer, Chief, USAF

Motion Picture Film Depot, Wright-Patterson AFB, Dayton, Ohio, I saw many reels of film, especially of the bombing tests of 1921 and 1923. I am indebted to Mrs. Burdette S. Wright of Leesburg, Va., for use of the diaries of her husband, long a Mitchell aide; and to Dr. Eugene Emme of Silver Spring, Md., for general advice; Dr. Adolph G. Bauemker of Bad Godesberg, West Germany; Gen. and Mrs. St. Clair Streett of Lusby, Md.; Gen. George Goddard, USAF (Ret.), of Washington; Edward Steichen of West Redding, Conn.; Gen. James H. Doolittle, USAF (Ret.), of Redondo Beach, Calif.; Col. C. H. M. Roberts, USA (Ret.), of Syracuse, N.Y.; Alfred Verville of San Diego, Calif.; Mrs. Robert Daniel of Brandon, Prince George County, Va.; Samuel F. Bemis of Richmond, Va.; Capt. Alvin S. Preil, USNR (Ret.), of Corpus Christie, Texas; Jerome C. Hunsaker of Boston; the late Maj. Gen. Orvil A. Anderson, USAF; Mrs. Frank R. Reid, Jr., member of Congress from Illinois; and Maj. Alfred Hurley, USAF. I owe a special debt to Marvin McFarland, Chief, Science & Technology Division, Libr. Congr., for his reading of a version of the manuscript; and to my editor, Robert D. Loomis, who conceived this book and persisted through six years of official discouragement to win permission for my use of the primary materials.

My wife, Evangeline, was in fact co-author, chief of research, and consultant.

Chapter Notes

CHAPTER 1 Mitchell's homecoming in 1919 is based on his war diary "From Start to Finish of Our Greatest War" and its edited version, *Memoirs of World War I;* on Percy Hammond's N.Y. *Herald* column of 1925 (n.d.), "Oddments & Raiments"; on the *N.Y. Times*, Mar. 1, 1919 (p. 4, col. 6); on recollections of Jerome S. Hunsaker as cited in *History of United States Naval Aviation,* by A. D. Turnbull and Clifford L. Lord (New Haven, 1949), and in correspondence with the author; and on correspondence with Mrs. Harriet M. Fladoes of Milwaukee, Mitchell's sister.

CHAPTER 2 The sketch of Mitchell's family background and youth is drawn largely from Ruth Mitchell's *My Brother Bill* and the biographies of Levine, Hurley and Burlingame. This period is also illuminated by hundreds of letters from Mitchell to his father and mother, in the Library of Congress collection. Mary Alexander's recollections of Mitchell's boyhood appeared in the Denver *Post,* May 12, 1926.

Mitchell's first publications were in the Denver *Times*, June 10, 1904, and the *National Geographic* (Sept. 1904); the *Cavalry Journal* carried his first public military prophecies in Apr. 1906.

His report on the armed forces of Japan, China and Russia, so important in his career, was made Jan. 2, 1912; it is in the National Archives, as General Staff Report 7027–1.

H. H. Arnold's recollections of Mitchell, beginning at College Park, Md., in 1912 and continuing through Mitchell's career, are from Arnold's *Global Mission* (N.Y., 1949).

Mitchell's first appearance before a congressional committee, in 1913, is detailed in *U.S. Congress, House Committee on Military*

Affairs. Hearings in Connection with H.R. 5304, 63rd Congress, 1st Session (pp. 77, 84, 88, 91).

Mitchell's early brush with his superiors about newspaper publicity is recorded in War College Papers, National Archives, and in the Washington *Herald,* Feb. 16, 1915; and his early critique, *Our Faulty Military Policy,* in mimeographed form, is in the same collection.

Mitchell's flying lessons were described by his instructor, Jimmy Johnson of Weslaco, Texas, in correspondence with the author, and by the late Walter Lees in letters to his friend Alfred Verville. Mrs. Walter Lees kindly granted permission to cite her husband's letters. A more general recollection of Mitchell's training as a pilot was left in OHP by T. deWitt Milling. The Smithsonian Air Museum, Washington, has documents on this phase of Mitchell's career.

CHAPTER 3 This brief account of Mitchell's career in World War I is drawn largely from his *Memoirs,* with use of letters to his mother in the Libr. Congr. collection. Important supplements were: Arnold's *Global Mission;* Mason Patrick's *The U.S. in the Air* (N.Y., 1928); James G. Harbord's *Leaves from a War Diary* (1925); H. A. Toulmin's *The Air Service, A.E.F., 1918* (N.Y., 1927); *A Brief History of the Air Service* (unpubl. MS., Mitchell Papers) by Clayton Bissell; and a variety of Mitchell's magazine articles.

Details of Mitchell's flight training in France are in his 201 file, and his rating as Junior Military Aviator dates from July 19, 1917.

The association between Mitchell and Sir Hugh Trenchard was sketched by Mitchell and, in a somewhat different vein, by Andrew Boyle in his *Trenchard* (London, 1962).

Mitchell's "will," undated, but obviously of 1917, is in Box 30 of his Papers.

The tangled skein of Air Service command, merely summarized here, is based largely on E. S. Gorrell's 24-vol., unpubl. history of the Air Service, on microfilm at the National Archives. A digest of the command sequence during the war, also by Gorrell, is in the author's collection.

Benjamin Foulois reported on his clash with Mitchell to Pershing on June 4, 1918; a copy is in Mitchell's 201 file.

The St. Mihiel summary is based on Mitchell's account, a full-length report written by Milling, on recollections by Elmer Haslett, and on memoirs of participants found in OHP—Carl Spaatz and Kenneth Littauer. Also valuable was the diary of Burdette S. Wright and the G-2 Summary of Air Information, A.E.F., Gen. Staff No. 47, of Sept. 17, 1918.

Pershing's order sending Mitchell to England to study the unified air arm is dated Jan 14, 1919, and a copy is in Part 7 of the 201 file. This document may have marked an important turn in Mitchell's career, leading to his later campaign for air power in the U.S.

CHAPTER 4 Mitchell's office diary, varied congressional committee reports, and the B. S. Wright diary were helpful in the narrative of this chapter. The Air Service reduction of 1919 is based on Menoher's testimony before the Senate Subcommittee on Military Affairs, 66th Congress, 1st Session, Part 1, p. 270–73. There is a bewildering body of statistics, often in conflict. Juliette Hennessy, in *The U.S. Army Air Arm Between the Wars,* says that of more than 220,000 men in the Bureau of Military Aeronautics, only 57 percent remained by March 1919—and that 94 percent of those in aircraft production had been mustered out.

Mitchell's speech to the Society of Automotive Engineers is mentioned in the N.Y. *Herald* of Mar. 8, 1919, and in his diary.

The abrupt reorganization of the air arm resulted from the transfer of the Air Service (which had never existed in the U.S.) from France. Mitchell's orders (Mar. 10, 1919) to become head of Military Aeronautics indicate that he was unaware of the change until the day it was made.

Reed Chambers left his account of Mitchell's whiskey still in the OHP.

The almost endless proposals for improving air power in the U.S., sent from Mitchell to his superiors, are found throughout his 201 file and are scattered in the poorly organized Mitchell Papers.

Alexander de Seversky's memoir of Mitchell appeared in *Air Power Historian* (Oct. 1956), and is the source of several incidents involving Mitchell and Seversky in this book.

Mitchell's designation as a Military Aviator is documented in his 201 file, Part 13.

The affair of the Crowell mission is drawn from several congressional committee reports, from Mitchell's office diaries, the diaries of Josephus Daniels, a letter from Gen. Patrick to Pershing, Nov. 11, 1919, and from *The Question of Autonomy for the U.S. Air Arm,* by R. Earl McClendon, Maxwell AFB, Ala., revised, 1951, and Turnbull and Lord, *History of U.S. Naval Aviation.*

Sec. Baker's ban on U.S. strategic bombing in WWI is in his dispatch to Gen. Peyton March, Chief of Staff, Nov. 4, 1918; Mitchell's own evasion of the issue, in which he spoke of industrial and civilian targets as "elements which are further back," is illustrated in his

"Proposed Aeronautical Organization for the U.S.," July 15, 1919.

Admiral Benson's comments following the Crowell report are cited in Levine, *op. cit.*, p. 183.

This version of Mitchell's disagreement with Franklin D. Roosevelt before the Senate Military Affairs Committee is based on published reports of hearings, and on a memorandum, Mitchell-Menoher, Dec. 3, 1919, in the Mitchell Papers.

The first challenge to the Navy by Mitchell, in which he quoted the Navy General Board, drew a protest from Sec. Daniels to Sec. Baker, Sept. 22, 1919, and a presumably immediate reply from Baker; both documents are in RG 72 of Old Navy Records, National Archives, the latter undated.

Mitchell's appearance before the House Committee considering Air Service reorganization in Dec. 1919 is based on published reports; the comment of Foulois upon Mitchell's reticence is in the former's memoirs in OHP.

CHAPTER 5 The sketch of Mitchell's work with Seversky's notes and drawings is from *My Brother Bill.*

Mitchell's office diary in his Papers and his correspondence with Thurman Bane give a picture of the variety of Mitchell's interests at this time. His first open attacks on the battleship were before the House Committee on Military Affairs in Feb. 1920.

Material on the U.S.S. *Indiana* test is from the author's interview with Col. C. H. M. Roberts, Mitchell's own report, from contemporary newspapers, and the press releases of Josephus Daniels. Mitchell's early preparations for the bombing tests, few of them cited in the narrative, are found in his Papers.

CHAPTER 6 One of the richest collections of material on Mitchell's career deals with the bombing tests. Most of these are in the Papers; a few scattered ones, some apparently unique, are in the 201 file.

The story of the development of the big bombs for Mitchell is based on interviews with Col. C. H. M. Roberts, correspondence with Harry S. Becker of Silver Spring, Md., and Frederick V. Ludden of Sepulveda, Calif., who took part in the project; and on Mitchell's own files and Ordnance Department publications.

Maj. Melvin Hall's report on Japanese purchase of aircraft in England is in the Mitchell Papers, as well as in the 201 file.

Mitchell's role in the miners' strike in W. Va. is detailed at length in the *Airpower Historian* (Apr. 1965), in a study by Dr. Maurer Maurer.

Most of the material on Adm. Moffett's personality is found in the memoirs of Eugene E. Wilson in OHP. Moffett's scathing report on Mitchell's activities is in Old Navy Records, National Archives, File RG 72 (3084–45).

The vivid report of Herbert Corey to Mitchell on the Navy's reaction to his campaign is in the Mitchell Papers, undated, but about Apr. 9, 1921; Mitchell replied on Apr. 11.

The bitter exchanges involving Menoher's effort to discipline Mitchell are in the Mitchell Papers, especially Menoher to Weeks of June 15 and 16, 1921. Sec. Weeks's statement on the affair is in Part 1 of the 201 file.

CHAPTER 7 The account of the bombing of the warships in the 1921 tests is based on official Air Service and Navy reports, especially the Project B records in Old Army Records, National Archives, and Mitchell's own report. That of Capt. Alfred Johnson is the most important Navy report. In addition, the recollections of Col. C. H. M. Roberts, Brig. Gen. George Goddard and Harriet Mitchell Fladoes were used. William B. Harward of the Martin Company, Baltimore, Md., provided details on the Martin bomber. Contemporary newspaper accounts depicted events aboard the observation ships.

CHAPTER 8 The Mitchell Papers tell the Air Service side of the controversy over results of the tests. Capt. Alfred Johnson put the Navy position in these words: "I think that our Navy learned as much about publicity from these experiments as it did about bombing battleships." Johnson thought Mitchell "distorted" results, and that his dispatch of eight planes loaded with 2000-pound bombs on the final day of the *Ostfriesland* test was "an unauthorized interference with my conduct of the experiments and a violation of the procedures he had agreed to." Johnson added: "Looking back, I don't see what else Mitchell could have done except keep on dropping bombs until the ship sank. If the ship had not sunk soon he would have been the object of ridicule . . . The operation would make him or break him. It made him." (From Johnson's "The Naval Bombing Experiments" for the Naval Historical Foundation, May 31, 1959).

Carbon copies of the "news stories" urging Mitchell's elevation to Chief of Air Service are in the Mitchell Papers. Gen. Patrick's assumption of the office, and his victory over Mitchell, are recounted in his own book, *The United States in the Air.*

CHAPTER 9 The Navy's delaying tactics in delivering the U.S.S. *Alabama* are revealed in the Mitchell Papers, and more thoroughly in the 201 file. The admonition to Mitchell, describing poor organization in the Langley Field mess, is in Part 10, 201 file.

The 201 file also contains the exchanges between Mitchell and the Adjutant General and between Mitchell and Patrick over the "leak" of Mitchell's bombing-test report. The *Alabama* bombing itself was completely described by Mitchell and Fullam, and by reporters who were present.

Jimmy Doolittle's recollection of his one day as Mitchell's aide is in OHP.

Arthur Christie's report to Mitchell on Japanese aircraft production and training of aviators is in the 201 file—as is the report of Army psychiatrists on Mitchell's emotional and mental condition.

The anecdote involving Mitchell and Adm. Moffett at the Limitation of Armaments Conference is recounted by Eugene E. Wilson in *Slipstream* magazine (n.d.), Dayton, Ohio.

CHAPTER 10 The chief source for this chapter is the four-volume report of the European tour, written by Alfred Verville, revised by Clayton Bissell, and published by the Air Service. Also used: Mitchell's office diary, his correspondence with Patrick en route, and with Thurman Bane before departure. Patrick's order of warning to Mitchell as the trip began is in Mitchell's 201 file, dated Dec. 7, 1921.

Mitchell's flight and other activities at the U.S. air base at Weissenthurm, Germany, are described in *Amaroc News,* a newspaper of the U.S. army of occupation in the Ruhr, Feb. 18, 1922.

Verville's memoir in OHP was used in the narrative of the Mitchell party's visit to Berlin, and to the plants of Dornier, Junkers and Fokker. Advisers on this material included Bart J. Slattery of NASA, Telford Taylor of N.Y.C., and Dr. Adolph G. Bauemker, consultant, R&D, USAF, Bad Godesberg, Germany.

A potentially valuable document, a complete diary of the inspection tour, once included in the Mitchell Papers, is now missing.

CHAPTER 11 Recollections of several of Mitchell's contemporaries are used in this chapter: Brig. Gen. Auby Strickland, USAF (Ret.), Arlington, Va.; Gen. Ira Eaker, Washington, D.C. (in OHP); Alfred Verville; Harriet Mitchell Fladoes; Spurgeon Phillips, Durham, N.C.;

Eugene E. Wilson (in OHP); and Alexander de Seversky.

Mitchell's fitness reports, like others used throughout this book, are from his 201 file; material on his divorce, little of it used here, is from the same source.

Incidental material, especially concerning Elizabeth Miller Mitchell, is from Ruth Mitchell's *My Brother Bill*, and from Levine, *op. cit.*

The 1923 bombing tests were fully documented in Mitchell's report, in his Papers as well as his 201 file; the subsequent controversy over release of the results is described by Samuel Taylor Moore in the Mitchell Papers of the Aerospace Studies Institute, Maxwell AFB, and in Levine, *op. cit.*

Mitchell's unremitting campaign to secure the old battleships as targets, and the Navy's resistance, is made clear in a memorandum: Patrick to Pershing, June 30, 1923, which is in Box 62 of RG 94, Old Army Records, National Archives.

CHAPTER 12 The account of Mitchell's wedding is drawn from his diary, and from Detroit newspaper accounts, some undated and unidentified, in Mitchell Papers. His correspondence with Patrick is in the same source, as is Patrick's exchange with Gen. Summerall. The San Francisco *Examiner* of Oct. 1, 1923, the Honolulu *Call-Bulletin* of Oct. 29, 30 and Nov. 6, 1923 and the Manila *Daily Bulletin* of Jan. 7, 1924 were useful in timing Mitchell's movements.

The narrative of Mitchell's Pacific tour in this and the next chapter is based on his "Report of Inspection of U.S. Possessions in the Pacific and Java, Singapore, India, Siam, China and Japan," dated Oct. 24, 1924. It was "Secret" until 1958, when it was declassified, and has not been used by other writers. The 323-page document consists of eighteen chapters and Conclusions, plus appendices. Of almost equal value were Mitchell's preliminary reports detailing his movements during the inspections, which were sent to Patrick in Dec. 1923 and Jan. 1924. All these documents are in the 201 file; a copy of the longer, formal report is at the USAF Academy in Colorado, but has been restricted. Mitchell's sparse diary of this period is in Box 5, in his Papers.

Mitchell's candor in presenting his inspection report to Hawaiian headquarters was revealed later by Lt. Col. Lesley J. McNair, then serving in Hawaii. McNair testified in the Mitchell court-martial.

The complaint about Mitchell's unorthodox uniform was made by Gen. J. L. Hines, Nov. 3, 1923, and Mitchell responded Dec. 13. The documents are in Part 1 of the 201 file; the newspaper photograph in question is missing.

The Summerall-Patrick correspondence concerning Mitchell's inspection is dated Jan. 1924, soon after Mitchell left his stinging report in Hawaii. Patrick's soothing reply to Summerall was written Jan. 26. The Chief's failure to support Mitchell's position in this private exchange probably had an important bearing on events which led to Mitchell's court-martial, since Patrick made it clear that Mitchell's "radical conclusions" were suspect in his own branch of the service.

Sources of the quotations from Mrs. MacArthur: *The Untold Story of Douglas MacArthur,* by Frazier Hunt (N.Y., 1954), pp. 124–25; *Douglas MacArthur,* by Clark Lee & Richard Henschel (N.Y., 1952), pp. 48–52.

Blasco Ibáñez commented on his encounter with Mitchell in his book, *La vuelta al mundo de un novelista.* The passage was located and translated through the kindness of Vicente Asensi Genoves of Valencia, Spain, and Dr. Meta H. Miller of Greensboro, N.C.

The confusion over Mitchell's exact movements in and out of Japan may result from missing or undiscovered documents. In Box 28 of the Mitchell Papers is a letter in his hand from Kobe, undated, but establishing his arrival there on Feb. 6, 1924. Box 10 of the Papers includes copies of diplomatic cables from Ambassador Cyrus Woods, Tokyo, to Washington; one of which, advising against Mitchell's visit, is dated May 16. By May 26, however, the U.S. legation at Peking telegraphed the consul general at Mukden, asking that Mitchell be advised that he might travel to Tokyo "unofficially as a tourist." Mitchell's own cables in this affair are in his 201 file. In any event, the Mitchells remained in the Far East throughout the nine months Oct. 1923–June 1924.

CHAPTER 13 This chapter consists almost entirely of selected quotations from Mitchell's "Report of Inspection."

His greeting to the British fleet was noted by the San Francisco *Chronicle,* July 8, 1924.

CHAPTER 14 The substantial file of War Department reactions to and comments upon Mitchell's Pacific report is scattered in the Mitchell 201 file, in Parts 6, 8 and 13. This chapter is built upon them, almost exclusively; no search was made for later Army documents, since only the immediate War Department reaction seemed to be germane. Until the court-martial itself, this exchange of documents between Mitchell and his adversaries within the Army hierarchy was the most complete and revealing clash of conflicting views on air power in Mitchell's career.

The sequence of events in this exchange is of importance. On Nov. 11, 1925, when Mitchell was being tried by court-martial, the Army traced the several copies of the report (some of them at distant airfields), to ascertain whether they had been marked "Secret."

It was the following week when Operations, Intelligence and War Plans commented on the report (and May of 1926 before Operations reported). Gen. Patrick had reported on Jan. 25, 1925, that he had had the report about ten days, but due to the pressing of "other matters," he could not respond before late February. It was Apr. 16, 1925, when Patrick sent in his comments.

Though it was beyond the scope of this book, future investigators may be able to piece together the complete course of official Army action on Mitchell's report in later years and to relate them to the state of unpreparedness in the Pacific in Dec. 1941.

The difficulty in determining Japanese plane production, even as late as 1941, is made patent in *U.S. Strategic Bombing Survey,* draft study, *Japanese Air Power* (Washington, 1946), p. 28.

CHAPTER 15 The comments of the Washington *Post* on U.S. mobilization plans, and the rejoinder of Adm. Fullam are in the *Post* of Jan. 11, 1924.

The brief summary of the Round the World flight is based on Mitchell's diary, the recollections of Leslie Arnold (in OHP) and of Spurgeon Phillips, on the Washington *Times* of Sept. 9, 1924, and on *The First World Flight,* by Lowell Thomas (Boston, 1925).

The affair of the controversial *Saturday Evening Post* articles by Mitchell is recounted here from Mitchell's diary, his version of the incident given to the House Aircraft Committee; from a memorandum, Gen. Patrick to the Adjutant General, Mar. 14, 1925 (in the Mitchell 201 file, Part 8 of 15); from the magazine itself, and from various contemporary newspaper accounts. A copy of the letter of permission to publish (President Coolidge to Mitchell), is in the Coolidge Papers, Library of Congress, Box 52, Item 25, Miscellaneous, dated Nov. 12, 1924. (It is not now possible to judge accurately the extent to which Mitchell used subterfuge in evading strict orders against such publications.)

The Navy's ordnance tests against the hull of the U.S.S. *Washington* and the resulting squabble were aired before successive committee hearings in early 1925, and were often commented upon by newspapers. Mitchell's personal file, as well as his Papers, has a wealth of reports on the matter.

The colorful sketch of Mitchell's office, just before his banishment, was by Oscar Cesare of the *N.Y. Times,* Mar. 8, 1925.

The beginning of the end for Mitchell in Air Service headquarters dates from his testimony before the Lampert committee of the House. On Jan. 29, 1925 Sec. Weeks, through the Adjutant General, demanded that Mitchell substantiate his statements. Mitchell replied to Patrick in a 15-page memorandum. These and related documents are in Part 8 of the 201 file, and illuminate the final stages of Mitchell's downfall much more thoroughly than was possible in this brief narrative. Old Navy Records in National Archives, RG 72, include correspondence between Secretaries Wilbur and Weeks; the general theme is bitter complaint by the Navy of Mitchell's testimony as "intentionally deceptive." One of Wilbur's memoranda was more than fifty pages, setting forth in parallel columns Mitchell's allegedly inaccurate statements and the Navy version of the facts.

The joint resolution of Mar. 11, 1925 by Sen. Lewis of Washington, a futile effort to save Mitchell, died in the Committee on Federal Relations. A copy is in the Mitchell Papers (Senate Joint Resolution No. 26).

The heated letter from Weeks to Coolidge, giving reasons why Mitchell was not to be reappointed, was dated Mar. 5, 1925; a copy is in Part 10 of Mitchell's 201 file.

Mitchell's farewell to Washington appeared in numerous newspapers; accounts of the farewell parties are drawn from Ruth Mitchell and H. H. Arnold.

CHAPTER 16 The flight of Mitchell and Will Rogers is described in *The Autobiography of Will Rogers,* Donald Day, ed. (Boston, 1949); other material from *Will Rogers,* by Donald Day (N.Y., 1962), p. 165, and *Will Rogers,* by Betty Rogers (Garden City, 1948).

His brief stay in San Antonio was described by his ex-secretary, Maydell Blackmon McDarment, of Austin, Tex., by Mitchell himself in letters to his wife, and, later, in court-martial testimony.

Patrick's reprimand to the commanding officer, Kelly Field, for permitting an "honor guard" to fly with Mitchell to a Dallas speech is in the 201 file, Part 7, Patrick-Col. C. C. Culver, Aug. 12, 1925.

Harry Bruno's anecdote about Mitchell's alleged choice of resignation or banishment is in Bruno's *Wings Over America* (N.Y., 1942), p. 151.

Mitchell's comments on his book *Winged Defense* appeared in the Kansas City *Star*, Sept. 3, 1925.

The account of the Navy's California-Hawaii flight is based on newspapers of the day and court-martial testimony; that of the loss of the *Shenandoah* owes much to court-martial and the naval court of inquiry—and to John Toland's *Ships in the Sky* (N.Y., 1957).

The two statements at San Antonio by Mitchell, on Sept. 5 and 9, 1925, became familiar to millions of his contemporaries; many newspapers published them in full. There are copies in his 201 file, in his Papers and in the court-martial record.

CHAPTER 17 Mitchell's letters to his wife, in the collection of William Mitchell, Jr., were used in the opening of this chapter. The *N.Y. Times* and the N.Y. *Herald*, and the Washington *Star* and *Post* in particular, were attentive to Mitchell, once he had reached Washington; this version of his welcome at Union Station and his Morrow Board appearance owe much to these sources.

Through the courtesy of Col. John A. Magruder, Jr., USMC, of Boyce, Va., the papers of the late Henry Leonard were used in describing the court of inquiry into the *Shenandoah* disaster.

Mitchell's pretrial letter to Patrick of Oct. 1, 1925, assuring the Chief that he did not seek his position, is in the 201 file, Part 7.

Frank Reid's oratory before the court-martial opened, at the end of this chapter, was published in the *N.Y. Times*, Oct. 25, 1925.

CHAPTER 18 The chief source for all chapters in this account of the court-martial is the extensive official record of the trial itself, sealed by the Army at the end of the court and until now never consulted by writers. (When Mitchell's sister Ruth wrote her book, she was under the impression that the record had been destroyed.) The record is stored in thirty-two archive boxes; one transcript, exclusive of stipulations, correspondence, exhibits and supporting documents, runs to about 4000 pages.

Other general sources are newspapers, cited in detail when appropriate; Ruth Mitchell's *My Brother Bill;* the biographies of Levine, Burlingame and Hurley (q.v.); and, of much value, the recollections of three who attended the trial—Mrs. Harriet Mitchell Fladoes, William H. Webb of Bethesda, Md., who aided in the defense, and Miss Eleanor Plain of Aurora, Ill., daughter of Judge Plain of defense counsel. Correspondence with Maj. Gens. Robert L. and

Hamilton Howze, USA (Ret.), sons of the court's president, was also helpful.

The opening scene of the trial is based on accounts in the Washington *Star, N.Y. Times, World* and *Sun* of Oct. 29, 1925, and subsequent dates, and on *My Brother Bill,* p. 318 ff.

Mrs. Mitchell's revelation that one of the judges, Gen. McCoy, and the law member, Col. Winship, were godfathers to the Mitchell children appeared in the Washington *Star,* May 22, 1951.

Gen. Wood's comment to Gen. McCoy on the burden of court-martial service, cited in Hurley (*op. cit.*), p. 109, is from Wood to McCoy, Nov. 12, 1925, in the Wood manuscripts, Libr. Congr.

CHAPTER 19 Mitchell's statement that his trial was "a necessary cog in the wheel of progress" is in his Papers, in a copy of an article written for the Bell Syndicate.

The testimony of Spaatz, Arnold, Schauffler, Chambers, Rickenbacker, et al., has been much condensed and rendered in highlight. No attempt has been made to indicate the wholesale deletions. Throughout, the aim has been to give a faithful account in summary, despite excisions for the sake of clarity.

The comments of Mrs. Arnold and Ira Eaker on Mitchell's attitude during the trial are from their recollections in OHP.

Pershing's absence from the court-martial was discussed in a Washington *Star* editorial, Nov. 3, 1925, and Pershing's comment to Gen. Wright on the "Bolshevik bug" (i.e., mutinous or revolutionary influences) in the Army is in the Pershing Papers, Libr. Congr.

The Armistice Day incident involving Mitchell and the American Legion post in N.Y. is based on the Coolidge Papers, Libr. Congr. (Folder 249, Box 159, Charles Matthews-Coolidge and D. E. Nolan to Everett Sanders, dates of Oct. 9 and 10 and Nov. 11, 1925); also on the Washington *Star,* Nov. 11 and 12, 1925.

A copy of the dispatch, Patrick to Col. C. C. Culver on the secret nature of Mitchell's Pacific report, is in Mitchell's 201 file, Part 8.

CHAPTER 20 The courtroom atmosphere of this phase of the narrative is drawn from the Washington *Star* and *Herald,* Nov. 13, 14 and 29, 1925; also from unidentified newspaper clippings of the period in the Mitchell Papers.

Witnesses quoted on the *Shenandoah* here have been selected, and testimony has been much abbreviated, since it was so extended, often technical in nature, repetitious and occasionally conflicting.

Sidney Miller's attempted payment of a fee to Frank Reid was recalled by Reid's secretary, Miss Frances Youker of Aurora, Ill., in a report to the author.

An occasional witness appears out of sequence in this narrative, but only for purposes of clarity. Admiral Sims, for example, appears out of chronological order so that all of the *Shenandoah* testimony might be read in sequence.

CHAPTER 21 The sketch of the defendant as he took the stand is based on a Washington *Star* story of Nov. 29, 1925. Mitchell's testimony opens on p. 1400 of the court-martial record; he spent more than a day and a half under direct, cross- and redirect examination.

The Navy's "spy reports" from the courtroom, of which the memorandum from Capt. Cook to War Plans is typical, are found in Old Navy Records, National Archives; Cook's is in RG 80 (6000-1424), date of Jan. 6, 1926.

Mitchell's reported heart condition is cited in Ruth Mitchell's *My Brother Bill,* p. 325.

CHAPTER 22 Mitchell's observation that MacArthur's features were "as cold as carved stone" during the trial is cited by Lee & Henschel, *Douglas MacArthur* (N.Y., 1952) p. 45.

Gen. King's attempted apology to Reid in the courtroom is described in the *N.Y. Times,* Nov. 30, 1925, after the paper had glossed over the incident in its report of Nov. 28.

The complaint of the unidentified judge as to hardships and expenses encountered during the trial is from the N.Y. *World,* Nov. 28, 1925; McCoy's housing problem is cited in Hurley, *op. cit.,* p. 104.

To modern readers, contemporary newspaper accounts of the trial seem curiously lacking in an awareness of the hostility of the court toward Mitchell's cause. It should be remembered that Mitchell's stature as a prophet dates from World War II in the mind of the American public, and that hindsight prevents the recapture of these weeks of 1925. Furthermore, most working reporters, hard put to write brief summaries of the tumultuous trial, were not only unfamiliar with aviation but also unacquainted with the practices of military justice.

CHAPTER 23 Will Rogers in the courtroom was sketched in the *N.Y. Times,* Dec. 12, and the Gridiron Club dinner in the same paper on Dec. 13, 1925.

The scene at the end of the trial, of which the official record says almost nothing, is most thoroughly depicted in the *N.Y. Times,* the

World and the Washington *Post* of Dec. 18, 1925, with numerous other newspapers reporting more briefly.

MacArthur's version of his role in the trial is described in his *Reminiscences* (N.Y., 1964), pp. 85–86; Mrs. Mitchell's statement is in the Washington *Star*, May 22, 1951; Ruth Mitchell comments in *My Brother Bill*, pp. 282–83.

The summary of national and world events at the end of the chapter is drawn from various issues of the *N.Y. Times*, especially from that of Dec. 18, 1925.

CHAPTER 24 Congressional reaction to the Mitchell verdict is drawn chiefly from the cited newspapers. Public reaction, not detailed here, was expressed in thousands of letters and telegrams to President Coolidge and the War Dept., almost all of them favorable to Mitchell. The record (Mitchell's 201 file, Part 3) notes that 410 such communications to the President were sent to storage in one day. A form letter from the Sec. of War went to these correspondents: "Your letter has been received. Please be assured that all questions relating to this matter will be handled in a fair and just manner."

The author is indebted to Glenn Tucker of Flat Rock, N.C., a White House correspondent of the time, for a copy of the release in which Coolidge "amended" the court's verdict.

The bitter comment of former Sec. of War Weeks on the Mitchell verdict is from an A.P. dispatch from Los Angeles of Jan. 29, 1926, in an unidentified newspaper clipping, Mitchell Papers.

Copies of Mitchell's resignation and its acceptance, and his farewell statement, are in the Mitchell Papers as well as in the 201 file.

The story of his speaking tour comes from scores of letters, Mitchell to his wife Feb.–May 1926, in the collection of William Mitchell, Jr., Boyce, Va.

The final settlement of Mitchell's accounts with the Army, and the incident of his denial of access to confidential matters, are documented in the 201 file. Numerous letters between Mitchell and the White House during the Roosevelt Administration are in the Mitchell Papers.

The recollections of Mrs. Arnold and Alfred Verville in this chapter are from OHP.

The account of Mitchell's death and funeral is drawn from contemporary newspapers, and from the recollections of Mrs. Harriet Mitchell Fladoes.

After a radio commentator charged that the Army had denied Mitchell's body a place in Arlington National Cemetery, Gen. Malin

Craig wrote Mrs. Mitchell: ". . . I have known Billy since he first came into the Army and served close to him on the Border, in the Philippines, in France and elsewhere. He was always my friend and a gallant, fearless soldier. Feeling as I do, I can only guess what his loss means to you.

"Billy's remains should lie in Arlington among those with whom he served and who knew him and loved him. He has every right to be there, and the matter is one which can be decided only by you."

Mrs. Mitchell replied somewhat later: ". . . Billy has always loved and admired you beyond most men, and counted on your friendship and as you know he always dearly loved the Army and the men he served with, and I was deeply distressed that Arlington came up as it did, with, I am sure, the best and friendliest intentions on the part of others. But I really had no choice, for he had told me several different times in the past two or three years that though for various reasons he would like to lie in Arlington, on deeper consideration he really wanted to go back to Wisconsin, the home of his family. So, at the end, there was no question of what to do . . . It seems impossible that he is gone, and I can only hope that I can bring our children up to love and serve their country with as true devotion as their father."

The exchange of letters is in the Mitchell 201 file, Part 5; Craig's letter is dated Feb. 21, 1926, and Mrs. Mitchell's reply is undated.

The log entry by Franklin D. Roosevelt at Adak in Aug. 1944, is cited in *White House Sailor,* by William H. Rigdon (N.Y., 1962), p. 108.

A copy of the verdict of Sec. James Douglas in declining to set aside the court-martial decision is in the author's collection.

Index

ABOUT THE AUTHOR

BURKE DAVIS is the author of four biographies—*Gray Fox, They Called Him Stonewall, The Last Cavalier* and *Marine!*—several military histories, including *To Appomattox* and *The Cowpers-Guilford Courthouse Campaign,* as well as four novels. *The Billy Mitchell Affair* is his fifteenth book. MR. DAVIS lives in Williamsburg, Virginia, is married, and has two children.